BK 891.713 L616M
MAJOR POETICAL WORKS
/LERMONTOV,
C1983 39.50 M

3000 663106 40013

D0848841

891.
LERM
MAJOR POETICAL WORKS

39.50

M

WITHDRAWN

St. Louis Community College

Library

5801 Wilson Avenue
St. Louis, Missouri 63110

St. Louis Community College
at Meramec
Library

MIKHAIL LERMONTOV

Major Poetical Works

Minnesota Publications in the Humanities, Volume Three

A series of books published with
the financial assistance of the Graduate School
and the College of Liberal Arts of
the University of Minnesota

Mikhail
Lermontov
Major Poetical Works

Translated from the Russian
with a biographical sketch
and an introduction and
commentary

by

Anatoly Liberman

*With the original poems
on facing pages and 65 illustrations*

University of Minnesota Press □ Minneapolis

Copyright © 1983 by the University of Minnesota.
All rights reserved.
Published by the University of Minnesota Press,
2037 University Avenue Southeast, Minneapolis, MN 55414
Printed in the United States of America.

Library of Congress Cataloging in Publication Data

Lermontov, Mikhail ĪŪr´evich, 1814-1841.
  Major poetical works.

  (Minnesota publications in the humanities; v. 3)
  English and Russian
  ''With the original poems on facing pages and 65
illustrations.''
    I. Liberman, Anatoly. II. Title.
PG3337.L4A253 1983   891.71'3   82-23798
ISBN 0-8166-1124-6

The University of Minnesota
is an equal-opportunity
educator and employer.

Acknowledgments

I began working on this book in December 1975 and owe a debt of gratitude to my students and colleagues at the University of Minnesota, who were my first listeners and readers. In 1976 I was no novice in poetical translation, some of my Russian translations from Shakespeare and the modern Icelandic author Jón Helgason having been published in the Soviet Union. I also had translated many lines from Coleridge, Robert Louis Stevenson, Byron, Kipling, and Oscar Wilde ("The Ballad of Reading Gaol"), but writing poetry in English was relatively new to me, and I would have desisted from further attempts, if my first American critics had disapproved of the experiment. Fortunately, they liked the lyrics, and roughly at the same time *Sequoia*, a literary magazine of Stanford University, published "January 1, 1840" (No. 55 in this volume), all of which helped to make my project a reality.

In May 1978, C. P. Snow came to Minneapolis, and I showed him some ten pages of my translations. He took them home, and in June I received a short letter from him, which contained these words, "Your translations of Lermontov are very much the best I have ever seen in English. If I can help in getting them published, do let me know." It is this letter that made me think of bringing out a book, even though at the time its outlines were not clear to me (for example, the idea of detailed notes came later). Beginning in June 1978, I devoted some time almost every day to translation, and by early spring of 1980, the work, except for *The Demon and Related Poetry,* had been completed. Shortly before his death, Lord Snow saw the entire manuscript and gave a very favorable report of it for the University of Minnesota Press.

In the spring of 1980 Joseph Brodsky recommended my translations to *Russian Literature Triquarterly*; their willingness to publish a large

Acknowledgments

selection was an important additional encouragement at the moment when I was grappling with *The Demon.*

Several other people supported me by their selfless interest and appreciation. Foremost among them were Roman Jakobson and Krystyna Pomorska-Jakobson.

I have been exceptionally lucky in getting the manuscript read by Professors Catherine V. Chvany, Paul Kiparsky (both from M.I.T.), and Stephen Rudy (New York University). The reports of Catherine Chvany and Stephen Rudy contained, among other things, numerous critical remarks, with almost all of which I agreed, and the book has gained immensely from their suggestions. My manuscript has also received its fair share of adverse criticism. I have learned a great deal from my opponents, and "A Note on the Translation" reflects my thoughts on their objections.

A number of colleagues at the University of Minnesota, especially Mr. Ian Ritchie and Ms. Hazel Hanley, helped me in my work, and the manuscript probably would have been shelved but for the enthusiastic support by Professors Wlad Godzich, Russel Hamilton, and J. Lawrence Mitchell at a critical moment. My cooperation with the staff of the University of Minnesota Press has been a source of real joy to me over the years, and I cannot thank enough the Interlibrary Loans Division at the University of Minnesota, without whose help half of the commentary would not have been written. In the spring of 1982 my friend Mr. Earl Buys read the translation, and I owe several improvements to his discerning ear. He collaborated with me in a program "Evening of Romantic Art," in which I recited several of Lermontov's masterpieces and he played Schumann and Chopin in his usual inspired way. This program was part of the tour I made in 1978-83 with my translations. The tour started in Minnesota and included "Voices in the Wind," M.I.T., the University of Michigan, and Cornell University.

I wish to extend my thanks to Ms. Mary Jane Craveiro, Ms. Patricia Haga, Ms. Nancy Lestina, and Ms. Terry Ruttger for typing the manuscript. The College of Liberal Arts and the Department of German of the University of Minnesota were most generous in providing secretarial help. My gratitude is also due the deans of the Graduate School and the College of Liberal Arts of the University of Minnesota for giving financial support for Minnesota Publications in the Humanities, and the Office of Research Development (College of Liberal Arts, University of Minnesota) for providing part of the funds for the illustrations.

Acknowledgments

This collection of Lermontov's poetry in translation is meant to be a messenger of Russian culture in the English-speaking world, but it is in equal measure a tribute to my friends and colleagues, whose love of literature, good will, and patience have made the appearance of this book possible.

Contents

Contents

Contents

xi

Contents

Illustrations

xii

Contents

xiii

INTRODUCTION

Biographical Sketch
Lermontov as a Poet
Note on the Translation

The music of heavenly grace

M. Yu. Lermontov Portrait by K. A. Gorbunov.

Biographical Sketch

. . . I was born with lava in my breast . . .

Mikhaíl Yúryevich Lérmontov (1814-1841), one of the most famous Russian poets, was born on October 2, 1814, in Moscow. The greatest historical event of that time was Napoleon's invasion of Russia. During the war and for ten years after it, the Russian monarch was Tsar Alexander I. The next Tsar, Nicholas I, ascended the throne in 1825. On December 14, 1825, when the army was to swear allegiance to Nicholas, a group of aristocrats made an abortive attempt to overthrow the regime. In Russian history the rebels have come to be known as the Decembrists. Five of them were hanged in 1826, and 120 were sent to Siberian mines. After the quelling of this earliest Russian revolution, the country was long ruled by the police. Marquis de Custine's *La Russie en 1839*, along with Hertzen's memoirs, gives an excellent idea of how that epoch was viewed by nonconforming observers.

For the sake of historical continuity, it may be useful to give the dates of birth of some other great Russian authors. Púshkin: 1799, Tyútchev: 1803, Gógol: 1809, Goncharóv: 1812, Turgénev: 1818, Tolstoy, 1828. None of them had as short a life as Lermontov, and none, including Pushkin, had begun to approach what he had done by the age of twenty-six.

Lermontov was several months old when his parents—Captain Yúry Petróvich Lérmontov and Maríya Mikháilovna Lérmontova (née Arsényeva)—moved to Tarkhány (in the Pénza region, not far from Moscow), the estate belonging to Elizavéta Alekséevna Arsényeva, the boy's maternal grandmother. Lermontov's childhood was spent on this

3

estate. The marriage of his parents was very unhappy. When Lermontov was two-and-a-half years old, his mother died on February 24, 1817, at the age of twenty-one. Arsenyeva hated her son-in-law but adored her grandson; she brought maximum pressure to bear on Yury Petrovich to make him renounce the child. In June 1817 she had a will drawn up, according to which her grandson would inherit all her property, if he stayed with her until he came of age. Otherwise, her property was to return to her family (the Stolýpins). Yury Petrovich was not rich; so he left his son in Tarkhany. The family strife poisoned Lermontov's childhood, and it is reflected in many of his early works. Father and son met occasionally, but Yury Petrovich (d. 1831) did not live to his son's majority.

Lermontov received his elementary education from private tutors. In 1828 he was sent to a boarding school for boys of noble birth, affiliated with the University of Moscow; he finished it in 1830, and became a University student. But in May 1832 he did not come to the spring examination and several days later left the University with a view of transferring to the University of St. Petersburg. The reason for this move, which influenced his entire life, is unknown. Later in the same summer he went to St. Petersburg, but the University refused to take into account his two years in Moscow. Even if he had entered, he would have had to begin his studies from scratch. Lermontov withdrew his application and entered the School of Military Cadets. He stayed there for two years.

Before 1833, Lermontov wrote some prose, about three hundred lyrics, three dramas, and eighteen narrative poems of varying length, few of them good. As a military cadet, he produced a series of longer poems, mainly known for their grossly scurrilous passages. These poems are, however, lively and witty, and some descriptions in them are excellent.

On November 22, 1834, Lermontov was made ensign and began the usual "merry" life of a well-to-do hussar. The next years, 1835-36, were comparatively unproductive ones in his literary career. The event that changed everything for him was the murder of Pushkin in a duel by Dantès (January 27, 1837). Lermontov reacted to the event with a lyric, "The Poet's Death," which made him famous and cost him an exile to the Caucausus. After that he wrote and published regularly until his death. Early in 1838, he returned to St. Petersburg and continued his service as an officer. The next catastrophe occurred on February 16, 1840, because of his duel with de Barante, the son of the French envoy.

4

A Biographical Sketch

The exact cause of the duel was not quite clear even to Lermontov's acquaintances: the quarrel may have had political overtones, but the outward provocation was a woman. Lermontov discharged his revolver into the air, and he himself received an insignificant scratch. Duels were prohibited by the Tsar, but Lermontov was punished with unexpected severity (despite Nicholas's hatred of the French): he was again sent to the Caucasus, this time to the most dangerous place, where he took part in several expeditions. The day after the duel, a censor signed for publication his novel *A Hero of Our Time*, and in his absence, his book of selected poems came out in St. Petersburg. The following pieces were included in it (the numbers refer to the translations in this volume): *A Song about Tsar Iván Vasílyevich, his Young Body-Guard, and the Valiant Merchant Kaláshnikov*, Nos. 30, 33, 37, 46, 26, 32, 49, "A Hebrew Melody (from Byron)," "An Album Piece (from Byron)," Nos. 50, 51, 52, 53, 55, 57, 63, 60, 56, 67, 65, 66, "From Goethe," Nos. 91, 35, 34, 36, 70.

At the beginning of 1841, he was allowed a short furlough and spent about three months in St. Petersburg. Before his return to the army, his friend V. F. Odóevsky gave him an empty album, and Lermontov wrote many poems in it: Nos. 79, 80, 81, 82, 83, 84, 85, 86, 87, 91, two epigrams, and "Encounters."

On July 13, 1841, in Pyatigórsk, Lermontov quarrelled with his fellow officer N. S. Martýnov, and in the duel two days later was killed on the spot. The circumstances of the duel, despite over a century of research, remain obscure, but what is known is not to Martynov's credit. It is an established fact that Tsar Nicholas rejoiced in the news from Pyatigorsk.

Most of what the modern reader finds in editions of Lermontov's complete works is pre-1837 juvenilia, never meant for publication. Lermontov himself, apart from the two books mentioned above (selected poems and a novel), and one childish lyric, published only Nos. 12, 40, 47, 61, 62, 69, 71, 72, 73, 74 and one narrative poem (in addition, one Caucasian poem was published against his will). A stream of posthumous works made him an active force in Russian literature for several more decades.

Lermontov, who could be gentle and tender, was often sarcastic, rude, and hard to get along with. His last duel, unlike Pushkin's, appears to be a sickening anticlimax: it could have been avoided so easily. But this is no place for a study of Lermontov's character. Instead, the reader is offered an extract from Pushkin's "Egyptian Nights." In the description of the poet Charsky, there are many obvious elements of self-parody and it gives us a brilliant picture of a poet at the time when both Pushkin and Lermontov were active. (Cf. also no. 63: 115ff.)

Charsky was a native of Petersburg. He was under thirty; he was unmarried; service life did not weigh too heavily upon him. His late uncle, who had been a vice-governor in the good old days, had left him a considerable fortune. His life could have been very pleasant; however, he had the misfortune to write and print verses. In magazines he was described as a poet, and among servants, as a storyteller.

Despite the great privileges enjoyed by poets (it must be stated that, apart from the right to use the accusative case in place of the genitive case and other similar so-called poetic licences, we know of no especial privileges accorded to Russian poets), despite every possible privilege, these persons are subjected to great disadvantages and unpleasantnesses. The bitterest evil of all and for the poet the most intolerable is the appellation with which he is branded, and from which he can never break away. The public look upon him as their own property; in their opinion, he was born for their *benefit and pleasure*. Should he return from the country, the first person he meets will ask:

"Haven't you got anything new for us?"

Should he seem pensive on account of the disorder of his affairs or the illness of some person dear to him, then instantly will a banal smile accompany the banal exclamation:

"Perhaps he's composing something!"

Should he fall in love, the object of his affections will buy herself an album at the English shop, and then await an elegy. Should he call upon a man almost unknown to him to discuss an important matter of business, the latter will call his son and command him to read the verses of so-and-so; and the boy will then treat the poet to a distorted reading of his own compositions. And these are the flowers of his art! What then must be the misfortunes? Charsky confessed that the compliments, the questions, the albums and the small boys irked him to such an extent that he was constantly forced to restrain himself from perpetrating some act of rudeness.

Charsky used every possible effort to rid himself of the intolerable appellation. He avoided the society of his literary brothers, preferring men of the world, even the most simple-minded, to their company. His conversation was extremely commonplace and never touched on literature. In his dress he always observed the very latest fashions, with the diffidence and superstition of a young Muscovite arriving in Petersburg for the first time in his life. In his study, which was furnished like a lady's bedroom, there was nothing to recall the writer: there were no books strewn about and beneath the tables; the sofa was not stained with ink; there was none of that disorder which marks the presence of the Muse and the absence of broom and brush. Charsky became quite downcast if any of his worldly friends happened to find him with a pen in his hand. It is difficult to believe

A Biographical Sketch

to what trifles a man, otherwise endowed with talent and soul, can descend. At one time he affected to be a passionate lover of horses, at another, a desperate gambler, and at another, a refined gastronome, even though he had never been able to distinguish between horses of mountain and Arab breed, could never remember what were trumps, and in secret preferred a baked potato to all the possible inventions of a French cuisine. He led a life of great distinction; he was to be seen at all the diplomatic dinners, and his presence at a soirée was as inevitable as that of ice-creams from Rezanov's.

However, he was a poet, and his passion was insuperable: when he found that his "silly mood" (so did he term his inspiration) was on him, Charsky would shut himself up in his study and write from morning until late at night. To his genuine friends he confessed that it was only on these occasions that he knew real happiness. The rest of his time was spent in strolling around, standing on ceremony, dissembling and constantly hearing the famous question:

"Haven't you written anything new?"

One morning Charsky felt that happy state of soul when one's imaginings take bodily shape in one's mind, when one finds bright, unexpected words to incarnate the visions, when verses flow easily from one's pen and sonorous rhythms fly to meet harmonious thoughts. Charsky was mentally plunged in sweet oblivion . . . and the world and the opinions of the world and his own personal whims no longer existed for him. He was writing verses. (*The Complete Prose Tales of Alexandr Sergeyevitch Pushkin*. Translated from the Russian by Gillon R. Aitkin. London: Barrie and Rockliff, 1966, pp. 320-21.)

What happened to Charsky that morning has no bearing on the story of Lermontov's life.

7

Lermontov as a Poet

Lermontov was confronted with the most difficult poetic task—to overcome the Pushkin canon (Eikhenbaum).

To be so dependent on Pushkin, so totally, so completely, so slavishly; and to shake off this dependence—this is where Lermontov's genius manifested itself (Anna Akhmatova, as reported by Lidia Chukovskaya).

The enormous literature on Lermontov falls roughly into six groups.

1) *Biography.* In 1841 Lermontov's readers knew nothing at all about his life. Even several decades later, the political scandal associated with his name sealed many mouths. His letters were destroyed, and his friends kept their recollections to themselves. At the same time his enemies spoke often and readily. Thanks to the toil of scholars, we now know Lermontov's biography rather well (including a lot of details that he would rather not have divulged). However, Lermontov's last duel is partly wrapped in mystery, and the dates of his works often remain unclear. The life of no other Russian author has given such impetus to the detective genre as it flourishes in Lermontov studies. An investigator can read hundreds of pages, race from town to town, peruse voluminous archives, and so on, to learn only that the name of the lady in whose house Lermontov stayed two days is beyond recovery but that both of her daughters seem to have died unmarried.

2) *Textology.* This is a traditional and indispensable area. It plays a very important role in Lermontov's case, for he was indifferent to the fate of his manuscripts, and his poems usually lack a definitive text. Most

of *The Demon* scholarship, for instance, consists in attempts to find such a text.

3) *Ideological interpretation.* Probably three-quarters of everything written on Lermontov falls under this rubric. Studies of Lermontov's religious views, moral attitudes, and political creed belong here. Every epoch and trend discovered in Lermontov what it needed, emphasizing in turn his mysticism, his atheism, his Slavophile bias, his dedication to Belinsky's cause and his influence on Belinsky, his melancholy, his militant spirit, his moral degradation, his tenderness and purity, or whatever. As a rule, Lermontov and his lyric hero have been treated as one person.

4) *Comparative literature.* Lermontov was a cultured man: He read poets in three European languages, apart from Russian, and his works are full of borrowings. Some of his predecessors played an outstanding role in his development. For years it was common to search for Lermontov's "sources." In the Soviet Union this practice came to an end with the official position that foreign influences on Russian authors are always questionable; also, Lermontov had been proclaimed a classic and as such was allowed a certain degree of independence. In recent years, sources of and parallels to Lermontov's work have again attracted some attention, and the *Lermontovskaya Èntsiklopediya* (1981) treats this subject with all the seriousness it deserves.

5) *Lermontov's artistic method.* Literary historians are seldom interested in literature itself. In Lermontov's case, they have always preferred to discuss his attitude toward his God, his monarch, and his female friends, rather than analyze his poetics. After reading hundreds of critical essays, one gathers the impression that Lermontov's principal merit is that he was very melancholy or very brave or very profound, that he sympathized with the mountaineers, loved liberty, and described the Caucasus. There are almost no works that question whether Lermontov was a great *poet* and whether his fame is deserved. Lermontov's contemporaries also treated his production in a strictly utilitarian way (for instance called it antipatriotic, immoral, etc.), and Belinsky, Lermontov's greatest supporter, was as utilitarian as any of them, only his approach was "progressive." The *Lermontovskaya Èntsiklopediya* is an important step forward.

6) *Popularization.* Lermontov is regularly studied in Soviet schools, colleges, and universities, and this fact has called forth numerous commentaries, bibliographies for teachers, children's editions, and the like.

Lermontov as a Poet

Here the most popular genre is a semischolarly book of the Great Lives type. A spate of monographs exists called *Lermontov*, but few of them are original.[1]

In the Commentary I drew on the observations of various people, regardless of their main sphere of interest, but this article will be devoted entirely to one subject: Lermontov's poetics. Section B is the result of my own research, and the few scholars who are my direct allies have been cited in full. My view of Lermontov's style is the translator's view and differs considerably from what students of Russian literature find in manuals and textbooks.

A. The World of Lermontov's Lyric Hero

Lermontov's lyric hero, " 'mid men a wanderer and stranger'' and a plaything of fate, is strongly attached to this life and craves the love of women and the friendship of men. But the women of his choice seldom want him. Overweening and smug, or simply indifferent, if not callous, they pass him by. He is haunted by the fear that he will finish his days on a scaffold and is sure that his death will shake the world; then the woman he has loved will be exposed to the mob's wrath—but let her not curse his memory. Although uncertain of himself, he can arouse love, but he is unable to reciprocate the woman's feeling and brings about her sorrow or death. His friends are few. The worthiest of them die young, others forget him the moment he is out of sight. The feast of life is forever going on, and he pretends to be part of it, but he knows that he is a stranger at this feast—an unbidden, bored guest.

All is rootless and volatile around him. Attachments, passions, and people are like clouds in the sky: the wind drives them on, but no one can guess whether or from whence. Nothing in the world leaves a trace. Nor does he; his many travels are useless, because he has no destination. Far, very far away, his true homeland lies in all its beauty. Perhaps long ago he was there; he seems to remember that land, but to return to it he must die. If it were possible to combine life and death: to die and not become dust! Other opposites meet: all things are amusing and sad at the same time; when in love, we are cold, though our blood is afire; the very mineral spring in the Caucasus is boiling ice; but the union of life and death will never come about, for dead men either cannot respond to other people's love, or fail to find the oblivion without which Paradise is worse than hell.

Earthly existence is full of noises: each object gives forth a rasping sound of its own. ''The music of heavenly grace'' is stronger, but this music can at times be drowned out by the cacophony of life. Everyone the hero meets wears a mask. It is hard to live among puppets, but this masquerade is a blessing in disguise. What would happen if we started exposing our sores to view? The hero is at peace with himself only when his soul merges with nature and becomes part of the universe. Then, tears flow from his eyes, and these tears are like the gentlest, the sweetest strains of music.

Lermontov's hero is doomed to be a poet and a prophet. Although he is solitary and sad, he is ready to tell the world his message; but the rabble will not listen, and his only reward is a wreath of thorns. Sometimes his pent-up passions, his thirst for activity will break through, and then leopards are not stronger than he.

This is not a sketch of Lermontov's own character, but of the inner world of his hero. The most noticeable feature of this hero is that he has almost no points of contact with the world of men. In his dealings with men, repulsion largely prevails over attraction, and he is pushed to the outskirts of life. He retains the sharpness of his vision but is made to look at everthing from a distance. Consequently, he always sees the whole better than details. It is my goal to show that, given the estrangement of Lermontov's lyric hero from his fellow men, Lermontov's poetic technique was the best possible.

B. Lermontov's Poetic Technique

At a technical level, half of the history of poetry is the history of the epithet, and nothing is more revealing in Lermontov's authorship than his use of the epithet. His texts are full of qualifying adjectives; in some poems there is one before each noun, but they are seldom informative. The sea in Lermontov's works is always blue, waves are also blue and constantly chase one another; sand is golden (and only golden), Chechens are angry, and horses raven black. Since in most cases Lermontov does not imitate folklore, these words lack the dignity of ''fixed'' epithets and sound repetitive and trivial. ''Eternal'' crops up in nearly half of his lyrics. Very many things are called mysterious (tale, saga, sadness, ideas, conversation, etc.), and wht is not ''mysterious'' tends to be *besplódny* ('arid, barren, futile': science, struggle, soil, fields, Russia herself). Some epithets are downright puzzling. A dead girl's shoulders (No. 52) are swarthy and pale at the same time. She has a fair-colored braid, but her head is white as snow. Teheran in ''The Debate'' (No.

80) dreams on a variegated divan before an emerald fountain, and an emerald fountain lulls the youth to sleep in the 1832 "Wish" (No. 20). Both times "an emerald fountain" must have been chosen for the sake of its verbal appeal. In the original of "Three Palms" most epithets are redundant: hard humps (about camels), swarthy arms (about women), and the like. In "The Terek's Gifts" (discussed a few lines above) we come across such dubious embellishments as "a noble trickle of burning blood" (on the dead Cabardinian's head) and "a crimson trickle of blood" (on the dead Cossack girl). The more one reads Lermontov's lyrics, the clearer it becomes that the poet was often indifferent to the exact meaning of his epithets. They are either too hackneyed to add anything, or too vague. But, indifferent to the epithet, he was extremely sensitive to other elements (see below), so the picture would emerge unexpectedly good. As pointed out in Section A, Lermontov had no other choice than to observe life from the outside, and therefore he saw the whole rather than the many details. He did not care whether each of his strokes was justified, as long as he made the finished canvas tell a convincing tale. If a term is needed, we can say that Lermontov was an impressionist.

From time to time scholars have realized this all-important circumstance, but either because the term impressionist has been applied to Tyutchev, Fet, and Ánnenesky but not to Lermontov,[2] or because it is unusual to find an impressionist so early—in an epoch usually typified by the question, "Romantic or Realist?"—the observations to this effect by several critics have hardly been understood, let alone developed.

In 1924 Eikhenbaum published his innovative book on Lermontov. In later days (until at least 1959, the year of Eikhenbaum's death), it was customary to treat this book with condescension; allegedly, it is full of Formalistic excesses (besides, Eikhenbaum had a low opinion of Belinsky's verbiage), which the distinguished author overcame in his subsequent works. In reality, strangled by a host of mediocre and self-seeking opponents, Eikhenbaum overcame his originality, his insights, and his intuition. Among other things, he said in 1924:

Lermontov writes in formulas that seem to hypnotize the author himself: he no longer feels semantic shades and details in them, they exist for him as abstract speech blocks, as *alloys* of words and not as concatenations. He is interested in the general emotional effect, as if he presupposed a quick reader who would not stop at details of meaning and syntax but would seek only the impression of the whole. The semantic base of words and word groups begins to dim, but

Lermontov as a Poet

then their declamatory coloring (that of sound and emotion) begins to shine with unprecedented brilliance. This shift in the very nature of the poetic language, the change of the dominant from the effects inherent in sing-song declamational verse, is the main peculiarity, strength, and essence of Lermontov's poetics. Herein lies the cause of his fascination with lyric formulas and his attitude toward them as permanent clichés. And this is the source of some of Lermontov's expressions and phrases, which are hard to notice—so strong is the emotional hypnosis of his speech.[3]

Soon after Eikhenbaum P. M. Bitsílli discovered the unusual quality of Lermontov's vision. If Eikhenbaum's book was dismissed as youthful folly, Bitsilli's article published in an emigrant edition remained quite unknown in the Soviet Union (even the 1981 *Lermontovskaya Èntsiklopediya*, which refers to non-Soviet sources in Russian, seems to have missed it). In Western works, too, references to it are incidental and rare. In my general evaluation of Lermontov, as is reflected in the Commentary, I am especially indebted to Bitsilli, whose analysis is deep, subtle, and to the point. Bitsilli's statements quoted below are a compression of several passages from his article.

In the world open to our feelings he seems lost, as if he could not see and hear well. When he tries to write like everybody else, the result is such: beautiful granite, high breast, white arms, black eyes, heavy storm, tall plane tree, mighty Kazbék; and this is not only in his childish works: the last three examples are from his masterpieces of the mature epoch. But he is at home in the world of echoes, glimmers, shadows, and wraiths created by imagination in the half-light of dawn, in the mist; in his symbolism very important are such expressions as "shadows of traces," "shadows of feelings," "shadows of clouds," "an echo of Paradise"; and the words "mist," "clouds," and so forth turn up all the time. To attract his attention, concrete objects must be grand, dazzling, . . . but then he sees things that nobody seems to have seen before him: he sees waves "singing a lullaby to the shadow of the cliff," he sees "clouds, wrapped in the mist, embrace and, intertwined like a heap of snakes, dream carefree on their rock" and finds connections between properties and things that nobody had ever found before him. . . . What in anyone else would be an expression of weakness, awkwardness, lack of talent, in Lermontov . . . testifies to his strength, genius, the exclusiveness of his poetic nature. . . . Lermontov is like a person looking at the Earth literally from some "interplanetary" point of view. . . . He is able, as it were, to occupy a position exterior to himself. . . . Among us he is like a far-sighted man among myopics: he sees distant objects better than what is near. . . . When it comes to things that surround us, that are close and visible to others, he is *blind*. . . . When he is at a distance from this world, which is too narrow for him, when he flies over it, he sees it all in perspective; changing

13

Lermontov as a Poet

epochs, historical and cosmic, open up to him . . . ; he sees the way to "the unknown land," . . . he waits for death in order to watch "a new world" that he has anticipated in his imagination. He treasures things around him, insofar as they are an image and likeness of the other world.[4]

With time Lermontov's artistic method was studied less and less by literary historians. "Formalism" was wiped out and the greatest concern of a whole army of scholars became to show what a brave man Lermontov had been, how he had hated the Tsar and how the Tsar had hated him. As in all Soviet humanistic studies, the main focus was shifted to matters historiographic and pseudo-sociological. An important exception was a long and interesting article by Pumpyansky (who wrote an illuminating essay on Tyutchev in 1928). In places, the article is somewhat rambling, but its idea is worthy of every consideration. According to Pumpyansky, two themes dominate Lermontov's authorship: that of unfulfilled social activity (one might perhaps say "of thirst for action and of social frustration") and that of *naródnost'* (relatedness to the people; see note on No. 73).

Two different styles and two different patterns of his poetic speech correspond to these two main themes. Of course, there is no clear-cut chronological border; beginning with 1837, the second style becomes more noticeable, but some of the best works of the first style, e.g., "In Memory of Odoevsky," were written just in the very last years. Quite provisionally and with reservations we will define this first style as a style of inexact wording, a style that certainly does not go back to Pushkin; the second style we will call exact, but its relative proximity to Pushkin's stylistic norm is in no way a return to Pushkin, it is a phenomenon peculiar to Lermontov.[5]

Examining the structure of "Mother of God, I Shall Pray in Humility" (No. 37), he went on,

Everything is insufficient and therefore requires immediate continuation, a hook-up, a helping hand, for separate notions to be able to move all together. The unit of style is not the line of verse, and within the line not the word, as with Pushkin, but the movement of speech (though, naturally, this juxtaposition is not absolute; different styles can in general be only relatively different). . . . We can see quite a new, autonomous phenomenon, autonomous in the etymological sense of the word, i.e., conforming to its own Lermontovian law. After B. M. Eikhenbaum's 1924 work it is well known that this law came as a result of a special trend in Russian poetry as far back as the Twenties and is represented by Kozlóv, Podolínsky, and very many others; but this only confirms the fact that this style was historically determined.[6]

14

Lermontov as a Poet

It is of course the style of inexact wording, the style in which movement alone defines the poetic effect that can be called impressionistic.[7]

To make our approach to Lermontov's poetic method more convincing, we can use a parallel from the sphere of comic art. Why is Gogol so irresistibly funny? His situations are either trivial (cf. the insignificant anecdotes that gave rise to *The Inspector General* and *Dead Souls*), or sad. The main source of merriment is his style. The stupid dialogue of his personages, the grotesque descriptions, and so on,[8] make everything he wrote funny. Critics have been wondering for years what attracts readers to the seemingly shallow Oscar Wilde. To be sure, Oscar Wilde was not at all shallow, but his magnetism does not depend on his intellectual depth; its secret should be sought in the beauty of his language. Gogol's immortality has nothing to do with his attitude toward bureaucracy; similarly, Lermontov's appeal to many generations of people is not fed by his melancholy or his hatred of Pushkin's murderers. Many cursed bureaucracy and the palace clique, and even more people were solitary and unhappy and put their feelings into versified lines. Nobody remembers them today. Lermontov, as well as Gogol, as well as any author, survives only because he is a great master. Such a conclusion would be self-evident in the history of painting or music, but it usually shocks literary historians.

Impressionism was a perfect medium for a poet with Lermontov's psyche and fate. The difference between him and the French impressionists, for example, Monet and Pissarro, is that the Frenchmen were aware of their method and their rupture with tradition; therefore, they took pride in their innovations. Lermontov's aesthetics, i.e., a system of conscious views on literature, cannot be reconstructed (the few attempts known to me were not worth making), but he must have looked upon himself mainly as Pushkin's follower. He learned from Pushkin and Byron and respected his predecessors. But in spite of his admiration of and indebtedness to Pushkin, he was the very opposite of Pushkin (as Eikhenbaum and Pumpyansky quite correctly pointed out). Pushkin and Lermontov exist side by side in human memory and university syllabi, and, when they are juxtaposed, critics usually contrast them with regard to their temperament. The polarities are expressed in terms of day versus night, sun versus moon, peace versus rebellion, relentless thought versus inner feeling, etc. But the two are not different thinkers, philosophers, or lovers; they are different poets, and the opposition between them rests on their different approach to language.

15

Lermontov as a Poet

Pushkin's epithet is varied and amazingly rich in overtones, but it is never ambiguous or imprecise. When Pushkin says in a lyric that a room is suffused with an amber light, he means exactly what he says, but when Lermontov writes that the eyes of his beloved are full of azure light (No. 55:28), this pronouncement is not a statement of fact. First, "full of azure light" is simply a figure of speech, another way of saying "blue"; secondly, *azure* is one of Lermontov's favorite words, and he endows everybody he loves with azure eyes. Lermontov is a whole stage closer to the Symbolists than Pushkin. He does not yet speak of the "shadows of uncreated creatures" like Bryusov (though remember his "shadows of traces" and "shadows of feelings"!), but, as we have seen, almost everything he describes becomes misty and mysterious. The outlines of the objects he studies are often vague. Russian Symbolists worshiped Pushkin, but, consciously or unconsciously, they owed much more to Lermontov. Blok is the best but not the only example of the link between Lermontov and the Symbolists. Andrey Bely cites admiringly the "azure light" in *The First Encounter* ('Pervoe Svidanie'), and, indeed, in the amber light of Pushkin's poetics he would have felt too exposed and uncomfortable.

Lermontov's impressionism is also evident from his choice of subject-matter and treatment of "plots." He likes landscape and all kinds of descriptions. "The Debate" (No. 80) is outwardly a long piece about the conquest of the Caucasus, but the political issue and even the philosophical theme (man versus nature) is little more than a frame: the poem seems to have been written for the sake of the strikingly memorable descriptive passages. Another example is "My Native Land" (No. 73). Again, it starts like a political lyric but after the first six lines becomes a beautiful—though slightly sentimental—landscape. Even "Borodino" (No. 30) abounds in descriptions and is not quite what it pretends to be, i.e., a ballad of a great battle. A glance at Lermontov's poem addressed to Countess Rostopchina (No. 76) shows how naturally landscape takes over in his works. "The Cliff" (No. 79) is a masterpiece that could have been put to music by Debussy, and the dedication to Vorontsova-Dashkova (No. 69), one of the most elegant poems written in Russian, is a perfect impressionistic portrait (note that it was inspired by a picture that is in no way impressionistic). More than half of Lermontov's lyrics can be analyzed along similar lines.

If we admit that Lermontov was an impressionist, we will be able partly to explain the main riddle of his maturation. The riddle is known to everybody who has read the complete Lermontov. Between 1828 and 1837 he wrote thousands of lines (counting only lyrics, but there were also dramas, long narrative poems, and novels). In this juvenilia one runs against several gems, such as "The Angel," "The Mermaid", and "The Sail" (Nos. 12, 26, 28), and a half-dozen touching love lyrics, but most of it is stodgy and dull. Then suddenly something happened: he exploded in "The Poet's Death" (No. 31) and after that never produced a bad poem. Moreover, what he wrote was becoming better and better. Nothing is easier than to show that almost every line in Lermontov's mature works derives from some place in or even occurs in his early works, but in doing so we only make the riddle more insoluble: if everything is the same, then why are the early poems bad and the later ones good? I can think of few cases in which art cries louder to be explained in terms of art. Lermontov's miracle is his discovery and conscious use of his own poetic style, "the style of inexact wording." If he had written only "The Poet's Death" (No. 31), "Meditation" (No. 46), and so forth, he would have been another author like Ryléev, Khomyakóv, or even Odóevsky, though obviously more talented. Lermontov, the great Russian lyric poet (for the moment I am leaving out of discussion his narrative poems, especially *The Demon*), is first and foremost a master of "inexact wording." When he had realized his main strength and become aware of his limitations, that is, learned to avoid doing what he could not do well, he stopped composing bad poetry. Nearly all his best lyrics written before 1837 are impressionistic, and that is why they are good.

There is nothing unique in Lermontov's experience. Hans Christian Andersen produced mediocre novels for years and would never have written a book worth reading if he had not discovered that he could tell a fairy tale. Corot was fond of painting "realistic" portraits of women (which made him famous), and even Levitán tried his hand at portraiture. If both had persisted in their folly, the nineteenth century would have lost two of its greatest landscape painters. Lermontov, in spite of his Romantic apprenticeship, did not know what to do with a love story, and this is another proof of his impressionistic sympathies. By 1837 at the latest Lermontov had realized that he must leave the love genre to others. His avoidance of love lyrics was an important victory at a time when everyone wrote them. Impressionism in poetry is an effective vehicle for the most tender lyrics because it is not encumbered with the ballast of details. One of the peaks of Lermontov's lyricism is his poem "In

Memory of A. I. Odoevsky'' (No. 53). On the face of it, the poem is about a dead friend, but this is almost an illusion. Only the beginning is really about Odoevsky; all the rest is about someone with azure eyes who had a warm and kind heart but was not spared by God or men, who died surrounded by callous fools and whose grave is in a beautiful corner of the earth. Part of it is the same as ''The Poet's Death'' (No. 31), part is close to the later ''All Alone Along the Road I Am Walking'' (No. 85), half is transposed from other poems. ''In Memory of A. I. Odoevsky'' is so good just because it is not a biography of any concrete man. Scholars are apt to apologize for Lermontov's habit of transferring lines and entire passages from poem to poem, but the essence of Lermontov's method was writing in lyric formulas, as Eikhenbaum called them, in huge blocks, and it is no wonder that those formulas (of any length) were transferable.

In a historical perspective, two important questions arise: (1) What makes Lermontov a great author if so many of his lines are traceable to somebody else? (2) How did he survive as a poet when behind him was Pushkin, who eclipsed all his contemporaries, and before him were such giants as Blok, Pasternak, Akhmatova, Mandelshtam? Actually, this is one question split into two. The answer can be given only if we realize the full extent of Lermontov's originality. As mentioned above, he was not a follower of Pushkin: he was a new page in Russian poetry. Anyone who tried ''to follow'' Pushkin suffered an immediate and dismal defeat, for there was nothing left for such a poet to do after Pushkin (compare Schubert's complaint, ''Beethoven has done it all!''). Lermontov says everything in his own way. Even when he repeats somebody's words, it matters little, because the familiar phrase becomes part of a different system and is almost impossible to recognize. It has taken critics more than a hundred years to notice that part of line 33 of No. 32 (''A Branch from Palestine'') is a direct quotation from Pushkin's *Bronze Horseman* (*prozrachny sumrak*). Lermontov's lyric poetry is a perfect unity of content and form: his impressionism was ideally suited to his message. Those who imitated him neither felt nor realized this fact: they parroted his formulas without sharing the peculiarities of his vision and invariably looked banal, approximately as a well-meaning professor of botany could if he set out to faithfully copy Monet. In Bitsilli's words, ''what in anyone else would be an expression of weakness, awkwardness, lack of talent, in Lermontov testifies to his strength, genius, the exclusiveness of his poetic nature.''

Lermontov as a Poet

Recognizing Lermontov's method is only the first step toward understanding him, because impressionism is too general a term. So far I have spoken of Lermontov's choice of words, specifically of epithets. Equally important are his technical predilections manifested in his syntax and metrics. I will barely touch on this subject, for neither a poet's syntax nor his metrics (let alone rhythm) can be studied in translation. The most important statements have been made by Eikhenbaum and Pumpyansky, both of whom have pointed out that the main unit of Lermontov's style is not the line of verse, and within the verse not the word, but the movement of speech.

Lermontov was very sensitive to the metrical arrangement of his lyrics, as could be expected from a poet who depended to such an extent on the movement of speech. Even in his earliest works he often experimented with unusual meters, but at that time the four-foot iamb remained his main medium. The situation changed after 1837, and one of the most important features of his mature style is great metrical variety. Almost every piece contains some novelty.

Yuly Aikhenval'd once remarked that Lermontov had a perfect ear. This is only partly true. To many things he was surprisingly deaf. Thus, he often did not hear jarring sound combinations in his lines, something like 'vnimál v nemóm blagogovénii' (No. 47:28 of the Russian text); such examples are rather numerous. He was indifferent to rhyme. It is good in his long narrative poems (in which his impressionism all but disappears) and unimaginative in his lyrics, but he took infinite care to organize a convincing and mellifluous whole. He was fond of parallel and symmetrical constructions, of mathematically exact antitheses, and pointed aphorisms at the end and resorted to the subtlest effects. Thus, at the beginning of "Tamara" (No. 82) the castle blackens on a black rock and at the very end something whitens from its window; at the beginning of "The Mermaid" (No. 26) the water maiden swims along a light-blue river, and in the finale the river is dark blue (I was unable to render the difference between *golubaya* and *sinyaya* in translation). He used to the full the force of anacrusis, the beauty of trochee and dactyl, the power of an unusual strophe (as in No. 53), the charm of multiple alliterations and recurring vowels. All these things he "heard." His ear was selective, and his goal directed his choices.

One of the traditional questions of Lermontov scholarship is whether he was a Romantic or a Realist. His development was not unlike Pushkin's (from "The Gypsies" to *Evgeny Onegin*) or Byron (from *Childe*

Lermontov as a Poet

Harold to *Don Juan*). Lermontov began with Romantic lyrics and ended up with *A Hero of Our Time* and the confession to Karamzina (No. 75); but *Mtsyri* (No. 91) and "Tamara" (No. 82) are equally late, and he kept working on his most romantic poem *The Demon* (No. 92) until 1839. At one time it was usual in Soviet criticism to praise Lermontov for his shift to realism, because realism was supposed to be a higher stage of literary evolution than Romanticism (Romanticism, "critical" realism, "socialist" realism). At present it is more customary to recognize the importance of Lermontov's Romanticism, though no conclusion has been reached as to how to classify *A Hero of Our Time*. The debate is scholastic (like all classificatory debates) and is fed by the indeterminacy of the main terms. The worst of them is *realism*, which is made to cover the phantasmagorical images of Gogol, Dickens's freaks, and Dostoevsky's devil, along with the dullest creations of fifth-rate authors, provided they are lifelike; but Romanticism is an equally vague term, and long ago Pushkin wondered what it meant.

For our evaluation of Lermontov's way we can easily do without definitions, but we have to distinguish between Romanticism as an approach to literature and art (philosophy) and Romanticism as a system of devices (style). Romanticism in its philosophical aspect is a victory of beauty and grandeur over ugliness and filth. It is a longing for the ideal and a superhuman attempt to find it. Romanticism normally accompanies transitional epochs and looks for a golden age—sometimes in the future, sometimes in the past. All religions and social utopias, as long as they offer a picture of Paradise, are children of the Romantic spirit.

Lermontov remained a militant Romantic all his life. As a literary movement, and more precisely, as a nineteenth-century movement, Romanticism had its favorite subjects, imagery, and devices. The devices included specific epithets and similes, recurring references, and so on. All of this is too well known to need recapitulation. This stylistic framework played its role and underwent utter degradation at the hands of epigones. Soon after the triumphs of the great masters it became common property, divorced from the spirit that had given it birth. Few literary movements knew such a speedy and catastrophic rupture between the original content and the hopelessly vulgarized form. No one with any aesthetic sense could have remained faithful to the conventional Romantic style after it had deteriorated into a set of clichés, totally predictable and mechanically reproduced. Romanticism, like many a trend before

Lermontov as a Poet

and after, was killed by the accessibility of its form. Pushkin was aware of it (hence his Lensky). Lermontov was aware of it, too. He was sorry that the style he loved had become ludicrous and renounced pseudo-Romantic phraseology but not Romanticism. His lifelong loyalty to the method that gave the world Byron and Delacroix is not fortuitous, for nineteenth-century Romanticism, with its taste for generalized descriptions in literature and contrasting masses of color in painting, is closer to Symbolism and impressionism than realism in its classic form ever was, and thus served as a good school and a proper source of inspiration for the poet who became the first impressionist in the history of Russian letters.

Notes

1. Far and away the best of them is L. (Ya) Ginzburg's study, *Tvorchesky put' Lermontova*, Leningrad: Khudozhestvennaya literatura, 1940. V. I. Korovin's book *Tvorchesky put' Lermontova*, Moscow: Prosveshchenie, 1973, can be recommended in parts. V. Arkhipov's thick volume (*M. Yu. Lermontov*, Moscow: Moskovsky rabochy, 1965) is obnoxious. Others usually repeat one another. Special monographs are often useful, but this is no place to list them. In recent years the best article on Lermontov I have read was devoted to a structural analysis of proper names in *The Masquerade*: A. B. Pen'kovsky, ''Antroponimicheskie zametki 1-2. O dvukx imenakh geroini 'Maskarada' '' [Anthroponymical notes on the heroine of *The Masquerade*'s two names], *Voprosy literatury (K stashestidesyatiletiyu so dnya rozhdeniya M. Yu. Lermontova)*, fasc. 10. Vladimir: Vladimirsky Gosudarstvenny Pedagogichesky Institut imeni P. I. Lebedeva-Polyanskogo, 1975, pp. 76-96.

2. Actually, V. M. Fisher does call Lermontov an impressionist (*Poètika Lermontova*, an article published in the excellent miscellany *Venok Lermontovu*. St. Petersburg-Moscow: Dumnov, 1914, p. 211), but he refers only to Lermontov's technique in describing landscapes. The only detailed discussion of Fisher's work in English and of Fisher's influence on Eikhenbaum can be found in John Garrard, *Mikhail Lermontov*. Boston: Twayne Publishers (1982), 76-78.

3. B. M. Eikhenbaum, *Lermontov. Opyt istoriko-literaturnoy otsenki*. Slavische Propyläen. Texte in Neu- und Nachdrucken. Bd. 35 [a photo reprint of the 1924 edition]. Munich: Wilhelm Fink, 1967, pp. 97-98. All the passages from the Russian critical works are given in my translation. At present, Eikhenbaum's book exists in English. See B. M. Eikhenbaum, *Lermontov. A Study in Literary-Historical Evaluation* Translated by Ray Parrott and Harry Weber. Ann Arbor: Ardis, 1981.

4. P. Bitsilli, *Mesto Lermontova v istorii russkoy poèzii*. In his: *Etyudy o russkoy poèzii*. Praha: Plamya, 1926, pp. 225-75 (see pp. 260-62, 266-67). (After the revolution Bitsilli

worked in Bulgaria and enjoyed great popularity among emigrant scholars. He wrote excellent works on Pushkin, Chekhov, and the development of the Russian literary language. In his method, he was close to the Prague Circle. Several of his works exist in English.

5. L. Pumpyansky, "Stikhovaya rech Lermontova." *Literaturnoe nasledstvo*, vol. 43-44. Moscow: AN SSSR, 1941, p. 390.

6. Ibid., p. 393.

7. Bitsilli's and Pumpyansky's ideas have not been developed in later scholarship, though Lermontov's style and especially his epithets have interested a number of scholars.

8. See A. D. Sinyavsky, *V teni Gogolya*. London: Overseas Publications Interchange: Collins, 1975.

Lermontov some time between 1830 and 1832. Portrait by Zabolótsky (1840) from a miniature by an anonymous painter.

Serednikovo. Photo taken in 1937 by V. G. Chudínov.

The poet's mother.

The poet's father.

"Ancestor Lerma."
Drawing by Lermontov.

Two anonymous portraits of Lermontov as a child.
Left: 1817-1818 (very little boys wore dresses in those days).
Right: 1820-1822.

Lermontov and other cadets in a tent, 1834.
Drawing by N. I. Polivánov.

Lermontov in 1837. Self-portrait.

Lermontov in 1839. Portrait
by A. Klyunder.

Pyatigorsk. The balcony of the house in which
Lermontov lived in 1841. Lithograph from a
drawing by A. I. Arnol`di.

The building of the "Ordonnanz-haus" (St. Petersburg, Sadóvaya Street) from an 1853 watercolor.

СТИХОТВОРЕНІЯ

М. Лермонтова.

СAНKТПЕТЕРВУРГЪ.
—
Въ типографіи Ильи Глазунова и К°.
1840.

The title page of Lermontov's 1840 book of selected poems.

Lermontov, 1840.
Drawing by D. P. Pálen.

The Karamzins' house (St. Petersburg, Gagárinskaya Street), from a 1947 watercolor.

Lermontov on his deathbed, July 1841.
Picture by R. Shvede.

Lermontov's grave in Pyatigorsk.
From a watercolor by A. I. Arnóldi (1841).

Note on the Translation

> Then the Bi-Coloured-Python-Rock-Snake scuffled down from the bank and said, "My Young Friend, if you do not now, immediately and instantly, pull as hard as ever you can, it is my opinion that your acquaintance in the large-pattern leather ulster" (and by this he meant the Crocodile) "will jerk you into yonder limpid stream before you can say Jack Robinson." This is the way Bi-Coloured-Python-Rock-Snakes always talk. (Rudyard Kipling).

This volume contains practically all of Lermontov's mature poetry. (The only serious exception is *The Song About Tsar Ivan Vasilyevich* . . . , which exists in several English versions. Unfortunately, it sounds silly even in the best translations because of its singsong *bylina* recitative verse, but it cannot be rendered without this meter.) The difficulties I experienced in translating Lermontov's works are known to everyone who has tried to make Russian authors "speak English."

Lermontov was one of the most musical Russian poets, and in a number of cases his poetic effects depended more on the sound shape of a line, a stanza, or even an entire lyric than on the actual wording. For this reason, I have invariably preserved the alliterative technique, sound symbolism, and the meter of the original, while remaining as close to Lermontov's meaning and imagery as possible. Some critics may believe that I have paid too great a price for my principles, so a short explanation is in order here.

English prosody differs from Russian in several respects.

23

A Note on the Translation

1) English allows rather free variations in the number of syllables and the place of stresses, though the rules (never too rigid) vary from author to author and genre to genre. For example,

> Was he /not born/ of wo(man)? /The spirits/ that know
> All mor/tal con/se(quences) have /pronounced/ me thus . . .

Shakespeare said *sp'rits*, but his *woman* was disyllabic, so that *-(man)* formed an extra syllable in the third foot; however, the line remained iambic. Likewise, the second line did not explode the iambic pentameter. Such examples can be found on every page of good English poetry. In Russian, an extra syllable, as we find it in *woman*, would ruin the line, and the two weak syllables of *consequences*, if simply added to a foot, would turn the verse into an alexandrine. Again, a passage like the following,

> My plenteous joys
> Wanton in fullness, seek to hide themselves
> In drops of sorrow. Sons, kinsmen, thanes . . .

if transplanted into Russian in its original form, would strike readers as prose: cf. the trochaic foot *wanton* (permissible but usually awkward in Russian), an isolated hypermetric verse (*themselves*), and a nine-syllable line (a syllable is missing after *sons*). Unstressed syllables are never elided in Russian poetry, but in English, *the, is, beneath, among*—pronounced as *th', 's, 'neath, 'mong*—is common practice.

2) Russian abounds in easy disyllabic and trisyllabic words stressed on their first syllables. In English they also exist but play a less significant role in poetry. Feminine rhyme is widespread but not so usual in English, in spite of the *Don Juan* stanza and other instances. One need only read Shakespeare's Sonnet 87 ("Farewell, thou art too dear for my possessing") to see both how beautiful an English poem in feminine rhyme can be and how this kind of rhyme depends on grammatical uniformity (twelve lines of fourteen end in *-ing*). Dactylic rhyme (*austerity-severity, intellectual-henpecked you all*, etc.) is rare in English, the more so because words like *severity* are supposed to be pronounced with two stresses (*sevéritỳ*) and traditionally rhyme with *be, see*, etc.; in Russian, dactylic rhyme is common enough (in Nekrasov, Blok, and many later authors).

Several other distinctions between Russian and English prosody must be made but none so conspicuous or important as the two mentioned above. (See Marina Tarlinskaja, *English Verse. Theory and History*. De

A Note on the Translation

proprietatibus litterarum. Series practica 117. The Hague, Paris: Mouton (1976), 1-14.) Ideally, a foreign poem translated into English should sound like genuine English poetry. However, this desire of the moth for the star can seldom, if ever, be realized. In too many cases the prosody of a foreign text is its integral and inalienable part. Homer's hexameters and the long leisurely lines of the *Kalevala* have no counterparts in English tradition, but if we want to read the *Odyssey* or Finnish runes in English, it seems that, in spite of Herder's strictures, we must put up with the unnatural media. *Beowulf* and the lays of *The Elder Edda* were composed in alliterative verses, and most translations reproduce this peculiarity, though in modern languages alliteration is a device of minor importance, not the prosodic backbone, as it was in ancient Germanic poetry. The skalds in medieval Iceland used internal rhyme, alliteration, and an extremely convoluted word order, and every translator makes more or less successful attempts to retain at least some of these features in English. I believe that since meter serves style in Lermontov's poetry, it should be preserved in translation inviolate. The same is true of Tyutchev, Blok, Pasternak, Mandelshtam, Akhmatova, and many, many others.

Thus Lermontov:

> In the middle of a jabbering mob,
> an ape-like masquerade—
> noble—parading
> like a nightmare, slobbering
> to music, prancing, whispering speeches
> stolen from books—
>
> (*Russian Poetry under the Tsars. An Anthology.*
> Translated and with an Introduction and Notes
> by Burton Raffel. Albany: State University of
> New York Press, 1971, p. 115 [= No. 55: 1-6
> of the present volume].)

and thus Tyutchev:

> The half-disclosures of the pale
> Glance past his eyes
> Where, cool and inaccessible,
> Shadows of trees and valley grass
> Spread through the parkland rural luxuries.
>
> (*Versions from Fyodor Tyutchev 1803-1873* by
> Charles Tomlinson. With an introduction by Henry
> Gifford. London, New York, Toronto: Oxford
> University Press, 1960, p. 38.)

25

seem to me a blind alley of modern translation, however convincing its theoretical foundations may be. Henry Gifford writes in his introduction to Tomlinson's book, "The aim of these translations has been to preserve not the metre, but the movement of each poem: its flight, or track through the mind" (p. 7). This is probably why *verses* became *versions*.

In my translations I have preserved not only Lermontov's meter, but also his enjambments and rhythm when they are stylistically significant: cf. short words in lines 1 and 9 of No. 31, No. 91:166 with its unusually long word, No. 76:23, where the line is cut into two symmetrical parts (a typical device in Lermontov's poetry), and the like. The syntactic structure of Lermontov's speech is reproduced faithfully in most cases.

As could be expected, my Lermontov does not always sound like an English-born Romantic, for Byron, Shelley, and Keats abided by partly different rules. Nor does he resemble Emily Dickinson, Robert Frost, or Yeats. He is definitely a Russian poet translated into English. "Translation is resurrection, but not of the body," says Gifford in the same introduction (p. 8). This is a good maxim for those who believe that the spirit of poetry is an entity separate from its body: I, for one, do not.

Half a century ago, Roman Jakobson remarked, "I think that we most approximate the art of the original when, to echo a foreign poetic work, a form is chosen which, in the sphere of forms of the given language, corresponds *functionally*, not merely externally, to the form of the original." This is undoubtedly true, but how is one to discover the functional counterpart? Luckily, in spite of all the divergencies, Russian and English prosody share many important features, for English poetry, from Chaucer to W. H. Auden, gives numerous excellent examples of very regular lines whose rhythm can be adapted for rendering Russian poetry. Compare:

> If thou survive my well-contended day,
> When that churl Death my bones with dust shall cover,
> And shalt by fortune once more resurvey
> These poor rude lines of thy diceasèd lover . . .
> (Shakespeare)

> Such shameless Bards we have; and yet 'tis true,
> There are as mad abandon'd Critics too.
> (Pope)

A Note on the Translation

Well didst thou loosen on this impious City
Thine angels of revenge: recall them now;
Thy worshippers, abased, here kneel for pity,
And bind their souls by an immortal vow . . .

(Shelley)

Fair youth, beneath the trees, thou canst not leave
   Thy song, nor ever can those trees be bare;
     Bold Lover, never, never canst thou kiss,
Though winning near the goal—yet, do not grieve;
   She cannot fade, though thou hast not thy bliss,
     For ever wilt thou love, and she be fair!

(Keats)

I want a hero: an uncommon want,
When every year and month sends forth a new one,
Till, after cloying the gazettes with cant,
The age discovers he is not the true one:
Of such as these I should not care to vaunt,
I'll therefore take our ancient friend Don Juan—
We all have seen him, in the pantomime,
Sent to the devil somewhat ere his time.

(Byron)

Books! 'tis a dull and endless strife:
Come, hear the woodland linnet,
How sweet his music! on my life,
There's more of wisdom in it.

(Wordsworth)

At the barren heart of midnight,
When the shadow shuts and opens
As the loud flames pulse and flutter,
I can hear a cistern breaking.

(Henley)

If you can fill the unforgiving minute
With sixty seconds' worth of distance run,
Yours is the earth and everything that's in it,
And—which is more—you'll be a Man, my son.

(Kipling)

Through winter-time we call on spring,
And through the spring on summer call,
And when abounding hedges ring

27

A Note on the Translation

Declare that winter's best of all . . .

(Yeats)

With conscience cocked to listen for the thunder,
He saw the Devil busy in the wind,
Over the chiming steeples and then under
The doors of nuns and doctors who had sinned.

(W. H. Auden)

Thus the "unnaturalness" of my translations (which, incidentally, I share with most translators from the Russian and other inflected languages) lies in my overconsistent use of one type of English line at the expense of the others.

Consider the practice of Babette Deutsch, Walter Arndt, and Sir Charles Johnston, three outstanding translators of *Evgeny Onegin*. All of them make free use of inverted (trochaic) feet in iambic lines (cf. *Porcelain and bronzes on the table*) and spondees, as has always been done in English poetry (nor do I avoid trochaic feet and spondees) and their scheme of permissible stresses is traditionally English, but they preserve Pushkin's number of syllables in a line, and this is exactly where the two schools of translation from the Russian agree to differ. Deutsch, Arndt, Johnston, and many others seem to feel that though *To see his ene(mies) writhe, and burn, and bleed* and *That night the Baron dreamt of many (a) woe* are quite at home in *The Revolt of Islam* and *The Eve of St. Agnes*, they will look "too English" in a translation from another language and that the only liberty that can be allowed under the circumstances is a weak schwa of the type designated in English poetry by the apostrophe (*whisp'ring*, and so forth); cf. *The fun(e)ral monument explains* (both Russian examples are from Sir Charles Johnston). I was guided by the same principles. See also Sir Charles Johnston's recent translation of *The Demon* in his *Rivers and Fireworks* (London, Sydney, Toronto: The Bodley Head), 1980, and of *Mtsyri* (Charles Johnston, *Talk about the Last Poet. A Novella in Verse and other Poems including 'Potted Memoirs' with new Verse Translations of 'The Bronze Horseman' by Alexander Pushkin & 'The Novice' by Michael Lermontov* and an introduction by Kyril Fitzlyon. London, Sydney, Toronto: The Bodley Head, 1981, 51-78.)

Controversies among translators are usually of no avail, and the merits of a translation cannot be assessed on theoretical grounds. In the final analysis, it is poetry, not principles, that should be judged by critics and readers, who usually do not (and are not supposed to) know the original.

A Note on the Translation

Poor production will not be saved by lofty considerations; perhaps if the above quotations from Lermontov and Tyutchev were convincing English poetry, I would have forgiven them their indifference to the beauty of the original.

So much for Lermontov's meter. His vocabulary is rich but repetitive, and he makes wide use of his favorite words. In several important instances I have succeeded in repeating the word where Lermontov repeats it, but in this area losses are the heaviest. In some places I used "poetic" words, such as *ounce* (notably in *Mtsyri*) or *guerdon*, if I knew that Byron or Shelley would have used them under similar circumstances, but such uses are rare, because the mature Lermontov kept clear of archaisms, even though he was fond of combining elevated and colloquial styles (cf., e.g., No. 31, with its characteristic mixture of pathos and irony, and his own self-parody in No. 97:198). Lermontov used many philosophical terms and other bookish words in his poems, especially verbal nouns of the type that would end in *-tion* in English. I tried to use *-tion* words only to render verbal nouns in the original.

Lermontov's rhyme is always correct but often unimaginative, even trivial, and the same is true of many poets who worked between the epochs of Pushkin and Blok. The age of Innokénty Ánnensky, Mayakovsky, Pasternak, etc. came much later (even Blok, in spite of all his innovative tendencies, did not mind rhyming *krov'* "blood" with *lyubóv'* "love," the paltriest pair in Russian (just as *Herz-Schmerz* is in German and *toujours-amour* in French), let alone *búri* "storms"—*lazúri* "azure" (the genitive case), which he used times without number, though this rhyme had become a worn-out cliché by the time Pushkin appeared on the scene. *Burn-yearn, love-above, anguish-languish, night-light-bright*, etc., which often turn up below, have been used deliberately. The constant occurrence of *story-glory* is a reminder that Lermontov was wont to employ the same rhyme in the most dissimilar works (his favorite pair was *bítva* "fight"-*molítva* "prayer"). However, the *granite-span it* type, as well as punning rhymes like *right-write*, both occur in the original (cf. 50:15-16, 90:1-3-5 of the Russian text).

My English is oriented toward the British norm. The years (since 1975) in the United States have made me well aware of the differences between "Standard" American and "Standard" British English. But I have retained my British accent and partly my British usage. This explains *harassment* in No. 51:9, which should rhyme with *embarrassment*, as it does in British English, and *clerk* (No. 63:45) pronounced as *clark*.

A Note on the Translation

Occasionally I also have rhymes like *calm-charm*; these words rhyme in British pronunciation and mine but seldom in American English. *Alley* in No. 55:24 is used in one of its British senses, viz. "garden walk" (not "street"). However, such instances are relatively few.

It is true that my Lermontov, though translated into English, remains a Russian poet on English soil; but "foreign," "artificial," or even "stylized" does not always mean "bad." Here is a passage from Gottfried's *Tristan*, as translated by A. T. Hatto, a recognized master of his art:

It is so this year, it was so last year and it will remain so among all lovers as long as Love endures, that while their affection is growing and bringing forth blossom and increase of all lovable things, they please each other more than ever they did when it first began to burgeon. Love that bears increase makes lovers fairer than at first. This is the seed of Love, from which it never dies. (Gottfried von Strassburg, *Tristan*, translated entire for the first time. With the surviving fragments of the Tristan of Thomas newly translated. With an Introduction by A. T. Hatto. Penguin Books, 1978, p. 197.)

It is beautiful English, but to appreciate its beauty we must remember that we are reading a medieval text translated into modern English; otherwise, it will strike us as a clever parody.

If my translation has retained at least a part of Lermontov's charm, my goal has been fulfilled. During the years of work on the book I kept repeating to myself that the time had definitely come for the geniuses of Russian poetry to move from the required reading lists of graduate courses into the wide world of the English-speaking public, as Gogol, Tolstoy, Dostoevsky, and Chekhov had done long ago, so that they could exercise the same influence there that Shakespeare and Byron had always exercised in the country of Pushkin, Lermontov, and Tyutchev.

LYRICS

By forceful words great thoughts are captured
As pearls are captured on a string.

ОСЕНЬ

Листья в поле пожелтели,
И кружатся, и летят;
Лишь в бору поникши ели
Зелень мрачную хранят.
Под нависшею скалою
Уж не любит, меж цветов,
Пахарь отдыхать порою
От полуденных трудов.
Зверь, отважный, поневоле
Скрыться где-нибудь спешит.
Ночью месяц тускл и поле
Сквозь туман лишь серебрит.

1. AUTUMN

Cruel winds benumb the country,
Leaves have turned from green to brown,
Every fir tree, every pine tree
Stands in silence with a frown.
5   And the plowman, tired of tilling,
From his many labors stiff,
Is unhappy—and unwilling
To recline beyond the cliff.
Forest creatures howl and shiver,
10 They are ready for the flight;
And the moon above the river
Sadly sheds its waning light.
1828

МОНОЛОГ

Поверь, ничтожество есть благо в здешнем свете.
К чему глубокие познанья, жажда славы,
Талант и пылкая любовь свободы,
Когда мы их употребить не можем?
Мы, дети севера, как здешние растенья,
Цветем недолго, быстро увядаем...
Как солнце зимнее на сером небосклоне,
Так пасмурна жизнь наша. Так недолго
Ее однообразное теченье...
И душно кажется на родине,
И сердцу тяжко, и душа тоскует...
Не зная ни любви, ни дружбы сладкой,
Средь бурь пустых томится юность наша,
И быстро злобы яд ее мрачит,
И нам горька остылой жизни чаша;
И уж ничто души не веселит.

2. A MONOLOGUE

Yes, mediocrity among us is a blessing.
What use are pride in deeper knowledge, lust for glory,
Unflinching love of liberty, and talent,
If in our world not one of us can use them!
5   We, children of the north, like native blossoms,
Burst into bloom, to wilt and wither quickly . . .
So like the winter sun against a gray horizon
Is our lack-luster life! Its tedious progress
Is equally monotonous and gloomy . . .
10 We seem to stifle in our Motherland;
The heart is heavy, and the soul is tortured . . .
Not knowing love, not knowing joys of friendship,
We spend our youth in foolish tempests pining;
By malice driven to the very brink,
15 We see our warmth and merriment declining,
And bitterness of life is all we drink.
1829

МОЛИТВА

Не обвиняй меня, всесильный,
И не карай меня, молю,
За то, что мрак земли могильный
С ее страстями я люблю;
За то, что редко в душу входит
Живых речей твоих струя,
За то, что в заблужденье бродит
Мой ум далеко от тебя;
За то, что лава вдохновенья
Клокочет на груди моей;
За то, что дикие волненья
Мрачат стекло моих очей;
За то, что мир земной мне тесен,
К тебе ж проникнуть я боюсь,
И часто звуком грешных песен
Я, боже, не тебе молюсь.

Но угаси сей чудный пламень,
Всесожигающий костер,
Преобрати мне сердце в камень,
Останови голодный взор;
От страшной жажды песнопенья
Пускай, творец, освобожусь,
Тогда на тесный путь спасенья
К тебе я снова обращусь.

3. A PRAYER

Oh Lord, forgive me, weak and erring.
I pray Thee: do not seal my doom
For all my passions, for preferring
To Thee and Heaven—earthly gloom;
5 For staying from Thy blessing distant,
For not consenting to recant,
For being stubbornly resistant
To all the wisdom Thou canst grant;
For the consuming inspiration
10 Whose stormy waves within me rise,
For every trouble and vexation
That dims the surface of my eyes;
For calling earth a narrow prison
But never seeking Thy reward,
15 For all my songs that should have risen
But did not rise to Thee, oh Lord.

Destroy my sight and crush my ardor
If for my sins I must atone,
Take out my heart to make it harder
20 And give it back, a piece of stone.
Stop once for all the yawning crater—
The source of my poetic heat,
Then I shall turn to Thee, Creator,
And seek salvation at Thy feet.
1829

КАВКАЗ

Хотя я судьбой на заре моих дней,
О южные горы, отторгнут от вас,
Чтоб вечно их помнить, там надо быть раз:
    Как сладкую песню отчизны моей,
    Люблю я Кавказ.

В младенческих летах я мать потерял.
Но мнилось, что в розовый вечера час
Та степь повторяла мне памятный глас.
За это люблю я вершины тех скал,
    Люблю я Кавказ.

Я счастлив был с вами, ущелия гор;
Пять лет пронеслось: всё тоскую по вас.
Там видел я пару божественных глаз;
И сердце лепечет, воспомня тот взор:
    Люблю я Кавказ!..

4. THE CAUCASUS

I came to your summits when I was a boy
And watched your impregnable pinnacles shine;
You live in my soul, and without you I pine:
   You are like one's motherland's music of joy,
5   Oh Caucasus mine!

Too early I was of my mother bereft,
But when in the evening the day would decline,
Her voice from the valley would give me a sign.
   For that I have worshipped your peaks since I left,
10   Oh Caucasus mine!

I loved, I adored every rock, every crest!
Five years have elapsed, and for others you shine . . .
I met there the eyes that I know were divine,
   Their beauty and brilliance are deep in my breast,
15   Oh Caucasus mine!
1830

ЕВРЕЙСКАЯ МЕЛОДИЯ

Я видал иногда, как ночная звезда
    В зеркальном заливе блестит;
Как трепещет в струях, и серебряный прах
    От нее рассыпаясь бежит.

Но поймать ты не льстись и ловить не берись:
    Обманчивы луч и волна.
Мрак тени твоей только ляжет на ней,
    Отойди ж — и заблещет она.

Светлой радости так беспокойный призрак
    Нас манит под хладною мглой;
Ты схватить — он шутя убежит от тебя!
    Ты обманут — он вновь пред тобой.

5. A HEBREW MELODY

I have seen from afar how a glittering star
  Has slept in a motionless bay;
But a breeze or a gust—and the silvery dust
  In a moment is carried away.

5   The reflection will sink, and you err if you think
  That close are the flash and the stream;
Your shadow will spread, and the light will be dead—
  Move away if you look for the gleam.

So it happens to most that, enticed by a ghost,
10   We chase our enjoyment in vain;
We discover its shape . . . and the ghost will escape!
  But deceived, we shall see it again.
1830

41

ЭПИТАФИЯ

Простосердечный сын свободы,
Для чувств он жизни не щадил;
И верные черты природы
Он часто списывать любил.

Он верил темным предсказаньям,
И талисманам, и любви,
И неестественным желаньям
Он отдал в жертву дни свои.

И в нем душа запас хранила
Блаженства, муки и страстей.
Он умер. Здесь его могила.
Он не был создан для людей.

D. V. Venevitinov, a possible
addressee of the poem.

6. AN EPITAPH

A simple-hearted son of freedom,
His soul for love he did not spare;
He knew some traits of life, could read them,
And could describe them and compare.

5   He'd trust a presage and an omen
And search for love on tortuous ways;
Himself, his one and only foeman,
He very strangely spent his days.

Within his heart there sang a chorus
10   Of anguish, tenderness, and scorn.
He died. His grave is there before us.
This man was not for people born.
1830

К ***

Не думай, чтоб я был достоин сожаленья,
Хотя теперь слова мои печальны; — нет;
Нет! все мои жестокие мученья —
Одно предчувствие гораздо больших бед.

Я молод; но кипят на сердце звуки,
И Байрона достигнуть я б хотел;
У нас одна душа, одни и те же муки;
О если б одинаков был удел!..

Как он, ищу забвенья и свободы,
Как он, в ребячестве пылал уж я душой,
Любил закат в горах, пенящиеся воды,
И бурь земных и бурь небесных вой.

Как он, ищу спокойствия напрасно,
Гоним повсюду мыслию одной.
Гляжу назад — прошедшее ужасно;
Гляжу вперед — там нет души родной!

7. TO***
(After reading Moore's *Life of Byron*)

Oh no, you must not think I need commiseration
Because my words are sad and I am looking glum!
My racking pain, my utter desperation
But presage harder days and darker things to come.

5   I hear my soul; its youthful sounds keep swelling.
To soar at Byron's summits is my aim.
Our nature is alike, we both have lived rebelling;
Oh, if our lot could also be the same!

For peace and liberty my soul has striven, once it
10   Discovered that, like his, it burned with youthful fire;
At sea it wants a storm, on peaks it loves a sunset,
In heaven and on earth it yearns for tempests dire.

I will not find relief—I am tired of trying;
I must, like Byron, stop the useless chase.
15   I seek my past—the past is terrifying;
I seek my future—not a friendly face.
1830

45

ПРЕДСКАЗАНИЕ

Настанет год, России черный год,
Когда царей корона упадет;
Забудет чернь к ним прежнюю любовь,
И пища многих будет смерть и кровь;
Когда детей, когда невинных жен
Низвергнутый не защитит закон;
Когда чума от смрадных, мертвых тел
Начнет бродить среди печальных сел,
Чтобы платком из хижин вызывать,
И станет глад сей бедный край терзать;
И зарево окрасит волны рек:
В тот день явится мощный человек,
И ты его узнаешь — и поймешь,
Зачем в руке его булатный нож:
И горе для тебя! — твой плач, твой стон
Ему тогда покажется смешон;
И будет всё ужасно, мрачно в нем,
Как плащ его с возвышенным челом.

8. A PROPHECY

A year will come—of Russia's blackest dread;
Then will the crown fall from the royal head,
The throne of tsars will perish in the mud,
The food of many will be death and blood;
5   Both wife and babe will vainly seek the law:
It will not shield the victims anymore;
The putrid, rotting plague will mow and cut
And boldly walk the road from hut to hut;
In people's sight its pallid face will float,
10   And hunger's hand will clutch them by the throat;
A scarlet sea will send its bloody surge;
A mighty man will suddenly emerge:
You'll recognize the man, you'll feel
That he has come to use a knife of steel;
15   Oh, horrid day! Your call, your groan, your prayer
Will only make him laugh at your despair;
And everything in his forbidding sight—
His brow, his cloak—will fill the land with fright.
1830

The autograph of Lermontov's poem
"Stanzas" with a drawing of E. A.
Sushkova-Khvostova.

НИЩИЙ

У врат обители святой
Стоял просящий подаянья
Бедняк иссохший, чуть живой
От глада, жажды и страданья.

Куска лишь хлеба он просил,
И взор являл живую муку,
И кто-то камень положил
В его протянутую руку.

Так я молил твоей любви
С слезами горькими, с тоскою;
Так чувства лучшие мои
Обмануты навек тобою!

E. A. Sushkova-Khvostova.

9. THE BEGGAR

Before the monastery gate
I saw a beggar half-demented—
A withered creature, crushed by fate,
By scorching heat and thirst tormented.

5   His gaze was like a silent moan,
A piece of bread was all he needed,
But someone gave the man a stone
Instead of food, for which he pleaded.

And I for love in sorrow yearned,
10   For love from you I pleaded kneeling,
But all the best in me you spurned
And coldly mocked my tender feeling.
1830

ЖЕЛАНИЕ

Зачем я не птица, не ворон степной,
Пролетевший сейчас надо мной?
Зачем не могу в небесах я парить
И одну лишь свободу любить?

На запад, на запад помчался бы я,
Где цветут моих предков поля,
Где в замке пустом, на туманных горах,
Их забвенный покоится прах.

На древней стене их наследственный щит
И заржавленный меч их висит.
Я стал бы летать над мечом и щитом
И смахнул бы я пыль с них крылом;

И арфы шотландской струну бы задел,
И по сводам бы звук полетел;
Внимаем одним, и одним пробужден,
Как раздался, так смолкнул бы он.

Но тщетны мечты, бесполезны мольбы
Против строгих законов судьбы.
Меж мной и холмами отчизны моей
Расстилаются волны морей.

Последний потомок отважных бойцов
Увядает средь чуждых снегов;
Я здесь был рожден, но нездешний душой...
О! зачем я не ворон степной?..

10. A WISH

Serednikovo, evening on the belvedere. July 29.

Why was I not born like a bird of the air,
Like the hawk that is vanishing there?
Why can I not soar over forest and sea
And be happy, unhampered, and free?

5   Away, to the West, to the West I would fly
Where the fields of my ancestors lie;
A castle deserted, a precipice steep
Is the place where my forefathers sleep.

I would see on the wall their inherited shield
10   And a sword from all strangers concealed;
The shield and the sword might be covered by rust—
With my wing I would brush off the dust.

The harp of the Scots I would touch with my wing
And wait for the echoes to ring;
15   The air in the vaults from this music would shake—
Some would sleep as before, some would wake.

But all supplications and dreams are in vain,
They are drowned by the billowy main;
I see it between us, tempestuous and great,
20   As relentless and cruel as fate.

The last of the youths who could argue with foes
Is expiring 'mid faraway snows;
Though here I was born, all my soul is elsewhere . . .
Ah, were I but a bird of the air!
1831

ЧАША ЖИЗНИ

1

Мы пьем из чаши бытия
С закрытыми очами,
Златые омочив края
Своими же слезами;

2

Когда же перед смертью с глаз
Завязка упадает,
И всё, что обольщало нас,
С завязкой исчезает;

3

Тогда мы видим, что пуста
Была златая чаша,
Что в ней напиток был — мечта
И что она — не наша!

11. THE CUP OF LIFE

1

When we are born, a cup appears:
It is the cup of being.
We wet its golden edge with tears
And drink from it unseeing.

2

5   But when the great delusion fails
And Father Death is calling,
When from our eyes—at last—the scales
Once and for all are falling;

3

We note that someone else's cup
10   Distracted us and tempted;
All was a dream, the game is up—
The cup of life is empty.
1831

АНГЕЛ

По небу полуночи ангел летел
    И тихую песню он пел;
И месяц, и звезды, и тучи толпой
Внимали той песне святой.

Он пел о блаженстве безгрешных духов
    Под кущами райских садов;
О боге великом он пел, и хвала
Его непритворна была.

Он душу младую в объятиях нес
    Для мира печали и слез,
И звук его песни в душе молодой
Остался — без слов, но живой.

И долго на свете томилась она,
    Желанием чудным полна;
И звуков небес заменить не могли
Ей скучные песни земли.

A baby reaching toward its mother.
Drawing by Lermontov, 1829.

12. THE ANGEL

The angel of Heaven was flying at night
And softly he sang in his flight.
The flickering stars and the cloud and the moon
Were wrapped in his beautiful tune.

5   He sang of the innocent spirits above,
Of blissful existence and love.
He sang of the Lord, of His will, and His ways,
And pure was the worshipper's praise.

He flew, and he tenderly carried a soul
10   For misery destined and dole.
It did not remember his singing, and yet—
That tune it could never forget.

It languished on earth, and by sufferings burned,
For things unattainable yearned;
15   But nothing it heard could destroy or replace
The music of heavenly grace.
1831

Я не люблю тебя; страстей
И мук умчался прежний сон;
Но образ твой в душе моей
Всё жив, хотя бессилен он;
Другим предавшися мечтам,
Я всё забыть его не мог;
Так храм оставленный — всё храм,
Кумир поверженный — всё бог!

13.

I do not love you; I have shed
The weight of longing and remorse.
But still your image is not dead:
It lives in me, devoid of force.
5 And in the passions' later play
I thought of you as only mine;
Thus to the fallen gods we pray
And kneel at a forsaken shrine.
1831

КРЕСТ НА СКАЛЕ

В теснине Кавказа я знаю скалу,
Туда долететь лишь степному орлу,
Но крест деревянный чернеет над ней,
Гниет он и гнется от бурь и дождей.

И много уж лет протекло без следов
С тех пор, как он виден с далеких холмов.
И каждая кверху подъята рука,
Как будто он хочет схватить облака.

О если б взойти удалось мне туда,
Как я бы молился и плакал тогда;
И после я сбросил бы цепь бытия,
И с бурею братом назвался бы я!

14. THE CROSS ON THE ROCK
(M-lle Souchkoff)

I once saw a rock of a terrible height,
Its pinnacle baffled the eagle in flight;
Yet someone erected a cross on that spot
And left it in tempests and rainstorms to rot.

5   Of years and of decades there is not a trace,
The cross is attached to its perilous place.
Its arms are uplifted, and, raised to the sky,
They seem to be grasping at clouds floating by.

Oh, if I could climb to that summit and stay,
10   I know I should weep, I should earnestly pray
And cast off my flesh with the fetters it brings,
For storms, like my brothers, would lend me their wings.
Between 1830 and 1832

ЗЕМЛЯ И НЕБО

Как землю нам больше небес не любить?
  Нам небесное счастье темно;
Хоть счастье земное и меньше в сто раз,
  Но мы знаем, какое оно.

О надеждах и муках былых вспоминать
  В нас тайная склонность кипит;
Нас тревожит неверность надежды земной,
  А краткость печали смешит.

Страшна в настоящем бывает душе
  Грядущего темная даль;
Мы блаженство желали б вкусить в небесах,
  Но с миром расстаться нам жаль.

Что во власти у нас, то приятнее нам,
  Хоть мы ищем другого порой,
Но в час расставанья мы видим ясней,
  Как оно породнилось с душой.

15. EARTH AND HEAVEN

Whoever needs Heaven when earth is so near?
   Heaven's light is a promise at best;
Though the joys of our earth are deplorably few,
   They are something that people can test.

5   Recollecting the anguish and hopes of the past
   Brings everyone secret relief;
We are worried that hopes which we cherish are vain,
   Yet, sadness is shockingly brief.

The soul is afraid when it suddenly sees
10   The future's unfathomable well;
We should like to partake of the heavenly fruit,
   But the earth's is attractive as well.

We are fond of the thing that we firmly possess,
   Though we wish for a loftier goal;
15   But when we must finally leave it behind,
   It already is part of the soul.
[?]1830, [?]1831

61

К ***

О, полно извинять разврат!
Ужель злодеям щит порфира?
Пусть их глупцы боготворят,
Пусть им звучит другая лира;
Но ты остановись, певец,
Златой венец — не твой венец.

Изгнаньем из страны родной
Хвались повсюду, как свободой;
Высокой мыслью и душой
Ты рано одарен природой;
Ты видел зло, и перед злом
Ты гордым не поник челом.

Ты пел о вольности, когда
Тиран гремел, грозили казни;
Боясь лишь вечного суда
И чуждый на земле боязни,
Ты пел, и в этом есть краю
Один, кто понял песнь твою.

A. I. Polezhaev in 1834, a possible
addressee of the poem.
Portrait by E. I. Bíbikova.

16. TO***

When tyrants sin, why make a plea,
Deferring to the royal banner?
Let others strum their lyres in glee,
Let fools in raptures cry Hosanna!
5   Oh, poet! Let them sing and clown:
A crown of gold is not your crown.

Your country banished you in hate;
Exult: at last you bought your freedom!
You saw through every deed and fate,
10   For in your youth you learned to read them.
When evil struck, you never bowed
But stood, as always, wise and proud.

You sang of liberty and pride,
You praised what villains would prohibit,
15   And only justice was your guide—
Not fear of chastisement or gibbet.
You sang, and someone in your land
Did hear your song and understand.
1832

63

К *

Я не унижусь пред тобою;
Ни твой привет, ни твой укор
Не властны над моей душою.
Знай: мы чужие с этих пор.
Ты позабыла: я свободы
Для заблужденья не отдам;
И так пожертвовал я годы
Твоей улыбке и глазам,
И так я слишком долго видел
В тебе надежду юных дней
И целый мир возненавидел,
Чтобы тебя любить сильней.
Как знать, быть может, те мгновенья,
Что протекли у ног твоих,
Я отнимал у вдохновенья!
А чем ты заменила их?
Быть может, мыслию небесной
И силой духа убежден,
Я дал бы миру дар чудесный,
А мне за то бессмертье он?
Зачем так нежно обещала
Ты заменить его венец,
Зачем ты не была сначала,
Какою стала наконец!
Я горд!.. прости! люби другого,
Мечтай любовь найти в другом;
Чего б то ни было земного
Я не соделаюсь рабом.
К чужим горам под небо юга
Я удалюся, может быть;
Но слишком знаем мы друг друга,

17. TO*

I will not humbly beg your favor;
Your angry look or friendly bow
Will never make me cry or waver,
For you and I are strangers now.
5   You thought that I should always falter
And sacrifice my life for guile.
Too long I worshipped at your altar
And sought redemption in your smile.
Too long indeed, and I am sorry
10   That for your sake I crushed my will,
That I rejected men and glory
To dote on you more blindly still.
Perhaps the days of adoration
That at your feet so swiftly flew
15   I took away from inspiration—
And what was the reward from you?
In peals of the Almighty's thunder
Or touched perhaps by Heaven's flame,
I could have wrought a work of wonder
20   And earned eternal grace and fame.
Why did you say that I was winning
Another wreath—a woman's heart?
Why were you not at the beginning
What you've become when we must part?
25   Farewell. May others seek your pleasure!
And may you others' worship crave!
I have not seen an earthly treasure
For which I will become a slave.
Perhaps to distant mountains southern,
30   To warmer climes my sail I'll set,
But much too well we know each other,

Чтобы друг друга позабыть.
Отныне стану наслаждаться
И в страсти стану клясться всем;
Со всеми буду я смеяться,
А плакать не хочу ни с кем;
Начну обманывать безбожно,
Чтоб не любить, как я любил;
Иль женщин уважать возможно,
Когда мне ангел изменил?
Я был готов на смерть и муку
И целый мир на битву звать,
Чтобы твою младую руку —
Безумец! — лишний раз пожать!
Не знав коварную измену,
Тебе я душу отдавал;
Такой души ты знала ль цену?
Ты знала — я тебя не знал!

N. F. Ivanova, a possible addressee of the poem.
Drawing by V. Binneman.

Ever each other to forget.
I shall enjoy myself hereafter
And promise love to all for fun.
35   I'll even join in people's laughter,
But cry . . . that I shall do with none.
I shall be cunning, false, affected,
And may my warmest feelings fade.
Oh Lord! Can women be respected,
40   If by a saint I was betrayed!
I would have let myself be tortured
Or fought to death the world of men,
To wander in your blooming orchard,
To press your gentle hand again.
45   Deceived, I loved you, and I tell you—
I offered you my soul and mind;
I wonder: did you know their value?
You did; but I was deaf and blind.
1832

Нет, я не Байрон, я другой,
Еще неведомый избранник,
Как он гонимый миром странник,
Но только с русскою душой.
Я раньше начал, кончу ране,
Мой ум не много совершит;
В душе моей, как в океане,
Надежд разбитых груз лежит.
Кто может, океан угрюмый,
Твои изведать тайны? кто
Толпе мои расскажет думы?
Я — или бог — или никто!

18.

No, I am not Byron, though I and he
Were both exposed to fame and danger;
'Mid men a wanderer and stranger,
I have a Russian soul in me.
5   I started young, I'll finish sooner,
In vain my mind for wisdom gropes;
My soul is like a shipwrecked schooner
That sank with all its broken hopes.
Who will, oh sea! your secrets fathom?
10   Who will you of your treasure rob?
And so my thoughts: alone I have them—
Myself and God, but not the mob.
1832

К *

Оставь напрасные заботы,
Не обнажай минувших дней:
В них не откроешь ничего ты,
За что б меня любить сильней!
Ты любишь — верю — и довольно;
Кого,— ты ведать не должна;
Тебе открыть мне было б больно,
Как жизнь моя пуста, черна.
Не погублю святое счастье
Такой души и не скажу,
Что недостоин я участья,
Что сам ничем не дорожу;
Что всё, чем сердце дорожило,
Теперь для сердца стало яд,
Что для него страданье мило,
Как спутник, собственность иль брат.
Промолвив ласковое слово,
В награду требуй жизнь мою;
Но, друг мой, не проси былого,
Я мук своих не продаю.

19. To*

I ask you to restrain your feeling,
Forget what happened long before:
I've hidden nothing worth revealing
For which you could have loved me more.
5   I would be sad if you insisted
And probed the man you love so well;
My soul, believe me, would be twisted
If you should see its blackest hell.
Your happiness I will not shatter,
10   I will not come to you and say
That things I treasure do not matter,
That for my peace you must not pray,
That I have taught my heart to smother
Old love, affections, wishes—all!
15   That more than to a friend or brother
It clings to sufferings and gall.
For just one word of yours so tender
Demand my life and all I've won—
But not my past; its sole defender,
20   I'll sell its grief and pain to none.
1832

71

V. A. Lopukhina, to whom this poem was
most probably dedicated. A drawing and a
portrait of her by Lermontov.

V. A. Lopukhina. Watercolor by Lermontov.

ЖЕЛАНЬЕ

Отворите мне темницу,
Дайте мне сиянье дня,
Черноглазую девицу,
Черногривого коня.
Дайте раз по синю полю
Проскакать на том коне;
Дайте раз на жизнь и волю,
Как на чуждую мне долю,
Посмотреть поближе мне.

Дайте мне челнок дощатый
С полусгнившею скамьей,
Парус серый и косматый,
Ознакомленный с грозой.
Я тогда пущуся в море
Беззаботен и один,
Разгуляюсь на просторе
И потешусь в буйном споре
С дикой прихотью пучин.

Дайте мне дворец высокой
И кругом зеленый сад,
Чтоб в тени его широкой
Зрел янтарный виноград;
Чтоб фонтан, не умолкая,
В зале мраморном журчал
И меня б в мечтаньях рая,
Хладной пылью орошая,
Усыплял и пробуждал...

20. A WISH

Open up my hateful prison,
Let me walk from fetters freed!
Oh, how high I could have risen
With my maiden on my steed!
5   Let the meadow open wider
For a new courageous guest;
Not a sad, enchained outsider,
But a dashing, happy rider
Would career from east to west.

10   Let me have a skiff half-shattered,
With a wooden thwart decayed,
With a sail by tempests tattered,
But of tempests unafraid.
I would leave behind my jailer
15   And would cross a raging sea
Like a weather-beaten sailor;
Thunder would not make me paler,
Whirlwinds would not frighten me.

Let me have a palace towering
20   On a solitary beach
And a shady orchard flowering,
Smelling sweet with pear and peach.
In a hall ornate and gleaming,
Where a fountain sends its spray,
25   To the sound of gentle streaming
I would wake and slumber, dreaming,
Every night and every day.
1832

К *

Печаль в моих песнях, но что за нужда?
Тебе не внимать им, мой друг, никогда.
Они не прогонят улыбку святую
С тех уст, для которых живу и тоскую.

К тебе не домчится ни слово, ни звук,
Отзыв беспокойный неведомых мук.
Певца твоя ласка утешить не может,
Зачем же он сердце твое потревожит?

О нет! одна мысль, что слеза омрачит
Тот взор несравненный, где счастье горит,
Безумные б звуки в груди подавила,
Хоть прежде за них лишь певца ты любила.

21. To*

My songs are all sadness, but let it be so;
They are not for you to think over or know.
I promise that ne'er shall I sing them or pen them
Nor ever distress you with drops of my venom.

5   And neither a word nor a sound will impart
The tortures and grief of a suffering heart.
Why should I disturb you and ask for your solace,
If nothing but sorrow and anguish befall us?

To think that your soul by my songs can be pained,
10   To think that your eyes by fond tears can be stained!
Oh, let me forget my poetical phrases,
The ones that you heard and rewarded with praises.
1832

ДВА ВЕЛИКАНА

В шапке золота литого
Старый русский великан
Поджидал к себе другого
Из далеких чуждых стран.

За горами, за долами
Уж гремел об нем рассказ,
И померяться главами
Захотелось им хоть раз.

И пришел с грозой военной
Трехнедельный удалец,
И рукою дерзновенной
Хвать за вражеский венец.

Но улыбкой роковою
Русский витязь отвечал:
Посмотрел — тряхнул главою...
Ахнул дерзкий — и упал!

Но упал он в дальнем море
На неведомый гранит,
Там, где буря на просторе
Над пучиною шумит.

22. TWO GIANTS

'Neath a cap of precious metal
Stood the Russian lord defiant,
For the time had come to settle
With the younger foreign giant.

5   By the warlike spirit prompted,
Rich in victories and might,
Both were heading for a combat,
Both were eager for a fight.

And he came, the three-week claimant,
10   All in splendor and renown,
Saw the Russian's royal raiment,
Jumped, and gripped the golden crown.

But the Russian giant, undaunted,
Smiled the fatal smile of war,
15   Shook his head—then he who vaunted
Fell subdued forevermore.

And he fell devoid of glory
On an island far away,
On the granite, bleak and hoary,
20   'Mid the breakers, cold and gray.
1832

К *

1

Прости! — мы не встретимся боле
Друг другу руки не пожмем;
Прости! — твое сердце на воле...
Но счастья не сыщет в другом.
Я знаю: с порывом страданья
Опять затрепещет оно,
Когда ты услышишь названье
Того, кто погиб так давно!

2

Есть звуки — значенье ничтожно
И презрено гордой толпой —
Но их позабыть невозможно:
Как жизнь, они слиты с душой;
Как в гробе, зарыто былое
На дне этих звуков святых;
И в мире поймут их лишь двое,
И двое лишь вздрогнут от них!

3

Мгновение вместе мы были,
Но вечность — ничто перед ним;
Все чувства мы вдруг истощили,
Сожгли поцелуем одним;
Прости! — не жалей безрассудно,
О краткой любви не жалей:
Расстаться казалось нам трудно,
Но встретиться было б трудней!

23. To*

Farewell! We are parting forever,
  With nothing to soften the pain,
The bonds of your heart you will sever,
  But will not be happy again.
5 Farewell! And I know you will cherish
  And will not forget to the end
The name of the man who will perish,
  The name of your lover and friend.

2

So often the meaning of speeches
10 Is hidden and foolishly mocked,
But souls that it timidly reaches
  Preserve it in secrecy locked.
These speeches conceal at the bottom
  The past irretrievably drowned;
15 The two of us never forgot them,
  And others are deaf to the sound.

3

Together we spent but a minute,
  A moment of heavenly bliss,
But lived through eternity in it
20 And burned in a passionate kiss.
Farewell!—it is useless lamenting
  That love is so brittle and fleet.
The parting was hard and tormenting—
  It would be much harder to meet!
1832

Она не гордой красотою
Прельщает юношей живых,
Она не водит за собою
Толпу вздыхателей немых.
И стан ее — не стан богини,
И грудь волною не встает,
И в ней никто своей святыни,
Припав к земле, не признает.
Однако все ее движенья,
Улыбки, речи и черты
Так полны жизни, вдохновенья,
Так полны чудной простоты.
Но голос душу проникает,
Как вспоминанье лучших дней,
И сердце любит и страдает,
Почти стыдясь любви своей.

24.

Her face is not the face of Venus,
That we should stand around in awe,
And she has hardly ever seen us
Extol her, worship, and adore.
5 A shapely nymph is more appealing,
Her breast is not a heaving wave,
So no one swept by violent feeling
Will kneel before her like a slave.
And yet her every little motion,
10 Her speech, her laughter, and her face—
All is exuberant emotion,
All is inimitable grace.
Her voice breaks through the soul's defenses,
As sunrays break through winter chill,
15 And once again revives the senses
And stirs the heart against its will.
1832

ТРОСТНИК

Сидел рыбак веселый
  На берегу реки;
И перед ним по ветру
  Качались тростники.
Сухой тростник он срезал
  И скважины проткнул;
Один конец зажал он,
  В другой конец подул.

И будто оживленный,
  Тростник заговорил;
То голос человека
  И голос ветра был.
И пел тростник печально:
«Оставь, оставь меня;
Рыбак, рыбак прекрасный
  Терзаешь ты меня!

И я была девицей,
  Красавица была,
У мачехи в темнице
  Я некогда цвела,
И много слез горючих
  Невинно я лила;
И раннюю могилу
  Безбожно я звала.

И был сынок любимец
  У мачехи моей;
Обманывал красавиц,
  Пугал честных людей.

25. THE REED

A fisherman was resting,
  He saw the river play;
The wind was blowing gently
  And made the rushes sway.
5 He chose a reed and cut it,
  And on it, all along,
He pierced some holes for music
  And tried a little song.

But, lo! as if by magic
10 The reed began its tale;
A human voice was in it,
  A melancholy wail.
The reed was singing sadly,
  "Oh, let me, let me be!
15 Oh, handsome youth, have mercy:
  You are tormenting me!

Yes, I was once a maiden,
  And, like a flower, I bloomed,
But by my stepmother cruel
20 I was to sorrow doomed.
I only wept and suffered—
  She grudged me light and breath—
And oh! I grieved so rashly:
  I asked the Lord for death!

25 She had a son belovèd—
  The apple of her eye;
With men he was dishonest,
  With beauties he was sly.

И раз пошли под вечер
    Мы на берег крутой,
Смотреть на сини волны,
    На запад золотой.

Моей любви просил он...
    Любить я не могла,
И деньги мне дарил он —
    Я денег не брала;
Несчастную сгубил он,
    Ударил в грудь ножом;
И здесь мой труп зарыл он
    На берегу крутом;

И над моей могилой
    Взошел тростник большой,
И в нем живут печали
    Души моей младой;
Рыбак, рыбак прекрасный,
    Оставь же свой тростник;
Ты мне помочь не в силах,
    А плакать не привык».

And once along the river
30 I walked with him for fun,
We watched the waves together,
We watched the setting sun.

He wanted me to love him—
His passion left me cold;
35 He tried to give me money—
I did not want his gold.
Then with a knife he struck me,
And to the ground I sank;
He dug a grave and buried
40 My body on the bank.

And on my grave so early,
A reed in summer rose;
A maiden's griefs are in it,
The soul's untimely woes.
45 So, handsome youth, have mercy
And let me quiet lie:
You cannot save or help me
Nor have you learned to cry.''
1832

РУСАЛКА

1

Русалка плыла по реке голубой,
Озаряема полной луной;
И старалась она доплеснуть до луны
Серебристую пену волны.

2

И шумя и крутясь колебала река
Отраженные в ней облака;
И пела русалка — и звук ее слов
Долетал до крутых берегов.

3

И пела русалка: «На дне у меня
Играет мерцание дня;
Там рыбок златые гуляют стада,
Там хрустальные есть города;

4

И там на подушке из ярких песков,
Под тенью густых тростников,
Спит витязь, добыча ревнивой волны,
Спит витязь чужой стороны...

5

Расчесывать кольца шелковых кудрей
Мы любим во мраке ночей,

26. THE MERMAID

1

The mermaid was splashing at night in the stream
In pursuit of a quivering beam.
She was swimming and hurling the silvery foam
To the moonbeam's invisible home.

2

5   As the river was flowing impatiently by,
It reflected the clouds and the sky;
The mermaid was swimming and singing a song
In a voice both appealing and strong.

3

And these were her words: "On the bottom, below,
10   Perpetual day is aglow,
The goldfish take pleasure in plunging adown
To the streets of the crystalline town.

4

And there, on a cushion of glittering sand,
A youth from some faraway land,
15   A youth from afar is asleep in his grave,
The prey of an envious wave.

5

At night, when the river embraces and rocks,
We tenderly play with his locks;

И в чело и в уста мы, в полуденный час,
Целовали красавца не раз.

6

Но к страстным лобзаньям, не знаю зачем,
Остается он хладен и нем;
Он спит,— и, склонившись на перси ко мне,
Он не дышит, не шепчет во сне».

7

Так пела русалка над синей рекой,
Полна непонятной тоской;
И шумно катясь, колебала река
Отраженные в ней облака.

"The Mermaid." Illustration by M. A. Vrubel'.

And at midday we dance all together and bow,
20   While kissing his mouth and his brow.

6

But passionate kisses, I cannot tell why,
    Do not make him respond or reply;
He lies; he immovably sleeps on my breast,
    Never breathing at all in his rest.''

7

25 The mermaid sang so, all enwrapped in the gleam;
    She sang of her longing and dream.
Beneath her the river reflected the sky,
    As it hurried impatiently by.
1832

91

Для чего я не родился
Этой синею волной?
Как бы шумно я катился
Под серебряной луной,
О! как страстно я лобзал бы
Золотистый мой песок,
Как надменно презирал бы
Недоверчивый челнок;
Всё, чем так гордятся люди,
Мой набег бы разрушал;
И к моей студеной груди
Я б страдальцев прижимал;
Не страшился б муки ада,
Раем не был бы прельщен;
Беспокойство и прохлада
Были б вечный мой закон;
Не искал бы я забвенья
В дальном северном краю;
Был бы волен от рожденья
Жить и кончить жизнь мою!

27.

What a pity that the Maker
Who created sea and shore
Did not let me be a breaker
Ever tossing with a roar.
5 I would come, a freeborn rebel,
To the sand behind the cliff;
I would fondle every pebble
But despise the timid skiff.
I would wildly hunt my quarry,
5 I would drown it and destroy,
But the sufferers I'd carry
On my liquid breast with joy;
I would laugh at pains infernal,
Paradise would leave me cool;
15 Streaming restlessness eternal
Would remain my only rule;
Then I would not seek oblivion
In a distant northern clime;
I would die, or I'd be living
20 Any place and any time.
1832

ПАРУС

Белеет парус одинокой
В тумане моря голубом!..
Что ищет он в стране далекой?
Что кинул он в краю родном?..

Играют волны — ветер свищет,
И мачта гнется и скрыпит...
Увы! он счастия не ищет
И не от счастия бежит!

Под ним струя светлей лазури,
Над ним луч солнца золотой...
А он, мятежный, просит бури,
Как будто в бурях есть покой!

The Sail. Drawing by Lermontov.

28. THE SAIL

A sail is gliding in the torrent,
Enveloped in a bluish haze.
What does it seek 'mid breakers foreign?
What did it leave in native bays?

5   The tempest roars, the sea is riven,
The mast gives in: it bends and creaks.
No, not by joy this sail is driven,
And 'tis not joy it vainly seeks!

Beneath, the stream is deep and quiet;
10   Above, the clouds are soft as fleece . . .
Alas! It longs for storms and riot,
As if a storm could bring it peace.
1832

1

Опять, народные витии,
За дело падшее Литвы
На славу гордую России
Опять шумя восстали вы.
Уж вас казнил могучим словом
Поэт, восставший в блеске новом
От продолжительного сна,
И порицания покровом
Одел он ваши имена.

2

Что это: вызов ли надменный,
На битву ль бешеный призыв?
Иль голос зависти смущенной,
Бессилья злобного порыв?..
Да, хитрой зависти ехидна
Вас пожирает; вам обидна
Величья нашего заря;
Вам солнца божьего не видно
За солнцем русского царя.

3

Давно привыкшие венцами
И уважением играть,
Вы мнили грязными руками
Венец блестящий запятнать.
Вам непонятно, вам несродно
Всё, что высоко, благородно;
Не знали вы, что грозный щит

29.

1

Again with swollen oratory
For Lithuania's hopeless cause
You open fire at Russia's glory,
Her sacred rights, and ancient laws.
5   You heard another poet's thunder
Not long ago; it was a wonder
That he awakened from his sleep
To castigate your thirst for plunder
And all your falsehoods, bold but cheap.

2

10   Is that a challenge to a battle,
A last attack on Russian might?
Or jealousy's embarrassed prattle,
A cry of impotence and spite?
Yes, envy gnaws you like an adder,
15   And nothing could have made you sadder
Than Russia with her glory new;
The sheen in which the Tsar has clad her
Eclipses Heaven's sheen for you.

3

You play one game and play it dully:
20   When wreaths are bright, you drag them down;
And you believed that you would sully,
That you would stain our shining crown!
Your tastes, your vulgar predilection
Shirks lofty aims and high perfection;
25   A villain never understands

Любви и гордости народной
От вас венец тот сохранит.

4

Безумцы мелкие, вы правы,
Мы чужды ложного стыда!

. . . .

5

Но честь России невредима.
И вам смеясь внимает свет...
Так в дни воинственные Рима,
Во дни торжественных побед,
Когда триумфом шел Фабриций
И раздавался по столице
Восторга благодарный клик,
Бежал за светлой колесницей
Один наемный клеветник.

That pride and popular affection
Can save a crown from greedy hands.

4

Indeed, 'tis true, oh petty madmen,
False shame is alien to us all!

. . . .

5

30   But Russia will not bow to foemen,
      And your reward is people's jibe;
      Thus, when Fabricius, the Roman,
      Returned from battles to his tribe,
      His triumph was unmarred and splendid;
35   But long before the day was ended,
      A dirty blackguard from the throng,
      A bribed nonentity offended
      The hero, as he rode along.
      [Before 1837]

БОРОДИНО

«Скажи-ка, дядя, ведь недаром
Москва, спаленная пожаром,
   Французу отдана?
Ведь были ж схватки боевые?
Да, говорят, еще какие!
Недаром помнит вся Россия
   Про день Бородина!»

— Да, были люди в наше время,
Не то, что нынешнее племя:
   Богатыри — не вы!
Плохая им досталась доля:
Не многие вернулись с поля...
Не будь на то господня воля,
   Не отдали б Москвы!

Мы долго молча отступали,
Досадно было, боя ждали,
   Ворчали старики:
«Что ж мы? на зимние квартиры?
Не смеют что ли командиры
Чужие изорвать мундиры
   О русские штыки?»

И вот нашли большое поле:
Есть разгуляться где на воле!
   Построили редут.
У наших ушки на макушке!
Чуть утро осветило пушки
И леса синие верхушки —
   Французы тут как тут.

30. BORODINO

—Say, uncle, *why* in spite of clashes
You gave up Moscow burnt to ashes
   And yielded to the foe.
I heard it that the French were rushing
5   But that your blows were also crushing,
For who will ever, if he is Russian,
   Forget Borodino!

—Yes, they were men who lived amongst us,
Not like the present breed of youngsters,
10   By battles never tossed!
Too few of them survived the fighting—
The soldiers marked by fate for smiting;
It was the will of God Almighty
   That Moscow should be lost!

15   For months we silently retreated.
We felt deceived but not defeated,
   We heard from every trench,
"Here's the reward for all our labors—
To live with enemies like neighbors!
20   Are Russian bayonets and sabers
   Too blunt to cut the French?"

Our battlefield was chosen later,
No field I'd ever seen was greater.
   We built a broad redoubt.
25   We listened closely for a warning,
And when the sun in early morning
Had lit the treetops, guns, and awning,
   The enemy was out.

Забил заряд я в пушку туго
И думал: угощу я друга!
  Постой-ка, брат, мусью!
Что тут хитрить, пожалуй к бою;
Уж мы пойдем ломить стеною,
Уж постоим мы головою
  За родину свою!

Два дня мы были в перестрелке.
Что толку в этакой безделке?
  Мы ждали третий день.
Повсюду стали слышны речи:
«Пора добраться до картечи!»
И вот на поле грозной сечи
  Ночная пала тень.

Прилег вздремнуть я у лафета,
И слышно было до рассвета,
  Как ликовал француз.
Но тих был наш бивак открытый:
Кто кивер чистил весь избитый,
Кто штык точил, ворча сердито,
  Кусая длинный ус.

И только небо засветилось,
Всё шумно вдруг зашевелилось,
  Сверкнул за строем строй.
Полковник наш рожден был хватом:
Слуга царю, отец солдатам...
Да, жаль его: сражен булатом,
  Он спит в земле сырой.

И молвил он, сверкнув очами:
«Ребята! не Москва ль за нами?
  Умремте ж под Москвой,
Как наши братья умирали!»
— И умереть мы обещали,
И клятву верности сдержали
  Мы в бородинский бой.

Ну ж был денек! Сквозь дым летучий
Французы двинулись, как тучи,
  И всё на наш редут.

I took a cannon ball and thrust it,
30   I thought, "Well, Frenchmen, you can trust it,
    And try to understand:
    You may be very strong and cunning,
    But we have stopped, we've done our running,
    We'll deal a blow that will be stunning
35   And save the Russian land."

    For three long days we fired at random,
    We knew that we had not unmanned them,
    And neither meant to yield.
    Each soldier thought it should be ended:
40   For had we fought or just pretended?
    And then it was that night descended
    Upon the fateful field.

    I dozed, like many, at my cannon;
    The grounds the French enclosed and ran on
45   Were loud from weapons hurled.
    But we were silent while they clattered,
    Some furbished shakos sadly battered,
    Some whetted bayonets half-shattered,
    And grumbled at the world.

50   But when the dark of night receded,
    All rose and mounted unimpeded;
    We saw the marching men.
    Our colonel was a man of mettle
    He led us like his sons in battle,
55   He served the Tsar, but, felled with metal,
    He'll never wake again.

    And thus he said, as would our father,
    "Boys, we are not retreating farther,
    Look, Moscow is behind!
60   Let's die, as others died before us!"
    "We will," we answered him in chorus,
    And when the battle tossed and tore us,
    We fought, to danger blind.

    That was a day! The French, exalting,
65   Like heavy clouds, began assaulting
    And aimed at our redoubt.

Уланы с пестрыми значками,
Драгуны с конскими хвостами,
Все промелькнули перед нами,
Все побывали тут.

Вам не видать таких сражений!..
Носились знамена, как тени,
В дыму огонь блестел,
Звучал булат, картечь визжала,
Рука бойцов колоть устала,
И ядрам пролетать мешала
Гора кровавых тел.

Изведал враг в тот день немало,
Что значит русский бой удалый,
Наш рукопашный бой!..
Земля тряслась — как наши груди,
Смешались в кучу кони, люди,
И залпы тысячи орудий
Слились в протяжный вой...

Вот смерклось. Были все готовы
Заутра бой затеять новый
И до конца стоять...
Вот затрещали барабаны —
И отступили басурманы.
Тогда считать мы стали раны,
Товарищей считать.

Да, были люди в наше время,
Могучее, лихое племя:
Богатыри — не вы.
Плохая им досталась доля:
Не многие вернулись с поля.
Когда б на то не божья воля,
Не отдали б Москвы!

We saw a picture wild and motley:
Dragoons and uhlans struggling hotly—
    The troops in smoke, intense and throttling,
70   All rushing, running out.

You'll never see such armies clashing,
The standards were like shadows dashing
    Through fire and screeching lead.
Each step was manfully contested,
75   The soldiers' fingers never rested,
And cannon balls would drop, arrested
    By masses of the dead.

We taught the enemy for ages
What is the Russian giant courageous,
80   When he has gone to war.
Earth shook like us—shot through and mangled,
We fell and fought, fatigued and strangled,
The field became a howling tangle—
    All thunder, fire, and roar.

85   Dusk came and stopped the shots and rattle;
We could have fought another battle
    Until its bitter end.
But then we heard that drums were beating,
And while the ruffians were retreating,
90   Our morning oaths we kept repeating
    And counted every friend.

Yes, they were men who lived amongst us,
Not like the present breed of youngsters . . .
    We were by battles tossed!
95   Too few of them survived the fighting—
The soldiers marked by fate for smiting;
It was the will of God Almighty
    That Moscow should be lost!
1837

СМЕРТЬ ПОЭТА

Отмщенья, государь, отмщенья!
Паду к ногам твоим:
Будь справедлив и накажи убийцу,
Чтоб казнь его в позднейшие века
Твой правый суд потомству возвестила,
Чтоб видели злодеи в ней пример.

Погиб поэт! — невольник чести —
Пал, оклеветанный молвой,
С свинцом в груди и жаждой мести,
Поникнув гордой головой!..
Не вынесла душа поэта
Позора мелочных обид,
Восстал он против мнений света
Один как прежде... и убит!
Убит!.. к чему теперь рыданья,
Пустых похвал ненужный хор
И жалкий лепет оправданья?
Судьбы свершился приговор!
Не вы ль сперва так злобно гнали
Его свободный, смелый дар
И для потехи раздували
Чуть затаившийся пожар?
Что ж? веселитесь...— он мучений
Последних вынести не мог:
Угас, как светоч, дивный гений,
Увял торжественный венок.

Его убийца хладнокровно
Навел удар... спасенья нет.
Пустое сердце бьется ровно,
В руке не дрогнул пистолет.

31. THE POET'S DEATH

Retaliation, Sire, retaliation!
You see me at your feet:
Be fair and let the murderer be punished,
And may his death in centuries to come
Proclaim to all posterity your justice,
That villains should not ever dare to kill.
(From a tragedy)

The poet fell, maligned by scandal,
Fell with a bullet in his breast,
Expired like a resplendent candle,
A slave to chivalry's behest.
5   He could not bear the shameless babble,
So, with a thirst for vengeance filled,
He threw his gauntlet to the rabble
And was dispassionately killed.
Killed, killed . . . you say your hearts are bleeding,
10   You praise in chorus, simper, prate . . .
Who needs your mumbling, childish pleading,
As if the murderer were fate!
Or were you not forever planning
To soil his genius and his name
15   And for your mean amusement fanning
A spark into a roaring flame?
Well! You can triumph: to his tortures
The man preferred eternal gloom;
Exult, for you extinguish torches
20   And smother fragrant wreaths in bloom.

The slayer, unmoved by the disaster,
Has taken aim—the deed is done;
His empty heart does not beat faster,
His hand is steady with the gun.

И что за диво?.. издалека,
Подобный сотням беглецов,
На ловлю счастья и чинов
Заброшен к нам по воле рока;
Смеясь, он дерзко презирал
Земли чужой язык и нравы;
Не мог щадить он нашей славы;
Не мог понять в сей миг кровавый,
На что он руку поднимал!..

И он убит — и взят могилой,
Как тот певец, неведомый, но милый,
Добыча ревности глухой,
Воспетый им с такою чудной силой,
Сраженный, как и он, безжалостной рукой.

Зачем от мирных нег и дружбы простодушной
Вступил он в этот свет завистливый и душный
Для сердца вольного и пламенных страстей?
Зачем он руку дал клеветникам ничтожным,
Зачем поверил он словам и ласкам ложным,
Он, с юных лет постигнувший людей?..

И прежний сняв венок,— они венец терновый,
Увитый лаврами, надели на него:
Но иглы тайные сурово
Язвили славное чело;
Отравлены его последние мгновенья
Коварным шепотом насмешливых невежд,
И умер он — с напрасной жаждой мщенья,
С досадой тайною обманутых надежд.
Замолкли звуки чудных песен,
Не раздаваться им опять:
Приют певца угрюм и тесен,
И на устах его печать.

*

А вы, надменные потомки
Известной подлостью прославленных отцов,
Пятою рабскою поправшие обломки
Игрою счастия обиженных родов!
Вы, жадною толпой стоящие у трона,
Свободы, Гения и Славы палачи!

25   Small wonder! From across the border,
     Like many others lacking pluck,
     In search of money, rank, and luck,
     He came to us, consumed with boredom.
     He mocked the alien tongue and mind,
30   And at that moment, grim and gory,
     He was not shaken, was not sorry
     To point his gun at Russia's glory—
     He was to fame and glory blind.

     He is killed and closed to consolation,
35   Like someone else, a child of his creation,
      A victim of the cold and cruel—
      A singer of poetic inspiration,
    Cut off like him in a relentless duel.

     Why did he leave behind the joys of adolescence?
40   Why did he want to learn the mortal lessons
     And live with people treacherous and vile?
     Why did he think—how could he think of running
     With petty slanderers, unscrupulous and cunning,
      He, who had always seen through every guile?

45   They took away his crown and gladly made it rougher,
     They put a laurel wreath with thorns upon his head
      And left him all alone to suffer,
      For no one wiped the brow that bled.
     Until the very end he saw the spurious glitter
50   And heard the falsehoods that had killed his art,
      And so he died, his sweetness turning bitter,
     His thirst for vengeance drying up his heart.
      We'll never learn, we'll never know it,
      What other songs he could have sung;
55   Deep in the ground they laid the poet,
      They sealed his lips and stopped his tongue.

*

     And you, so arrogant and bloated,
     Whose fathers' villainy has carried far and wide,
     You trample underfoot the clans on which you doted
60   The moment fortune brushes them aside.
     You, greedy, hungry pack, corrupters of the palace,
     You, murderers of Freedom, Genius, Fame!

Таитесь вы под сению закона,
Пред вами суд и правда — всё молчи!..
Но есть и божий суд, наперсники разврата!
Есть грозный суд: он ждет;
Он не доступен звону злата,
И мысли и дела он знает наперед.
Тогда напрасно вы прибегнете к злословью:
Оно вам не поможет вновь,
И вы не смоете всей вашей черной кровью
Поэта праведную кровь!

The laws you write have made you bold and callous,
Both truth and justice are for you a game!
65 But God will judge you all for every crime committed,
Yes, He will judge: He waits;
He will not be by you outwitted:
This time your clinking gold will not avert your fate.
In vain you will pretend that you are smart and clever,
70 This will not help you anymore;
In all eternity, your loathsome blood will never
Wash off the poet's righteous gore!

1837

A. S. Pushkin. Portrait by O. Kiprensky.

(?) Svyatoslav Raevsky (1836). Portrait by
Lermontov. He played an outstanding role
in disseminating the poem.

Moika. In this house Pushkin had his last apartment.

Natalya Nikolaevna, Pushkin's wife.

ВЕТКА ПАЛЕСТИНЫ

Скажи мне, ветка Палестины:
Где ты росла, где ты цвела?
Каких холмов, какой долины
Ты украшением была?

У вод ли чистых Иордана
Востока луч тебя ласкал,
Ночной ли ветр в горах Ливана
Тебя сердито колыхал?

Молитву ль тихую читали
Иль пели песни старины,
Когда листы твои сплетали
Солима бедные сыны?

И пальма та жива ль поныне?
Всё так же ль манит в летний зной
Она прохожего в пустыне
Широколиственной главой?

Или в разлуке безотрадной
Она увяла, как и ты,
И дольний прах ложится жадно
На пожелтевшие листы?..

Поведай: набожной рукою
Кто в этот край тебя занес?
Грустил он часто над тобою?
Хранишь ты след горючих слез?

Иль, божьей рати лучший воин,
Он был, с безоблачным челом,

32. A BRANCH FROM PALESTINE

Oh branch, recount to me the story
Of where you bloomed, of where you grew . . .
What hills, what valley used to glory
In having such a bough as you?

5 The sun that touched the Jordan lightly
Might kiss you too 'mid other trees.
Or did you bend when winds came nightly
And cooled the mountains Lebanese?

Who wove your leaves? An Arab peasant
Who worked and chanted songs of old?
10 He prayed perhaps . . . . And were you present
When of his woes he softly told?

And has the palm survived? And is it
As lush as it has always been?
15 Do weary men still love to visit
The hidden shelter of its green?

Perhaps the palmtree fades uprooted,
And, like yourself, in exile grieves;
Perhaps, deserted and polluted,
20 It gathers dust upon its leaves . . .

Who brought you to us with devotion?
Who plucked you in the Holy Land?
Did you observe his deep emotion
When he caressed you with his hand?

25 Or by his faith inspired and driven,
All doubts and hesitations gone,

115

Как ты, всегда небес достоин
Перед людьми и божеством?..

Заботой тайною хранима
Перед иконой золотой
Стоишь ты, ветвь Ерусалима,
Святыни верный часовой!

Прозрачный сумрак, луч лампады,
Кивот и крест, символ святой...
Всё полно мира и отрады
Вокруг тебя и над тобой.

Like you, a favorite of Heaven,
He lived and died a paragon?

Oh, noble branch, who would not liken
30 You to a sentinel of prayer,
As now you stand before an icon
Preserved by someone's secret care!

The melting dusk, the candle's waver,
The lighted cross—a simple sign—
35 The sacred image of the Savior,
All merge with you in peace divine.
1837

The corner in Muravyov's icon room that allegedly inspired
Lermontov to write "The Branch from Palestine." The
photo is given in Kushnerev's edition (see Note on No. 26)
and is very seldom (if ever) reproduced.

УЗНИК

Отворите мне темницу,
Дайте мне сиянье дня,
Черноглазую девицу,
Черногривого коня!
Я красавицу младую
Прежде сладко поцелую,
На коня потом вскочу,
В степь, как ветер, улечу.

*

Но окно тюрьмы высоко,
Дверь тяжелая с замком;
Черноокая далеко,
В пышном тереме своем,
Добрый конь в зеленом поле
Без узды, один, по воле
Скачет весел и игрив,
Хвост по ветру распустив.

*

Одинок я — нет отрады:
Стены голые кругом,
Тускло светит луч лампады
Умирающим огнем;
Только слышно: за дверями,
Звучномерными шагами,
Ходит в тишине ночной
Безответный часовой.

33. THE PRISONER

Open up my hateful prison,
Let me walk, from fetters freed!
Oh, how high I could have risen
With my maiden on my steed!
5   Come, my Black Eyes, blithe and sprightly,
I will kiss and hold you tightly;
Come, my black-maned neighing horse,
Fly with me through heath and gorse!

                *

But the locks are deaf to pity,
10   Thick and heavy is the bar,
And my Black Eyes, spry and pretty,
Hides her beauty very far.
And my steed, uncombed and idle,
Never sees his rein and bridle;
15   When he runs through hill and dale,
Winds alone caress his tail . . .

                *

Joy and hope are soon relinquished
In this cell obscure and damp;
Evening has well-nigh extinguished
20   My unsteady icon lamp;
In the stillness all-surrounding
Someone's steps I hear resounding;
'Tis the ever-silent guard
Slowly walking in the yard.
1837

119

СОСЕД

Кто б ни был ты, печальный мой сосед,
Люблю тебя, как друга юных лет,
   Тебя, товарищ мой случайный,
Хотя судьбы коварною игрой
Навеки мы разлучены с тобой
   Стеной теперь — а после тайной.

Когда зари румяный полусвет
В окно тюрьмы прощальный свой привет
   Мне умирая посылает
И, опершись на звучное ружье,
Наш часовой, про старое житье
   Мечтая, стоя засыпает,

Тогда, чело склонив к сырой стене,
Я слушаю — и в мрачной тишине
   Твои напевы раздаются.
О чем они — не знаю; но тоской
Исполнены, и звуки чередой,
   Как слезы, тихо льются, льются...

И лучших лет надежды и любовь
В груди моей всё оживает вновь,
   И мысли далеко несутся,
И полон ум желаний и страстей,
И кровь кипит — и слезы из очей,
   Как звуки, друг за другом льются.

34. THE NEIGHBOR

My gloomy neighbor, who and what are you?
I love you like my dearest friend, I do . . .
   One jailer, I believe, has seen us,
But we shall never meet, in jail or free:
5 Today a solid wall, then fate's decree—
   But something always stands between us.

When dusk is near and daylight melts away,
When in my cell I catch the scarlet ray
   And see the sun in glory sinking,
10 And when the guard just leans upon his gun,
Recalling things that he has known and done,
   And quietly dozes off, unthinking—

Then to the wall my burning brow I press.
The purport of your songs is hard to guess;
15   I listen long to them, not knowing
What tales they tell; their sounds are tragic all,
They float and reach me through the prison wall,
   Like tears, in sadness flowing, flowing . . .

And then again I want to love and strive;
20 My memories come throbbing and alive,
   I feel my world expanding, growing . . .
My blood is hot, my mind is free from fears,
I triumph, and I see my grateful tears,
   Like sounds, in sweet succession flowing.
1837

Когда волнуется желтеющая нива
И свежий лес шумит при звуке ветерка,
И прячется в саду малиновая слива
Под тенью сладостной зеленого листка;

Когда росой обрызганный душистой,
Румяным вечером иль утра в час златой,
Из-под куста мне ландыш серебристый
Приветливо кивает головой;

Когда студеный ключ играет по оврагу
И, погружая мысль в какой-то смутный сон,
Лепечет мне таинственную сагу
Про мирный край, откуда мчится он, —

Тогда смиряется души моей тревога,
Тогда расходятся морщины на челе, —
И счастье я могу постигнуть на земле,
И в небесах я вижу бога...

35.

When in a field of grain the wheat and rye wave yellow,
And to a passing wind the tranquil woods respond,
When on a bending tree a purple plum turns mellow
And hides itself, of the protecting branches fond;

5   When bathed in dew and from its fragrance tender
At early golden dawn or late at sunset red,
Serene and silvery in every tendril,
A lily of the valley bows its head;

When murmuring its tale, a rivulet meanders
10   And lulls my brain into an almost magic sleep
By telling me of secret, distant wonders,
Of peaceful mountains and of torrents deep,

Then do I feel that frosts are not so blasting;
All burdens lift and leave my forehead smooth,
15   And I perceive on earth both happiness and truth
And see above the Everlasting . . .
1837

Расстались мы; но твой портрет
Я на груди моей храню:
Как бледный призрак лучших лет,
Он душу радует мою.

И новым преданный страстям,
Я разлюбить его не мог:
Так храм оставленный — всё храм,
Кумир поверженный — всё бог!

36.

We parted, but your likeness stays
Forever hidden on my breast;
A vision from my older days,
It brings my soul content and rest.

5   And in the passions' later play
I always think of you as mine;
Thus to the fallen gods we pray
And kneel at a forsaken shrine.
1837

МОЛИТВА

Я, матерь божия, ныне с молитвою
Пред твоим образом, ярким сиянием,
Не о спасении, не перед битвою,
Не с благодарностью иль покаянием,

Не за свою молю душу пустынную,
За душу странника в свете безродного;
Но я вручить хочу деву невинную
Теплой заступнице мира холодного.

Окружи счастием душу достойную;
Дай ей сопутников, полных внимания,
Молодость светлую, старость покойную,
Сердцу незлобному мир упования.

Срок ли приблизится часу прощальному
В утро ли шумное, в ночь ли безгласную,
Ты восприять пошли к ложу печальному
Лучшего ангела душу прекрасную.

37. A PRAYER

Mother of God, I shall pray in humility,
Pray to Thine image in all its beatitude,
Not for amends or invulnerability,
Neither repenting my sins nor in gratitude;

5   Not for my soul, unprotected and shivering,
Barren of gladness, benumbed, and insensible,
But for a maid whom to you I am delivering—
Grant her defense in this world indefensible.

Grant her enjoyment and love and serenity,
10   Friends who are selfless, and worthy companionship,
Spring's satisfaction and autumn's amenity,
And for her graciousness give her Thy championship.

Early or late, at her moment of severance,
Think of this maid in Thy blessed maternity;
15   Let the devoutest of angels, with reverence,
Carry her soul to repose in eternity.
1837

127

Я не хочу, чтоб свет узнал
Мою таинственную повесть;
Как я любил, за что страдал,
Тому судья лишь бог да совесть!..

Им сердце в чувствах даст отчет;
У них попросит сожаленья;
И пусть меня накажет тот,
Кто изобрел мои мученья;

Укор невежд, укор людей
Души высокой не печалит;
Пускай шумит волна морей,
Утес гранитный не повалит;

Его чело меж облаков,
Он двух стихий жилец угрюмый,
И кроме бури да громов
Он никому не вверит думы...

38.

I am unwilling to disclose
My guarded tale and late repentance;
My love, my anguish—over those
Let God and conscience pass their sentence.

5   The heart will ask them to relent
When it has finished its confession,
And He, by Whom my pain was sent,
May judge and punish my transgression.

Reproofs of men, reproofs of knaves—
10   To noble souls, what do they matter?
Let oceans roar and rush their waves,
A cliff is not for them to shatter.

A sea cliff hides in clouds its peak,
Two worlds abide upon its granite;
15   With tempests only will it speak,
The howling wind alone will span it.
[?]1837

129

Спеша на север издалека,
Из теплых и чужих сторон,
Тебе, Казбек, о страж востока,
Принес я, странник, свой поклон.

Чалмою белою от века
Твой лоб наморщенный увит,
И гордый ропот человека
Твой гордый мир не возмутит.

Но сердца тихого моленье
Да отнесут твои скалы
В надзвездный край, в твое владенье,
К престолу вечному Аллы.

Молю, да снидет день прохладный
На знойный дол и пыльный путь,
Чтоб мне в пустыне безотрадной
На камне в полдень отдохнуть.

Молю, чтоб буря не застала,
Гремя в наряде боевом,
В ущелье мрачного Дарьяла
Меня с измученным конем.

Но есть еще одно желанье!
Боюсь сказать! — душа дрожит!
Что если я со дня изгнанья
Совсем на родине забыт!

39.

Before I've made my northern entry
And parted with the alien sun,
Kazbék! The Orient's watchful sentry!
I've come to greet you like a son.

5   Forever does a snow-white turban
Your wrinkled brow from people hide;
You disregard our vain disturbance,
And do not see it in your pride.

But may my humble supplications
10   Soar upward to your cloudy height,
And farther on, through constellations,
Where Allah sits in all His might.

I pray that midday should be colder
And cool descend on dale and road,
15   That I might sit upon a boulder
And rest awhile without my load.

And may the storm and thunder rumbling,
Pass by me on my peaceful course,
And may it never send us tumbling—
20   Myself and my exhausted horse.

But I am torn by hesitation;
I wonder: shall I travel forth?
This is the end of separation . . .
But do they want me in the North?

Найду ль там прежние объятья?
Старинный встречу ли привет?
Узнают ли друзья и братья
Страдальца, после многих лет?

Или среди могил холодных
Я наступлю на прах родной
Тех добрых, пылких, благородных,
Деливших молодость со мной?

О если так! своей метелью,
Казбек, засыпь меня скорей
И прах бездомный по ущелью
Без сожаления развей.

25   Shall I recover any traces
     Of friendships and attachments past?
     Will tender greetings and embraces
     Repay the trials through which I passed?

     Or no one's master, no one's servant,
30   I'll find my friends and brethren dead?
     The noble, charitable, fervent,
     With whom I lived and looked ahead . . .

     Should this be true, then, like a wizard,
     Kazbék, tell all your winds to blow,
35   And let a devastating blizzard
     Enwrap my homeless dust in snow.
     1837

КИНЖАЛ

Люблю тебя, булатный мой кинжал,
Товарищ светлый и холодный.
Задумчивый грузин на месть тебя ковал,
На грозный бой точил черкес свободный.

Лилейная рука тебя мне поднесла
В знак памяти, в минуту расставанья,
И в первый раз не кровь вдоль по тебе текла,
Но светлая слеза — жемчужина страданья.

И черные глаза, остановясь на мне,
Исполненны таинственной печали,
Как сталь твоя при трепетном огне,
То вдруг тускнели, то сверкали.

Ты дан мне в спутники, любви залог немой,
И страннику в тебе пример не бесполезный:
Да, я не изменюсь и буду тверд душой,
Как ты, как ты, мой друг железный.

Tiflis. An armorer's shop. Drawing by G. G.
Gagarin. (Prince Gagarin, a talented amateur,
was a close friend of Lermontov's and they
made several pictures together.)

40. THE DAGGER

My faithful dagger, bright and unsubdued,
You are my comrade, cool and biting.
A pensive Georgian forged you for his feud,
A freeborn Cherkess whetted you for fighting.

5   You were a gift to me, a priceless souvenir,
Before the parting on a murky morrow,
And for this once it was not blood, it was a tear
That dripped upon your steel, the brightest pearl of sorrow.

Her black, her thoughtful eyes were on me all that night,
With doleful mystery behind her lashes—
10   Just like your surface in a trembling light:
Now dim, now bursting into flashes.

Reminding me of love, you are its silent pledge,
And your example makes the wanderer still braver.
15   My friend of iron, I'll be like your unyielding edge:
Like you, like you, I'll never waver.
1838

135

Гляжу на будущность с боязнью,
Гляжу на прошлое с тоской
И, как преступник перед казнью,
Ищу кругом души родной;
Придет ли вестник избавленья
Открыть мне жизни назначенье,
Цель упований и страстей,
Поведать — что мне бог готовил,
Зачем так горько прекословил
Надеждам юности моей.

Земле я отдал дань земную
Любви, надежд, добра и зла;
Начать готов я жизнь другую,
Молчу и жду: пора пришла;
Я в мире не оставлю брата,
И тьмой и холодом объята
Душа усталая моя;
Как ранний плод, лишенный сока,
Она увяла в бурях рока
Под знойным солнцем бытия.

41.

My past is sad; I leave it, dreading
My future with its black disgrace.
A felon at his own beheading,
I try to find a friendly face.
5   Will someone take me off the scaffold,
Explaining things that left me baffled:
The aim of life, the way to truth,
My fate, as the Almighty meant it,
And why he bitterly resented
10 The hopes and strivings of my youth?

Of love and hope, of good and malice
I've paid the earth its earthly due;
My time is ripe, full is the chalice,
I only wait to say adieu.
15 I will not part with kin or lover;
I feel that cold and darkness cover
My soul exhausted by the strife;
A sapless fruit, an early comer,
It wilted in the storms of summer,
20 In the relentless sun of life.
1838

137

Она поет — и звуки тают,
Как поцелуи на устах,
Глядит — и небеса играют
В ее божественных глазах;
Идет ли — все ее движенья,
Иль молвит слово — все черты
Так полны чувства, выраженья,
Так полны дивной простоты.

42.

She sings: each sound I hear her singing
Melts like a kiss of gentle love,
She looks: I think of her as bringing
The beauty of the sky above.
5   She walks: her every little motion—
She speaks: her animated face—
All is expression and emotion,
All is inimitable grace.
1838

Слышу ли голос твой
Звонкий и ласковый,
Как птичка в клетке
Сердце запрыгает;

Встречу ль глаза твои
Лазурно-глубокие,
Душа им навстречу
Из груди просится,

И как-то весело,
И хочется плакать,
И так на шею бы
Тебе я кинулся.

43.

Speak with your voice to me,
Clear and melodious,
My heart then will leap
Like a bird in captivity;

5   Look with your eyes at me,
Lucid and azure-like,
My soul, when it meets them,
Sunders its manacles;

Life is all merriment,
10 And tears begin flowing;
I could die happy
Were I embracing you.
1838

Как небеса, твой взор блистает
Эмалью голубой,
Как поцелуй, звучит и тает
Твой голос молодой;

За звук один волшебной речи,
За твой единый взгляд
Я рад отдать красавца сечи,
Грузинский мой булат;

И он порою сладко блещет,
И сладостней звучит,
При звуке том душа трепещет
И в сердце кровь кипит.

Но жизнью бранной и мятежной
Не тешусь я с тех пор,
Как услыхал твой голос нежный
И встретил милый взор.

44.

Your eyes, like blue enamel gleaming,
    Are heaven's bright abyss;
Your voice, enveloping and streaming,
    Melts like a lover's kiss.

5   Without your speech I am a martyr,
    And for one look of yours
My Georgian dagger I would barter,
    That handsome tool of wars.

It also gleams with strange attraction,
10   It sings a song of steel,
It clings, it stirs to life and action,
    It warms by its appeal.

But to display its tempered splendor
    It has not had a chance,
15 Since I first heard your voice so tender
    And met your gentle glance.
1838

143

<А. Г. ХОМУТОВОЙ>

Слепец, страданьем вдохновенный.
Вам строки чудные писал,
И прежних лет восторг священный,
Воспоминаньем оживленный,
Он перед вами изливал.
Он вас не зрел, но ваши речи,
Как отголосок юных дней,
При первом звуке новой встречи
Его встревожили сильней.
Тогда признательную руку
В ответ на ваш приветный взор
Навстречу радостному звуку
Он в упоении простер.

И я, поверенный случайный
Надежд и дум его живых,
Я буду дорожить, как тайной,
Печальным выраженьем их.
Я верю, годы не убили,
Изгладить даже не могли,
Всё, что вы прежде возбудили
В его возвышенной груди.
Но да сойдет благословенье
На вашу жизнь, за то, что вы
Хоть на единое мгновенье
Умели снять венец мученья
С его преклонной головы.

I. I. Kozlov, "The blind man."

45. < TO A. G. KHOMUTOVA >

The blind man, purged by his reflection,
Admired you, blessed you, and extolled;
He bathed again in your perfection
And quickened by the recollection
5   Felt strong and happy as of old.
He did not see you, but he heard you
And opened to your greeting word;
In bitter frost, a sprig of verdure—
It brought him spring and deeply stirred.
10   And to the voice that held him captured,
Attracted by the joyful sound,
He stretched his hand, enthralled, enraptured,
And full of gratitude profound.

And I, who lovingly regarded,
15   Who saw his ardent hopes and flight,
Will keep from everybody guarded
The sad abandon of his fight.
I know that time could never ruin,
It could not possibly destroy
20   The gifts that you were fond of strewing
When life for him was sun and joy.
And may both grace and benediction
Be yours for what you did and said:
For one brief moment, your conviction
25   Removed the wreath of sad affliction
From his tormented, aging head.
1838

145

ДУМА

Печально я гляжу на наше поколенье!
Его грядущее — иль пусто, иль темно,
Меж тем, под бременем познанья и сомненья,
В бездействии состарится оно.
Богаты мы, едва из колыбели,
Ошибками отцов и поздним их умом,
И жизнь уж нас томит, как ровный путь без цели,
Как пир на празднике чужом.
К добру и злу постыдно равнодушны,
В начале поприща мы вянем без борьбы;
Перед опасностью позорно-малодушны,
И перед властию — презренные рабы.
Так тощий плод, до времени созрелый,
Ни вкуса нашего не радуя, ни глаз,
Висит между цветов, пришлец осиротелый,
И час их красоты — его паденья час!

Мы иссушили ум наукою бесплодной,
Тая завистливо от ближних и друзей
Надежды лучшие и голос благородный
Неверием осмеянных страстей.
Едва касались мы до чаши наслажденья,
Но юных сил мы тем не сберегли;
Из каждой радости, бояся пресыщенья,
Мы лучший сок навеки извлекли.

Мечты поэзии, создания искусства
Восторгом сладостным наш ум не шевелят;
Мы жадно бережем в груди остаток чувства -
Зарытый скупостью и бесполезный клад.

46. MEDITATION

Oh, sadly do I view the present generation
With its unpromising and uninspiring growth!
Oppressed by heavy doubts and sterile education,
It ages fast in idleness and sloth.
5 Upon us all our fathers have been pouring
The warnings of the weak and wisdom's late behests;
The life that faces us is long and deadly boring—
A banquet for unbidden guests.
We wither young, submissive and unhardened;
10 Good does not bring us joy, nor evil bring remorse.
By danger instantly, ingloriously disheartened,
We are obsequious slaves of every frowning force.
A fruit hangs so sometimes in early summer,
Precocious, thin, offensive to the eye and taste,
15 Among the blossoms hid, a pitiful newcomer,
By nature's triumph, by autumn's yield disgraced.

We study useless things, unpractical and arid,
But deep within, from everybody locked,
We keep our nobler hopes and have since childhood carried
20 The voice of passions ridiculed and mocked.
We touched the cup of ecstasy with trepidation
And thought to put our strength to better use;
And every joy we've had, afraid of satiation,
We've robbed forever of its precious juice.

25 The dreams of poetry have ceased to give us pleasure,
We are indifferent to genius and to art,
But miser-like we guard our last and worthless treasure,
The relics of the warmth once buried in the heart.

147

И ненавидим мы, и любим мы случайно,
Ничем не жертвуя ни злобе, ни любви,
И царствует в душе какой-то холод тайный,
Когда огонь кипит в крови.
И предков скучны нам роскошные забавы,
Их добросовестный, ребяческий разврат;
И к гробу мы спешим без счастья и без славы,
Глядя насмешливо назад.

Толпой угрюмою и скоро позабытой
Над миром мы пройдем без шума и следа,
Не бросивши векам ни мысли плодовитой,
Ни гением начатого труда.
И прах наш, с строгостью судьи и гражданина,
Потомок оскорбит презрительным стихом,
Насмешкой горькою обманутого сына
Над промотавшимся отцом.

We even hate by chance, and love will seldom bless us,
30   For we are loath to risk for love's or hatred's sake.
Some ruthless, secret frost congeals our soul's recesses,
  When burning passions are at stake.
Our fathers' daring sins make an insipid story.
  Those sumptuous revelries, that studied, childish lust!
35   The road we slowly tread has neither joy nor glory,
  And yesterday is simply dust.

A mirthless, sullen crowd, by people soon forgotten,
  We'll vanish from this world without a noise or trace,
Without a masterpiece by miracle begotten,
40   Or anything to save the human race.
When judged by better men and offspring coming after,
  We all shall be condemned in a derisive verse;
We'll quit like spendthrifts 'mid disdainful laughter
  And take with us our children's curse.
1838

ПОЭТ

Отделкой золотой блистает мой кинжал;
   Клинок надежный, без порока;
Булат его хранит таинственный закал —
   Наследье бранного востока.

Наезднику в горах служил он много лет,
   Не зная платы за услугу;
Не по одной груди провел он страшный след
   И не одну прорвал кольчугу.

Забавы он делил послушнее раба,
   Звенел в ответ речам обидным.
В те дни была б ему богатая резьба
   Нарядом чуждым и постыдным.

Он взят за Тереком отважным казаком
   На хладном трупе господина,
И долго он лежал заброшенный потом
   В походной лавке армянина.

Теперь родных ножон, избитых на войне,
   Лишен героя спутник бедный;
Игрушкой золотой он блещет на стене —
   Увы, бесславный и безвредный!

Никто привычною, заботливой рукой
   Его не чистит, не ласкает,
И надписи его, молясь перед зарей,
   Никто с усердьем не читает...

———

В наш век изнеженный не так ли ты, поэт,
   Свое утратил назначенье,

47. THE POET

A favorite of war, my sharp, unblemished blade,
    It did not ever bend or waver;
Long, long ago in Eastern smithies it was made
    And worked upon by an engraver.

5   By a Caucasian mountaineer it was possessed
    And left its victims dead and riven;
It did not seek rewards for thrusting through a breast
    Or ripping coats of mail to ribbons.

It shared its master's joys like an obedient slave
10   And boldly wrought retaliation;
To set it then in gold, embellish, and engrave
    Was but a waste of decoration.

A Cossack raised it too, to cut at war and chop
    (He took it off its owner's body);
15   It later gathered dust in an Armenian's shop
    With other goods, unused and shoddy.

Its scabbard, scratched and scarred, was lost for good and all;
    Without a sheath in which to sink it,
It glitters pleasantly—a toy upon the wall,
20   An unheroic, harmless trinket.

And no one's loving hand, with interest and care,
    Will clean again the dagger proudly,
And no one's lips will say a fervent morning prayer
    While reading its inscriptions loudly.

20   You, poet, too, in this unmanly age of ours
    Have, like that dagger, lost your station

151

На злато променяв ту власть, которой свет
Внимал в немом благоговенье?

Бывало, мерный звук твоих могучих слов
Воспламенял бойца для битвы;
Он нужен был толпе, как чаша для пиров,
Как фимиам в часы молитвы.

Твой стих, как божий дух, носился над толпой;
И, отзыв мыслей благородных,
Звучал, как колокол на башне вечевой,
Во дни торжеств и бед народных.

Но скучен нам простой и гордый твой язык,—
Нас тешат блестки и обманы;
Как ветхая краса, наш ветхий мир привык
Морщины прятать под румяны...

Проснешься ль ты опять, осмеянный пророк?
Иль никогда на голос мщенья
Из золотых ножон не вырвешь свой клинок,
Покрытый ржавчиной презренья?

And traded off for gold the sacred ancient power
  That filled the world with adoration.

It happened in the past that combatants went up
30   To your majestic steady rhythm;
  Your trenchant word was like a sacrificial cup,
    Which stayed in war and worship with them.

Your verse would cover all with its gigantic wing,
  It moved like the Almighty's spirit,
35 And you yourself were like a bell whose sound would ring,
    So men in joy and grief could hear it.
  But proud and simple words today annoy and bore,
    We love the bell that only tinkles;
  Alas! Our wilted age is like a wilted whore
40   That tries to hide with rouge her wrinkles.

Oh, prophet ridiculed! When will your dagger thrust?
  When shall we witness the explosion
At which your noble blade will leave its bed of rust,
  Its shameful scabbard of corrosion?
1838

Ребенка милого рожденье
Приветствует мой запоздалый стих.
Да будет с ним благословенье
Всех ангелов небесных и земных!
Да будет он отца достоин,
Как мать его, прекрасен и любим;
Да будет дух его спокоен
И в правде тверд, как божий херувим.
Пускай не знает он до срока
Ни мук любви, ни славы жадных дум;
Пускай глядит он без упрека
На ложный блеск и ложный мира шум;
Пускай не ищет он причины
Чужим страстям и радостям своим,
И выйдет он из светской тины
Душою бел и сердцем невредим!

48.

A darling child I am addressing;
This late epistle is to wish him joy,
And may there come a tender blessing
From every angel to the newborn boy.
5   I wish the baby would inherit
His mother's beauty and his father's worth,
And may he always use his merit
For shielding truth and godliness on earth.
I wish he would not start too early
10   To weep from jealousy or run for fame;
May falsehoods never make him surly,
For falsehood-mongers can't be put to shame.
And let him never seek a reason
For people's passions or a happy mood,
15   And may he pass through dirt and treason
And keep his faith in purity and good.
1839

НЕ ВЕРЬ СЕБЕ

Que nous font après tout les vulgaires abois
De tous ces charlatans qui donnent de la voix,
Les marchands de pathos et les faiseurs d'emphase
Et tous les baladins qui dansent sur la phrase?

A. Barbier.

Не верь, не верь себе, мечтатель молодой,
    Как язвы, бойся вдохновенья...
Оно — тяжелый бред души твоей больной
    Иль пленной мысли раздраженье.
В нем признака небес напрасно не ищи —
    То кровь кипит, то сил избыток!
Скорее жизнь свою в заботах истощи,
    Разлей отравленный напиток!

Случится ли тебе в заветный, чудный миг
    Отрыть в душе давно безмолвной
Еще неведомый и девственный родник,
    Простых и сладких звуков полный,—
Не вслушивайся в них, не предавайся им,
    Набрось на них покров забвенья:
Стихом размеренным и словом ледяным
    Не передашь ты их значенья.

Закрадется ль печаль в тайник души твоей,
    Зайдет ли страсть с грозой и вьюгой,
Не выходи тогда на шумный пир людей
    С своею бешеной подругой;
Не унижай себя. Стыдися торговать

49. DO NOT TRUST YOURSELF

Que nous font après tout les vulgaires abois
De tous ces charlatans qui donnent de la voix,
Les marchands de pathos et les faiseurs d'emphase
Et tous les baladins qui dansent sur la phrase?

Auguste Barbier

Oh, do not trust yourself, young dreamer, do not trust!
    Avoid, like poison, inspiration . . .
It is a sickness of your soul, its raving lust,
    Or captive reason's irritation.
5   You think it's Heaven's gift, but do not hope in vain:
    It's nothing but your heart's emotion!
In labor spend your life, exhaust yourself in pain,
    And quickly spill the mortal potion!

Should suddenly your barren soul begin to sing
10 At a divine and happy minute,
Should from within your depths there gush a virgin spring
    With sweet and simple music in it,
Forget it once for all, forget what you have heard,
    Ignore its harmony and splendor:
15 Its hidden meaning is not for an icy word
    Or for a measured rhyme to render.

Should sorrow grip your soul and make you sob
    Or passion come with storm and thunder,
Beware and do not show them to the feasting mob—
20 What is to you its childish wonder?
Do not debase yourself, remember not to trade

157

То гневом, то тоской послушной
И гной душевных ран надменно выставлять
На диво черни простодушной.

Какое дело нам, страдал ты или нет?
    На что нам знать твои волненья,
Надежды глупые первоначальных лет,
    Рассудка злые сожаленья?
Взгляни: перед тобой играючи идет
    Толпа дорогою привычной;
На лицах праздничных чуть виден след забот,
    Слезы не встретишь неприличной.

А между тем из них едва ли есть один,
    Тяжелой пыткой не измятый,
До преждевременных добравшийся морщин
    Без преступленья иль утраты!..
Поверь: для них смешон твой плач и твой укор,
    С своим напевом заученным,
Как разрумяненный трагический актер,
    Махающий мечом картонным...

In wrath or sadness with the rabble,
And do not let your sores be haughtily displayed,
For men will only gape and babble.

25   You may have suffered much, but graceful or uncouth,
      Why seek among us a physician?
   Who cares a bit for someone's silly hopes of youth,
      For reason's impotent contrition?
   Just look attentively and you will see a crowd,
30   All laughter, like a painted arras;
   Each looks so well-content, so satisfied, and proud,
      With not a tearstain to embarrass.

   But almost all of them have known a heinous crime
      Or have been shattered by misfortune,
35   Their furrows made them old before they'd reached their prime—
      A trace of agony and torture.
   Believe me: they'll despise your bitterness and rage;
      For them you are a shameless aper,
   A mime, a tragic actor painted for the stage,
40   Who brandishes a sword of paper.
   1839

ТРИ ПАЛЬМЫ

(Восточное сказание)

В песчаных степях аравийской земли
Три гордые пальмы высоко росли.
Родник между ними из почвы бесплодной
Журча пробивался волною холодной,
Хранимый, под сенью зеленых листов,
От знойных лучей и летучих песков.

И многие годы неслышно прошли;
Но странник усталый из чуждой земли
Пылающей грудью ко влаге студеной
Еще не склонялся под кущей зеленой,
И стали уж сохнуть от знойных лучей
Роскошные листья и звучный ручей.

И стали три пальмы на бога роптать:
«На то ль мы родились, чтоб здесь увядать?
Без пользы в пустыне росли и цвели мы,
Колеблемы вихрем и зноем палимы,
Ничей благосклонный не радуя взор?..
Не прав твой, о небо, святой приговор!»

И только замолкли — в дали голубой
Столбом уж крутился песок золотой,
Звонков раздавались нестройные звуки,
Пестрели коврами покрытые вьюки,
И шел колыхаясь, как в море челнок,
Верблюд за верблюдом, взрывая песок.

Мотаясь висели меж твердых горбов
Узорные полы походных шатров;

50. THREE PALMS

(An Oriental Legend)

In far-off Arabia, surrounded by sand,
Three palms grew together, majestic and grand.
A spring ran among them; it gurgled and carried
Cool waves through the desert forbidding and arid.
5   It purled, of the pitiless rays unafraid,
Forgetful of dangers and hid in the shade.

Thus centuries noiselessly flew o'er the palms,
And nothing disturbed the magnificent calm.
And never a camel's or wanderer's traces
10   Appeared on the land of the tranquil oasis,
But often the wind on its murderous wing
Would play with the leaves and the murmuring spring.

The trees, discontented, began to repine,
"Or, Lord, was it really Thy will and design
15   That we should be born in the this ruinous furnace
For whirlwinds to shake us and sunrays to burn us?
We stand in the desert and wither in vain;
Unjustly, oh Heaven, you rule and ordain!"

And when they had finished their plaintive reproof,
20   The sand was disrupted by foot and by hoof;
They saw through the emptiness many a camel,
The teeth of the drivers were shining enamel,
And each of the animals moved with a sway,
Resembling a boat on its watery way.

25   The camels were burdened by carpeted packs;
Marquees for the travelers swung on their backs,

161

Их смуглые ручки порой подымали,
И черные очи оттуда сверкали...
И стан худощавый к луке наклоня,
Араб горячил вороного коня.

И конь на дыбы подымался порой,
И прыгал, как барс, пораженный стрелой;
И белой одежды красивые складки
По плечам фариса вились в беспорядке;
И с криком и свистом несясь по песку,
Бросал и ловил он копье на скаку.

Вот к пальмам подходит шумя караван:
В тени их веселый раскинулся стан.
Кувшины звуча налилися водою,
И гордо кивая махровой главою,
Приветствуют пальмы нежданных гостей,
И щедро поит их студеный ручей.

Но только что сумрак на землю упал,
По корням упругим топор застучал,
И пали без жизни питомцы столетий!
Одежду их сорвали малые дети,
Изрублены были тела их потом,
И медленно жгли их до утра огнем.

Когда же на запад умчался туман,
Урочный свой путь совершал караван;
И следом печальным на почве бесплодной
Виднелся лишь пепел седой и холодный;
И солнце остатки сухие дожгло,
А ветром их в степи потом разнесло.

И ныне всё дико и пусто кругом —
Не шепчутся листья с гремучим ключом:
Напрасно пророка о тени он просит —
Его лишь песок раскаленный заносит,
Да коршун хохлатый, степной нелюдим,
Добычу терзает и щиплет над ним.

At times they would open, and from them in flashes
Young eyes could be seen under beautiful lashes;
An Arab on horseback, impatient for speed,
30 Would hustle and hasten his raven black steed.

The high-mettled stallion would whinny and bounce,
Rear up like a wounded and desperate ounce,
And fly picturesquely, compliant to urging,
The man and the stallion triumphantly merging;
35 The rider would reach for his spear and in fun
Would hurl it and catch it again on the run.

The men and the animals stopped by the trees,
The branches protected the splendid marquees,
'Mid laughter and shouting the pitchers were filling,
40 The generous water was flowing and spilling,
The palm trees complacently nodded their crests:
They welcomed the strangers, they bowed to the guests.

Refreshed by the shade was the great caravan,
Then merciless felling and hacking began;
45 The axes demolished the centuries' beauty,
The children got hold of the branches for booty,
The trunks were dismembered and chopped into logs,
To burn in the darkness and scatter the fogs.

And then, with the earliest glimmer of day,
50 The people on camels continued their way,
And all that was left in the ruined oasis
Were smouldering brands and the travelers' traces;
But even the coals were invisible soon,
All mixed with the sand by the howling simoon.

55 The place is deserted and desolate now,
And leaves on the trees never whisper or sough,
The spring for some coolness beseeches the Prophet,
But Heaven sends sandstorms to bury and scoff it,
And over its banks uninviting and gray
60 The vulture is busy devouring its prey.
1839

МОЛИТВА

В минуту жизни трудную
Теснится ль в сердце грусть:
Одну молитву чудную
Твержу я наизусть.

Есть сила благодатная
В созвучье слов живых,
И дышит непонятная,
Святая прелесть в них.

С души как бремя скатится,
Сомненье далеко —
И верится, и плачется,
И так легко, легко...

51. A PRAYER

In sadness or anxiety,
When all is gloom and grief,
A prayer I murmur quietly
That brings my soul relief.

5   There is a sweet simplicity
In every sacred phrase,
The promise of felicity,
A secret, healing grace.

The heart forgets its hárassment,
10   The stone is off the chest—
No burden, no embarrassment,
And all is peace and rest . . .
1839

ДАРЫ ТЕРЕКА

Терек воет, дик и злобен,
Меж утесистых громад,
Буре плач его подобен,
Слезы брызгами летят.
Но, по степи разбегаясь,
Он лукавый принял вид
И, приветливо ласкаясь,
Морю Каспию журчит:

«Расступись, о старец-море,
Дай приют моей волне!
Погулял я на просторе,
Отдохнуть пора бы мне.
Я родился у Казбека,
Вскормлен грудью облаков,
С чуждой властью человека
Вечно спорить был готов.
Я, сынам твоим в забаву,
Разорил родной Дарьял
И валунов, им на славу,
Стадо целое пригнал».

Но, склонясь на мягкий берег,
Каспий стихнул, будто спит,
И опять ласкаясь Терек
Старцу на ухо журчит:

«Я привез тебе гостинец!
То гостинец не простой:
С поля битвы кабардинец,
Кабардинец удалой.

52. THE TEREK'S GIFTS

Down has plunged the Terek, sweeping
All he meets upon his way;
Like a storm he rushes weeping—
Every tear is foamy spray.
5   But through steppes and valleys rolling,
He is wondrous tame and meek;
Gurgling tenderly, cajoling,
To the sea he starts to speak:

"Let me enter, oh my master,
10   Open up your mighty breast,
I was fiercer, louder, faster,
Now I need a little rest.
By the clouds beloved and suckled,
I, Kazbék's unbridled son,
15   To a tyrant never truckled,
Never cringed to anyone.
See the stones upon my shoulders?
That's a goodly load to lift!
I have robbed Daryál of boulders,
20   Just to bring your sons this gift."

But around his beaches curling,
Caspy rests upon his cheek,
And the Terek, sweetly purling,
Tries again with him to speak:

25   "Something else from my dominion
I am carrying on my wave;
I have fetched a Cabardinian,
He was handsome, young, and brave.

167

Он в кольчуге драгоценной,
В налокотниках стальных:
Из Корана стих священный
Писан золотом на них.
Он угрюмо сдвинул брови,
И усов его края
Обагрила знойной крови
Благородная струя;
Взор открытый, безответный
Полон старою враждой;
По затылку чуб заветный
Вьется черною космой».

Но, склонясь на мягкий берег,
Каспий дремлет и молчит;
И волнуясь буйный Терек
Старцу снова говорит:

«Слушай, дядя: дар бесценный!
Что другие все дары?
Но его от всей вселенной
Я таил до сей поры.
Я примчу к тебе с волнами
Труп казачки молодой,
С темно-бледными плечами,
С светло-русою косой.
Грустен лик ее туманный,
Взор так тихо, сладко спит,
А на грудь из малой раны
Струйка алая бежит.
По красотке-молодице
Не тоскует над рекой
Лишь один во всей станице
Казачина гребенской.
Оседлал он вороного,
И в горах, в ночном бою,
На кинжал чеченца злого
Сложит голову свою».

Замолчал поток сердитый,
И над ним, как снег бела,
Голова с косой размытой
Колыхаяся всплыла.

See the precious corselet glitter?
30   See the chain mail on the man?
On the plates a verse is written
All in gold from the Koran.
He has knit his eyebrows frowning,
Though his life released its grip,
35   And his scarlet blood is drowning
The moustache upon his lip.
Things indelible and sacred
Are reflected in his stare,
On his forehead sealed by hatred
40   There's a fringe of jet-black hair.''

But impenetrably languid,
Caspy dozes, soft and sleek,
And the Terek, getting angry,
Starts again with him to speak:

45   ''Uncle, something really pleasant
I am carrying to your shore,
I have hidden such a present,
As you've never seen before.
On my waves a Cossack's daughter
50   Sleeps immovable but sweet,
Pale and swarthy in the water,
With a plait like ripening wheat.
In her eyes serene and musing
Once there lived a trustful soul,
55   Now her blood is slowly oozing
From a tiny evil hole.
She's the treasure of my pillage!
All the Cossacks grieve and cry,
Though I saw that in her village
60   One is calm; his eyes are dry,
He is riding in his saddle,
Riding forward, firm and fast;
Night will come, and in the battle
He will gladly die at last.''

65   So the Terek spoke to Caspy,
So he argued, smooth and swift,
While his hungry waves were clasping
The incomparable gift.

И старик во блеске власти
Встал, могучий, как гроза,
И оделись влагой страсти
Темно-синие глаза.

Он взыграл, веселья полный, —
И в объятия свои
Набегающие волны
Принял с ропотом любви.

And in his majestic fashion
70   Did the old man Caspy rise;
Shining bright and moist with passion
Were his blue engulfing eyes.

Roused and merry, all a-tingle,
Caspy opened his embrace
75   And allowed the waves to mingle,
Full of longing, full of grace.
1839

ПАМЯТИ А. И. О<ДОЕВСКО>ГО

1

Я знал его: мы странствовали с ним
В горах востока, и тоску изгнанья
Делили дружно; но к полям родным
Вернулся я, и время испытанья
Промчалося законной чередой;
А он не дождался минуты сладкой:
Под бедною походною палаткой
Болезнь его сразила, и с собой
В могилу он унес летучий рой
Еще незрелых, темных вдохновений,
Обманутых надежд и горьких сожалений!

2

Он был рожден для них, для тех надежд,
Поэзии и счастья... Но, безумный —
Из детских рано вырвался одежд
И сердце бросил в море жизни шумной,
И свет не пощадил — и бог не спас!
Но до конца среди волнений трудных,
В толпе людской и средь пустынь безлюдных,
В нем тихий пламень чувства не угас:
Он сохранил и блеск лазурных глаз,
И звонкий детский смех, и речь живую,
И веру гордую в людей и жизнь иную.

3

Но он погиб далеко от друзей...
Мир сердцу твоему, мой милый Саша!

53. IN MEMORY OF A. I. O<DOEVSK>Y

1

I knew him well—we traveled many miles
In distant mountains, and, like loving brothers,
We shared our exile, but to native isles
I set my sail and left my friend to others.
5 I suffered with him but survived the storm,
While he—he never met a better morning;
A tent, a camp bed, and a roof of awning
Were with him to the last. He failed to find a form
For the enormous, buzzing, half-born swarm
10 Of his obscure poetic inspirations.
He died with hopes deceived, with sadness and frustrations.

2

Oh, he was born for them, for passions wild,
For life and love, but early was he ready
To throw away the garments of a child
15 And cast his heart into the worldly eddy.
Men were not merciful, God did not save!
But when he faced injustice, pain, and violence,
In noisy crowds or all immersed in silence,
His inner feeling kept him warm and brave;
20 His azure eyes were shiny till the grave,
He kept his youthful smile and lively manner,
And noble faith in men he carried like a banner.

You died alone, in sickness and distress . . .
Your heart is buried far away from Russia;

173

Покрытое землей чужих полей,
Пусть тихо спит оно, как дружба наша
В немом кладбище памяти моей!
Ты умер, как и многие, без шума,
Но с твердостью. Таинственная дума
Еще блуждала на челе твоем,
Когда глаза закрылись вечным сном;
И то, что ты сказал перед кончиной,
Из слушавших тебя не понял ни единый...

4

И было ль то привет стране родной,
Названье ли оставленного друга,
Или тоска по жизни молодой,
Иль просто крик последнего недуга,
Кто скажет нам?.. Твоих последних слов
Глубокое и горькое значенье
Потеряно... Дела твои, и мненья,
И думы, — всё исчезло без следов,
Как легкий пар вечерних облаков:
Едва блеснут, их ветер вновь уносит —
Куда они? зачем? откуда? — кто их спросит...

5

И после их на небе нет следа,
Как от любви ребенка безнадежной,
Как от мечты, которой никогда
Он не вверял заботам дружбы нежной...
Что за нужда? Пускай забудет свет
Столь чуждое ему существованье:
Зачем тебе венцы его вниманья
И терния пустых его клевет?
Ты не служил ему. Ты с юных лет
Коварные его отвергнул цепи:
Любил ты моря шум, молчанье синей степи —

6

И мрачных гор зубчатые хребты...
И, вкруг твоей могилы неизвестной,

174

25   A foreign field is all it will possess,
      And may it sleep in peace, my darling Sasha,
      As does our friendship in my mind's recess.
      You died without a pose or affectation,
      But manfully. A secret meditation
30   Was trying from your hidden depths to rise,
      When sleep eternal gently closed your eyes;
      And those who heard by chance your final message,
      They did not understand what it could mean or presage.

                              4

      Perhaps a greeting home you tried to send
35   Or called a name that one remembers ever;
      Or was it grief at your untimely end,
      Or just the pain inflicted by the fever?
      Today, who can interpret or appraise
      The deep and bitter sense of your predictions?
40   To things you did and to your past convictions
      There are, alas! no longer tracks, no ways.
      Like floating vapors, like an evening haze,
      They flash and die, their path is short and checkered . . .
      Whence are they? Why? Where now? Whoever keeps the record . . .

                              5

45   And not a trace is from them anywhere,
      As from a love that feeds on its rejection,
      As from a dream, which he would never share,
      Would not entrust to friendship or affection.
      Who cares! Who is the worse that people will not deign
50   To recognize a spirit proud and foreign?
      What are to you the thorns of their abhorrence
      Or wreaths of praises, equally inane?
      Not them you served; you managed to remain
      Free from the world and its corroding illness;
55   You loved the ocean's surge, the steppe's expanse and stillness—

                              6

      Caucasian peaks and jagged summits high . . .
      And all of it would after death await you;

                             175

Всё, чем при жизни радовался ты,
Судьба соединила так чудесно:
Немая степь синеет, и венцом
Серебряным Кавказ ее объемлет;
Над морем он, нахмурясь, тихо дремлет,
Как великан, склонившись над щитом,
Рассказам волн кочующих внимая,
А море Черное шумит не умолкая.

It all embraced the grave in which you lie,
Miraculously joined in one by nature.
60 As far as one can see, a silent field
And farther still, in shadows evanescent,
The Caucasus surrounds it in a crescent;
It dozes like a giant upon his shield,
It quietly stands, to breakers' tales attending—
65 The waves are running fast, the tales are never-ending.
1839

A. I. Odoevsky. Portrait by N. A.
Bestuzhev, 1833. (Bestuzhev's watercolor
is lost; extant is only A. Skino's
lithograph of it.)

На буйном пиршестве задумчив он сидел
Один, покинутый безумными друзьями,
И в даль грядущую, закрытую пред нами,
    Духовный взор его смотрел.

И помню я, исполненны печали,
Средь звона чаш, и криков, и речей,
И песен праздничных, и хохота гостей,
    Его слова пророчески звучали.

Он говорил: ликуйте, о друзья!
Что вам судьбы дряхлеющего мира?..
Над вашей головой колеблется секира,
    Но что ж!.. Из вас один ее увижу я.

54.

He sat all lost in thought on happy, feasting days
And used the eerie gift that he uniquely wielded:
He had a prophet's vision, and the future yielded
Its secrets to his inner gaze.

5   The words of his address were full of sadness,
He spoke and did not even raise his voice;
He let the others stupidly rejoice,
Carouse and laugh 'mid universal madness.

He said, "Feast on, my friends, without a care;
10   Your fate is sealed, you shall not overstep it.
Forget this world unworthy and decrepit,
But I, alas! can see a poleax in the air."
1839

Как часто, пестрою толпою окружен,
Когда передо мной, как будто бы сквозь сон,
  При шуме музыки и пляски,
При диком шепоте затверженных речей,
Мелькают образы бездушные людей,
  Приличьем стянутые маски,

Когда касаются холодных рук моих
С небрежной смелостью красавиц городских
  Давно бестрепетные руки,—
Наружно погружась в их блеск и суету,
Ласкаю я в душе старинную мечту,
  Погибших лет святые звуки.

И если как-нибудь на миг удастся мне
Забыться,— памятью к недавней старине
  Лечу я вольной, вольной птицей;
И вижу я себя ребенком; и кругом
Родные всё места: высокий барский дом
  И сад с разрушенной теплицей;

Зеленой сетью трав подернут спящий пруд,
А за прудом село дымится — и встают
  Вдали туманы над полями.
В аллею темную вхожу я; сквозь кусты
Глядит вечерний луч, и желтые листы
  Шумят под робкими шагами.

И странная тоска теснит уж грудь мою:
Я думаю об ней, я плачу и люблю,
  Люблю мечты моей созданье
С глазами, полными лазурного огня,

55.

How very often at a fashionable ball,
As in a dream, I stand surrounded by them all,
   Amid the noise and whispered speeches;
And guests in masks with hostesses and hosts
5 Slide quickly past like pallid, bloodless ghosts,
   Inanimate and doll-like creatures.

The bold and vicious dames with all-too-ready charms
Unhesitantly lay their hands upon my arms—
   The perfumed hands devoid of feeling;
10 Immersed in merriment and music I may seem
But from my ruined past I nurse a tender dream,
   Those sacred murmurs, old and healing.

And if sometimes I manage to forget the din
And let my memory just for a moment win,
15   It flies unfettered, freely, fleetly.
I am again a little boy and see around
The mansion and the greenhouse sinking to the ground
   And all the garden smelling sweetly.

The pond is sleeping in a bed of weeds and sedge,
20 The village roofs and smoke are seen beyond its edge,
   A mist envelops distant valleys.
The sun is setting; it is twilight in the park;
The yellow leaves are rustling gently in the dark,
   As I am passing through the alleys.

25 And then for tenderness and love my bosom yearns;
I think of her, I love, my fancy brightly burns—
   The fancy that I keep adorning.
Her eyes are beautiful and filled with azure light,

181

С улыбкой розовой, как молодого дня
     За рощей первое сиянье.

Так царства дивного всесильный господин —
Я долгие часы просиживал один,
     И память их жива поныне
Под бурей тягостных сомнений и страстей,
Как свежий островок безвредно средь морей
     Цветет на влажной их пустыне.

Когда ж, опомнившись, обман я узнаю,
И шум толпы людской спугнет мечту мою,
     На праздник незванную гостью,
О, как мне хочется смутить веселость их
И дерзко бросить им в глаза железный стих,
     Облитый горечью и злостью!..

Her smile is luminous, as roseate and bright,
30   As brilliant sunrays in the morning.

Thus did I hours in this enchanted kingdom stay,
Alone its overlord, my wishes holding sway.
     I still remember that emotion . . .
It passed through storms of love, through treachery and guile
35   And has survived intact, a fresh and flowering isle,
     Amid the desert of the ocean.

But when the dream is gone and all is feast and dance
Or if the merry tumult frightens it by chance,
     My strange and uninvited vision,
40   Oh, how I wish to see their mirth and laughter dead,
To stop and startle them with verses made of lead
     And charged with hatred and derision!
1840

И СКУЧНО И ГРУСТНО

И скучно и грустно, и некому руку подать
    В минуту душевной невзгоды...
Желанья!.. что пользы напрасно и вечно желать?..
    А годы проходят — все лучшие годы!

Любить... но кого же?.. на время — не стоит труда,
    А вечно любить невозможно.
В себя ли заглянешь? — там прошлого нет и следа:
    И радость, и муки, и всё там ничтожно...

Что страсти? — ведь рано иль поздно их сладкий недуг
    Исчезнет при слове рассудка;
И жизнь, как посмотришь с холодным вниманьем
                               вокруг,—
    Такая пустая и глупая шутка...

56. OH, BOREDOM AND SADNESS

Oh, boredom and sadness! And no one will rescue or save
  From this unendurable being . . .
My cravings? . . . Why should I forever and uselessly crave,
  When youth, the most beautiful season, is fleeing?

5 To love? . . . But whomever? If briefly, it does not avail,
  And loving forever is stifling . . .
I search in my soul; to the past I can see not a trail:
  Both anguish and joy in it—all is so trifling.

Sweet passions? But sooner or later a sobering word
10 Will cure them and easily scatter;
And life, if one cares to examine intently the world,
  Is only a joke . . . and a joke does not matter.
1840

КАЗАЧЬЯ КОЛЫБЕЛЬНАЯ ПЕСНЯ

Спи, младенец мой прекрасный,
    Баюшки-баю.
Тихо смотрит месяц ясный
    В колыбель твою.
Стану сказывать я сказки,
    Песенку спою;
Ты ж дремли, закрывши глазки,
    Баюшки-баю.

По камням струится Терек,
    Плещет мутный вал;
Злой чечен ползет на берег,
    Точит свой кинжал;
Но отец твой старый воин,
    Закален в бою:
Спи, малютка, будь спокоен,
    Баюшки-баю.

Сам узнаешь, будет время,
    Бранное житье;
Смело вденешь ногу в стремя
    И возьмешь ружье.
Я седельце боевое
    Шелком разошью...
Спи, дитя мое родное,
    Баюшки-баю.

Богатырь ты будешь с виду
    И казак душой.
Провожать тебя я выйду —
    Ты махнешь рукой...

57. A COSSACK LULLABY

Sleep, my darling, all is sleeping,
    Lulla, lulla-by.
High above, the moon is peeping
    From the peaceful sky.
5   I will sing and tell you stories
    Of the days gone by.
Close your eyes, forget your worries,
    Lulla, lulla-by.

I can see the Terek falling
10   Over rocks and land
And an angry Chechen crawling,
    Crawling knife in hand.
But your father is a soldier,
    Brave and sharp of eye.
15   Sleep, my darling, as I told you,
    Lulla, lulla-by.

You will grow and go to battle
    With the Cossack force;
I will decorate the saddle
20   For your handsome horse.
You yourself will pull the trigger;
    Time will quickly fly—
Only wait till you are bigger,
    Lulla, lulla-by.

25   You'll be strong and tough, my baby,
    Like a Cossack, brave;
I will watch you leave, and maybe
    You will turn and wave.

Сколько горьких слез украдкой
   Я в ту ночь пролью!..
Спи, мой ангел, тихо, сладко,
   Баюшки-баю.

Стану я тоской томиться,
   Безутешно ждать;
Стану целый день молиться,
   По ночам гадать;
Стану думать, что скучаешь
   Ты в чужом краю...
Спи ж, пока забот не знаешь.
   Баюшки-баю.

Дам тебе я на дорогу
   Образок святой:
Ты его, моляся богу,
   Ставь перед собой;
Да готовясь в бой опасный,
   Помни мать свою...
Спи, младенец мой прекрасный,
   Баюшки-баю.

You'll be gone, and I'll stay grieving;
30   I will think and cry—
Sleep, my boy, you aren't yet leaving,
   Lulla, lulla-by.

And my grief will never lessen,
   Never will abate;
35 May the Lord then send His blessing,
   While I pray and wait.
I will fear that you are lonely,
   That for home you sigh.
Sleep, my angel, one and only,
40   Lulla, lulla-by.

With an icon of your mother's
   You will ride away;
Keep it, while you serve with others,
   And before it pray.
45 Think of me, when night is creeping
   Or when foes are nigh.
Sleep, my darling, all is sleeping,
   Lulla, lulla-by.
[?]1840

189

<М. А. ЩЕРБАТОВОЙ>

На светские цепи,
На блеск утомительный бала
Цветущие степи
Украйны она променяла,

Но юга родного
На ней сохранилась примета
Среди ледяного,
Среди беспощадного света.

Как ночи Украйны,
В мерцании звезд незакатных,
Исполнены тайны
Слова ее уст ароматных,

Прозрачны и сини,
Как небо тех стран, ее глазки;
Как ветер пустыни,
И нежат и жгут ее ласки.

И зреющей сливы
Румянец на щечках пушистых,
И солнца отливы
Играют в кудрях золотистых.

И следуя строго
Печальной отчизны примеру,
В надежду на бога
Хранит она детскую веру;

58. <TO M. A. SHCHERBATOVA>

For fetters of duty,
For ballrooms and wearisome dances
She bartered the beauty
Of boundless Ukrainian expanses.

5   But something primeval
She saved as a Southerner's token;
Surrounded by evil,
She carried it fresh and unbroken.

The shimmer of vagrant,
Mysterious stars over beaches
10   Is hid in the fragrant
Ukrainian appeal of her speeches.

From under the lashes
Her eyes look as blue as her heaven,
15   She'll burn you to ashes
Or promise the dream of a haven.

Her cheeks are as wondrous,
As ripening plums in the autumn,
Her curls play with sunrays
20   And seem to have easily caught them.

Her faith, like a jewel,
She brought from her homeland and hoarded;
A wall 'gainst the cruel,
It guards her from all that is sordid.

Как племя родное,
У чуждых опоры не просит
И в гордом покое
Насмешку и зло переносит;

От дерзкого взора
В ней страсти не вспыхнут пожаром,
Полюбит не скоро,
Зато не разлюбит уж даром.

25   When she is with strangers
       Her kin are her mainstay and anchor;
         She passes through dangers,
       Untouched by derision and rancor.

       Bold glances and ruses
30   Will leave her impassive and frozen;
         She is slow when she chooses,
       But lucky is he who is chosen!
       1840

M. A. Shcherbatova in the Forties.

Есть речи — значенье
Темно иль ничтожно,
Но им без волненья
Внимать невозможно.

Как полны их звуки
Безумством желанья!
В них слезы разлуки,
В них трепет свиданья.

Не встретит ответа
Средь шума мирского
Из пламя и света
Рожденное слово;

Но в храме, средь боя
И где я ни буду,
Услышав, его я
Узнаю повсюду.

Не кончив молитвы,
На звук тот отвечу
И брошусь из битвы
Ему я навстречу.

59.

So many are speeches
Whose meaning is hidden,
Like magic they reach us,
Uncanny, unbidden.

5   The phrases come throbbing
With love and frustration,
Of misery sobbing
Or singing salvation.

A word born of lightning,
10   A luminous bubble
Will perish in fighting,
In tumult and trouble.

But calm or in battle,
When weaker or firmer,
15   In silence or rattle,
I'll answer its murmur.

I'll turn from the altar
To hear and to meet it,
My voice will not falter
20   In combat to greet it.
1840

ВОЗДУШНЫЙ КОРАБЛЬ

(Из Зейдлица)

По синим волнам океана,
Лишь звезды блеснут в небесах,
Корабль одинокий несется,
Несется на всех парусах.

Не гнутся высокие мачты,
На них флюгера не шумят,
И молча в открытые люки
Чугунные пушки глядят.

Не слышно на нем капитана,
Не видно матросов на нем;
Но скалы и тайные мели,
И бури ему нипочем.

Есть остров на том океане —
Пустынный и мрачный гранит;
На острове том есть могила,
А в ней император зарыт.

Зарыт он без почестей бранных
Врагами в сыпучий песок,
Лежит на нем камень тяжелый,
Чтоб встать он из гроба не мог.

И в час его грустной кончины,
В полночь, как свершается год,
К высокому берегу тихо
Воздушный корабль пристает.

60. THE GHOST SHIP

(from Zedlitz)

When darkness descends on the ocean
And stars in the firmament shine,
A battleship glides unattended,
Full sail through the billowy brine.

5   Its vanes do not turn in the tempest,
Its masts in the storm do not bend,
Its hatchways are open forever
For motionless guns to defend.

The ship is disowned by the captain,
10   Its course by the pilot unlaid,
But boldly it crosses the current,
Of breakers and shoals unafraid.

An island there is in that ocean,
As bleak as the land of the dead;
15   A grave has been dug in its quicksands,
And this is the Emperor's bed.

He sleeps by his enemies buried,
Unhonored by banner or mound,
A stone is on top of his coffin
20   To keep him for aye in the ground.

But once every May, just at midnight,
A battleship starts like a ghost,
It starts on the Emperor's death day
And lands at the ominous coast.

197

Из гроба тогда император,
Очнувшись, является вдруг;
На нем треугольная шляпа
И серый походный сюртук.

Скрестивши могучие руки,
Главу опустивши на грудь,
Идет и к рулю он садится
И быстро пускается в путь.

Несется он к Франции милой,
Где славу оставил и трон,
Оставил наследника-сына
И старую гвардию он.

И только что землю родную
Завидит во мраке ночном,
Опять его сердце трепещет
И очи пылают огнем.

На берег большими шагами
Он смело и прямо идет,
Соратников громко он кличет
И маршалов грозно зовет.

Но спят усачи-гренадеры —
В равнине, где Эльба шумит,
Под снегом холодной России,
Под знойным песком пирамид.

И маршалы зова не слышат:
Иные погибли в бою,
Другие ему изменили
И продали шпагу свою.

И топнув о землю ногою,
Сердито он взад и вперед
По тихому берегу ходит,
И снова он громко зовет:

Зовет он любезного сына,
Опору в превратной судьбе;
Ему обещает полмира,
А Францию только себе.

25 The Emperor quietly awakens
And rises alone from the dead;
His gray-colored tunic is on him,
His three-cornered hat on his head.

He crosses his arms with an effort,
30 And, walking as if in a dream,
He noiselessly reaches the vessel
And pushes it into the stream.

To France, his belovèd, he hurries,
Again to his glory and throne,
35 Again to his son and his comrades,
Back home to the land of his own.

And when through the vaporous darkness
It suddenly springs into sight,
His spirit revives in his bosom,
40 His glance is triumphant and bright.

He is quick and courageous, he marches,
He firmly approaches the shore,
He calls his attendants and marshals,
He calls his compeers as of yore.

45 But over his former companions
The Elbe imperturbably flows,
The desert unleashes its sandstorms,
And Russia, her pitiless snows.

And deaf to his call are the marshals:
50 Some perished in battles, deplored,
While others are serving new masters
And selling their saber and sword.

Bewildered and hurt by the treason,
He walks on the desolate shore,
55 He watches and waits for an answer
And angrily calls as before.

He waits for a last consolation
And loudly addresses his son;
He'll give him the world for the asking,
60 Yet, France he can promise to none.

Но в цвете надежды и силы
Угас его царственный сын,
И долго, его поджидая,
Стоит император один —

Стоит он и тяжко вздыхает,
Пока озарится восток,
И капают горькие слезы
Из глаз на холодный песок,

Потом на корабль свой волшебный,
Главу опустивши на грудь,
Идет и, махнувши рукою,
В обратный пускается путь.

But robbed of his kingdom and glory,
Expired at the zenith his heir;
The Emperor paces and listens,
But no one will come to him there.

65 He stands, and he sighs, and he watches,
Till morning returns to the land;
Then tears from his eyes drop unnoticed
And heavily fall to the sand.

In silence he turns to the ocean,
70 And, walking as if in a dream,
He noiselessly reaches his vessel
And pushes it into the stream.
1840

The Ghost Ship.
Illustration by I. Ya. Bilibin.

СОСЕДКА

Не дождаться мне видно свободы,
А тюремные дни будто годы;
И окно высоко над землей!
И у двери стоит часовой!

Умереть бы уж мне в этой клетке,
Кабы не было милой соседки!..
Мы проснулись сегодня с зарей,
Я кивнул ей слегка головой.

Разлучив, нас сдружила неволя,
Познакомила общая доля,
Породнило желанье одно
Да с двойною решеткой окно;

У окна лишь поутру я сяду,
Волю дам ненасытному взгляду...
Вот напротив окошечко: стук!
Занавеска подымется вдруг.

На меня посмотрела плутовка!
Опустилась на ручку головка,
А с плеча, будто сдул ветерок,
Полосатый скатился платок,

Но бледна ее грудь молодая,
И сидит она долго вздыхая,
Видно, буйную думу тая,
Всё тоскует по воле, как я.

Не грусти, дорогая соседка...
Захоти лишь — отворится клетка,

61. MY NEIGHBOR

They will keep me forever in prison,
In my cell I shall wither and wizen;
And the window is far from the ground,
And the sentry is always around.

5   But my cage would be darker and grimmer
If her face right across did not glimmer;
Every day by this face I am drawn,
And I nod to her gently at dawn.

It is prison that shortened my tether,
10 And it's prison that brought us together;
For the same we are destined to long,
But the bars on the windows are strong.

Once I sat at the window and waited,
With a gaze that can never be sated.
15 Lo! I saw that your fingers were quick,
And your window was pushed with a click.

Such a rogue! Who could look at me bolder!
And she lowered her head on her shoulder!
Was it windy? Or why did it fall—
20 Tell me why you let go of your shawl!

She is bold, but she hopes for my valor;
All her features are sadness and pallor,
And I feel that she yearns to be free:
She is tethered and fettered like me.

25 Oh, my neighbor! This cage can't be grimmer;
You must try it, and freedom will glimmer,

И, как божии птички, вдвоем
Мы в широкое поле порхнем.

У отца ты ключи мне украдешь,
Сторожей за пирушку усадишь,
А уж с тем, что поставлен к дверям,
Постараюсь я справиться сам.

Избери только ночь потемнея,
Да отцу дай вина похмельнея,
Да повесь, чтобы ведать я мог,
На окно полосатый платок.

And, like God's little birds, you and I,
To the fields we shall merrily fly.

Steal the keys from your father, my darling,
30 Leave the sentries carousing or snarling,
And the one at the door of my cell
I shall probably manage quite well.

Of the nights choose the darkest and longest,
Of the wines for the guards choose the strongest.
35 As to signs for myself through the wall,
Simply hang on the window your shawl.
1840

ПЛЕННЫЙ РЫЦАРЬ

Молча сижу под окошком темницы;
Синее небо отсюда мне видно:
В небе играют всё вольные птицы;
Глядя на них, мне и больно и стыдно.

Нет на устах моих грешной молитвы,
Нету ни песни во славу любезной:
Помню я только старинные битвы,
Меч мой тяжелый да панцирь железный.

В каменный панцирь я ныне закован,
Каменный шлем мою голову давит,
Щит мой от стрел и меча заколдован,
Конь мой бежит, и никто им не правит.

Быстрое время — мой конь неизменный,
Шлема забрало — решетка бойницы,
Каменный панцирь — высокие стены,
Щит мой — чугунные двери темницы.

Мчись же быстрее, летучее время!
Душно под новой бронею мне стало!
Смерть, как приедем, подержит мне стремя;
Слезу и сдерну с лица я забрало.

62. A CAPTIVE KNIGHT

Quiet and sad is the cell in my prison,
High is the window, and far is my guerdon.
Free are the birds that have gracefully risen—
They add to my shame, my distress, and my burden.

5   Prayers never come to the lips of the sinner,
Neither do songs of my mistress's glory;
Combats that brought me the fame of a winner
Will be my last, undefeatable story.

Tight is my helmet, my armor is narrow,
10   Prisoners' panoply should not be wider;
Charmed is my shield 'gainst the sword and the arrow,
Swift is my horse, though unspurred by a rider.

Time is my chosen, unwavering charger,
Bars are my visor, secure and unyielding,
15   Walls are the armor that will not get larger,
Doors with a lock are my durable shielding.

Hurry, oh time! Do not squander a second!
Grim is my visor: it stifles and smothers.
Death from afar has obligingly beckoned,
20   Ready to free me as kindly as others.
1840

ЖУРНАЛИСТ, ЧИТАТЕЛЬ И ПИСАТЕЛЬ

Les poètes ressemblent aux ours,
qui se nourrissent en suçant leur
patte.

Inédit.

(Комната писателя; опущенные шторы. Он сидит в больших
креслах перед камином. Читатель, с сигарой, стоит спиной к
камину. Журналист входит.)

Журналист

Я очень рад, что вы больны:
В заботах жизни, в шуме света
Теряет скоро ум поэта
Свои божественные сны.
Среди различных впечатлений
На мелочь душу разменяв,
Он гибнет жертвой общих мнений.
Когда ему в пылу забав
Обдумать зрелое творенье?..
Зато какая благодать,
Коль небо вздумает послать
Ему изгнанье, заточенье,
Иль даже долгую болезнь:
Тотчас в его уединенье
Раздастся сладостная песнь!
Порой влюбляется он страстно
В свою нарядную печаль...
Ну, что вы пишете? нельзя ль
Узнать?

63. THE JOURNALIST, THE READER, AND THE WRITER

Les poètes ressemblent aux ours, qui se nourris-
sent en suçant leur patte.

Inédit.

*(Writer's room, the blinds are down. He is
sitting in a broad armchair before the
fireplace; Reader, cigar in mouth, is stand-
ing with his back to the fireplace. Enter
Journalist.)*

Journalist

Hello! You are unwell? That's fine!
In troubles that beset us daily
The poet, living fast and gaily,
Will quickly lose his dreams divine.
5　When petty interests restrict him,
The mob's abominable taste
Can make of him an easy victim;
And worldly joys are such a waste:
They kill the spirit of creation!
10　But what a blessing in disguise,
If Heaven checks him in some wise:
By banishment or isolation—
Or sends a long disease to him.
The author, barred from each temptation,
15　At once begins to sing a hymn.
His very grief is often pretty;
He sees it and begins to flirt . . .
And how are you? I hope, alert?
Write something?

Писатель

Да ничего...

Журналист

Напрасно!

Писатель

О чем писать? Восток и юг
Давно описаны, воспеты;
Толпу ругали все поэты,
Хвалили все семейный круг;
Все в небеса неслись душою,
Взывали с тайною мольбою
К N. N., неведомой красе, —
И страшно надоели все.

Читатель

И я скажу — нужна отвага,
Чтобы открыть... хоть ваш журнал
(Он мне уж руки обломал):
Во-первых, серая бумага,
Она, быть может, и чиста;
Да как-то страшно без перчаток...
Читаешь — сотни опечаток!
Стихи — такая пустота;
Слова без смысла, чувства нету,
Натянут каждый оборот;
Притом — сказать ли по секрету?
И в рифмах часто недочет.
Возьмешь ли прозу? Перевод.
А если вам и попадутся
Рассказы на родимый лад —
То, верно, над Москвой смеются
Или чиновников бранят.
С кого они портреты пишут?
Где разговоры эти слышат?
А если и случалось им,
Так мы их слышать не хотим...

Writer

Nothing . . .

Journalist

20   What a pity!

Writer

What shall I sing? The East? The South?
The raptures of a happy marriage?
The mob is easy to disparage . . .
But that you've heard from every mouth!
25   All have been skyward nobly soaring,
All have been plaintively imploring
For love from winsome Miss N. N. . . .
You want some more of it again?

Reader

Yes! Take your journal; few are duller.
30   One should be very brave indeed
To choose a book like yours to read.
Look at the paper's grayish color:
It may be clean, I am not certain,
But gloves, I think, can hardly hurt one.
35   Besides, the words are all misspelt.
When I was reading it, I felt
That, though some lines are glib and rapid,
Your poets have not learned to rhyme.
The thoughts are, too, jejune and vapid . . .
40   To publish them is just a crime.
And prose? Translations all the time!
And when you treat a native topic,
It is on Moscow sharp remarks
Or something grimly misanthropic
45   Concerning offices and clerks.
Who are the models for these pictures?
What are the reasons for these strictures?
They may have heard such talks themselves,
But do we want them on our shelves?

211

Когда же на Руси бесплодной,
Расставшись с ложной мишурой,
Мысль обретет язык простой
И страсти голос благородный?

Журналист

Я точно то же говорю.
Как вы, открыто негодуя,
На музу русскую смотрю я.
Прочтите критику мою.

Читатель

Читал я. Мелкие нападки
На шрифт, виньетки, опечатки,
Намеки тонкие на то,
Чего не ведает никто.
Хотя б забавно было свету!..
В чернилах ваших, господа,
И желчи едкой даже нету —
А просто грязная вода.

Журналист

И с этим надо согласиться.
Но верьте мне, душевно рад
Я был бы вовсе не браниться —
Да как же быть?.. меня бранят!
Войдите в наше положенье!
Читает нас и низший круг:
Нагая резкость выраженья
Не всякий оскорбляет слух;
Приличье, вкус — всё так условно;
А деньги все ведь платят ровно!
Поверьте мне: судьбою несть
Даны нам тяжкие вериги.
Скажите, каково прочесть
Весь этот вздор, все эти книги,—
И всё зачем? чтоб вам сказать,
Что их не надобно читать!..

50   When will this country, sad and arid,
      Learn to distinguish gems from junk?
      And when will Russia's speech and spunk,
      Her tongue and dignity be married?

Journalist

      That is what I myself discussed:
55   The Russian Muse, her sloth eternal . . .
      When I contribute to the journal,
      I voice, like you, my frank disgust.

Reader

      Oh yes, I saw you boldly facing
      The problem of vignettes and spacing;
60   You curse the misprints and allude
      To some obscure and stupid feud.
      If what you write were simply witty
      Or if your ink were mixed with gall!
      But no, it is not. Such a pity:
65   It's dirty water—that is all.

Journalist

      Oh, I would like to be objective
      And not to sound disgruntled, but . . .
      What can I do? I need invective,
      For *I* am everybody's butt!
70   Besides, my friend, the lower orders
      Enjoy and fatten on abuse;
      Politeness, with its laws and borders,
      Is, as a concept, very loose.
      Some find us crude, some find us funny
75   But pay the same subscription money!
      The critic's lot is really bitter:
      I am supposed to be a judge,
      But all my life I read this litter,
      As if I were a common drudge.
80   And later, all that can be said
      Is that it's better left unread!

Читатель

Зато какое наслажденье,
Как отдыхает ум и грудь,
Коль попадется как-нибудь
Живое, свежее творенье!
Вот, например, приятель мой:
Владеет он изрядным слогом,
И чувств и мыслей полнотой
Он одарен всевышним богом.

Журналист

Всё это так,— да вот беда:
Не пишут эти господа.

Писатель

О чем писать?.. Бывает время,
Когда забот спадает бремя,
Дни вдохновенного труда,
Когда и ум и сердце полны,
И рифмы дружные, как волны,
Журча, одна вослед другой
Несутся вольной чередой.
Восходит чудное светило
В душе проснувшейся едва:
На мысли, дышащие силой,
Как жемчуг нижутся слова...
Тогда с отвагою свободной
Поэт на будущность глядит,
И мир мечтою благородной
Пред ним очищен и обмыт.
Но эти странные творенья
Читает дома он один,
И ими после без зазренья
Он затопляет свой камин.
Ужель ребяческие чувства,
Воздушный, безотчетный бред
Достойны строгого искусства?
Их осмеет, забудет свет...

Бывают тягостные ночи:
Без сна, горят и плачут очи,

But think how great is the elation,
What an enjoyment for the heart,
When you approach a work of art,
85   A child of wit and inspiration.
I have a friend of whom I'm proud,
His style is brilliant and appealing;
By God Himself he is endowed
With rare intelligence and feeling.

Journalist

90   Perhaps. But such distinguished men
Are too refined to use their pen.

Writer

What should they sing? It happens often
That something in the soul will soften:
The poet wants to work again.
95   This spirit comes like an obsession,
And rhymes, like waves, in quick succession,
Unhampered, by their sisters chased,
Rush forward, piling up in haste.
And then within his soul enraptured
100   The bells of dawn and sunrise ring,
By forceful words great thoughts are captured,
As pearls are captured on a string.
His new, unconquerable boldness
With every noble task can cope;
105   The world, in spite of all its coldness,
Is brightened by the poet's hope . . .
There is not anything to hinder
Or check the produce of this mood—
But later, when in need of tinder,
110   He uses it to kindle wood.
For do the phantoms born of fever
Belong with art? They cannot stay.
The world, a mocking disbeliever,
Will scorn this childish, weak display.

115   There are some nights, when tears come streaming,
When anguish crushes sleep and dreaming,

На сердце — жадная тоска;
Дрожа холодная рука
Подушку жаркую объемлет;
Невольный страх власы подъемлет;
Болезненный, безумный крик
Из груди рвется — и язык
Лепечет громко, без сознанья,
Давно забытые названья;
Давно забытые черты
В сиянье прежней красоты
Рисует память своевольно:
В очах любовь, в устах обман —
И веришь снова им невольно,
И как-то весело и больно
Тревожить язвы старых ран...
Тогда пишу. Диктует совесть,
Пером сердитый водит ум:
То соблазнительная повесть
Сокрытых дел и тайных дум;
Картины хладные разврата,
Преданья глупых юных дней,
Давно без пользы и возврата
Погибших в омуте страстей,
Средь битв незримых, но упорных,
Среди обманщиц и невежд,
Среди сомнений ложно черных
И ложно радужных надежд.
Судья безвестный и случайный,
Не дорожа чужою тайной,
Приличьем скрашенный порок
Я смело предаю позору;
Неумолим я и жесток...
Но, право, этих горьких строк
Неприготовленному взору
Я не решуся показать...
Скажите ж мне, о чем писать?

К чему толпы неблагодарной
Мне злость и ненависть навлечь,
Чтоб бранью назвали коварной
Мою пророческую речь?
Чтоб тайный яд страницы знойной
Смутил ребенка сон покойный

When greedy pain and grief are such
That icy, trembling fingers clutch
But cannot cool the burning pillow,
120 And fear comes sweeping like a billow;
A wild, inhuman cry is wrung
Right from the tortured breast; the tongue
Pronounces loudly, half delirious,
Some names, forgotten and mysterious;
125 A face, forgotten, dead for years,
In splendor once again appears—
A smiling, shining apparition.
Its eyes are warm, its heart is cold;
One loves again in meek submission,
130 And pain is mixed with sweet contrition,
While surging in the wounds of old.
Then does my pen obey my feeling,
And all I write my conscience reads.
My story tempts the world, revealing
135 My hidden thoughts and secret deeds,
My love and lust with which I trifled,
The youthful tales I learned in vain—
Now all irrevocably stifled
In passions' roaring hurricane,
140 In fights, invisible but draining,
'Mid dolls and knaves devoid of shame,
In doubts, unworthy of sustaining,
In hopes, unworthy of the name.
A judge dispassionate and lowly,
145 I laugh at things considered holy,
At the dissembler's solemn shrine,
And at the vice that looks like virtue;
Assurance, firmness, strength are mine—
But not for you I write this line:
150 You are naive, it won't convert you,
You'll only feel its deadly sting . . .
So tell me now: what shall I sing?

Why should I say my words pathetic?
They will incense the mob and tempt;
155 The world will take my speech prophetic
For an expression of contempt.
My poisoned page will, like an adder,
Disturb a child and make it sadder

217

И сердце слабое увлек
В свой необузданный поток?
О нет! преступною мечтою
Не ослепляя мысль мою,
Такой тяжелою ценою
Я вашей славы не куплю...

Or to a trusting heart dictate
160   The canons of contagious hate.
Oh, no!—it is not my ambition
To lead astray and to entice;
Your paltry fame and recognition
I will not buy at such a price.
1840

M. A. Vrubel'
Illustration to "The Journalist, the Reader, and the Writer." From
Kushnerev's edition (see Note on No. 26). Represented are (from left
to right) Lermontov, Belinsky, and Panaev.

\<М. П. СОЛОМИРСКОЙ\>

Над бездной адскою блуждая,
Душа преступная порой
Читает на воротах рая
Узоры надписи святой.

И часто тайную отраду
Находит муке неземной,
За непреклонную ограду
Стремясь завистливой мечтой.

Так, разбирая в заточенье
Досель мне чуждые черты,
Я был свободен на мгновенье
Могучей волею мечты.

Залогом вольности желанной,
Лучом надежды в море бед
Мне стал тогда ваш безымянный,
Но вечно-памятный привет.

64. <TO M. P. SOLOMIRSKAYA>

A felon's soul in heavy fetters,
When through infernal voids it flies,
Can find by chance redeeming letters
Upon the gate of Paradise.

5   And in its pain and desolation,
In all its punishment immense,
It seeks some secret consolation
By casting looks beyond the fence.

And thus in jail, when I was reading
10   Your hand, unknown to me but bold,
I saw the prison walls receding
And for a moment felt consoled.

Your note, mysteriously handed,
At once dispersed the mists of night—
15   That nameless greeting, warm and candid,
A pledge of joy, a ray of light.
1840

ОТЧЕГО

Мне грустно, потому что я тебя люблю,
И знаю: молодость цветущую твою
Не пощадит молвы коварное гоненье.
За каждый светлый день иль сладкое мгновенье
Слезами и тоской заплатишь ты судьбе.
Мне грустно... потому что весело тебе.

65. WHEREFORE?

I am disconsolate, because I love you so,
Because the wicked world, unscrupulous and low,
Will crush your bloom, inflicting pain and torment.
You'll pay with misery for every tender moment,
5   For every happy day, for every joy on earth;
I am disconsolate . . . because I see your mirth.
1840

БЛАГОДАРНОСТЬ

За всё, за всё тебя благодарю я:
За тайные мучения страстей,
За горечь слез, отраву поцелуя,
За месть врагов и клевету друзей;
За жар души, растраченный в пустыне,
За всё, чем я обманут в жизни был...
Устрой лишь так, чтобы тебя отныне
Недолго я еще благодарил.

66. THANKSGIVING

For all to Thee my gratitude I offer:
For every pain that tortures me and bends,
For poisoned kisses, insults of the scoffer,
For foes' revenge and the deceit of friends;
5   For passions' warmth expended in the desert,
For all the treasons life has kept in store . . .
But only grant (Thy humble servant says it):
Please, do not let me thank Thee anymore.
1840

225

РЕБЕНКУ

О грезах юности томим воспоминаньем,
С отрадой тайною и тайным содроганьем,
Прекрасное дитя, я на тебя смотрю...
О, если б знало ты, как я тебя люблю!
Как милы мне твои улыбки молодые,
И быстрые глаза, и кудри золотые,
И звонкий голосок! — Не правда ль, говорят,
Ты на нее похож? — Увы! года летят;
Страдания ее до срока изменили,
Но верные мечты тот образ сохранили
В груди моей; тот взор, исполненный огня,
Всегда со мной. А ты, ты любишь ли меня?
Не скучны ли тебе непрошеные ласки?
Не слишком часто ль я твои целую глазки?
Слеза моя ланит твоих не обожгла ль?
Смотри ж, не говори ни про мою печаль,
Ни вовсе обо мне. К чему? Ее, быть может,
Ребяческий рассказ рассердит иль встревожит...

Но мне ты всё поверь. Когда в вечерний час
Пред образом с тобой заботливо склонясь,
Молитву детскую она тебе шептала
И в знаменье креста персты твои сжимала,
И все знакомые родные имена
Ты повторял за ней,— скажи, тебя она
Ни за кого еще молиться не учила?
Бледнея, может быть, она произносила
Название, теперь забытое тобой...
Не вспоминай его... Что имя? — звук пустой!
Дай бог, чтоб для тебя оно осталось тайной.
Но если как-нибудь, когда-нибудь, случайно
Узнаешь ты его,— ребяческие дни
Ты вспомни и его, дитя, не прокляни!

67. TO A CHILD

When of my past I think, all lost in meditation,
At times with secret joy, at times with detestation,
My child, my darling boy, I like to look at you . . .
How fond of you I am! Oh, if you only knew!
5   How very much I like to see you coyly smiling,
I love your eyes, your golden locks—for reconciling
My life and me. I hear your gentle voice and think,
"They say, he is like her." You're a living link
Between us . . . Time flies very fast and is a niggard!
10   Her face is, as I've heard, by sufferings disfigured . . .
But dreams, my faithful dreams, preserve her fiery gaze,
Her image, quite unchanged, within me always stays.
And do you love me? When I am with you, I soften.
Are you not bored? Perhaps I kiss your eyes too often?
15   When kissing you, I cry; my tears might burn your cheek.
Still when you talk to her, I beg you: do not speak
Of me or of my grief . . . Why tell her that? Your story
May take away her peace, may even make her sorry . . .

But open up to me and say: When day is done,
20   And when she comes and prays with you, her only son,
And whispers sacred words to you and lingers
To make you cross yourself with your obedient fingers,
When she pronounces names, the names that you repeat,
The ones you cherish both—for they are dear and sweet—
25   Perhaps she taught you, child, her voice and courage failing,
To pray for somebody whose name to you seemed alien,
For someone still alive whose name you had not heard?
Do not remember it. What is a name? A word!
God grant that it remain from you well kept and hidden . . .
30   But if by accident, unwanted and unbidden,
It comes to you one day, have mercy—if you can.
Recall your childish prayers and do not curse the man!
1840

227

А. О. СМИРНОВОЙ

В простосердечии невежды
Короче знать вас я желал,
Но эти сладкие надежды
Теперь я вовсе потерял.
Без вас — хочу сказать вам много,
При вас — я слушать вас хочу:
Но молча вы глядите строго,
И я, в смущении, молчу!
Что делать? — речью безыскусной
Ваш ум занять мне не дано...
Всё это было бы смешно,
Когда бы не было так грустно.

A. O. Smirnova.
Portrait by P. F. Sokolov.

68. TO A. O. SMIRNOVA

[So artless and naive and open,
I wanted to become your friend;
Alas! Those dreams were all utopian,
And I have shed them in the end.]
5   Without you, words stand by me boldly,
But they betray me when you come;
You look reprovingly and coldly,
Which is enough to strike me dumb.
What can I do? I am not cunning,
10   My words are innocent. Too bad!
If all of it were not so sad,
Perhaps it even would be funny.
1840

229

The miniature of A. K. Vorontsova-
Dashkova that inspired the poem.

К ПОРТРЕТУ

Как мальчик кудрявый, резва,
Нарядна, как бабочка летом;
Значенья пустого слова
В устах ее полны приветом.

Ей нравиться долго нельзя:
Как цепь, ей несносна привычка,
Она ускользнет, как змея,
Порхнет и умчится, как птичка.

Таит молодое чело
По воле — и радость и горе.
В глазах — как на небе светло,
В душе ее темно, как в море!

То истиной дышит в ней всё,
То всё в ней притворно и ложно!
Понять невозможно ее,
Зато не любить невозможно.

Detail of the miniature.

69. TO A PORTRAIT

A butterfly sent by the south,
Vivacious and playful as Cupid,
Whatever she says—in her mouth
It cannot be paltry or stupid.

5   Inconstant and charming to all,
She shrinks from the fetters of habit;
Away like a snake she will crawl,
Escape like a scampering rabbit.

She can be incredibly sly
10 Or promise reward and devotion;
Her eyes are as blue as the sky,
Her soul is as dark as the ocean.

Her frankness and beautiful calm
Can turn into anger and treason.
15 She may be a puzzle to reason,
But reason is nothing to charm.
1840

231

ТУЧИ

Тучки небесные, вечные странники!
Степью лазурною, цепью жемчужною
Мчитесь вы, будто как я же, изгнанники
С милого севера в сторону южную.

Кто же вас гонит: судьбы ли решение?
Зависть ли тайная? злоба ль открытая?
Или на вас тяготит преступление?
Или друзей клевета ядовитая?

Нет, вам наскучили нивы бесплодные...
Чужды вам страсти и чужды страдания;
Вечно холодные, вечно свободные,
Нет у вас родины, нет вам изгнания.

70. CLOUDS

Heaven's inhabitants, friends of diversity,
Aimlessly roaming in endless variety!
Can you be exiles and prey to adversity,
Fleeing, like me, in regret and anxiety?

5   Why from your home in the South are you traveling?
Is it a crime that has made of you wanderers?
Destiny's verdict? Or venomous caviling?
Thrusts of your friends? Or the malice of slanderers?

No, you are bored by the world's immobility;
10   Easily forming and easily vanishing,
Heedless of friendliness, deaf to hostility—
No one is driving you, no one is banishing.
1840

233

ЗАВЕЩАНИЕ

Наедине с тобою, брат,
Хотел бы я побыть:
На свете мало, говорят,
Мне остается жить!
Поедешь скоро ты домой:
Смотри ж... Да что? моей судьбой,
Сказать по правде, очень
Никто не озабочен.

А если спросит кто-нибудь...
Ну, кто бы ни спросил,
Скажи им, что навылет в грудь
Я пулей ранен был;
Что умер честно за царя,
Что плохи наши лекаря
И что родному краю
Поклон я посылаю.

Отца и мать мою едва ль
Застанешь ты в живых...
Признаться, право, было б жаль
Мне опечалить их;
Но если кто из них и жив,
Скажи, что я писать ленив,
Что полк в поход послали
И чтоб меня не ждали.

Соседка есть у них одна...
Как вспомнишь, как давно
Расстались!.. Обо мне она
Не спросит... всё равно,
Ты расскажи всю правду ей,
Пустого сердца не жалей;
Пускай она поплачет...
Ей ничего не значит!

71. TESTAMENT

Please, could I have perhaps a word
With you alone, my friend?
From many people I have heard
That I am near my end.
5   You'll soon be home, and you may tell . . .
Although, as I remember well,
They won't be in a hurry
To look for me or worry.

Should someone ask you questions still,
10   Whoever that may be,
Explain that bullets hit and kill,
And one was meant for me;
That for the Tsar I waged my head,
That doctors are not worth their bread,
15   And that while I was dying,
My thoughts were homeward flying.

By now my parents, I believe,
Have died, for they were old.
It's just as well: they both would grieve,
20   Should all the truth be told.
If one of them is living, say
That I am fighting far away
And that it would be better
Not to expect a letter.

25   They had a neighbor, lived next door . . .
So many years have passed!
She never thinks of me or war,
But speak to her unasked.
Just tell her all, and let her smart,
30   It cannot break the empty heart.
She'll cry perhaps and chatter,
Which really doesn't matter.
1840

ОПРАВДАНИЕ

Когда одни воспоминанья
О заблуждениях страстей,
На место славного названья,
Твой друг оставит меж людей, —

И будет спать в земле безгласно
То сердце, где кипела кровь,
Где так безумно, так напрасно
С враждой боролася любовь, —

Когда пред общим приговором
Ты смолкнешь, голову склоня,
И будет для тебя позором
Любовь безгрешная твоя, —

Того, кто страстью и пороком
Затмил твои младые дни,
Молю: язвительным упреком
Ты в оный час не помяни.

Но пред судом толпы лукавой
Скажи, что судит нас иной
И что прощать святое право
Страданьем куплено тобой.

72. A PLEA

When time has finally extinguished
All recollections of my pride,
When, once respected and distinguished,
My name has been to folly tied;

5 And when my heart in mute submission
Has plunged into eternal sleep,
So love and hatred and contrition
Can make it neither laugh nor weep;

When overwhelmed by vile attention,
10 You bend despondently your head,
Afraid to speak, afraid to mention
Your love for someone who is dead,

Your love for someone, who, though sinning,
Eclipsed your younger, better years,
15 Then do not curse your bright beginning
And do not show the mob your tears.

Just tell the wicked, sly, and hardened
To put aside their spite and grudge;
You suffered long and will be pardoned
20 By Him Who is a milder judge.
1840

237

РОДИНА

Люблю отчизну я, но странною любовью!
Не победит ее рассудок мой.
　　Ни слава, купленная кровью,
Ни полный гордого доверия покой,
Ни темной старины заветные преданья
Не шевелят во мне отрадного мечтанья.

　　Но я люблю — за что, не знаю сам —
　　Ее степей холодное молчанье,
　　Ее лесов безбрежных колыханье,
Разливы рек ее, подобные морям;
Проселочным путем люблю скакать в телеге
И, взором медленным пронзая ночи тень,
Встречать по сторонам, вздыхая о ночлеге,
Дрожащие огни печальных деревень.
　　Люблю дымок спаленной жнивы,
　　В степи ночующий обоз
　　И на холме средь желтой нивы
　　Чету белеющих берез.
С отрадой многим незнакомой
Я вижу полное гумно,
Избу, покрытую соломой,
С резными ставнями окно;
И в праздник, вечером росистым,
Смотреть до полночи готов
На пляску с топаньем и свистом
Под говор пьяных мужичков.

238

73. MY NATIVE LAND

I love my native land but love it strangely; reason
  Has vainly tried to make this love less strange:
    The glory bought by blood and treason,
The proud serenity that will not pass or change,
5 The sacred chronicles of the heroic nation—
None ever strikes a spark in my imagination.

  How odd that I am moved by simpler things!
    By rustling woods on infinite expanses,
    The silent steppe that neither speaks nor answers,
10 The overflowing streams that swell like seas in spring.
I also like to ride through country starkness
And from the cart to look at the surrounding sights;
To dream of restful sleep and search the gloomy darkness
For mournful villages with ever-trembling lights.
15 I love the smoke of burning stubble,
    The steppe and drays, the midnight sky,
    And on a hill a tender couple—
    Two birches, white in yellow rye.
    Perhaps like few, I find it pleasant
20 To see a garner full of grain,
    Carved shutters made by patient peasants,
    The thatch resisting snow and rain.
    And when the countryside rejoices,
    When Sunday night is fresh and damp,
25 I love to hear men's drunken voices
    And see them whistle, dance, and stamp.
1841

ЛЮБОВЬ МЕРТВЕЦА

Пускай холодною землею
    Засыпан я,
О друг! всегда, везде с тобою
    Душа моя.
Любви безумного томленья,
    Жилец могил,
В стране покоя и забвенья
    Я не забыл.

*

Без страха в час последней муки
    Покинув свет,
Отрады ждал я от разлуки —
    Разлуки нет.
Я видел прелесть бестелесных
    И тосковал,
Что образ твой в чертах небесных
    Не узнавал.

*

Что мне сиянье божьей власти
    И рай святой?
Я перенес земные страсти
    Туда с собой.
Ласкаю я мечту родную
    Везде одну;
Желаю, плачу и ревную,
    Как в старину.

74. A DEAD MAN'S LOVE

Yes, it is true that I was swallowed
    By clammy death,
But from my grave I've watched and followed
    Your every breath.
5   I do not bide among the living,
    But passions' thrust
I saved from darkness and oblivion,
    From death and dust.

*

When from this world I once departed
10   To sleep and rot,
I thought and hoped that we had parted,
    But we did not.
Through fields of Paradise I plodded
    And grieved anew;
15 What are to me the disembodied?
    I needed you!

*

I do not want the saints' quietus
    For all its worth:
The human pangs that gnaw and eat us
20   I brought from earth.
One single dream I am used to nursing,
    One single woe;
I love; I hate my rivals, cursing
    As long ago.

*

Коснется ль чуждое дыханье
    Твоих ланит,
Моя душа в немом страданье
    Вся задрожит.
Случится ль, шепчешь засыпая
    Ты о другом,
Твои слова текут пылая
    По мне огнем.

*

Ты не должна любить другого,
    Нет, не должна,
Ты мертвецу, святыней слова,
    Обручена.
Увы, твой страх, твои моленья
    К чему оне?
Ты знаешь, мира и забвенья
    Не надо мне!

*

25 A stranger's breath may touch your forehead—
Then I will start:
A jealous flame will scorch me torrid
And burn my heart.
The face you dream of may be someone's
30 Who is not dead;
Your dream for me is like a summons
In molten lead.

*

No other man must make you merry;
Before I died,
35 You swore to me that we should marry.
You are my bride!
Alas, your fear and desperation—
Who wants your plea?
You know: oblivion and salvation
40 Are not for me!
1841

Portrait of S. N. Karamzina
by P. N. Orlov.

\<ИЗ АЛЬБОМА С. Н. КАРАМЗИНОЙ\>

Любил и я в былые годы,
В невинности души моей,
И бури шумные природы,
И бури тайные страстей.

Но красоты их безобразной
Я скоро таинство постиг,
И мне наскучил их несвязный
И оглушающий язык.

Люблю я больше год от году,
Желаньям мирным дав простор,
Поутру ясную погоду,
Под вечер тихий разговор,

Люблю я парадоксы ваши,
И ха-ха-ха, и хи-хи-хи,
Смирновой штучку, фарсу Саши
И Ишки Мятлева стихи...

S. N. Karamzina in the Forties.
Portrait by T. Wright.

75. <FROM THE ALBUM OF
S. N. Karamzina>

In years gone by (you've spoken truly!)
I also loved, as do the young,
Loud storms of nature, things unruly,
And stormy passions' secret tongue.
5   But later I have been unwilling
To trust and use their secret trick,
Their thunder seems no longer thrilling,
Their ugly beauty makes me sick.

So now that years have marched together
10   I give to peaceful wishes flight:
At sunrise, calm and tranquil weather,
A quiet and steady talk at night.

To me your puns are interesting,
And ha-ha-ha! you funny folks!
15   Smirnóva's quips and Sásha's jesting,
And Íshka Myátlev's clever jokes.
1841

Countess E. P. Rostopchina.

ГРАФИНЕ РОСТОПЧИНОЙ

Я верю: под одной звездою
Мы с вами были рождены;
Мы шли дорогою одною,
Нас обманули те же сны.
Но что ж! — от цели благородной
Оторван бурею страстей,
Я позабыл в борьбе бесплодной
Преданья юности моей.
Предвидя вечную разлуку,
Боюсь я сердцу волю дать;
Боюсь предательскому звуку
Мечту напрасную вверять...

Так две волны несутся дружно
Случайной, вольною четой
В пустыне моря голубой:
Их гонит вместе ветер южный;
Но их разрознит где-нибудь
Утеса каменная грудь...
И, полны холодом привычным,
Они несут брегам различным,
Без сожаленья и любви,
Свой ропот сладостный и томный,
Свой бурный шум, свой блеск заемный
И ласки вечные свои.

The Countess at a later age (drawing by
E. A. Mertvago, née Soimonova).

76. TO COUNTESS ROSTOPCHINA

    I've always known: one star received us
When first we saw the light of day;
When we were young, one dream deceived us,
One road was paved for us, one way.
5   Alas for me! Of passions' battle
I paid the overwhelming cost:
In useless strife and vapid prattle
My noble goals I dropped and lost.
Too soon I'll part from you forever;
10   I feel it, and my words are terse:
I am afraid that time will sever
My hope from my inconstant verse . . .

    Two ocean waves run so embracing,
And driven by the southern breeze
15   They cross the desert of the seas,
Unthinkingly and gaily racing.
But far away a cliff or ledge
Will come between them like a wedge . . .
And then devoid of agitation
20   They hurry on in separation,
Forgetful of the broken bliss;
They carry forth their roaring clamor,
Their languid whisper, borrowed glamour,
And ever-ready liquid kiss.
1841

ДОГОВОР

Пускай толпа клеймит презреньем
Наш неразгаданный союз,
Пускай людским предубежденьем
Ты лишена семейных уз.

Но перед идолами света
Не гну колени я мои;
Как ты, не знаю в нем предмета
Ни сильной злобы, ни любви.

Как ты, кружусь в веселье шумном,
Не отличая никого:
Делюся с умным и безумным,
Живу для сердца своего.

Земного счастья мы не ценим,
Людей привыкли мы ценить:
Себе мы оба не изменим,
А нам не могут изменить.

В толпе друг друга мы узнали;
Сошлись и разойдемся вновь.
Была без радости любовь,
Разлука будет без печали.

77. THE PACT

Oh, let the world torment and hate us
And probe our secret with a knife,
And let it rob you of the status
Of a respected, honest wife!

5   We both despise the proud and idle—
The rabble's gods of love and hate;
Let someone else create an idol
To bow before and venerate.

Like you, I think, I have forever
10   Through dancing and enjoyment whirled;
Some men are foolish, some are clever,
But all are welcome to my world.

For earthly gains we do not bother,
By goodness only are we swayed;
15   We two who won't betray each other
By men can never be betrayed.

We met by chance 'mid noise and madness,
We met and we shall come apart.
The love was joyless from the start,
20   The parting will not bring us sadness.
1841

249

Прощай, немытая Россия,
Страна рабов, страна господ,
И вы, мундиры голубые,
И ты, им преданный народ.

Быть может, за стеной Кавказа
Сокроюсь от твоих пашей,
От их всевидящего глаза,
От их всеслышащих ушей.

78.

Farewell, my Russia, sad and sordid!
To slaves and masters my adieu.
Farewell, blue uniforms—and lord it
Over the men that cringe to you.

5   Who knows? Perhaps 'mid brave Caucasians
I'll hide myself from your viziers,
From searching eyes on all occasions,
From ever-present, open ears.
1841

УТЕС

Ночевала тучка золотая
На груди утеса-великана;
Утром в путь она умчалась рано,
По лазури весело играя;

Но остался влажный след в морщине
Старого утеса. Одиноко
Он стоит, задумался глубоко,
И тихонько плачет он в пустыне.

79. THE CLIFF

On the bosom of a cliff deserted,
Slept a cloudlet, beautiful and pearly,
But she left him in the morning, early:
Flew away and with the azure flirted.

5   And a gentle trace of moisture only
Stayed till later in his furrow hidden;
In the wilderness he towers lonely,
Lost in thought and dropping tears unbidden.
1841

СПОР

Как-то раз перед толпою
Соплеменных гор
У Казбека с Шат-горою *
Был великий спор.
«Берегись! — сказал Казбеку
Седовласый Шат, —
Покорился человеку
Ты недаром, брат!
Он настроит дымных келий
По уступам гор;
В глубине твоих ущелий
Загремит топор;
И железная лопата
В каменную грудь,
Добывая медь и злато,
Врежет страшный путь.
Уж проходят караваны
Через те скалы,
Где носились лишь туманы
Да цари-орлы.
Люди хитры! Хоть и труден
Первый был скачок,
Берегися! многолюден
И могуч Восток!»
— Не боюся я Востока! —
Отвечал Казбек, —
Род людской там спит глубоко
Уж девятый век.
Посмотри: в тени чинары

---

* Шат — Елбрус. (*Примечание Лермонтова*).

80. THE DEBATE

Once it was that Shat, the mountain,[1]
  And Kazbék the Great
In a thunderous encounter
  Held a loud debate.
5 Long they argued with each other;
  Said the white-haired Shat,
"You have bowed to man, oh brother,
  You will smart for that.
Man will build his smoky hovels
10 And destroy your pride,
He will cut with heavy shovels
  Through your stony side.
Once he comes to you and settles
  In your granite core,
15 He will break your breast for metals,
  Mining gold and ore.
Look! Across your summits regal
  Camels pass in crowds;
This is where a lonely eagle
20 Used to fly through clouds.
Men are crafty. The beginning
  Took them very long,
But remember: they are winning,
  For the East is strong."
25 Said Kazbék, "The East is hazy;
  Drop your groundless fears,
In the East they have been lazy
  For a thousand years.
There's a Georgian by the plantain:

---

[1]Shat is Elbrus. (Lermontov's note.)

255

Пену сладких вин
На узорные шальвары
Сонный льет грузин;
И склонясь в дыму кальяна
На цветной диван,
У жемчужного фонтана
Дремлет Тегеран.
Вот — у ног Ерусалима,
Богом сожжена,
Безглагольна, недвижима
Мертвая страна;
Дальше, вечно чуждый тени,
Моет желтый Нил
Раскаленные ступени
Царственных могил.
Бедуин забыл наезды
Для цветных шатров
И поет, считая звезды,
Про дела отцов.
Всё, что здесь доступно оку,
Спит, покой ценя...
Нет! не дряхлому Востоку
Покорить меня!

«Не хвались еще заране! —
Молвил старый Шат, —
Вот на севере в тумане
Что-то видно, брат!»

Тайно был Казбек огромный
Вестью той смущен;
И, смутясь, на север темный
Взоры кинул он;
И туда в недоуменье
Смотрит, полный дум:
Видит странное движенье,
Слышит звон и шум.
От Урала до Дуная,
До большой реки,
Колыхаясь и сверкая,
Движутся полки;
Веют белые султаны,
Как степной ковыль;

30 In his sunlit land,
   He has put aside his lantern,
      Dozing, jug in hand.
   See the hookahs smoking slowly?
      This is Teheran
35 Dreaming by its fountains holy
      On a soft divan.
   And the land beyond the Jordan,
      Flattened like a shelf,
   Is asleep where deserts broaden,
40   Burnt by God Himself.
   Farther on the Nile has tarried,
      And its yellow waves
   Crawl through acres hot and arid,
      Licking royal graves.
45 Bedouins never raid or ravage,
      Never fight for fame;
   Nomads' songs are bold and savage—
      They themselves are tame.
   The decrepit East will slumber,
50   Full of rosy hopes;
   Not such forces will outnumber
      My ravines and slopes."

   "Brother, this is foolish vaunting"—
      Said the mighty Shat—
55 "Northern forces are not wanting.
      Have you noticed that?"

   Shat pronounced his admonition,
      And Kazbék annoyed,
   Cast his glances with suspicion
60   Through the northern void.
   There he noticed in an instant,
      Saw with sudden fright
   In a country, huge and distant,
      Motion, changes, light.
65 From the Urals' barren ridges
      To the Danube's banks,
   Crossing valleys, crossing bridges,
      Soldiers move in ranks.
   Plumes are low on every helmet,
70   For the wind is strong,

Мчатся пестрые уланы,
    Подымая пыль;
Боевые батальоны
    Тесно в ряд идут,
Впереди несут знамены,
    В барабаны бьют;
Батареи медным строем
    Скачут и гремят,
И дымясь, как перед боем,
    Фитили горят.
И испытанный трудами
    Бури боевой,
Их ведет, грозя очами,
    Генерал седой.
Идут все полки могучи,
    Шумны, как поток,
Страшно-медленны, как тучи,
    Прямо на восток.

И томим зловещей думой,
    Полный черных снов,
Стал считать Казбек угрюмый —
    И не счел врагов.
Грустным взором он окинул
    Племя гор своих,
Шапку * на́ брови надвинул —
    И навек затих.

---

* Горцы называют шапкою облака, постоянно лежащие на вершине Казбека. *(Примечание Лермонтова).*

But the uhlans overwhelm it,
Rushing all along.

Bravely marching war battalions
Are resolved to win;
75 Mounted batteries, on stallions,
Ride amid the din.
Old Kazbék is looking puzzled:
Drummers beat with sticks,
Heavy cannons, open-muzzled,
80 Roll with smoking wicks.
The commander, wise and hardened,
Though his head is white,
Is as ever strong and ardent,
With his eyes alight.
85 Onward crawls the mighty army,
Like a cloud released;
Dark, enveloping, alarming,
Heading for the East.

And the great Caucasian mountain,
90 Gloomy and morose,
Tried but could not finish counting
The advancing rows.
Sad, he glanced where eagles hovered,
Shuddered in dismay,
95 With a cap[2] his eyebrows covered
And was still for aye.
1841

---

[2]A cap, in the speech of mountaineers, is
the clouds always lying on Kazbék's sum-
mit. (Lermontov's note.)

"The Debate"
Illustration by V. D. Polenov

"The Debate"
Illustration by D. I. Mitrokhin.

СОН

В полдневный жар в долине Дагестана
С свинцом в груди лежал недвижим я;
Глубокая еще дымилась рана,
По капле кровь точилася моя.

Лежал один я на песке долины;
Уступы скал теснилися кругом,
И солнце жгло их желтые вершины
И жгло меня — но спал я мертвым сном.

И снился мне сияющий огнями
Вечерний пир в родимой стороне.
Меж юных жен, увенчанных цветами,
Шел разговор веселый обо мне.

Но в разговор веселый не вступая,
Сидела там задумчиво одна,
И в грустный сон душа ее младая
Бог знает чем была погружена;

И снилась ей долина Дагестана;
Знакомый труп лежал в долине той;
В его груди дымясь чернела рана,
И кровь лилась хладеющей струей.

81. THE DREAM

Deep in a dale, immovable and choking,
I lay alone, my breast by bullets ripped;
At scorching noon my open wound was smoking,
And drop by drop my blood congealed and dripped.

5   The dale was empty after the invasion,
The mountains stood inhospitably steep,
Their summits cracked in midday heat Caucasian,
But I was cold in my unbroken sleep.

I slept and dreamed that women decked with roses
10   Had come together for a merry feast;
They drank and laughed and sat in languid poses.
They talked of me; their talking never ceased.

But 'mid the guests there was a silent maiden
Who did not laugh and did not talk or dance.
15   The table stood with rich refreshments laden,
But something plunged her feelings in a trance.

She dreamed of someone motionless and choking;
A man she knew was dying in a dale,
At scorching noon his open wound was smoking,
20   And all his blood became congealed and stale.
1841

263

ТАМАРА

В глубокой теснине Дарьяла,
Где роется Терек во мгле,
Старинная башня стояла,
Чернея на черной скале.

В той башне высокой и тесной
Царица Тамара жила:
Прекрасна, как ангел небесный,
Как демон, коварна и зла.

И там сквозь туман полуночи
Блистал огонек золотой,
Кидался он путнику в очи,
Манил он на отдых ночной.

И слышался голос Тамары:
Он весь был желанье и страсть,
В нем были всесильные чары,
Была непонятная власть.

На голос невидимой пери
Шел воин, купец и пастух;
Пред ним отворялися двери,
Встречал его мрачный евнух.

На мягкой пуховой постели,
В парчу и жемчуг убрана,
Ждала она гостя. Шипели
Пред нею два кубка вина.

Сплетались горячие руки,
Уста прилипали к устам,

82. TAMÁRA

High up, o'er the gorges that slacken
The rush of the Terek's assault
A castle eternally blackened,
As black as its rock of basalt.

5   That tower on the desperate Terek
Belonged to Tamara, the Queen;
Her beautiful face was angelic,
Her spirit demonic and mean.

A traveler, lost and benighted,
10   Would notice a light from the top—
It glimmered, it called, it invited,
It tempted and begged him to stop.

A voice through the darkness was soaring
With passion and yearning replete;
15   It was irresistibly luring,
It was indescribably sweet.

A warrior, a herdsman, a merchant
Would hear the invisible call,
Its plea overwhelmingly urgent . . .
20   A eunuch would open the hall:

Tamara awaited reclining
In garments of majesty dressed;
Beside her two goblets were shining,
Prepared for herself and the guest.

25   The arms were like snakes interwoven,
The lips were dissolved in a kiss,

И странные, дикие звуки
Всю ночь раздавалися там.

Как будто в ту башню пустую
Сто юношей пылких и жен
Сошлися на свадьбу ночную,
На тризну больших похорон.

Но только что утра сиянье
Кидало свой луч по горам,
Мгновенно и мрак и молчанье
Опять воцарялися там.

Лишь Терек в теснине Дарьяла
Гремя нарушал тишину;
Волна на волну набегала,
Волна погоняла волну;

И с плачем безгласное тело
Спешили они унести;
В окне тогда что-то белело,
Звучало оттуда: прости.

И было так нежно прощанье,
Так сладко тот голос звучал,
Как будто восторги свиданья
И ласки любви обещал.

Daryal and "Tamara's Castle."
Drawing by Lermontov.

The silence all over was cloven
By moans of attainment and bliss.

There seemed to have swarmed to the gorges
30 Impetuous women and men,
Who gathered for feasting and orgies,
Who reveled again and again.

But lo! when at dawn the next morning
The sunrays illumined the scene,
35 The quiet of gloomiest mourning
Enfolded the home of the queen.

The Terek, unbridled and crushing,
Alone in the stillness would rave,
A wave to a wave would be rushing,
40 A wave would be driving a wave.

The torrent despairingly tightened
And closed on the body anew.
A face or a handkerchief whitened,
And somebody whispered "adieu."

45 It was so caressing and tender,
That whisper that came from above,
As if it had promised surrender
And raptures of passionate love.
1841

267

ЛИСТОК

Дубовый листок оторвался от ветки родимой
И в степь укатился, жестокою бурей гонимый;
Засох и увял он от холода, зноя и горя
И вот наконец докатился до Черного моря.

У Черного моря чинара стоит молодая;
С ней шепчется ветер, зеленые ветви лаская;
На ветвях зеленых качаются райские птицы;
Поют они песни про славу морской царь-девицы.

И странник прижался у корня чинары высокой;
Приюта на время он молит с тоскою глубокой,
И так говорит он: «Я бедный листочек дубовый,
До срока созрел я и вырос в отчизне суровой.

Один и без цели по свету ношуся давно я,
Засох я без тени, увял я без сна и покоя.
Прими же пришельца меж листьев своих
                                 изумрудных,
Немало я знаю рассказов мудреных и чудных».

— На что мне тебя? — отвечает младая чинара,
Ты пылен и желт,— и сынам моим свежим не пара.
Ты много видал — да к чему мне твои небылицы?
Мой слух утомили давно уж и райские птицы.

Иди себе дальше; о странник! тебя я не знаю!
Я солнцем любима, цвету для него и блистаю;
По небу я ветви раскинула здесь на просторе,
И корни мои умывает холодное море.

83. THE LEAF

A leaf blew away from the oak tree that nursed it and mothered;
It rolled through the steppe, by the tempest tormented and smothered,
It faded and shriveled, a plaything of hailstorms and breezes,
And rolled to the waters protected by mountains from freezes.

5   It came to a beautiful plantain that stood by the ocean,
The wind wooed its branches and whispered a tale of devotion;
The sweetest of birds, in its boughs intertwining and shady,
Incessantly sang of a strange, unattainable lady.

The wanderer pressed to the root; for a minute it halted
10   And begged for a respite, entreating the beauty exalted;
It said to the plantain, "I fell from an oak tree; have pity:
The tempest has blown me through many a village and city.

Too soon I matured, and today I am homeless and nameless;
I wilted and withered, my roamings are grievous and aimless.
15   I pray you: allow me to rest 'mid your emerald glory,
I've seen divers lands, and of each I shall tell you a story."

"Away," said the plantain and looked neither charming nor pensive,
"You are dusty and old, to my children your sight is offensive;
You think you can stand with your long-winded stories before me,
20   When even the silver-tongued warblers of Paradise bore me!

Continue your way and, oh wanderer! spare me your whining;
The sun is my lover, that's why all my blossoms are shining;
My branches are tall; it's the sky that my rustle addresses,
And deep are my roots that the ocean surrounds and caresses."
1841

1

Нет, не тебя так пылко я люблю,
Не для меня красы твоей блистанье:
Люблю в тебе я прошлое страданье
И молодость погибшую мою.

2

Когда порой я на тебя смотрю,
В твои глаза вникая долгим взором:
Таинственным я занят разговором,
Но не с тобой я сердцем говорю.

3

Я говорю с подругой юных дней;
В твоих чертах ищу черты другие;
В устах живых уста давно немые,
В глазах огонь угаснувших очей.

84.

1

No, 'tis not you for whom I am aflame,
Your shining beauty will not make me languish.
In you I love my deeply buried anguish,
My ruined youth with all its pain and shame.

2

5 And when at times I look into your eyes
And meet your glance with glances long and seeking,
I feel my heart mysteriously speaking,
But not for you my words in secret rise.

3

They go to her, my love of younger days;
10 Her face alone I seek behind your features;
Her long-dead laughter in your merry speeches,
Her vanished look behind your fiery gaze.
1841

1

Выхожу один я на дорогу;
Сквозь туман кремнистый путь блестит;
Ночь тиха. Пустыня внемлет богу,
И звезда с звездою говорит.

2

В небесах торжественно и чудно!
Спит земля в сиянье голубом...
Что же мне так больно и так трудно?
Жду ль чего? жалею ли о чем?

3

Уж не жду от жизни ничего я,
И не жаль мне прошлого ничуть;
Я ищу свободы и покоя!
Я б хотел забыться и заснуть!

4

Но не тем холодным сном могилы...
Я б желал навеки так заснуть,
Чтоб в груди дремали жизни силы,
Чтоб дыша вздымалась тихо грудь;

5

Чтоб всю ночь, весь день мой слух лелея,
Про любовь мне сладкий голос пел,
Надо мной чтоб вечно зеленея
Темный дуб склонялся и шумел.

85.

1

All alone along the road I am walking,
In the haze the moonbeams shed their light.
High above the stars are quietly talking,
The Almighty rules the silent night.

2

5   Heaven breathes solemnity and wonder,
And the earth is sleeping in a mist.
What is it that tears my heart asunder?
Barren hopes? Regrets of something missed?

3

In my bosom not a hope is living,
10   And my past has ceased to cause regret.
All I need is freedom and oblivion,
And I wish to sleep and to forget.

4

But I fear the frosty sleep eternal . . .
I would like to have a peaceful rest
15   And preserve my life-bestowing kernel
With some breath and warmth within my breast.

5

I would like a melody unending
Day and night to sing of happy love
And an oak, its heavy branches bending,
20   To caress me gently from above.
1841

МОРСКАЯ ЦАРЕВНА

В море царевич купает коня;
Слышит: «Царевич! взгляни на меня!»

Фыркает конь и ушами прядет,
Брызжет и плещет и дале плывет.

Слышит царевич: «Я царская дочь!
Хочешь провесть ты с царевною ночь?»

Вот показалась рука из воды,
Ловит за кисти шелко́вой узды.

Вышла младая потом голова;
В косу вплелася морская трава.

Синие очи любовью горят;
Брызги на шее, как жемчуг, дрожат.

Мыслит царевич: «Добро же! постой!»
За косу ловко схватил он рукой.

Держит, рука боевая сильна:
Плачет и молит и бьется она.

К берегу витязь отважно плывет;
Выплыл; товарищей громко зовет.

«Эй вы! сходитесь, лихие друзья!
Гляньте, как бьется добыча моя...

Что ж вы стоите смущенной толпой?
Али красы не видали такой?»

86. THE SEA PRINCESS

Far in the sea waves the prince bathes his steed.
Suddenly somebody calls him: "Give heed!"

Snorting, the stallion swims forward, decoyed,
Quickly obeying the call from the void.

5   "Welcome, my prince," says the voice from the deep,
"Look at my palace, and then we will sleep."

Someone is stretching a hand from the main,
Someone is catching the silk of the rein.

Who is the maiden that comes from beneath?
10   Seaweed adheres to her head like a wreath.

Burning with love are the eyes of the girl,
Drops on her shoulders are brighter than pearl.

"Wait you, my sweetest!" The prince, unafraid,
Seizes the maiden and pulls at her braid.

15   Strongly he holds her—his fingers are tight—
Letting her writhe on his saddle and fight.

Back to his friends he returns through the spray,
Eager to show his companions the prey.

"Hurry, my comrades, oh, hurry to me,
20   Look what a treasure I've caught in the sea!

Why do you gloomily stand on the shore?
Haven't you seen such a beauty before?"

275

Вот оглянулся царевич назад:
Ахнул! померк торжествующий взгляд.

Видит: лежит на песке золотом
Чудо морское с зеленым хвостом;

Хвост чешуею змеиной покрыт,
Весь замирая, свиваясь дрожит;

Пена струями сбегает с чела,
Очи одела смертельная мгла.

Бледные руки хватают песок;
Шепчут уста непонятный упрек...

Едет царевич задумчиво прочь.
Будет он помнить про царскую дочь!

Angry, he glances away from the crowd:
Heavens! What is it that makes him so proud?

25   Panting, there shivers, defenseless and pale,
Only a beast with an emerald tail.

Scaly all over, this tail of a snake,
Tries to uncoil with a torturous shake.

Water has mingled with foam on her head,
30   Light in her eyes is extinguished and dead.

Weakly she clutches the gold of the sand,
Strange are the words of her whispered demand.

Homeward is riding the prince in regret.
This is a wooing he'll never forget!
1841

277

ПРОРОК

С тех пор как вечный судия
Мне дал всеведенье пророка,
В очах людей читаю я
Страницы злобы и порока.

Провозглашать я стал любви
И правды чистые ученья:
В меня все ближние мои
Бросали бешено каменья.

Посыпал пеплом я главу,
Из городов бежал я нищий,
И вот в пустыне я живу,
Как птицы, даром божьей пищи.

Завет предвечного храня,
Мне тварь покорна там земная;
И звезды слушают меня,
Лучами радостно играя.

Когда же через шумный град
Я пробираюсь торопливо,
То старцы детям говорят
С улыбкою самолюбивой:

«Смотрите: вот пример для вас!
Он горд был, не ужился с нами.
Глупец, хотел уверить нас,
Что бог гласит его устами!

Смотрите ж, дети, на него:
Как он угрюм и худ и бледен!
Смотрите, как он наг и беден,
Как презирают все его!»

87. THE PROPHET

When people's eyes I learned to read
With the omniscience of a prophet,
I noticed malice, envy, greed,
And a disgraceful thirst for profit.

5   The truth of friendship I proclaimed—
Alas for my misguided labor!
I was tormented and defamed
By every relative and neighbor.

And then with ashes on my head
10   I left the town, my courage failing;
Now in the wilderness my bread
Is what the Lord can give me daily.

Unharmed by beasts and snakes, I preach;
I speak, and silent planets listen;
15   My words as far as Heaven reach,
And stars in satisfaction glisten.

But when I cross a noisy street
And move along, morose and ugly,
The elders, bursting with conceit,
20   Address their youngsters, grinning smugly,

"Just look at him! How high he soared!
He treated all of us like vermin.
He thought that the Almighty Lord
Proclaimed commandments through his sermon.

25   But look at what the man has done!
Today he is hungry, gaunt, dejected,
Despised by everyone, rejected,
A naked wretch, a friend to none."
1841

279

Из-под таинственной холодной полумаски
Звучал мне голос твой отрадный, как мечта,
Светили мне твои пленительные глазки
И улыбалися лукавые уста.

Сквозь дымку легкую заметил я невольно
И девственных ланит и шеи белизну.
Счастливец! видел я и локон своевольный,
Родных кудрей покинувший волну!..

И создал я тогда в моем воображенье
По легким признакам красавицу мою:
И с той поры бесплотное виденье
Ношу в душе моей, ласкаю и люблю.

И всё мне кажется: живые эти речи
В года минувшие слыхал когда-то я;
И кто-то шепчет мне, что после этой встречи
Мы вновь увидимся, как старые друзья.

88.

A half-mask on your face, mysterious and teasing,
Concealed your charming smile, invisible but coy;
I heard your dreamy voice, alluring and appeasing,
I saw your gleaming eyes that promised love and joy.

5   I saw unwittingly, when lights around us wavered,
The pallor of your neck, your cheeks and forehead white,
I even saw a curl, adventurous and wayward,
That left its wave of locks and boldly took to flight.

And soon I could create in my imagination
10   A vision beautiful—from every gentle line;
And ever since we met, this nebulous creation
Has lived within my soul, beloved and only mine.

As years are rolling by, I cannot stop repeating
That I've already heard your accents warm and sweet;
15   I trust the voice which says that after such a meeting
I'll meet you once again, as only friends can meet.
[?]

NARRATIVE POEMS

That voice seductive and disturbing . . .

БЕГЛЕЦ

(Горская легенда)

Гарун бежал быстрее лани,
Быстрей, чем заяц от орла;
Бежал он в страхе с поля брани,
Где кровь черкесская текла;
Отец и два родные брата
За честь и вольность там легли,
И под пятой у сопостата
Лежат их головы в пыли.
Их кровь течет и просит мщенья,
Гарун забыл свой долг и стыд;
Он растерял в пылу сраженья
Винтовку, шашку — и бежит!

И скрылся день; клубясь, туманы
Одели темные поляны
Широкой белой пеленой;
Пахнуло холодом с востока,
И над пустынею пророка
Встал тихо месяц золотой!..

Усталый, жаждою томимый,
С лица стирая кровь и пот,
Гарун меж скал аул родимый
При лунном свете узнает;
Подкрался он, никем не зримый...
Кругом молчанье и покой,
С кровавой битвы невредимый
Лишь он один пришел домой.

89. THE DESERTER

(A mountaineers' legend)

He scurried doe-like, ever faster,
As would a rabbit from a kite;
He left his tribesmen in disaster
And let them curse and fall and fight.
5   His father and his elder brothers
Had joined the battle hot and just,
And now their heads, with many others,
Lay trampled in the native dust.
They called for swift retaliation;
10 He saw the blood his kin had shed,
But kinship, duty, obligation—
He cast them to the winds and fled.

When dusk descended quietly breathing,
It brought the mists, opaque and wreathing,
15 Which covered dale and bird and beast;
The scorching heat of day subsided,
The crescent shone and shadows glided
Above the desert of the East.

The night was slowly getting shorter,
20 When all in sweat, his corselet torn,
Exhausted, yearning for some water,
He reached the place where he was born;
He who had been his kin's supporter
Returned a wretched, trembling man,
25 Returned unwounded from the slaughter—
The only remnant of his clan.

И к сакле он спешит знакомой,
Там блещет свет, хозяин дома;
Скрепясь душой, как только мог,
Гарун ступил через порог;
Селима звал он прежде другом,
Селим пришельца не узнал;
На ложе, мучимый недугом,
Один,— он, молча,— умирал...
«Велик Аллах, от злой отравы
Он светлым ангелам своим
Велел беречь тебя для славы!»
«Что нового?» — спросил Селим,
Подняв слабеющие вежды,
И взор блеснул огнем надежды!..
И он привстал, и кровь бойца
Вновь разыгралась в час конца.
«Два дня мы билися в теснине;
Отец мой пал, и братья с ним;
И скрылся я один в пустыне,
Как зверь, преследуем, гоним,
С окровавленными ногами
От острых камней и кустов,
Я шел безвестными тропами
По следу вепрей и волков;
Черкесы гибнут — враг повсюду...
Прими меня, мой старый друг;
И вот пророк! твоих услуг
Я до могилы не забуду!..»
И умирающий в ответ:
«Ступай — достоин ты презренья.
Ни крова, ни благословленья
Здесь у меня для труса нет!..»

Стыда и тайной муки полный,
Без гнева вытерпев упрек,
Ступил опять Гарун безмолвный
За неприветливый порог.

И, саклю новую минуя,
На миг остановился он,
И прежних дней летучий сон
Вдруг обдал жаром поцелуя
Его холодное чело;

A neighbor's house. He knew its master;
What made his heart beat ever faster?
A brother's door is never shut . . .
30   He sighed and stepped into the hut.
He found his former friend Selím
Upon his lonely deathbed lying;
In pain, the helpless man was dying
And neither heard nor noticed him.
35   "Oh, great is Allah! From diseases
He'll make His angels save you soon,
He'll show His mercy if it pleases . . . "
"Just tell me what's the news, Haroun."
The news . . . Selim began to weaken,
40   But here his guest stood like a beacon,
A man who'd met the deadly storm!
It made him happy, strong, and warm.
"Two days we fought by cannons stunted;
My father and my brothers fell.
45   I left the gorge, pursued and hunted,
And saved myself from knife and shell.
Through shrubs and rocks, through wasteland muddy,
Half-deafened by the battle's roar,
I crawled, my feet and fingers bloody,
50   As would a hungry wolf or boar.
For us this massacre is fateful . . .
I pray, receive me, oh my friend,
And, by the Prophet, to the end
I shall be truly, deeply grateful."
55   His words were checked by a reproof.
The dying man in anger glowered:
"Away, you miserable coward,
And never seek my love or roof."

He heard the wrathful accusation;
60   Consumed with torture and disgrace,
He turned away in resignation
And left the grim, unfriendly place.

Another hut . . . it may be kinder!
He lingered, and to him it seemed
65   That of his distant past he dreamed;
It all returned like a reminder;
It kissed, it cooled his burning brow,

И стало сладко и светло
Его душе; во мраке ночи,
Казалось, пламенные очи
Блеснули ласково пред ним;
И он подумал: я любим;
Она лишь мной живет и дышит...
И хочет он взойти — и слышит,
И слышит песню старины...
И стал Гарун бледней луны:

Месяц плывет
Тих и спокоен,
А юноша воин
На битву идет.
Ружье заряжает джигит,
А дева ему говорит:
Мой милый, смелее
Вверяйся ты року,
Молися востоку,
Будь верен пророку,
Будь славе вернее.
Своим изменивший
Изменой кровавой,
Врага не сразивши,
Погибнет без славы,
Дожди его ран не обмоют,
И звери костей не зароют.
Месяц плывет
И тих и спокоен,
А юноша воин
На битву идет.

Главой поникнув, с быстротою
Гарун свой продолжает путь,
И крупная слеза порою
С ресницы падает на грудь...

Но вот от бури наклоненный
Пред ним родной белеет дом;
Надеждой снова ободренный,
Гарун стучится под окном.
Там, верно, теплые молитвы
Восходят к небу за него;

And almost pacified was now
His soul. He saw a maid Circassian:
70 Her eyes were all agleam with passion.
He thought, "She is my faithful bride,
I am her light, her world, her pride;
She can't become her love's tormentor."
He hurries forth, he wants to enter . . .
75 She sings. Then he will come and hail . . .
Oh, not this song! Haroun turned pale.

    "Bright is the moon,
    Soft and caressing;
    The warrior is dressing:
80 The battle is soon.
    He carries his gun, unafraid,
    And these are the words of his maid:
    'Speak not of surrender
    And think of preserving
85 The faith you are serving;
    Be brave and deserving,
    Be Allah's defender.
    A coward and traitor,
    All glory he'll forfeit.
90 Both men and the Prophet
    Will banish him later.
    His pitiable spirit will shirk us,
    And no one will care for this Cherkess.'
    Bright is the moon,
95 Soft and caressing;
    The warrior is dressing:
    The battle is soon!"

He sadly hung his head while trying
To mollify the spiteful skies;
100 He did not know that he was crying,
But tears were dropping from his eyes.

Here is a house by tempests battered,
And by the sun of summers bleached;
Upon its roof all rains have pattered . . .
105 It is his home that he has reached.
He knocks. By others shunned and hated,
He is his mother's son, her own;

Старуха-мать ждет сына с битвы,
Но ждет его не одного!..

«Мать — отвори! я странник бедный,
Я твой Гарун, твой младший сын;
Сквозь пули русские безвредно
Пришел к тебе!»
              — «Один?»
                       — «Один!»
  — «А где отец и братья?» —
                       — «Пали!
Пророк их смерть благословил,
И ангелы их души взяли».
  — «Ты отомстил?»
                 — «Не отомстил...
Но я стрелой пустился в горы,
Оставил меч в чужом краю,
Чтобы твои утешить взоры
И утереть слезу твою...»
«Молчи, молчи! гяур лукавый,
Ты умереть не мог со славой,
Так удались, живи один.
Твоим стыдом, беглец свободы,
Не омрачу я стары годы,
Ты раб и трус — и мне не сын!..»
Умолкло слово отверженья,
И всё кругом объято сном.
Проклятья, стоны и моленья
Звучали долго под окном;
И наконец удар кинжала
Пресек несчастного позор...
И мать поутру увидала...
И хладно отвернула взор.
И труп, от праведных изгнанный,
Никто к кладбищу не отнес,
И кровь с его глубокой раны
Лизал рыча домашний пес;
Ребята малые ругались
Над хладным телом мертвеца,
В преданьях вольности остались
Позор и гибель беглеца.
Душа его от глаз пророка
Со страхом удалилась прочь;

She must have prayed, she must have waited . . .
But waited not for him alone!

110 "Oh, mother, look into the garden!
Thy youngest son has come to thee;
Unhurt, by Russian bullets pardoned,
I have returned."—
"Just you?"
115 —"Just me!"
"And where are all the others?"—
"Fallen!
The joys of Heaven are their lot;
This fate could only have befallen . . . "
120 "Did you revenge?"
—"No, I did not . . .
I darted like the swiftest arrow
And let the battle roar and rage.
My death . . . I knew that it would harrow
125 A loving mother at your age!"
"Hush, crafty giaour, do not continue!
A thirst for glory was not in you;
You are a slave, you lost your gun,
You left your brothers and your father!
130 I'd live alone without you, rather
Than take a traitor for a son."
Such was the sentence that she uttered,
He wept and moaned, and prayed, and stuttered,
Attempting to avert his doom.
135 When nothing helped, he thrust his dagger
And stopped his misery and shame;
She saw him later, proud and haggard,
But looked away and stayed the same.
And no one searched for an enclosure
140 To hide the sinner's cold remains;
A dog rejoiced at the exposure
And licked the wound unwashed by rains.
The children mocked and stamped, while spitting
At the deserter's tortured face;
145 There was not anyone to pity—
Yet, all remembered his disgrace.
From Allah's anger, just and frightful,
His soul in shyness sped away,

И тень его в горах востока
Поныне бродит в темну ночь,
И под окном поутру рано
Он в сакли просится стуча,
Но внемля громкий стих Корана,
Бежит опять, под сень тумана,
Как прежде бегал от меча.

But people say that, grim and spiteful,
150 His ghost is often seen today.
At night his grief and pain he nurses
And roams, by everyone abhorred;
At dawn he knocks, but sacred verses
155 Will make him run away with curses,
As once he ran from gun and sword.

Я к вам пишу случайно; право,
Не знаю как и для чего.
Я потерял уж это право.
И что скажу вам? — ничего!
Что помню вас? — но, боже правый,
Вы это знаете давно;
И вам, конечно, всё равно.

И знать вам также нету нужды,
Где я? что я? в какой глуши?
Душою мы друг другу чужды,
Да вряд ли есть родство души.
Страницы прошлого читая,
Их по порядку разбирая
Теперь остынувшим умом,
Разуверяюсь я во всем.
Смешно же сердцем лицемерить
Перед собою столько лет;
Добро б еще морочить свет!
Да и притом что пользы верить
Тому, чего уж больше нет?..
Безумно ждать любви заочной?
В наш век все чувства лишь на срок;
Но я вас помню — да и точно,
Я вас никак забыть не мог!

Во-первых, потому, что много
И долго, долго вас любил,
Потом страданьем и тревогой
За дни блаженства заплатил;
Потом в раскаянье бесплодном
Влачил я цепь тяжелых лет;

90. <VALERIK>

I write to you and truly wonder
What in the world has made me write.
For you, I've gone away and under
And must have forfeited this right.
5 You know that, though we are asunder,
Your image was too much to lose.
Of course, you do! Such boring news . . .

Between attacks and other dangers
I live in God-forsaken holes.
10 But do you care? Our souls are strangers—
Indeed, a normal case with souls.
Today I read my past; its pages
Narrate some half-forgotten rages,
And each is like a feeble wraith
15 In which I have not any faith.
It's ludicrous to keep deceiving,
To fool oneself for years and years.
If it were meant for someone's ears!
But really, what's the good believing
20 In vanished love and dried-up tears?
This age disloyal is the sternest
To those of us who go away.
But I remember you in earnest.
(I mean, believe me, what I say.)

25 I loved you deeply, long, sincerely.
But let me also tell you this:
I paid as always very dearly
For every single day of bliss.
Contrite, in fruitless abnegation,
30 I cursed my anguish and my doom

И размышлением холодным
Убил последний жизни цвет.
С людьми сближаясь осторожно,
Забыл я шум младых проказ,
Любовь, поэзию,— но вас
Забыть мне было невозможно.

И к мысли этой я привык,
Мой крест несу я без роптанья:
То иль другое наказанье?
Не всё ль одно. Я жизнь постиг;
Судьбе, как турок иль татарин,
За всё я ровно благодарен;
У бога счастья не прошу
И молча зло переношу.
Быть может, небеса востока
Меня с ученьем их пророка
Невольно сблизили. Притом
И жизнь всечасно кочевая,
Труды, заботы ночь и днем,
Всё, размышлению мешая,
Приводит в первобытный вид
Больную душу: сердце спит,
Простора нет воображенью...
И нет работы голове...
Зато лежишь в густой траве
И дремлешь под широкой тенью
Чинар иль виноградных лоз;
Кругом белеются палатки;
Казачьи тощие лошадки
Стоят рядком, повеся нос;
У медных пушек спит прислуга,
Едва дымятся фитили;
Попарно цепь стоит вдали;
Штыки горят под солнцем юга.
Вот разговор о старине
В палатке ближней слышен мне;
Как при Ермолове ходили
В Чечню, в Аварию, к горам;
Как там дрались, как мы их били,
Как доставалося и нам;
И вижу я неподалеку
У речки, следуя пророку,

And killed with barren meditation
Both life's and love's remaining bloom.
It happened that, for pranks too clever
And open to a chosen few,
35   I quite forgot my past, but you . . .
You could not be forgotten—ever.

I grieve but have to compromise.
I bear my cross without denial:
This or perhaps another trial—
40   What difference? And I am wise.
So wise that like a Turk or Tartar
I never think myself a martyr.
I am content, I've curbed my pride
And take injustice in my stride.
45   Perhaps in Eastern climate gentle
I have become an Oriental,
The Prophet's follower. Besides,
My life, unsettled and nomadic,
My constant troubles, labor, rides,
50   Make thinking processes sporadic
And very easily reduce
A complex soul to simple use.
I feel composure slowly wrapping
My heart, my fantasy, my head;
55   I do not want to strive—instead
I lie in grassy corners napping.
In plantains' shade all dreams are sweet.
Around, the field is white with awning;
Thin horses, dappled, gray, and tawny,
60   Stand brooding sadly in the heat.
The gunners are asleep, reclining
Beside the cannons they will use,
A chain far off keeps watch in twos,
On bayonets the sun is shining.
65   In one of the adjoining tents
The soldiers speak of past events.
Chechnyá, Avaria, mountain ranges—
Those needed just Yermólov's pluck.
But then, who has not heard of changes
70   Of wayward military luck!
Close to the riverbank, just off it,
A Muslim faithful to the Prophet,

297

Мирной татарин свой намаз
Творит, не подымая глаз;
А вот кружком сидят другие.
Люблю я цвет их желтых лиц,
Подобный цвету ноговиц,
Их шапки, рукава худые,
Их темный и лукавый взор
И их гортанный разговор.
Чу — дальний выстрел! прожужжала
Шальная пуля... славный звук...
Вот крик — и снова всё вокруг
Затихло... но жара уж спáла,
Ведут коней на водопой,
Зашевелилася пехота;
Вот проскакал один, другой!
Шум, говор. Где вторая рота?
Что, вьючить? — что же капитан?
Повозки выдвигайте живо!
Савельич! Ой ли? — Дай огниво! —
Подъем ударил барабан —
Гудит музыка полковая;
Между колоннами въезжая,
Звенят орудья. Генерал
Вперед со свитой поскакал...
Рассыпались в широком поле,
Как пчелы, с гиком казаки;
Уж показалися значки
Там на опушке — два, и боле.
А вот в чалме один мюрид
В черкеске красной ездит важно,
Конь светло-серый весь кипит,
Он машет, кличет — где отважный?
Кто выдет с ним на смертный бой!..
Сейчас, смотрите: в шапке черной
Казак пустился гребенской;
Винтовку выхватил проворно,
Уж близко... выстрел... легкий дым...
Эй вы, станичники, за ним...
Что? ранен!.. — Ничего, безделка...
И завязалась перестрелка...

Но в этих сшибках удалых
Забавы много, толку мало;

A peaceful Tartar, quietly prays,
Forgetful of the beating rays.
75   Some other Tartars sit together . . .
The sight is soothing, it relieves.
I like their caps and worn-out sleeves
And faces as of yellow leather,
Their smiling eyes that often glow,
80   Their accent, guttural and low . . .
A crack—it is a bullet whizzing.
A proper sound—a random shot!
We wait. . . . It has become less hot,
The people do not feel so dizzy.
85   The infantry is up and stirs,
The men take horses to the river;
The noise of shouting, neighing, spurs . . .
Reports are ready to deliver.
—Where is the Captain? —Here he comes!
90   —Hey, second squad! —What? —We are packing!
—All wagons out! —Why are you backing?
And finally I hear the drums.
The band strikes up. Here are some pennons,
The gunners move their heavy cannons;
95   The general has ridden near,
His officers bring up the rear.
The yelling Cossacks, right before us,
Are scattered everywhere like bees;
More pennons: both among the trees
100   And at the edges of the forest.
A tall muríd begins to wave:
Important, dressed in native fashion,
His handsome horse in pent-up passion . . .
He looks for someone really brave.
105   Who'll meet him for a mortal fight?
His manly call is not a trifle!
A Cossack runs, and come what might!
The black-cap quickly grabs the rifle;
He's close to him! A click, a shot . . .
110   —Hey, Cossacks, brothers, help him! —What?
—He's wounded! . . —Lightly! —Stop your hooting!
And then some foolish random shooting.

Such skirmishes are mostly fun,
Whichever army may be losing:

Прохладным вечером, бывало,
Мы любовалися на них
Без кровожадного волненья,
Как на трагический балет;
Зато видал я представленья,
Каких у вас на сцене нет...

Раз — это было под Гихами,
Мы проходили темный лес;
Огнем дыша, пылал над нами
Лазурно-яркий свод небес.
Нам был обещан бой жестокий.
Из гор Ичкерии далекой
Уже в Чечню на братний зов
Толпы стекались удальцов.
Над допотопными лесами
Мелькали маяки кругом;
И дым их то вился столпом,
То расстилался облаками;
И оживилися леса;
Скликались дико голоса
Под их зелеными шатрами.
Едва лишь выбрался обоз
В поляну, дело началось;
Чу! в арьергард орудья просят;
Вот ружья из кустов выносят,
Вот тащат за ноги людей
И кличут громко лекарей;
А вот и слева, из опушки,
Вдруг с гиком кинулись на пушки;
И градом пуль с вершин дерев
Отряд осыпан. Впереди же
Всё тихо — там между кустов
Бежал поток. Подходим ближе.
Пустили несколько гранат;
Еще подвинулись; молчат;
Но вот над бревнами завала
Ружье как будто заблистало;
Потом мелькнуло шапки две;
И вновь всё спряталось в траве.
То было грозное молчанье,
Не долго длилося оно,
Но в этом странном ожиданье

115 Quite useless, even if amusing.
    We'd watch them when the work was done.
    This theater left us unexcited:
    Too petty to arouse a rage . . .
    But many times we were invited
120 To plays that would not fit your stage . . .

    It was at Ghikhi. Every minute
    We thought the natives would assault.
    The wood we crossed had no light in it,
    But all aflame was Heaven's vault.
125 We knew that losses would be heavy,
    Both sides would pay an awful levy:
    For hosts of Muslims, brave in wars,
    Had gathered to defend their cause.
    Ichkerians, each a famous killer,
130 Were coming to Chechnyá in crowds.
    On signal towers, smoke spread like clouds
    Or rose and hovered like a pillar;
    The ancient forest came alive,
    As would a huge and angry hive,
135 With voices getting ever shriller.
    At last the transport left the wood . . .
    Then hell broke loose! Some cannons stood
    In front, but they were moved and shifted
    Back, to the rear; the guns were lifted . . .
140 Ho! Some are wounded, many fall,
    Some groan and for a doctor call.
    They have attacked us from a shelter!
    The men were running helter-skelter
    When from the treetops bullets fell
145 Like hail. . . . The front was unassaulted
    And moved until they reached the dell
    And saw a stream by which they halted.
    We all drew close, they hurled some shells.
    Deep silence. Neither shots nor yells.
150 We stand together, wait and listen.
    Lo! Polished muzzles seem to glisten
    Where logs and trunks have blocked the pass . . .
    Two caps have flitted through the grass . . .
    The pause was fraught with death and violence.
    How long could such a respite last?
    We waited in the eery silence,

Забилось сердце не одно.
Вдруг залп... глядим: лежат рядами,
Что нужды? здешние полки
Народ испытанный... В штыки,
Дружнее! раздалось за нами.
Кровь загорелася в груди!
Все офицеры впереди...
Верхом помчался на завалы,
Кто не успел спрыгнуть с коня...
Ура — и смолкло.— Вон кинжалы,
В приклады! — и пошла резня.
И два часа в струях потока
Бой длился. Резались жестоко,
Как звери, молча, с грудью грудь,
Ручей телами запрудили.
Хотел воды я зачерпнуть...
(И зной и битва утомили
Меня), но мутная волна
Была тепла, была красна.

    На берегу, под тенью дуба,
Пройдя завалов первый ряд,
Стоял кружок. Один солдат
Был на коленах; мрачно, грубо
Казалось выраженье лиц,
Но слезы капали с ресниц,
Покрытых пылью... на шинели,
Спиною к дереву, лежал
Их капитан. Он умирал;
В груди его едва чернели
Две ранки; кровь его чуть-чуть
Сочилась. Но высоко грудь
И трудно подымалась, взоры
Бродили страшно, он шептал...
«Спасите, братцы.— Тащат в горы.
Постойте — ранен генерал...
Не слышат...» Долго он стонал,
Но всё слабей и понемногу
Затих и душу отдал богу;
На ружья опершись, кругом
Стояли усачи седые...
И тихо плакали.... потом
Его остатки боевые

And many hearts were beating fast.
A volley! Yes, we see them hiding!
To bayonets! The soldiers run—
160 These men have often fought and won.
The officers come quickly riding.
The fight is on: to bear its brunt
They hurry forward to the front.
Those few who had not yet dismounted
165 All rushed together—to a man.
It was the daggers first that counted . . .
To arms! The massacre began.
Two hours it lasted in the torrent.
We cut and tore (it was abhorrent!)
170 Like beasts, in silence, breast to breast.
The corpses nearly dammed the water;
I dipped my hand . . . I needed rest,
Exhausted by the heat and slaughter.
But from the bodies of the dead
175 The stream was warm, the stream was red.

Beneath an oak, a few short paces
From the obstructions, in a group,
I saw a man kneel down and stoop;
The soldiers' weather-beaten faces
180 Seemed rough and motionless, and yet
The dust upon their eyes was wet.
They gathered 'round their captain lying
And tossing on a bloodstained cloak.
His wound was small and did not smoke,
185 But it was clear that he was dying.
Blood from the tiny hole still dripped;
His breath came heavy, he was gripped
By visions of some great disaster.
His stifled mutterings were slow,
190 "Help, brothers! Drag them! higher . . . faster . . .
The general is wounded! No!
I say . . . " His words were coming low.
His raving speech remained unended
Before eternal peace descended.
195 The soldiers, old, from battles gray,
Surrounded silently their captain . . .
They cried but did not speak or pray:
Just raised the cloak the man was wrapped in

Накрыли бережно плащом
И понесли. Тоской томимый,
Им вслед смотрел я недвижимый.
Меж тем товарищей, друзей
Со вздохом возле называли;
Но не нашел в душе моей
Я сожаленья, ни печали.
Уже затихло всё; тела
Стащили в кучу; кровь текла
Струею дымной по каменьям,
Ее тяжелым испареньем
Был полон воздух. Генерал
Сидел в тени на барабане
И донесенья принимал.
Окрестный лес, как бы в тумане,
Синел в дыму пороховом.
А там вдали грядой нестройной,
Но вечно гордой и спокойной,
Тянулись горы — и Казбек
Сверкал главой остроконечной.
И с грустью тайной и сердечной
Я думал: жалкий человек.
Чего он хочет!.. небо ясно,
Под небом места много всем,
Но беспрестанно и напрасно
Один враждует он — зачем?
Галуб прервал мое мечтанье,
Ударив по плечу; он был
Кунак мой: я его спросил,
Как месту этому названье?
Он отвечал мне: «*Валерик*,
А перевесть на ваш язык,
Так будет речка смерти: верно,
Дано старинными людьми».
— А сколько их дралось примерно
Сегодня? — Тысяч до семи.
— А много горцы потеряли?
— Как знать? — зачем вы не считали!
«Да! будет,— кто-то тут сказал,—
Им в память этот день кровавый!»
Чеченец посмотрел лукаво
И головою покачал.

And gently carried him away.
200 From scenes of death and anguish hollow,
I let my wearied glances follow
The tragic group. A dreadful toll
Of former friends the fight had taken,
But strangely empty was my soul—
205 I did not feel depressed or shaken.
The fight was over. All was still.
The bodies made a grisly hill.
Blood trickled from them, steaming, smoking,
And in its vapors we were choking.
210 Deep in the shade, upon a drum,
Alone, the general was seated
And waited for reports to come.
In powder smoke, by sunrays heated,
The wood seemed hidden in a mist.
215 The mountains, grand, uneven, crowded,
But peaceful and in ices shrouded,
Loomed far away; Kazbék stood high
In all its shining might and glitter.
My thoughts were sorrowful and bitter:
220 "Oh, human weakling! Tell me, why,
Why are you such? Since tranquil heaven
To everybody is the same,
Why do you fight, by hatred driven?
What do you want? What is your aim?"
225 The cool of evening made me shiver.
—Hey! Who has slapped me on the back?
—Galoob? . . . Just tell me, my kunák,
What do they call this little river?
—They call it *Valerik*—he said,—
230 Which means "the river of the dead."
Those men who named it are in Heaven . . .
—How many of us fought today?
—I do not know, but I would say
That many thousand . . . maybe seven.
235 —Their losses, I believe, amounted
To greater numbers. . . . No one counted.
Then someone else's voice I heard,
"This day is for the war decisive."
I caught the Chéchen's glance derisive:
240 He grinned but did not say a word.

Но я боюся вам наскучить,
В забавах света вам смешны
Тревоги дикие войны;
Свой ум вы не привыкли мучить
Тяжелой думой о конце;
На вашем молодом лице
Следов заботы и печали
Не отыскать, и вы едва ли
Вблизи когда-нибудь видали,
Как умирают. Дай вам бог
И не видать: иных тревог
Довольно есть. В самозабвенье
Не лучше ль кончить жизни путь?
И беспробудным сном заснуть
С мечтой о близком пробужденье?

Теперь прощайте: если вас
Мой безыскусственный рассказ
Развеселит, займет хоть малость,
Я буду счастлив. А не так? —
Простите мне его как шалость
И тихо молвите: чудак!..

I have descriptions even rougher,
But of my tales you have no need,
For in the merry life you lead
Your mind was never made to suffer
245   From thoughts of death, and on your face
There probably is not a trace
Of torture, sadness, or affliction.
In your refined and guarded diction
Death is a literary fiction.
250   And let it be this way! In life
So many other woes are rife!
It's sweet to laugh at every warning,
Enjoyment from deception reap,
And fall into a dreamless sleep
255   With dreams of an approaching morning . . .

Farewell! I've finished. If you feel
That I have not misspent my zeal
And have not made you melancholic,
I shall be glad. But, if displeased,
260   Dismiss my story like a frolic
And whisper, "He has always teased. . . ."

General A. V. Galafeev ("the general on the drum"). Watercolor by D. P. Palen, 1840.

Valerik, an episode. Drawing by Lermontov.

Valerik, an episode. Watercolor by Lermontov and Gagarin.

Valerik, burying the dead. Drawing by
Lermontov.

МЦЫРИ [1]

Вкушая, вкусих мало меда и се аз умираю.

1-я Книга царств.

1

Немного лет тому назад,
Там, где сливаяся шумят,
Обнявшись, будто две сестры,
Струи Арагвы и Куры,
Был монастырь. Из-за горы
И нынче видит пешеход
Столбы обрушенных ворот,
И башни, и церковный свод;
Но не курится уж под ним
Кадильниц благовонный дым,
Не слышно пенье в поздний час
Молящих иноков за нас.
Теперь один старик седой,
Развалин страж полуживой,
Людьми и смертию забыт,
Сметает пыль с могильных плит,
Которых надпись говорит
О славе прошлой — и о том,
Как удручен своим венцом,
Такой-то царь, в такой-то год
Вручал России свой народ.

———

И божья благодать сошла
На Грузию! — она цвела

---

[1] *Мцыри* на грузинском языке значит «неслужащий монах», нечто вроде «послушника». *(Примечание Лермонтова).*

91. MTSYRI[1]

While partaking, I have partaken of little
honey, and behold: now I am dying.

(1 Kings)

1

Not very many years ago,
Where two Caucasian rivers flow
And meet in sisterly embrace
And, having merged, together race,
5   There was a cloister; from that place
One still can see the ruined gate,
The pillars, as they stood of late,
The vault and turrets spared by fate.
But monks in cassocks never halt
10   To talk or pray within this vault,
And fragrant incense does not rise
From smoking vessels to the skies.
Today an aged man alone,
The feeble guard of crumbling stone,
15   By death forgotten and by men,
Will walk 'mid tombstones now and then
And clean their legends, telling when
Some king, in glory and renown,
But sadly burdened by his crown,
20   Gave up his subjects and his star
To humbly serve the Russian Tsar.

———

And Georgia after that was blessed;
Her thriving land enjoyed a rest,

---

[1]Mtsyri in Georgian means a non-ordained
monk, something like a novice. (Lermontov's
note.)

С тех пор в тени своих садов,
Не опасаяся врагов,
За гранью дружеских штыков.

2

Однажды русский генерал
Из гор к Тифлису проезжал;
Ребенка пленного он вез.
Тот занемог, не перенес
Трудов далекого пути.
Он был, казалось, лет шести;
Как серна гор, пуглив и дик
И слаб и гибок, как тростник.
Но в нем мучительный недуг
Развил тогда могучий дух
Его отцов. Без жалоб он
Томился — даже слабый стон
Из детских губ не вылетал,
Он знаком пищу отвергал,
И тихо, гордо умирал.
Из жалости один монах
Больного призрел, и в стенах
Хранительных остался он,
Искусством дружеским спасен.
Но, чужд ребяческих утех,
Сначала бегал он от всех,
Бродил безмолвен, одинок,
Смотрел вздыхая на восток,
Томим неясною тоской
По стороне своей родной.
Но после к плену он привык,
Стал понимать чужой язык,
Был окрещен святым отцом,
И, с шумным светом незнаком,
Уже хотел во цвете лет
Изречь монашеский обет,
Как вдруг однажды он исчез
Осенней ночью. Темный лес
Тянулся по горам кругом.
Три дня все поиски по нем
Напрасны были, но потом
Его в степи без чувств нашли

Unmuddied stayed her cooling source,
25 The country quietly ran its course,
Protected by a friendly force.

2

A Russian general one day
Through mountains slowly made his way.
He had a captive boy with him;
30 The child fell ill; too small and slim
He was to travel, ride, or drive;
The boy was six or even five,
Shy as the mountain chamois's breed
And frail and supple as a reed.
35 But his disease, his sorry plight
Awakened in him all the might
His tribe possessed. His racking pain
Would never make the child complain;
He never groaned and never cried,
40 He pushed his food and drink aside,
And, proud and silent, nearly died.
A kindly monk began to tend
The patient; and, indeed, his end
He warded off. Thus, saved by care,
45 The boy survived and grew up there.
But having never learned to play,
From everyone he'd run away,
Avoid the brothers and the priest
And cast long glances to the East.
50 It made him deeply, strangely sad
To see the home he could have had.
But he succumbed, for he was young,
And learned to speak the alien tongue.
Baptized, he lived like a recluse;
55 Life was for him of little use,
And long before its cup was drunk
He knew that he would be a monk.
But suddenly, one autumn night,
The brothers missed him. Filled with fright,
60 They searched the woody slopes around.
For three long days he was not found,
When, finally, upon the ground
They saw the youngster in a swoon

И вновь в обитель принесли;
Он страшно бледен был и худ
И слаб, как будто долгий труд,
Болезнь иль голод испытал.
Он на допрос не отвечал,
И с каждым днем приметно вял;
И близок стал его конец.
Тогда пришел к нему чернец
С увещеваньем и мольбой;
И, гордо выслушав, больной
Привстал, собрав остаток сил,
И долго так он говорил:

3

«Ты слушать исповедь мою
Сюда пришел, благодарю.
Всё лучше перед кем-нибудь
Словами облегчить мне грудь;
Но людям я не делал зла,
И потому мои дела
Не много пользы вам узнать;
А душу можно ль рассказать?
Я мало жил, и жил в плену.
Таких две жизни за одну,
Но только полную тревог,
Я променял бы, если б мог.
Я знал одной лишь думы власть,
Одну — но пламенную страсть:
Она, как червь, во мне жила,
Изгрызла душу и сожгла.
Она мечты мои звала
От келий душных и молитв
В тот чудный мир тревог и битв,
Где в тучах прячутся скалы,
Где люди вольны, как орлы.
Я эту страсть во тьме ночной
Вскормил слезами и тоской;
Ее пред небом и землей
Я ныне громко признаю
И о прощенье не молю.

And to the cloister brought him soon.
65   He looked so gaunt and pale and tense,
As though he'd done some work immense
Or had been dangerously ill.
He lay indifferent and still,
Devoid of interest and will.
70   And when they saw how low he'd sunk
There came to him his Father monk
And begged him to disclose the truth.
The weak and almost dying youth
Collected all his ebbing strength
75   And proudly spoke to him at length.

3

"You've come to hear what I can tell.
I thank you for it: you mean well.
And I believe, if I confess,
My burden will torment me less.
80   But what's my tale to such as you?
I never harmed the men I knew,
I never killed and never stole . . .
And who can tell the world his soul!
I lived a wretched captive boy.
85   Two lives like mine I'd give with joy
For one and even shorter life,
If it were only filled with strife.
I knew one passion's mighty surge,
A single but consuming urge;
90   At first a tiny seed, a germ,
It burned and gnawed me like a worm,
But with it I was strong and firm,
For in my dingy, stuffy cell
It called upon me to rebel,
95   To seek the world of rock and cloud,
The world of men, like eagles, proud.
This urge would torture me and rend,
But I have fed it to the end;
Let earth and heaven now attend—
100 I say aloud: The dream was mine,
I loved it, and I don't repine.

4

«Старик! я слышал много раз,
Что ты меня от смерти спас —
Зачем?.. угрюм и одинок,
Грозой оторванный листок,
Я вырос в сумрачных стенах,
Душой дитя, судьбой монах.
Я никому не мог сказать
Священных слов — «отец» и «мать».
Конечно, ты хотел, старик,
Чтоб я в обители отвык
От этих сладостных имен.
Напрасно: звук их был рожден
Со мной. Я видел у других
Отчизну, дом, друзей, родных,
А у себя не находил
Не только милых душ — могил!
Тогда, пустых не тратя слез,
В душе я клятву произнес:
Хотя на миг когда-нибудь
Мою пылающую грудь
Прижать с тоской к груди другой,
Хоть незнакомой, но родной.
Увы, теперь мечтанья те
Погибли в полной красоте,
И я, как жил, в земле чужой
Умру рабом и сиротой.

5

«Меня могила не страшит:
Там, говорят, страданье спит
В холодной, вечной тишине;
Но с жизнью жаль расстаться мне.
Я молод, молод... Знал ли ты
Разгульной юности мечты?
Или не знал, или забыл,
Как ненавидел и любил;
Как сердце билося живей
При виде солнца и полей
С высокой башни угловой,
Где воздух свеж и где порой
В глубокой скважине стены,

4

"Old man! I often heard it said
That you had saved me from the dead.
Why did you? Somber and forlorn,
105 A tiny leaf by tempests torn,
I've grown behind this cheerless gate,
A child by soul, a monk by fate.
My Father . . . mother . . . neither word
I ever said or even heard.
110 I know how glad you would have been,
If in the cloister-life routine
I had forgotten, like my games,
Those sweet and stirring sacred names.
Oh, labor lost! I used to roam
115 And saw that men had kin and home,
That only I was robbed by doom
Of parents' love and parents' tomb.
I saw it all and cried no more,
But to myself an oath I swore
120 That once, just once, my burning breast
To someone else's would be pressed
And that the man who'd see me bend
Might be a stranger but a friend.
Alas, the dream that fed my oath
125 Is checked in all its blooming growth,
And in an alien land, my grave
Will hide a wretched, orphaned slave.

5

"I do not fear it; dust to dust . . .
The grave protects from torture's thrust,
130 Its cold and quiet end our strife,
But I am grieved to part with life.
I am young, so young. . . . Say, did you know
The dreams of youth, their sweeping flow?
Perhaps you didn't—or forgot
135 How love and hatred tie a knot;
How fast the heart in you would beat,
When from a height your eye would meet
The freshness of a sunlit field
And mountains standing like a shield;
140 Or when you notice from above

4

317

Дитя неведомой страны,
Прижавшись, голубь молодой
Сидит, испуганный грозой?
Пускай теперь прекрасный свет
Тебе постыл: ты слаб, ты сед,
И от желаний ты отвык.
Что за нужда? Ты жил, старик!
Тебе есть в мире что забыть,
Ты жил,— я также мог бы жить!

6

«Ты хочешь знать, что видел я
На воле? — Пышные поля,
Холмы, покрытые венцом
Дерев, разросшихся кругом,
Шумящих свежею толпой,
Как братья, в пляске круговой.
Я видел груды темных скал,
Когда поток их разделял,
И думы их я угадал:
Мне было свыше то дано!
Простерты в воздухе давно
Объятья каменные их
И жаждут встречи каждый миг;
Но дни бегут, бегут года —
Им не сойтися никогда!
Я видел горные хребты,
Причудливые, как мечты,
Когда в час утренней зари
Курилися, как алтари,
Их выси в небе голубом,
И облачко за облачком,
Покинув тайный свой ночлег,
К востоку направляло бег —
Как будто белый караван
Залетных птиц из дальних стран!
В дали я видел сквозь туман,
В снегах, горящих как алмаз,
Седой, незыблемый Кавказ;
И было сердцу моему
Легко, не знаю почему.
Мне тайный голос говорил,

A guest from far away, a dove,
Who in a crevice found a seat
And waits for thunder to retreat.
Of course, today it leaves you cold:
145 You are decrepit, gray, and old.
Your former yearnings must have ceased;
But what of that? You lived at least!
At least you soared before you fell.
You lived. I could have lived as well.

6

150 "What did I see when I was free?
A waving field came close to me,
A sloping hill, a rustling wood,
With trees that in a circle stood.
So young and happy brothers stand
155 And dance together, hand in hand.
I saw two rocks, each with its crest,
And a ravine that cut their breast;
And lo! their secret thoughts I guessed.
God let me guess them in His grace!
160 The rocks have opened their embrace
And wait forever, day and night:
They long to meet and to unite;
But ages pass, for time is fleet—
The parted rocks will never meet.
165 I saw some ridges, sharp and tall,
Like dreams, phantasmagorical.
When morning brought its azure cloak,
Their lofty peaks began to smoke
Like solemn altars lifted high;
170 Then fleecy cloudlets in the sky
Could leave their shelter for the night
And gently start their eastward flight.
I saw them float in pearly lines,
Like migrant birds from distant climes;
175 And through the mist I saw at times
How unassailable, in snows,
The Caucasus in glory rose.
What happened then I can't relate:
My soul, I felt, threw off its weight,
180 I heard a voice in me which told

Что некогда и я там жил,
И стало в памяти моей
Прошедшее ясней, ясней.

7

«И вспомнил я отцовский дом,
Ущелье наше, и кругом
В тени рассыпанный аул;
Мне слышался вечерний гул
Домой бегущих табунов
И дальний лай знакомых псов.
Я помнил смуглых стариков,
При свете лунных вечеров
Против отцовского крыльца
Сидевших с важностью лица;
И блеск оправленных ножон
Кинжалов длинных... и, как сон,
Всё это смутной чередой
Вдруг пробегало предо мной.
А мой отец? он как живой
В своей одежде боевой
Являлся мне, и помнил я
Кольчуги звон, и блеск ружья,
И гордый непреклонный взор,
И молодых моих сестер...
Лучи их сладостных очей
И звук их песен и речей
Над колыбелию моей...
В ущелье там бежал поток,
Он шумен был, но не глубок;
К нему, на золотой песок,
Играть я в полдень уходил
И взором ласточек следил,
Когда они, перед дождем,
Волны касалися крылом.
И вспомнил я наш мирный дом
И пред вечерним очагом
Рассказы долгие о том,
Как жили люди прежних дней,
Когда был мир еще пышней.

That it is there I'd lived of old;
And from my half-forgotten past
A misty veil was dropped at last.

7

"My father's house I could recall,
185   Our native gorge, the village small,
Enclosed by overhanging rocks,
The evening din of running flocks . . .
Again I heard the horses neigh
And barking dogs along the way.
190   Old men sat there, from battles gray;
I knew what they had come to say.
They talked of things that they had seen
With tranquil dignity of mien.
I loved their daggers and the gleam
185   Of splendid sheaths . . . as in a dream
So many a forgotten thing
Would pass before me in a string—
To each I would with fondness cling.
I heard my father's corselet ring,
200   When he appeared before his son—
A doughty warrior with a gun;
He was invincible in all.
My sisters, too, I would recall,
Their shining eyes, so large and deep,
205   Their songs of war and mountains steep,
As they were rocking me to sleep . . .
Just where our houses used to stand
A torrent ran; it was not grand,
But both its banks were golden sand;
210   I liked to come and frolic there
And watch quick swallows in the air,
When feeling the approaching rain
They dashed to clouds and dipped again . . .
New pictures floated in my brain—
215   Of men who came to entertain
With ancient stories and explain
How they had lived in days of yore
When things were fresh and glittered more.

«Ты хочешь знать, что делал я
На воле? Жил — и жизнь моя
Без этих трех блаженных дней
Была б печальней и мрачней
Бессильной старости твоей.
Давным-давно задумал я
Взглянуть на дальние поля,
Узнать, прекрасна ли земля,
Узнать, для воли иль тюрьмы
На этот свет родимся мы.
И в час ночной, ужасный час,
Когда гроза пугала вас,
Когда, столпясь при алтаре,
Вы ниц лежали на земле,
Я убежал. О, я как брат
Обняться с бурей был бы рад!
Глазами тучи я следил,
Рукою молнию ловил...
Скажи мне, что средь этих стен
Могли бы дать вы мне взамен
Той дружбы краткой, но живой,
Меж бурным сердцем и грозой?..

«Бежал я долго — где, куда,
Не знаю! ни одна звезда
Не озаряла трудный путь.
Мне было весело вдохнуть
В мою измученную грудь
Ночную свежесть тех лесов,
И только. Много я часов
Бежал, и наконец, устав,
Прилег между высоких трав;
Прислушался: погони нет.
Гроза утихла. Бледный свет
Тянулся длинной полосой
Меж темным небом и землей,
И различал я, как узор,
На ней зубцы далеких гор;
Недвижим, молча, я лежал.

"What did I do when I was free?
220 I lived! My life without those three,
Three blessed days of fight and thrill
Would have been sadder, bleaker still
Than yours with its pervading chill.
It has been long since first I planned
225 To see the fields and mountains grand,
To learn if beauty filled the land,
To learn, if joy or jail from birth
Is human destiny on earth.
And on that night, that dreadful night,
230 When all the cloister shook with fright,
When at the altar, meek and cowed,
You lay prostrated in a crowd,
I ran away. The world's unrest
To me was like my brother's breast.
235 I saw the clouds that would not calm,
And lightnings danced upon my palm.
What could you give me to replace
That wild and passionate embrace,
That God-like friendship, short but warm
240 Between a bursting heart and storm?

9

"I ran and was already far.
I know not where, for not a star
Broke through the curtain of the night,
But freshness reached me from the height
245 And made my breathing soft and light.
The wood was fragrant, and its smell
I felt in every glade and dell
That in my flight I had to pass.
At last, exhausted, in the grass
250 I lay and listened: no pursuit.
The storm had stopped, the sky was mute.
The light above was one long streak,
And both the sky and earth were bleak;
But I could see a jagged line,
255 Where summits formed their odd design.
I lay immovable and still;

Порой в ущелии шакал
Кричал и плакал, как дитя,
И гладкий чешуей блестя,
Змея скользила меж камней;
Но страх не сжал души моей:
Я сам, как зверь, был чужд людей
И полз и прятался, как змей.

10

«Внизу глубоко подо мной
Поток, усиленный грозой,
Шумел, и шум его глухой
Сердитых сотне голосов
Подобился. Хотя без слов,
Мне внятен был тот разговор,
Немолчный ропот, вечный спор
С упрямой грудою камней.
То вдруг стихал он, то сильней
Он раздавался в тишине;
И вот, в туманной вышине
Запели птички, и восток
Озолотился; ветерок
Сырые шевельнул листы;
Дохнули сонные цветы,
И, как они, навстречу дню,
Я поднял голову мою...
Я осмотрелся; не таю:
Мне стало страшно; на краю
Грозящей бездны я лежал,
Где выл, крутясь, сердитый вал;
Туда вели ступени скал;
Но лишь злой дух по ним шагал,
Когда, низверженный с небес,
В подземной пропасти исчез.

11

«Кругом меня цвел божий сад;
Растений радужный наряд
Хранил следы небесных слез,
И кудри виноградных лоз
Вились, красуясь меж дерёв

In the ravine, below the hill,
A jackal, like a baby, wept,
A scaly snake beside me crept,
260 And pebbles rustled in its wake.
I watched it fearless, wide awake,
For, like a beast, I nursed my ache
And hid from people, like a snake.

10

"A torrent ran beneath my dell;
265 The heavy rain had made it swell,
And I could hear its roaring well.
I understood this wordless roar:
It was the old unending war
Between a freshet, fierce and deep,
270 And boulders crowded in a heap;
The torrent's blocked and tortuous flow
Was fast at times, more often slow;
It ran and rumbled on its way.
At last I saw a distant ray:
275 The night had passed; the dripping trees
Received the gentle morning breeze.
Each flower awoke upon its stalk,
And birds resumed their merry talk.
I also left my grassy bed
280 And toward the heavens raised my head.
I viewed my recent path with dread,
For to a precipice it led,
And on its very brink I'd slept.
Below, a stream in fury leapt;
285 Its jutting rocks meant death, except
That once a demon on them stepped,
When, having lost eternal bliss,
He sank into a dark abyss.

11

"All bloomed and breathed upon the ground;
290 The rainbow garb of plants around
Was wet with Heaven's tears; the rocks
Stood green with grapevines' curly locks;
Each tendril twisted on a trunk,

Прозрачной зеленью листов;
И грозды полные на них,
Серег подобье дорогих,
Висели пышно, и порой
К ним птиц летал пугливый рой.
И снова я к земле припал,
И снова вслушиваться стал
К волшебным, странным голосам;
Они шептались по·кустам,
Как будто речь свою вели
О тайнах неба и земли;
И все природы голоса
Сливались тут; не раздался
В торжественный хваленья час
Лишь человека гордый глас.
Всё, что я чувствовал тогда,
Те думы — им уж нет следа;
Но я б желал их рассказать,
Чтоб жить, хоть мысленно, опять.
В то утро был небесный свод
Так чист, что ангела полет
Прилежный взор следить бы мог;
Он так прозрачно был глубок,
Так полон ровной синевой!
Я в нем глазами и душой
Тонул, пока полдневный зной
Мои мечты не разогнал,
И жаждой я томиться стал.

12

«Тогда к потоку с высоты,
Держась за гибкие кусты,
С плиты на плиту я, как мог,
Спускаться начал. Из-под ног
Сорвавшись, камень иногда
Катился вниз — за ним бразда
Дымилась, прах вился столбом;
Гудя и прыгая, потом
Он поглощаем был волной;
И я висел над глубиной,
Но юность вольная сильна,
И смерть казалась не страшна!

Each was with dew and raindrops drunk.
295 Like earrings in their graceful shapes,
There hung sweet-smelling, heavy grapes;
Birds for the amber berries searched,
Flew 'round the clusters, sang, and perched.
I lay again and stretched myself
300 And listened like a wary elf.
I heard the voice of every twig,
Of trees and bushes, small and big;
They seemed to whisper and rehearse
The secrets of the universe.
305 But when the world awoke and sang,
One voice there was that never rang:
When nature's solemn hymn began,
It lacked the mighty voice of man.
Those things for which I dared to yearn
310 Have vanished never to return,
But I am glad to say it all:
I live again when I recall.
The vault of Heaven was so blue,
That even if an angel flew,
315 The human eye, intent and keen,
Could have observed it in the sheen—
So clear it was and so profound;
My eyes and soul were in it drowned.
So did I lie upon the ground,
320 Till from the heat my dreams dispersed;
My mouth and throat were sealed with thirst.

12

"Then, holding on to every vine,
I ventured down the steep incline:
From rock to rock, from plate to plate.
325 A stone, unsettled by my weight,
Would move and roll at breakneck speed,
With pebbles following its lead.
Still faster, faster it would dash,
And then a cloud of dust, a splash—
330 The waves would part, the river's breast
Would open for the reckless guest.
I also like a pebble hung,
But what is danger to the young!

327

Лишь только я с крутых высот
Спустился, свежесть горных вод
Повеяла навстречу мне,
И жадно я припал к волне.
Вдруг голос — легкий шум шагов...
Мгновенно скрывшись меж кустов,
Невольным трепетом объят,
Я поднял боязливый взгляд,
И жадно вслушиваться стал.
И ближе, ближе всё звучал
Грузинки голос молодой,
Так безыскусственно живой,
Так сладко вольный, будто он
Лишь звуки дружеских имен
Произносить был приучен.
Простая песня то была,
Но в мысль она мне залегла,
И мне, лишь сумрак настает,
Незримый дух ее поет.

13

«Держа кувшин над головой,
Грузинка узкою тропой
Сходила к берегу. Порой
Она скользила меж камней,
Смеясь неловкости своей.
И беден был ее наряд;
И шла она легко, назад
Изгибы длинные чадры
Откинув. Летние жары
Покрыли тенью золотой
Лицо и грудь ее; и зной
Дышал от уст ее и щек.
И мрак очей был так глубок,
Так полон тайнами любви,
Что думы пылкие мои
Смутились. Помню только я
Кувшина звон,— когда струя
Вливалась медленно в него,
И шорох... больше ничего.
Когда же я очнулся вновь
И отлила от сердца кровь,

At last I finished my descent;
335 The rapid, foaming river sent
Its cool and freshness to the bank,
And long and greedily I drank,
When someone's voice and steps I heard
And sought the bushes like a bird.
340 With an involuntary dread
I raised my eyes and looked ahead.
It seemed I heard a woman climb;
The steps were closer all the time,
And soon I saw a Georgian maid;
345 Vivacious, free, and unafraid,
She sang. Her gentle voice caressed,
As though the men it had addressed
Had always been the very best.
She sang a simple, artless strain,
350 But deep it sits within my brain,
And every night, before the moon,
Some spirit hums to me its tune.

13

"She held a pitcher on her head
And chose the path that downward led.
355 I could observe her cautious tread
On shaky pebbles. When her foot
Would stumble at a stone or root,
Her clumsiness would make her smile.
I saw her modest clothes meanwhile
360 And viewed her face, for her yashmak—
Both parts of it—she'd folded back.
The sun that warmed and burned her land
Had made her cheeks and forehead tanned.
Her glowing face and mouth breathed heat,
365 Her eyes were with it so replete,
So full of passion deeply hid
That things I felt and thought and did
Lost every meaning. From the bank
I heard the pitcher gently clank;
370 I also heard a pebble fall—
And then a rustle. That was all.
When I had managed to regain
My senses and my breath again,

329

Она была уж далеко;
И шла хоть тише,— но легко,
Стройна под ношею своей,
Как тополь, царь ее полей!
Недалеко, в прохладной мгле,
Казалось, приросли к скале
Две сакли дружною четой;
Над плоской кровлею одной
Дымок струился голубой.
Я вижу будто бы теперь,
Как отперлась тихонько дверь...
И затворилася опять!..
Тебе, я знаю, не понять
Мою тоску, мою печаль;
И если б мог,— мне было б жаль:
Воспоминанья тех минут
Во мне, со мной пускай умрут.

14

«Трудами ночи изнурен,
Я лег в тени. Отрадный сон
Сомкнул глаза невольно мне...
И снова видел я во сне
Грузинки образ молодой.
И странной, сладкою тоской
Опять моя заныла грудь.
Я долго силился вздохнуть —
И пробудился. Уж луна
Вверху сияла, и одна
Лишь тучка кралася за ней,
Как за добычею своей,
Объятья жадные раскрыв.
Мир темен был и молчалив;
Лишь серебристой бахромой
Вершины цепи снеговой
Вдали сверкали предо мной,
Да в берега плескал поток.
В знакомой сакле огонек
То трепетал, то снова гас:
На небесах в полночный час
Так гаснет яркая звезда!
Хотелось мне... но я туда

She was too far. Behind the trees
375 She slowly walked with grace and ease;
Herself, I think, she could have been
A poplar and the poplars' queen.
Close by me, on a mountain, stood
Two humble huts together glued.
380 They stood like tender sisters twain,
A smoke was rising in a skein
And slowly floating to the plain . . .
You need not listen in surprise:
I see it all before my eyes;
385 I saw her push the door and then
All was immovable again.
Old man! Oh, if you only knew . . .
But no! this tale is not for you.
Let all I wished and all I saw
390 Stay buried in me evermore.

14

"Fatigued, I wandered on and strayed,
Until at last I found some shade.
And then I slept; my dreams were kind
And sent her image to my mind.
395 The vision came and danced and rose,
Sweet anguish tortured my repose;
At times it seemed that I would choke,
But with an effort I awoke
And looked about. The moon was high;
400 Above me, in the darkened sky,
A hungry cloud was on its way
And chased the moon, its lawful prey.
I saw it open its embrace
And drift in haste through boundless space.
405 With silent stars the sky was strewn,
And far away, beyond the moon,
The summits formed a long festoon.
I heard the stream through mountains cut;
A candle in the flat-roofed hut
410 Would brighten up, then flicker low . . .
A midnight star may twinkle so
And die, extinguished in the air.
I wished, I wished . . . but did not dare

Взойти не смел. Я цель одну,
Пройти в родимую страну,
Имел в душе,— и превозмог
Страданье голода, как мог.
И вот дорогою прямой
Пустился, робкий и немой.
Но скоро в глубине лесной
Из виду горы потерял
И тут с пути сбиваться стал.

15

«Напрасно в бешенстве, порой,
Я рвал отчаянной рукой
Терновник, спутанный плющом:
Всё лес был, вечный лес кругом,
Страшней и гуще каждый час;
И миллионом черных глаз
Смотрела ночи темнота
Сквозь ветви каждого куста...
Моя кружилась голова;
Я стал влезать на дерева;
Но даже на краю небес
Всё тот же был зубчатый лес.
Тогда на землю я упал;
И в исступлении рыдал,
И грыз сырую грудь земли,
И слезы, слезы потекли
В нее горючею росой...
Но верь мне, помощи людской
Я не желал... Я был чужой
Для них навек, как зверь степной;
И если б хоть минутный крик
Мне изменил — клянусь, старик,
Я б вырвал слабый мой язык.

16

«Ты помнишь детские года:
Слезы не знал я никогда;
Но тут я плакал без стыда.
Кто видеть мог? Лишь темный лес,
Да месяц, плывший средь небес!

332

To go that way, for in my soul
415   I had one aim, one sacred goal—
To find my land. So, starved and weak,
I went to look for it, to seek . . .
I did, believe me, all I could.
I stepped into the murky wood,
420   But 'round me trees in silence stood.
The distant mountains stayed away,
And I began to lose my way.

15

"The vines were thick; I madly tore,
Until my hands and arms were sore,
425   But thorn and ivy made a fence
Across the forest dark and dense.
I saw it stretch and sway and rise;
A million of the blackest eyes
Among the boughs of every tree
430   Intently watched and followed me.
My head, I felt, began to swim.
I climbed a pine, but, black and grim,
The wood stretched like a massive wall;
It had no end, it covered all.
435   In vain a path in it I sought;
I fell, bewildered and distraught,
I fell to weep, to gnaw and bite
The breast of earth with all my might.
My tears gushed forth, like scalding dew;
440   But help from men, from such as you,
I did not want. Alone I grew
And all alone was breaking through.
My tongue suppressed my every shout,
And if it had not—do not doubt:
445   I would myself have torn it out.

16

"Remember? Neither pain nor fear
Had ever made me shed a tear.
But then I wept. For who could hear?
The gloomy oaks from near and far
450   And in the sky a distant star . . .

333

Озарена его лучом,
Покрыта мохом и песком,
Непроницаемой стеной
Окружена, передо мной
Была поляна. Вдруг по ней
Мелькнула тень, и двух огней
Промчались искры... и потом
Какой-то зверь одним прыжком
Из чащи выскочил и лег,
Играя, навзничь на песок.
То был пустыни вечный гость —
Могучий барс. Сырую кость
Он грыз и весело визжал;
То взор кровавый устремлял,
Мотая ласково хвостом,
На полный месяц, — и на нем
Шерсть отливалась серебром.
Я ждал, схватив рогатый сук,
Минуту битвы; сердце вдруг
Зажглося жаждою борьбы
И крови... да, рука судьбы
Меня вела иным путем...
Но нынче я уверен в том,
Что быть бы мог в краю отцов
Не из последних удальцов.

17

«Я ждал. И вот в тени ночной
Врага почуял он, и вой
Протяжный, жалобный, как стон,
Раздался вдруг... и начал он
Сердито лапой рыть песок,
Встал на дыбы, потом прилег,
И первый бешеный скачок
Мне страшной смертию грозил...
Но я его предупредил.
Удар мой верен был и скор.
Надежный сук мой, как топор,
Широкий лоб его рассек...
Он застонал, как человек,
И опрокинулся. Но вновь,

334

Where I was hiding, right across,
Half-buried in the sand and moss,
There was a glade; by tree roots split,
It lay enclosed and dimly lit.
455 All seemed to sleep, but in the dark
I saw a flash, a double spark;
A shadow flitted, and a bounce
Brought forward a majestic ounce.
The desert's guest, he came alone,
460 But in his teeth he had a bone.
His bloody meal was finished soon.
He roared, contented, at the moon,
Then rolled, and stretched his paws, and played,
Of beasts and people unafraid.
465 I heard him scratch the ground and purr,
And moonbeams shone upon his fur,
Whenever he would only stir.
I held a stick: sharp end and knob;
I watched. My heart began to throb.
470 I wanted blood, I could not wait!
Today I know: the hand of fate
Has pushed me jealously aside.
But I can say with glowing pride
That in the land from which I came
475 My courage would not bring me shame.

17

"Protected by the shade, I stood
Until he sensed me. Then the wood
Shook with his howl. It rent the air,
As might a groan of wild despair.
480 The cautious beast was getting hot,
I saw him look at me and squat.
He could have killed me on the spot,
So powerful was his jump, so quick;
But I was ready with my stick
485 And never let my grip relax;
My knobby weapon, like an ax,
Cut through his forehead to the bone.
He gave an almost human moan
And fell upon his back; his blood

Хотя лила из раны кровь
Густой, широкою волной,
Бой закипел, смертельный бой!

18

«Ко мне он кинулся на грудь;
Но в горло я успел воткнуть
И там два раза повернуть
Мое оружье... Он завыл,
Рванулся из последних сил,
И мы, сплетясь, как пара змей,
Обнявшись крепче двух друзей,
Упали разом, и во мгле
Бой продолжался на земле.
И я был страшен в этот миг;
Как барс пустынный, зол и дик,
Я пламенел, визжал, как он;
Как будто сам я был рожден
В семействе барсов и волков
Под свежим пологом лесов.
Казалось, что слова людей
Забыл я — и в груди моей
Родился тот ужасный крик,
Как будто с детства мой язык
К иному звуку не привык...
Но враг мой стал изнемогать,
Метаться, медленней дышать,
Сдавил меня в последний раз...
Зрачки его недвижных глаз
Блеснули грозно — и потом
Закрылись тихо вечным сном;
Но с торжествующим врагом
Он встретил смерть лицом к лицу,
Как в битве следует бойцу!..

19

«Ты видишь на груди моей
Следы глубокие когтей;
Еще они не заросли
И не закрылись; но земли
Сырой покров их освежит,

490   Gushed mixing with the moss and mud;
       But he got up, and in the night
       The fight went on—a mortal fight.

18

       "His paws were on me like a vice,
       But soon he paid the awful price:
495   I thrust my stick and turned it twice
       Inside his throat. His howl was deep,
       He rolled, then gave a flying leap,
       And we, like writhing snakes entwined,
       Like friends whom love and passion bind,
500   Both fell to earth. Another bound,
       And we continued on the ground.
       You should have seen my thrust and pounce!
       As wild and awful as the ounce,
       I jumped and shrieked by madness torn,
505   As though I, too, had once been born
       Not as a child like other men
       But in a wolf's or panther's den.
       I did not need the human tongue,
       And from my breast a shriek was wrung,
510   A horrid, awe-inspiring shriek,
       As though, when I was small and weak,
       I had not even learned to speak.
       My foe upon the reddened moss
       Began in agony to toss;
515   He pressed me feebly, tried to rise,
       The pupils of his yellow eyes
       Flashed once again as long before,
       And shut to open nevermore.
       He perished and he lost his war,
520   But in his mortal, last embrace
       He met the winner face to face.

19

       "Look: you can see upon my breast
       The marks still forcibly impressed.
       They are not covered by a crust,
525   They smart and bleed. But earthly dust
       Will let their burning heat subside,

И смерть навеки заживит.
О них тогда я позабыл,
И, вновь собрав остаток сил,
Побрел я в глубине лесной...
Но тщетно спорил я с судьбой:
Она смеялась надо мной!

20

«Я вышел из лесу. И вот
Проснулся день, и хоровод
Светил напутственных исчез
В его лучах. Туманный лес
Заговорил. Вдали аул
Куриться начал. Смутный гул
В долине с ветром пробежал...
Я сел и вслушиваться стал;
Но смолк он вместе с ветерком.
И кинул взоры я кругом:
Тот край, казалось, мне знаком.
И страшно было мне, понять
Не мог я долго, что опять
Вернулся я к тюрьме моей;
Что бесполезно столько дней
Я тайный замысел ласкал,
Терпел, томился и страдал,
И всё зачем?.. Чтоб в цвете лет,
Едва взглянув на божий свет,
При звучном ропоте дубрав,
Блаженство вольности познав,
Унесть в могилу за собой
Тоску по родине святой,
Надежд обманутых укор
И вашей жалости позор!..
Еще в сомненье погружен,
Я думал — это страшный сон...
Вдруг дальний колокола звон
Раздался снова в тишине —
И тут всё ясно стало мне...
О! я узнал его тотчас!
Он с детских глаз уже не раз
Сгонял виденья снов живых
Про милых ближних и родных,

And death will heal them all and hide.
But I forgot about them then.
I gathered all my strength again
530 And wandered on. Alas! Too late,
For useless was my game with fate:
I could not overcome its hate.

20

"I left the wood and came to meet
The rising sun. The jealous suite
535 Of constellations disappeared
Before its rays. Somber and weird,
The forest spoke. A village small
Began to smoke, and through it all
The wind came rustling to the land.
540 I tried but could not understand.
The sun above me was aglow;
I looked attentively, and lo!
This place, this wood I seemed to know.
Faint noises floated through the air . . .
545 I guessed of course but did not dare
To say that I had reached my jail;
That all my pains would not avail,
That everything I'd fondly planned,
My dreams, my wishes, sweet and grand,
550 Had failed, and that my humble lot
Was early death; that I would not
Break through or conquer fate's decree,
That just for once I had been free,
But that the end of bitter strife
555 Was broken hopes, a ruined life,
The insult of a stupid chase,
And your compassion's dark disgrace.
I thought my spinning head would swell,
Or could the nightmare finish well?
560 But suddenly I heard a bell.
It reached me, and its measured boom
Forever sealed for me my doom.
I listened to the toll spellbound:
How often in the past this sound
565 Would drive my childish dreams away,
The dreams of freedom, friends, and play,

339

Про волю дикую степей,
Про легких, бешеных коней,
Про битвы чудные меж скал,
Где всех один я побеждал!..
И слушал я без слез, без сил.
Казалось, звон тот выходил
Из сердца — будто кто-нибудь
Железом ударял мне в грудь.
И смутно понял я тогда,
Что мне на родину следа
Не проложить уж никогда.

21

«Да, заслужил я жребий мой!
Могучий конь в степи чужой,
Плохого сбросив седока,
На родину издалека
Найдет прямой и краткий путь...
Что я пред ним? Напрасно грудь
Полна желаньем и тоской:
То жар бессильный и пустой,
Игра мечты, болезнь ума.
На мне печать свою тюрьма
Оставила... Таков цветок
Темничный: вырос одинок
И бледен он меж плит сырых,
И долго листьев молодых
Не распускал, всё ждал лучей
Живительных. И много дней
Прошло, и добрая рука
Печалью тронулась цветка,
И был он в сад перенесен,
В соседство роз. Со всех сторон
Дышала сладость бытия...
Но что ж? Едва взошла заря,
Палящий луч ее обжег
В тюрьме воспитанный цветок...

22

«И, как его, палил меня
Огонь безжалостного дня.
Напрасно прятал я в траву

Of native home, of older days,
Of dashing horses' heat and craze,
Of battles and of combats' din,
570   Of wars that I would always win.
That toll! . . . It made me writhe and smart,
For it was coming from my heart,
As if a blade anew, anew
Were cutting up my breast in two.
575   And then I understood at last
That, whether I was slow or fast,
I should not find my home and past.

21

"I know that I've deserved my lot;
A mighty steed would boldly trot
580   And find his home from any steppe,
But if the rider is inept,
He'd throw him off and run alone.
And I? My heart is like a stone,
My soul is striving ever higher—
585   An impotent and useless fire,
The dream's deceit, the mind's disease.
The prison put me on my knees;
I bear its imprint, like a flower
That grew in jail, forlorn and sour.
590   It waited long, it opened late
Its home was on a barren plate,
It hoped for summer warmth and rays:
To draw their strength. So many days
Had passed, until a kindly hand
595   Transferred it to another land.
A blooming garden was around,
With fragrant roses; on the ground
All seemed for joy and pleasure born.
So what? It perished in the morn!
600   It burned: the earliest rays beguiled
This prison plant, this captive child.

22

"The sun was rising, and I feared
That like that plant I should be seared.
In vain I desperately tried

341

Мою усталую главу;
Иссохший лист ее венцом
Терновым над моим челом
Свивался, и в лицо огнем
Сама земля дышала мне.
Сверкая быстро в вышине,
Кружились искры; с белых скал
Струился пар. Мир божий спал
В оцепенении глухом
Отчаянья тяжелым сном.
Хотя бы крикнул коростель,
Иль стрекозы живая трель
Послышалась, или ручья
Ребячий лепет... Лишь змея,
Сухим бурьяном шелестя,
Сверкая желтою спиной,
Как будто надписью златой
Покрытый донизу клинок,
Браздя рассыпчатый песок,
Скользила бережно; потом,
Играя, нежася на нем,
Тройным свивалася кольцом;
То, будто вдруг обожжена,
Металась, прыгала она
И в дальних пряталась кустах...

23

«И было всё на небесах
Светло и тихо. Сквозь пары
Вдали чернели две горы,
Наш монастырь из-за одной
Сверкал зубчатою стеной.
Внизу Арагва и Кура,
Обвив каймой из серебра
Подошвы свежих островов,
По корням шепчущих кустов
Бежали дружно и легко...
До них мне было далеко!
Хотел я встать — передо мной
Всё закружилось с быстротой;
Хотел кричать — язык сухой
Беззвучен и недвижим был...

605   To stay in taller grass and hide.
      I seemed to walk through molten lead;
      A withered leaf upon my head
      Was like a wreath of thorns. With dread
      I felt that earth had come aflame;
610   Some shining sparks from heaven came
      And whirled in circles. Whitish steam
      Concealed the rocks. Plunged in a dream,
      The world seemed sleeping, and its sleep
      Was, like its consternation, deep.
615   If only birds were not so still,
      Or if a dragonfly would trill!
      Or if a stream would gently fall!
      But no! a snake alone would crawl
      And squirm, indifferent to all.
620   Its back was like a dagger's shaft
      Embellished by a master's craft.
      The snake crawled rustling in the weeds,
      And sandgrains fell away like seeds
      Through its elaborate advance;
625   I saw it pause as in a trance,
      Then start a quick and eery dance,
      Then look for something on the soil,
      Then twist in loops, again uncoil,
      And to the distant bushes hie . . .

                    23

630   "Yet, all was tranquil in the sky.
      Through vapors, at the very back,
      Two mountains stood morose and black.
      Close to the second, looking small,
      I saw our monastery wall.
635   The sister rivers were the same;
      Each, like a gleaming silver frame,
      Encircled many islets fresh;
      Across the roots' entwining mesh
      They hurried gaily to the sea . . .
640   But they were far, so far from me!
      I tried to rise, but in the sun
      The earth before me whirled and spun!
      I could not shout, for thirst had won:
      It parched my tongue and burned it dry . . .

                    343

Я умирал. Меня томил
Предсмертный бред!
                        Казалось мне,
Что я лежу на влажном дне
Глубокой речки — и была
Кругом таинственная мгла.
И, жажду вечную поя,
Как лед холодная струя,
Журча, вливалася мне в грудь...
И я боялся лишь заснуть,
Так было сладко, любо мне...
А надо мною в вышине
Волна теснилася к волне,
И солнце сквозь хрусталь волны
Сияло сладостней луны...
И рыбок пестрые стада
В лучах играли иногда.
И помню я одну из них:
Она приветливей других
Ко мне ласкалась. Чешуей
Была покрыта золотой
Ее спина. Она вилась
Над головой моей не раз,
И взор ее зеленых глаз
Был грустно нежен и глубок...
И надивиться я не мог:
Ее сребристый голосок
Мне речи странные шептал,
И пел, и снова замолкал.

Он говорил: „Дитя мое,
    Останься здесь со мной:
В воде привольное житье
    И холод и покой.

              *

„Я созову моих сестер:
    Мы пляской круговой
Развеселим туманный взор
    И дух усталый твой.

              *

„Усни, постель твоя мягка,
    Прозрачен твой покров.

645   Half-stifled, I began to die.
      Strange visions came.
                    I had a dream
      That I was lying in a stream.
      The heat was gone, the sun had set,
      The bottom of the stream was wet.
650   In water blissfully immersed,
      I felt it quench my scorching thirst.
      The spurt was cold as ice and deep . . .
      I only feared to fall asleep:
      It was so sweet to lie, to rave . . .
655   And high above my fluid grave
      A wave would chase another wave,
      And through the roof of my lagoon
      The sun shone milder than the moon.
      Illumined by a wayward ray
660   A flock of fish began to play.
      I saw that one had whisked her tail
      And moved to me; her every scale
      Was glittering gold. She'd leap and rise
      And gently look into my eyes
665   With hers, which were like seaweeds green—
      Such tender eyes I'd never seen.
      I did not know what she could mean:
      On me alone she seemed to dote,
      And close to me she'd swim and float.
670   She sang, and from her silver throat
      There came a whisper, then a song,
      First low and weak, then loud and strong.

      I heard the words, 'My darling boy,
         My darling child, I pray,
675   Stay in the water and enjoy
         A life of peace for aye.

                *

      I'll call my sisters: wait awhile!
         We'll dance for you and dive;
      And then your mournful eyes will smile,
680   Your spirit will revive.

                *

      Your roof is like transparent glass,
      Your bed is washed by streams,

Пройдут года, пройдут века
Под говор чудных снов.

＊

„О милый мой! не утаю,
Что я тебя люблю,
Люблю как вольную струю,
Люблю как жизнь мою...‘‘

И долго, долго слушал я;
И мнилось, звучная струя
Сливала тихий ропот свой
С словами рыбки золотой.
Тут я забылся. Божий свет
В глазах угас. Безумный бред
Бессилью тела уступил...

24

«Так я найдёп и поднят был...
Ты остальное знаешь сам.
Я кончил. Верь моим словам
Или не верь, мне всё равно.
Меня печалит лишь одно:
Мой труп холодный и немой
Не будет тлеть в земле родной,
И повесть горьких мук моих
Не призовет меж стен глухих
Вниманье скорбное ничье
На имя темное мое.

25

«Прощай, отец... дай руку мне;
Ты чувствуешь, моя в огне...
Знай, этот пламень с юных дней,
Таяся, жил в груди моей;
Но ныне пищи нет ему,
И он прожег свою тюрьму
И возвратится вновь к тому,
Кто всем законной чередой
Дает страданье и покой...

And days will pass, and years will pass
To murmurs of your dreams.

*

685 Believe me, darling, it is true:
  I am in love with you,
  I love you like the river blue,
   Like pleasures, old and new . . . '

  I lay and listened very long,
690 And everything—the quiet song,
  The gurgle of the stream around
  Became a single, lulling sound.
  And then I fainted. Day and light
  Went out; my raving visions' might
695 Was in my body's weakness drowned . . .

24

  "And so, unconscious, I was found.
  You know the rest, and if you can,
  Believe my artless tale, old man,
  Or if you can't, then don't believe.
700 There's something else that makes me grieve.
  I grieve that after all my toil
  I shall not sleep in native soil,
  And in these walls, behind this gate
  The story of my bitter fate
705 Will kindle no one's sacred flame
  Or bring attention to my name.

25

  "I've finished. Father, touch my hand:
  It's hot; this fire I cannot stand;
  Concealed from people and suppressed,
710 It glowed too long within my breast
  And burned its jail; I've come to learn
  That it has nothing else to burn,
  And now at last it will return
  To Him whose will is to dispose
715 And send us anguish or repose.

347

Но что мне в том? — пускай в раю,
В святом, заоблачном краю
Мой дух найдет себе приют...
Увы! — за несколько минут
Между крутых и темных скал,
Где я в ребячестве играл,
Я б рай и вечность променял...

26

«Когда я стану умирать,
И, верь, тебе не долго ждать —
Ты перенесть меня вели
В наш сад, в то место, где цвели
Акаций белых два куста...
Трава меж ними так густа,
И свежий воздух так душист,
И так прозрачно золотист
Играющий на солнце лист!
Там положить вели меня.
Сияньем голубого дня
Упьюся я в последний раз.
Оттуда виден и Кавказ!
Быть может, он с своих высот
Привет прощальный мне пришлет,
Пришлет с прохладным ветерком...
И близ меня перед концом
Родной опять раздастся звук!
И стану думать я, что друг
Иль брат, склонившись надо мной,
Отер внимательной рукой
С лица кончины хладный пот,
И что вполголоса поет
Он мне про милую страну...
И с этой мыслью я засну,
И никого не прокляну!»

But do I care, if in the skies,
Among the souls of Paradise
My spirit finds a quiet abode?
Ah! For a minute on the road
720 Where stones shone brighter than a hoard,
O'er which an eagle boldly soared
I'd gladly forfeit that reward . . .

26

"When I begin to die (alas!
It will, I know, soon come to pass),
725 I pray, remember my bequest:
I want to breathe my last and rest
In that secluded piece of land
Where two acacia bushes stand
In snow-white blossoms every May,
730 Where grass and flowers so gently sway,
Where leaves turn golden from a ray.
Please, let the brothers take me there.
Once more I'll drink the fragrant air,
Enveloped in its piercing sheen.
735 From there, the Caucasus is seen!
Who knows? Before I take my leave
Perhaps its greeting I'll receive;
A gentle wind that stroked its peaks
May touch and cool my burning cheeks . . .
740 And then a song, serene and soft,
Will float caressingly aloft,
As though a brother or a friend
Were come to me before my end,
A brother whom I never met
745 But who will come to wipe my sweat.
He'll sing to me of home again;
I'll fall asleep to his amen
And will not curse the world of men."

Ruins on the bank of the Aragva in Georgia.
Drawing by Lermontov.

"Mtsyri."
Illustration by Zamirailo.

Mtsyri watching a Georgian girl.
Drawing by Polyakov.

The Georgian Military Road near Mtskhet. Picture by Lermontov.

THE DEMON AND RELATED POETRY

I am the cause of each upheaval . . .

ДЕМОН

Восточная повесть

ЧАСТЬ I

I

Печальный Демон, дух изгнанья,
Летал над грешною землей,
И лучших дней воспоминанья
Пред ним теснилися толпой;
Тех дней, когда в жилище света
Блистал он, чистый херувим,
Когда бегущая комета
Улыбкой ласковой привета
Любила поменяться с ним,
Когда сквозь вечные туманы,
Познанья жадный, он следил
Кочующие караваны
В пространстве брошенных светил;
Когда он верил и любил,
Счастливый первенец творенья!
Не знал ни злобы, ни сомненья,
И не грозил уму его
Веков бесплодных ряд унылый...
И много, много... и всего
Припомнить не имел он силы!

II

Давно отверженный блуждал
В пустыне мира без приюта:
Вослед за веком век бежал,

92. THE DEMON

An Oriental Tale

Part I

I

The gloomy Demon, lorn and banished,
Flew high above this vale of woe,
Immersed in thought of what had vanished,
Of things and scenes of long ago.
5   His past before his eyes was fleeting,
When he enjoyed his Maker's grace,
When comets, gladdened by the meeting,
Would smile at him in tender greeting
Upon their way through empty space;
10   When from his habitation holy
Through cosmic mists he could perceive
The distant stars migrating slowly;
When ardent, glowing, and naive,
He learned to worship and believe—
15   The happy firstborn of creation!
Exempt from evil and negation,
He had not known that time could mean
A chain of ages, vainly crawling . . .
But all the pictures he had seen
20   He felt too sad to keep recalling.

II

His world was a gigantic cage,
And aimlessly he wandered in it;
An age would chase another age,

Как за минутою минута,
Однообразной чередой.
Ничтожной властвуя землей,
Он сеял зло без наслажденья.
Нигде искусству своему
Он не встречал сопротивленья —
И зло наскучило ему.

III

И над вершинами Кавказа
Изгнанник рая пролетал:
Под ним Казбек, как грань алмаза,
Снегами вечными сиял,
И, глубоко внизу чернея,
Как трещина, жилище змея,
Вился излучистый Дарьял,
И Терек, прыгая, как львица
С косматой гривой на хребте,
Ревел,— и горный зверь, и птица,
Кружась в лазурной высоте,
Глаголу вод его внимали;
И золотые облака
Из южных стран, издалека
Его на север провожали;
И скалы тесною толпой,
Таинственной дремоты полны,
Над ним склонялись головой,
Следя мелькающие волны;
И башни замков на скалах
Смотрели грозно сквозь туманы —
У врат Кавказа на часах
Сторожевые великаны!
И дик, и чуден был вокруг
Весь божий мир; но гордый дух
Презрительным окинул оком
Творенье бога своего,
И на челе его высоком
Не отразилось ничего.

IV

И перед ним иной картины
Красы живые расцвели:

As would a minute chase a minute—
25 They came and went and came again . . .
He was unchallenged in his reign:
Like a dispassionate intriguer,
He scattered evil and discord;
For both the world was always eager—
30 And soon he was by evil bored.

III

He flew, indifferent and placid,
O'er the Caucasian shining snows:
Below him, like a diamond's facet,
Kazbék in all its grandeur rose,
35 And farther down, in depths abysmal,
In a crevasse, obscure and dismal,
Daryál its home 'mid serpents chose;
The Terek, like a lioness leaping,
Its foamy mane in fury shook;
40 Wild beasts, reclining, running, creeping,
And birds in every distant nook
To its incessant roar attended;
The fluffy clouds, like golden fleece,
From southern lands, from climes of peace
45 Their way above the river wended.
The mountains stood in serried ranks,
As though bewitched by a magician;
They viewed the Terek from its banks
And dozed from endless repetition.
50 Upon the rocks, by nature barred,
The castles, gloomy and defiant,
Stood grim like sentinels on guard,
Each like an ever-watchful giant.
God's world was splendid, wild, and great,
55 But with disdain the child of hate
His Maker's universe inspected,
It did not make him happy now,
And not a feeling was reflected
Upon his high, unruffled brow.

IV

60 Still farther on the vales of Georgia's
Among the mountains could be seen;

357

Роскошной Грузии долины
Ковром раскинулись вдали;
Счастливый, пышный край земли!
Столпообразные раины,
Звонко-бегущие ручьи
По дну из камней разноцветных,
И кущи роз, где соловьи
Поют красавиц, безответных
На сладкий голос их любви;
Чинар развесистые сени,
Густым венчанные плющом,
Пещеры, где палящим днем
Таятся робкие олени;
И блеск, и жизнь, и шум листов,
Стозвучный говор голосов,
Дыханье тысячи растений!
И полдня сладострастный зной,
И ароматною росой
Всегда увлаженные ночи,
И звезды яркие, как очи,
Как взор грузинки молодой!..
Но, кроме зависти холодной,
Природы блеск не возбудил
В груди изгнанника бесплодной
Ни новых чувств, ни новых сил;
И всё, что пред собой он видел,
Он презирал иль ненавидел.

V

Высокий дом, широкий двор
Седой Гудал себе построил...
Трудов и слез он много стоил
Рабам послушным с давних пор.
С утра на скат соседних гор
От стен его ложатся тени.
В скале нарублены ступени;
Они от башни угловой
Ведут к реке, по ним мелькая,
Покрыта белою чадрой,[1]
Княжна Тамара молодая
К Арагве ходит за водой.

---

[1] Покрывало. *(Примечание Лермонтова)*.

Instead of dark, forbidding gorges,
There spread a carpet, lush and green:
A happy land, a peaceful scene!
65 Beneath were huts and smoking forges,
Luxuriant poplars, purling rills,
Through variegated pebbles ringing;
And roses blooming on the hills
Where nightingales were sweetly singing
70 Of beauty and of passion's thrills;
Majestic plantains, which arose
All overhung by sprawling ivy,
Well-hidden caves where timid does
Were often seen for shelter diving;
75 Light, life, and groves of swaying trees,
The din of beasts and birds, and bees,
And plants, on slopes and meadows thriving;
The dazzling sun, each morning new,
At night the smell of fragrant dew,
80 And stars—a wondrous distant cluster—
That shine with almost human luster:
So looks a Georgian maid at you!
But nature's luxury and glitter
Struck in the exile not a spark;
85 He stayed resentful, dry, and bitter,
Impassive, arrogant, and dark.
And all that was unstained or sacred
Aroused in him contempt and hatred.

V

A sturdy castle, broad and tall,
90 The very best among its neighbors,
The fruit of slaves' unending labor . . .
It is the home of Prince Goudál.
Close to the mountain is its wall;
The rocky steps, rough-hewn by axes,
95 Give to the river easy access.
In this secluded, guarded place
The aged ruler's only daughter,
Princess Tamára, full of grace,
From the Arágva carries water;
100 A white yashmak[1] conceals her face.

_____
[1] A kind of veil. (Lermontov's note.)

VI

Всегда безмолвно на долины
Глядел с утеса мрачный дом;
Но пир большой сегодня в нем —
Звучит зурна́, [1] и льются ви́ны —
Гудал сосватал дочь свою,
На пир он созвал всю семью.
На кровле, устланной коврами,
Сидит невеста меж подруг:
Средь игр и песен их досуг
Проходит. Дальними горами
Уж спрятан солнца полукруг;
В ладони мерно ударяя,
Они поют — и бубен свой
Берет невеста молодая.
И вот она, одной рукой
Кружа его над головой,
То вдруг помчится легче птицы,
То остановится,— глядит —
И влажный взор ее блестит
Из-под завистливой ресницы;
То черной бровью поведет,
То вдруг наклонится немножко,
И по ковру скользит, плывет
Ее божественная ножка;
И улыбается она,
Веселья детского полна.
Но луч луны, по влаге зыбкой
Слегка играющий порой,
Едва ль сравнится с той улыбкой,
Как жизнь, как молодость живой.

VII

Клянусь полночною звездой,
Лучом заката и востока,
Властитель Персии златой
И ни единый царь земной
Не целовал такого ока;
Гарема брызжущий фонтан
Ни разу жаркою порою

---

[1] Вроде волынки. (*Примечание Лермонтова*).

VI

Inside the castle on the mountain
That always looked morose and gray
Zournáhs[1] and flutes compete today,
And wines are lavished in a fountain.
105   Goudál has called his tribe with pride:
His daughter has become a bride.
While in the hall the men are drinking,
She and her maidens, richly dressed,
Upon the roof, on carpets, rest
110   And play; the solar disk is sinking
Beyond the summits in the west.
The maidens sing; for better rhythm
They clap their hands and forward lean;
And now Tamara, who is with them,
115   Right in the middle of the scene
Stands up and lifts her tambourine.
First like a bird she swiftly dashes,
Then stops arrested in her flight;
Her shining eyes are moist and bright,
120   Half-hidden by the jealous lashes.
She bends, she gives a tiny shrug,
Her eyes are with enjoyment brimming,
Her foot divine upon the rug
Is gliding, sliding, almost swimming;
125   And on her lips a childish smile
Plays full of mirth, devoid of guile.
That smile is gentle and disarming
Beyond description or compare;
In its appeal of youth more charming
130   Than all the moonbeams of the air.

VII

I could have sworn by every star
By morning young and evening weary
That golden Persia's mighty shah
Or any past or present Tsar
135   Had hardly fondled such a peri.
The iridescent fountain spray
Had never played with such a shoulder,

---

[1]Resemble bagpipes. (Lermontov's note.)

Своей жемчужною росою
Не омывал подобный стан!
Еще ничья рука земная,
По милому челу блуждая,
Таких волос не расплела;
С тех пор как мир лишился рая,
Клянусь, красавица такая
Под солнцем юга не цвела.

VIII

В последний раз она плясала.
Увы! заутра ожидала
Ее, наследницу Гудала,
Свободы резвую дитя,
Судьба печальная рабыни,
Отчизна, чуждая поныне,
И незнакомая семья.
И часто тайное сомненье
Темнило светлые черты;
И были все ее движенья
Так стройны, полны выраженья,
Так полны милой простоты,
Что если б Демон, пролетая,
В то время на нее взглянул,
То, прежних братий вспоминая,
Он отвернулся б — и вздохнул...

IX

И Демон видел... На мгновенье
Неизъяснимое волненье
В себе почувствовал он вдруг.
Немой души его пустыню
Наполнил благодатный звук —
И вновь постигнул он святыню
Любви, добра и красоты!..
И долго сладостной картиной
Он любовался — и мечты
О прежнем счастье цепью длинной,
Как будто за звездой звезда,
Пред ним катилися тогда.
Прикованный незримой силой,

While making languid harems colder
Upon a blazing summer day.
140 A lover's hand, that sweet offender,
Had not yet touched her forehead tender
Or run with passion through her braid;
Since God created woman's gender
A maid more beautiful and slender
145 Had never danced, had never played.

VIII

Her mirth she seemed from day to borrow,
Though deep within her heart was sorrow:
She smiled but knew that in the morrow
She, freedom's joyous, willful pet,
150 Would leave her home and occupations
To humbly serve her new relations,
To serve the clan she'd never met.
This secret thought, a bitter potion,
Would often cloud her shining face;
155 But when she danced, her every motion
Was full of such intense emotion,
Of such inimitable grace
That if the Demon, slowly flying,
Had noticed her by any chance,
160 He would have thought of love—and, sighing,
Would not have liked to watch the dance.

IX

And lo! He saw the maiden plighted
And felt ineffably excited,
Surprised and touched against his will.
165 He closely viewed the bride and tarried,
And blessèd sounds began to fill
His silent soul for ages arid.
Love, goodness came to him again
Revived by innocent perfection;
170 He watched the peaceful scene, and then
An endless string of recollections
Rolled on before his inner eye,
Like planets in the misty sky.
His feeling pierced him like a rivet

Он с новой грустью стал знаком;
В нем чувство вдруг заговорило
Родным когда-то языком.
То был ли признак возрожденья?
Он слов коварных искушенья
Найти в уме своем не мог...
Забыть? — забвенья не дал бог:
Да он и не взял бы забвенья!..
. . . .

X

Измучив доброго коня,
На брачный пир к закату дня
Спешил жених нетерпеливый.
Арагвы светлой он счастливо
Достиг зеленых берегов.
Под тяжкой ношею даров
Едва, едва переступая,
За ним верблюдов длинный ряд
Дорогой тянется, мелькая:
Их колокольчики звенят.
Он сам, властитель Синодала,
Ведет богатый караван.
Ремнем затянут ловкий стан;
Оправа сабли и кинжала
Блестит на солнце; за спиной
Ружье с насечкой вырезной.
Играет ветер рукавами
Его чухи,¹— кругом она
Вся галуном обложена.
Цветными вышито шелками
Его седло; узда с кистями;
Под ним весь в мыле конь лихой
Бесценной масти, золотой.
Питомец резвый Карабаха
Прядет ушьми и, полный страха,
Храпя косится с крутизны
На пену скачущей волны.
Опасен, узок путь прибрежный!
Утесы с левой стороны,

175 Yet did not make him grieve or smart:
This feeling wanted him to give it
A piece of his awakened heart.
What did it mean? Renunciation?
The evil phrases of temptation
180 Within him of a sudden died;
Oblivion? That he was denied
And would have spurned such expiation.

. . . .

X

The youth was hastening to his bride;
The horse, exhausted by the ride,
185 At sunset reached the blue Arágva,
Whose grassy banks reposed in languor.
Along the road a caravan
Accompanied the happy man.
The camels by the drivers goaded,
190 Moved on; there tinkled silver bells.
With many costly presents loaded,
They'd covered plains and slopes and dells.
It was becoming dark and cooler,
Too slowly did the camels tread;
195 The bridegroom stopped and looked ahead—
Great Sinodál's illustrious ruler.
His mounted blade shines like the sun,
And fine-chased is his proven gun.
He has a long chukháh[1] on, which is
200 All fringed with braid; the bridle, too,
Has tassels, beautiful and new;
The precious saddle from his riches
Is well adorned with silken stitches.
His priceless, agile sorrel steed
205 Is of the famous Karabakh breed.
The horse is shy, and by the river,
Excited, he begins to shiver,
To stamp his foot and prance and snort;
He is afraid that he is caught
210 Upon a pathway steep and winding
That will not give his foot support;

---

[1] A cloak with loose sleeves. (Lermontov's note.)

Направо глубь реки мятежной.
Уж поздно. На вершине снежной
Румянец гаснет; встал туман...
Прибавил шагу караван.

XI

И вот часовня на дороге...
Тут с давних лет почиет в боге
Какой-то князь, теперь святой,
Убитый мстительной рукой.
С тех пор на праздник иль на битву,
Куда бы путник ни спешил,
Всегда усердную молитву
Он у часовни приносил;
И та молитва сберегала
От мусульманского кинжала.
Но презрел удалой жених
Обычай прадедов своих.
Его коварною мечтою
Лукавый Демон возмущал:
Он в мыслях, под ночною тьмою,
Уста невесты целовал.
Вдруг впереди мелькнули двое,
И больше — выстрел! — что такое?..
Привстав на звонких [1] стременах,
Надвинув на брови папах,[2]
Отважный князь не молвил слова;
В руке сверкнул турецкий ствол,
Нагайка щелк — и, как орел,
Он кинулся... и выстрел снова!
И дикий крик, и стон глухой
Промчались в глубине долины —
Недолго продолжался бой:
Бежали робкие грузины!

XII

Затихло всё; теснясь толпой,
На трупы всадников порой
Верблюды с ужасом глядели;

He sees the stream untamed by bridges . . .
It's late; the sun has touched the ridges,
Its crimson light will soon be gone;
215 The men and camels hurry on.

XI

They reached a chapel, where for ages
Had slept a murdered prince courageous.
His tragic death or last complaint
Made of the prince a local saint.
220 All men around were used to trust him
And to his relics humbly pray—
Such was an immemorial custom
Of travelers upon that way.
The prayer would serve as a protection
225 Against a Muslim insurrection.
But quickly past the saint's abode
The bridegroom in his hurry rode,
For tempted by the jealous Demon,
By him in secret envy loathed,
230 He saw himself a happy leman
Already kissing his betrothed . . .
What's this? A man? Another figure?
A rifle shot! Who pulled the trigger?
A running brigand . . . more of those . . .
235 The youth upon his stirrups rose;
Not for a moment did he falter:
He struck his stallion with a lash,
Pulled on his cap and made a dash,
Hawklike, to meet the chief assaulter.
240 A shot, a shriek . . . another gun . . .
A stifled groan across a distance . . .
The timid Georgian drivers run
Without a fight, without resistance!

XII

The camels looked in silent fear
245 At many corpses lying near
And at the sand by blood besprinkled;

367

И глухо в тишине степной
Их колокольчики звенели.
Разграблен пышный караван;
И над телами христиан
Чертит круги ночная птица!
Не ждет их мирная гробница
Под слоем монастырских плит,
Где прах отцов их был зарыт;
Не придут сестры с матерями,
Покрыты длинными чадрами,
С тоской, рыданьем и мольбами,
На гроб их из далеких мест!
Зато усердною рукою
Здесь у дороги, над скалою
На память водрузится крест;
И плющ, разросшийся весною,
Его, ласкаясь, обовьет
Своею сеткой изумрудной;
И, своротив с дороги трудной,
Не раз усталый пешеход
Под божьей тенью отдохнет...

XIII

Несется конь быстрее лани,
Храпит и рвется, будто к брани;
То вдруг осадит на скаку,
Прислушается к ветерку,
Широко ноздри раздувая;
То, разом в землю ударяя
Шипами звонкими копыт,
Взмахнув растрепанною гривой,
Вперед без памяти летит.
На нем есть всадник молчаливый!
Он бьется на седле порой,
Припав на гриву головой.
Уж он не правит поводами,
Задвинул ноги в стремена,
И кровь широкими струями
На чепраке его видна.
Скакун лихой, ты господина
Из боя вынес, как стрела,
Но злая пуля осетина
Его во мраке догнала!

The only sound that one could hear
Was from the bells that shook and tinkled.
The sumptuous caravan was sacked;
250 The Christians, heinously attacked,
Would soon be carrion for the vulture!
A crypt, a plaque, a modest sculpture
Would not allay these people's doom;
Not one would share his father's tomb.
255 By fate unmerciful and wayward
These wretched victims were not favored:
Their mothers in a cloister graveyard
Would not bemoan the awful loss.
But someone, diligent and pious,
260 Exempt from worldly cares and bias,
Would on the rock set up a cross.
Then blooming spring, while passing by us,
Would leave the cross in close embrace
With ivy stalks, with verdant ravels,
265 And weary men, fatigued by travels,
Would come and slacken here their pace
To seek oblivion in this place.

XIII

The noble stallion wildly dashes,
Affrighted by the shrieks and clashes:
270 One minute fast, another slow,
It stops, then rushes like a doe,
Its flanks and back all hot and steaming;
Its shaggy mane is wildly streaming,
Its feet, before the journey shod,
275 Stamp madly at the sand and clod;
Its eyes dilate, its nostrils widen,
It carries an immobile rider
Who can no longer touch the rein;
His head is buried in the mane.
280 He does not feel his charger flying,
His lifeless legs hang down like lead;
Upon the horsecloth, blood is drying—
The blood that he has bravely shed.
Oh, handsome steed! You saved your master,
285 When like the swiftest wind you ran,
But the Ossetian shot was faster:
The bullet hit and killed the man.

XIV

В семье Гудала плач и стоны,
Толпится на дворе народ:
Чей конь примчался запаленный
И пал на камни у ворот?
Кто этот всадник бездыханный?
Хранили след тревоги бранной
Морщины смуглого чела.
В крови оружие и платье;
В последнем бешеном пожатье
Рука на гриве замерла.
Недолго жениха младого,
Невеста, взор твой ожидал:
Сдержал он княжеское слово,
На брачный пир он прискакал...
Увы! но никогда уж снова
Не сядет на коня лихого!..

XV

На беззаботную семью,
Как гром, слетела божья кара!
Упала на постель свою,
Рыдает бедная Тамара;
Слеза катится за слезой,
Грудь высоко и трудно дышит;
И вот она как будто слышит
Волшебный голос над собой:
«Не плачь, дитя! не плачь напрасно!
Твоя слеза на труп безгласный
Живой росой не упадет:
Она лишь взор туманит ясный,
Ланиты девственные жжет!
Он далеко, он не узнает,
Не оценит тоски твоей;
Небесный свет теперь ласкает
Бесплотный взор его очей;
Он слышит райские напевы...
Что жизни мелочные сны,
И стон, и слезы бедной девы
Для гостя райской стороны?
Нет, жребий смертного творенья,

Goudal is pale. His joy has withered,
His household in the courtyard groans.
290 What fell event has brought them thither?
Whose horse has fallen on the stones?
Who is that rider sadly thwarted?
He does not breathe; his face distorted
Retains the traces of the pain.
295 His weapon and his clothes are gory,
His frenzied hand still tells the story
Of how he clutched his stallion's mane.
He did not live to see his idyll,
His smile became a corpse's wince,
300 But to the merry banquet bridal
He came—the noble, loyal prince . . .
Alas! His steed will now be idle:
His master will not touch the bridle.

XV

The peaceful home is crushed by doom,
305 God's wrath destroyed the happy wedding!
Princess Tamara, in her room,
Lies, tears of bitter sorrow shedding.
She wrings her hands, her breast heaves high,
But lo! With magical insistence
310 A voice is coming from a distance,
From the remote and tranquil sky.
"Cry not, oh child, cry not in anguish,
The ghost of death you will not vanquish,
Your tears are not life-giving dew,
315 In futile mourning you will languish,
Your virgin cheeks will lose their hue.
He is too far for curse or blessing,
He is beyond your groans and cries,
The light of heaven is caressing
320 His incorporeal, empty eyes.
Around him angels sing in chorus . . .
What is to us a maiden's tear,
When shining Eden is before us
And all its ecstasies are near?
325 My earthly angel, let me tell you:

371

Поверь мне, ангел мой земной,
Не стоит одного мгновенья
Твоей печали дорогой!

«На воздушном океане,
Без руля и без ветрил,
Тихо плавают в тумане
Хоры стройные светил;
Средь полей необозримых
В небе ходят без следа
Облаков неуловимых
Волокнистые стада.
Час разлуки, час свиданья —
Им ни радость, ни печаль;
Им в грядущем нет желанья
И прошедшего не жаль.
В день томительный несчастья
Ты об них лишь вспомяни;
Будь к земному без участья
И беспечна, как они!

«Лишь только ночь своим покровом
Верхи Кавказа осенит,
Лишь только мир, волшебным словом
Завороженный, замолчит;
Лишь только ветер над скалою
Увядшей шевельнет травою,
И птичка, спрятанная в ней,
Порхнет во мраке веселей;
И под лозою виноградной,
Росу небес глотая жадно,
Цветок распустится ночной;
Лишь только месяц золотой
Из-за горы тихонько встанет
И на тебя украдкой взглянет,—
К тебе я стану прилетать;
Гостить я буду до денницы
И на шелковые ресницы
Сны золотые навевать...»

XVI

Слова умолкли в отдаленье,
Вослед за звуком умер звук.

Of all the mortal things you know
There is not even one whose value
Is great enough to cause your woe.

On the infinite expanses
330   Of the boundless cosmic void
Planets dance their measured dances,
Unconducted, undeployed.
On the drift, forever aimless,
Fibrous clouds invade the sky,
335   Unattainable and nameless,
Slowly floating, flocklike, by.
Cold when touching, cold when thronging,
They disperse at every blast,
For the future never longing,
340   Never caring for the past.
On the day of tribulation
Think of clouds upon their way,
Do not wish for consolation
But remain as cool as they.
345   When night has come, and darkness, creeping,
Has wrapped the lofty peaks around,
When all the world is quietly sleeping,
Enchanted by the magic sound;
When evening winds, in secret passes,
350   Have rustled through the faded grasses
And when a warbler, hidden there,
Has shot, disturbed, into the air;
When heat has finally abated
And when, by moisture saturated,
355   A flower has opened up at night;
As soon as from its dizzy height
The moon has sent its golden lances
And looked at you with tender glances,
Then wait for me; upon the beams
360   I'll stay until by morning banished;
And all your sorrows will have vanished
Before my songs of golden dreams . . . ''

XVI

Deep silence fell. The great temptation,
Like a mirage, was gone and dead.

373

Она вскочив глядит вокруг...
Невыразимое смятенье
В ее груди; печаль, испуг,
Восторга пыл — ничто в сравненье.
Все чувства в ней кипели вдруг;
Душа рвала свои оковы,
Огонь по жилам пробегал,
И этот голос чудно-новый,
Ей мнилось, всё еще звучал.
И перед утром сон желанный
Глаза усталые смежил;
Но мысль ее он возмутил
Мечтой пророческой и странной.
Пришлец туманный и немой,
Красой блистая неземной,
К ее склонился изголовью;
И взор его с такой любовью,
Так грустно на нее смотрел,
Как будто он об ней жалел.
То не был ангел-небожитель,
Ее божественный хранитель:
Венец из радужных лучей
Не украшал его кудрей.
То не был ада дух ужасный,
Порочный мученик — о нет!
Он был похож на вечер ясный:
Ни день, ни ночь,— ни мрак, ни свет!..

———

ЧАСТЬ II

I

«Отец, отец, оставь угрозы,
Свою Тамару не брани;
Я плачу: видишь эти слезы,
Уже не первые они.
Напрасно женихи толпою
Спешат сюда из дальних мест...
Немало в Грузии невест;
А мне не быть ничьей женою!..
О, не брани, отец, меня.
Ты сам заметил: день от дня
Я вяну, жертва злой отравы!

365   The words dissolved, as if unsaid . . .
    In mute surprise, in consternation
    She looked around. It was not dread,
    Nor was it feelings' agitation
    That stormed her heart and turned her head.
370   Her soul broke every bond and fetter,
    She was aflame and deeply stirred,
    His speech seemed stranger, sweeter, better
    Than anything she'd ever heard.
    Sleep came at last, her passions curbing;
375   It came at dawn and sealed her eyes,
    But still she seemed to recognize
    That voice, seductive and disturbing.
    By some mysterious forces sent,
    He walked into her room and bent,
380   And looked at her—unearthly handsome.
    What did he want? A sound? A ransom?
    He stood so loving, so forlorn,
    His grief seemed of compassion born.
    He will not be her guardian later,
385   He was not sent by the Creator,
    For light and radiance did not spread
    From the intruder's chiseled head.
    And yet, his features lacked the starkness
    Of those who are the Devil's prey.
390   He was like twilight: neither darkness
    Nor sunshine; neither night nor day . . .

———

Part II

I

    "O Father, Father! Stop your scolding.
    I beg you: do not storm or fret.
    You've seen me weep, my tears are scalding,
395   You will not dry them by a threat.
    In vain the eager suitors carry
    Their signs of reverence to you;
    There are so many brides to woo . . .
    And I do not intend to marry.
400   You must not scold your wretched maid;
    You see: from day to day I fade.
    A victim of an evil spirit,

Меня терзает дух лукавый
Неотразимою мечтой;
Я гибну, сжалься надо мной!
Отдай в священную обитель
Дочь безрассудную свою;
Там защитит меня Спаситель,
Пред ним тоску мою пролью.
На свете нет уж мне веселья...
Святыни миром осеня,
Пусть примет сумрачная келья,
Как гроб, заранее меня...»

II

И в монастырь уединенный
Ее родные отвезли,
И власяницею смиренной
Грудь молодую облекли.
Но и в монашеской одежде,
Как под узорною парчой,
Всё беззаконною мечтой
В ней сердце билося, как прежде.
Пред алтарем, при блеске свеч,
В часы торжественного пенья,
Знакомая, среди моленья,
Ей часто слышалася речь.
Под сводом сумрачного храма
Знакомый образ иногда
Скользил без звука и следа
В тумане легком фимиама;
Сиял он тихо, как звезда;
Манил и звал он... но — куда?..

III

В прохладе меж двумя холмами
Таился монастырь святой.
Чинар и тополей рядами·
Он окружен был — и порой,
Когда ложилась ночь в ущельи,
Сквозь них мелькала, в окнах кельи,
Лампада грешницы младой.
Кругом, в тени дерев миндальных,
Где ряд стоит крестов печальных,

I dread his speech but always hear it;
He comes and tempts me every night.
405 Take pity on my sorry plight.
You are surprised at my behavior,
But let me leave your home in peace.
Perhaps our Lord, the mighty Savior,
Will grant that all my woes should cease.
410 My joyous days are dead, believe me;
My mirth is broken; I have done.
And let a holy cell receive me,
As may the grave receive a nun. . . . ''

II

And to a distant sacred dwelling
415 Her kinsmen took her as she bid
And gave her sackcloth rough—for quelling
The passions that her bosom hid.
But in this coarse and humble raiment,
As formerly in rich brocade,
420 The heart of the unhappy maid
Still beat for the rebellious claimant.
And when the sisters would rejoice
In worshiping and chanting anthems,
She would perceive familiar phantoms
425 And tremble at the pleading voice.
In vaulted space, obscure and murky,
She saw his features in the air
And could not start her fervent prayer;
He seemed in clouds of incense lurking,
430 His beauty was beyond compare,
And he invited her . . . but where?

III

The holy convent stood secluded,
By groves protected from the sun,
By planes' and poplars' branches hooded.
435 And oftentimes, when day was done,
When evening winds came blowing quicker,
One saw inside a trembling flicker—
The lantern of the sinful nun.
'Mid trees where birds in chorus warble,
440 'Mid crosses made of wood and marble

Безмолвных сторожей гробниц,
Спевались хоры легких птиц.
По камням прыгали, шумели
Ключи студеною волной
И под нависшею скалой,
Сливаясь дружески в ущелье,
Катились дальше, меж кустов,
Покрытых инеем цветов.

IV

На север видны были горы.
При блеске утренней Авроры,
Когда синеющий дымок
Курится в глубине долины,
И, обращаясь на восток,
Зовут к молитве муэцины,
И звучный колокола глас
Дрожит, обитель пробуждая;
В торжественный и мирный час,
Когда грузинка молодая
С кувшином длинным за водой
С горы спускается крутой,
Вершины цепи снеговой
Светло-лиловою стеной
На чистом небе рисовались,
И в час заката одевались
Они румяной пеленой;
И между них, прорезав тучи,
Стоял, всех выше головой,
Казбек, Кавказа царь могучий,
В чалме и ризе парчевой.

V

Но, полно думою преступной,
Тамары сердце недоступно
Восторгам чистым. Перед ней
Весь мир одет угрюмой тенью;
И всё ей в нем предлог мученью —
И утра луч и мрак ночей.
Бывало только ночи сонной
Прохлада землю обоймет,
Перед божественной иконой

(Those gloomy guards of silent tombs),
Where almond in its beauty blooms,
Along the many winding passes,
All white with flying spray and foam,
445   Springs leaped on rocks and hurried home
Into the bottomless crevasses
And flowed, forgetful of the roar,
In fragrant pollen, as in hoar.

IV

North of the place one saw the ridges.
450   When morning rays, like rosy bridges,
Were from the cloudy heights released,
When bluish smoke enveloped valleys,
And the muezzins looking east
Called on the pious men of Allah's;
455   When from the monastery tower
The bell had boomed its waking cadence;
In the serene and solemn hour,
When, in the village, Georgian maidens
Had risen at the break of day
460   To start with jugs their usual way
Along the slope of stone and clay,
Then did the purple color play
Upon the crests and summits lofty;
But when the sun was sinking softly,
465   Then crimson shone its parting ray,
And, open only to the eagle,
Kazbék, impregnable and regal,
Did o'er the Caucasus hold sway
In sparkling holiday array.

V

470   But, full of sinful meditation,
She stays away from contemplation,
She is to nature's beauty blind.
When night descends or day approaches
All objects send her their reproaches,
475   All set aflame her tortured mind.
And often, while the world was sleeping,
When on the mountains darkness fell,
She started passionately weeping

Она в безумье упадет
И плачет; и в ночном молчанье
Ее тяжелое рыданье
Тревожит путника вниманье;
И мыслит он: «То горный дух,
Прикованный в пещере, стонет!»
И, чуткий напрягая слух,
Коня измученного гонит...

VI

Тоской и трепетом полна,
Тамара часто у окна
Сидит в раздумье одиноком
И смотрит в даль прилежным оком,
И целый день, вздыхая, ждет...
Ей кто-то шепчет: он придет!
Недаром сны ее ласкали,
Недаром он являлся ей,
С глазами, полными печали,
И чудной нежностью речей.
Уж много дней она томится,
Сама не зная почему;
Святым захочет ли молиться —
А сердце молится *ему;*
Утомлена борьбой всегдашней,
Склонится ли на ложе сна:
Подушка жжет, ей душно, страшно,
И вся, вскочив, дрожит она;
Пылают грудь ее и плечи,
Нет сил дышать, туман в очах,
Объятья жадно ищут встречи,
Лобзанья тают на устах...

. . . .
. . . .

VII

Вечерней мглы покров воздушный
Уж холмы Грузии одел.
Привычке сладостной послушный,
В обитель Демон прилетел.
Но долго, долго он не смел
Святыню мирного приюта

Before the icon in her cell.
480 And then a traveler benighted,
Surprised, embarrassed, and affrighted,
Would spur and urge his horse excited—
And think he had his life to save
From a malicious, groaning devil
485 Who languished fettered in his cave,
A conquered and imprisoned rebel.

VI

A victim to her restless moods,
Tamara often sits and broods
And does not fight her strange emotion.
490 She peers into the aereal ocean,
She sighs and looks beyond the gate,
And something tells her, "Only wait.
He'll come. Believe his secret message,
Believe the visions you have had,
495 Your longing soul's unspoken presage,
His tender glances, deep and sad."
This restlessness in her kept surging
And tearing her for many days.
She kneels before the Holy Virgin
500 But it's to *him* she really prays.
By blessed martyrs unenlightened,
Upon her bed, in bitter throes,
She tosses, pale, exhausted, frightened,
Deprived of comfort and repose.
505 She burns, she sees contorted faces,
She stifles under passion's whips,
Her breast and shoulders seek embraces,
His kisses melting on her lips.
. . . .
. . . .

VII

When night's impenetrable cover
510 Fell on the hills of Georgia fair,
The Demon, like a faithful lover,
Flew swiftly through the darkened air
To her abode. He did not dare
To go inside and for a second

Нарушить. И была минута,
Когда казался он готов
Оставить умысел жестокой.
Задумчив, у стены высокой
Он бродит: от его шагов
Без ветра лист в тени трепещет.
Он поднял взор: ее окно,
Озарено лампадой, блещет;
Кого-то ждет она давно!
И вот средь общего молчанья
Чингура ¹ стройное бряцанье
И звуки песни раздались;
И звуки те лились, лились,
Как слезы, мерно друг за другом;
И эта песнь была нежна,
Как будто для земли она
Была на небе сложена!
Не ангел ли с забытым другом
Вновь повидаться захотел,
Сюда украдкою слетел
И о былом ему пропел,
Чтоб усладить его мученье?..
Тоску любви, ее волненье
Постигнул Демон в первый раз;
Он хочет в страхе удалиться...
Его крыло не шевелится!
И, чудо! из померкших глаз
Слеза тяжелая катится...
Поныне возле кельи той
Насквозь прожженный виден камень
Слезою жаркою, как пламень,
Нечеловеческой слезой!..

VIII

И входит он, любить готовый,
С душой, открытой для добра,
И мыслит он, что жизни новой
Пришла желанная пора.
Неясный трепет ожиданья,

515 He hesitated, thought, and reckoned.
Uncertain, pensive, like a thief
He paces up and down and ponders
And through the shady garden wanders;
At every step a hanging leaf
520 Disturbed by him in stillness trembles.
The Demon looks. . . . Her candle burns,
She waits for someone! She resembles
A saint in love! The Demon turns,
And lo! the silent night is woken,
525 Its peace and sanctity are broken
By a chingár.[1] To the abode
The sounds in slow succession flowed.
They flowed like tears and never ended;
The song he sang, the tune he played
530 Was sweet, as though in Heaven made
For an adoring earthly maid.
As though an angel had descended
From heavenly expanses vast
And met a long-lost friend at last
535 To sing him gently of the past,
To comfort him in deprivation.
Both passion's pain and exaltation
Did grip with might and almost sear
His heart, and futile was his trying
540 To move away, to vanish flying.
A single bright and heavy tear
Dropped from his eye unused to crying.
And where that tear in anguish fell,
The tear which let the Demon enter,
545 A stone, burned through the very center,
Still stands before Tamara's cell!

VIII

And in he comes, his heart appealing
To love and truth, and—what is more!—
He has a strange and joyous feeling
550 That nothing will be as before.
Since the beginning of creation

---

[1] A kind of guitar. (Lermontov's note.)

Страх неизвестности немой,
Как будто в первое свиданье
Спознались с гордою душой.
То было злое предвещанье!
Он входит, смотрит — перед ним
Посланник рая, херувим,
Хранитель грешницы прекрасной,
Стоит с блистающим челом
И от врага с улыбкой ясной
Приосенил ее крылом;
И луч божественного света
Вдруг ослепил нечистый взор,
И вместо сладкого привета
Раздался тягостный укор:

IX

«Дух беспокойный, дух порочный,
Кто звал тебя во тьме полночной?
Твоих поклонников здесь нет,
Зло не дышало здесь поныне;
К моей любви, к моей святыне
Не пролагай преступный след.
Кто звал тебя?»
            Ему в ответ
Злой дух коварно усмехнулся;
Зарделся ревностию взгляд;
И вновь в душе его проснулся
Старинной ненависти яд.
«Она моя! — сказал он грозно,—
Оставь ее, она моя!
Явился ты, защитник, поздно,
И ей, как мне, ты не судья.
На сердце, полное гордыни,
Я наложил печать мою;
Здесь больше нет твоей святыни,
Здесь я владею и люблю!»
И Ангел грустными очами
На жертву бедную взглянул
И медленно, взмахнув крылами,
В эфире неба потонул.
· · · · · · · · · ·

The Demon had not yet allowed
Such doubts and fear and adoration
To storm his bosom cold and proud.
555 But oh! The future tribulation . . .
He enters. But he has to meet
An angel rising to his feet.
Tamara's heavenly defender,
With wings miraculously large,
560 Emerged in all his dazzling splendor
To struggle for his sinful charge.
The Demon angered by the meeting
Stood still under the convent's roof,
And what he heard was not a greeting
565 But a contemptuous, harsh reproof.

IX

"Oh King of evil, King of riot!
Who conjured you in midnight quiet?
In this abode they never sinned,
They never breathed contempt or hatred.
570 Their faith is strong, their faith is sacred . . .
You've come upon an evil wind.
Who conjured you?''
              The Demon grinned.
His grin was chilling and malicious,
His eyes were full of hate and pain,
575 And all within him that was vicious
Suffused his poisoned heart and brain.
"She is mine," he cried, "I am the winner,
To me she gave her silent oath;
Too late you've come to save your sinner!
580 And who are you to judge us both?
The heart that lies before us naked
I branded and forever sealed,
It bursts with pride, you will not take it.
This maid is mine to love and wield!''
585 The angel, in the cell unholy,
Looked at her with a wistful gaze,
Then beat his wings and slowly, slowly
Dissolved among the shining rays.
. . . .

X

Тамара

О! Кто ты? речь твоя опасна!
Тебя послал мне ад иль рай?
Чего ты хочешь?..

Демон

Ты прекрасна!

Тамара

Но молви, кто ты? отвечай...

Демон

Я тот, которому внимала
Ты в полуночной тишине,
Чья мысль душе твоей шептала,
Чью грусть ты смутно отгадала,
Чей образ видела во сне.
Я тот, чей взор надежду губит;
Я тот, кого никто не любит;
Я бич рабов моих земных,
Я царь познанья и свободы,
Я враг небес, я зло природы,
И, видишь, — я у ног твоих!
Тебе принес я в умиленье
Молитву тихую любви,
Земное первое мученье
И слезы первые мои.
О! выслушай — из сожаленья!
Меня добру и небесам
Ты возвратить могла бы словом.
Твоей любви святым покровом
Одетый, я предстал бы там,
Как новый ангел в блеске новом;
О! только выслушай, молю, —
Я раб твой, — я тебя люблю!
Лишь только я тебя увидел —
И тайно вдруг возненавидел
Бессмертие и власть мою.

X

Tamara

Who are you? What's your awful duty?
590 Are you from Heaven or from hell?
What do you want from me?

The Demon

Your beauty!

Tamara

Who are you? Tell me! Will you tell?

The Demon

I am the one whose plea unending
Destroyed at midnight your repose,
595 Whose voice you heard with God contending,
Whose secret grief you kept defending,
Whose face before you always rose.
I am with malice never sated,
I am by everybody hated,
600 I only kill and never save.
I am the cause of each upheaval,
Both Heaven's foe and nature's evil,
But at your feet I am a slave.
I've brought my love for ages dormant,
605 My prayer, for you alone to hear,
My first, my piercing earthly torment,
My first, my scalding earthly tear.
I beg you: listen for a moment!
A word from you and I'll repine,
610 Forget my hatred, dull and sterile,
And, shielded from revenge and peril,
Shall, as before, 'mid angels shine—
A seraph new in new apparel.
Oh listen! I am evil's prince,
615 But I have loved you ever since
I saw you in your castle's portal.
I do not want my strength immortal,
My strife with Heaven makes me wince.

Я позавидовал невольно
Неполной радости земной;
Не жить, как ты, мне стало больно,
И страшно — розно жить с тобой.
В бескровном сердце луч нежданый
Опять затеплился живей,
И грусть на дне старинной раны
Зашевелилася, как змей.
Что без тебя мне эта вечность?
Моих владений бесконечность?
Пустые звучные слова,
Обширный храм — без божества!

Тамара

Оставь меня, о дух лукавый!
Молчи, не верю я врагу...
Творец... Увы! я не могу
Молиться... гибельной отравой
Мой ум слабеющий объят!
Послушай, ты меня погубишь;
Твои слова — огонь и яд...
Скажи, зачем меня ты любишь!

Демон

Зачем, красавица? Увы,
Не знаю!.. Полон жизни новой,
С моей преступной головы
Я гордо снял венец терновый,
Я всё былое бросил в прах:
Мой рай, мой ад в твоих очах.
Люблю тебя нездешней страстью,
Как полюбить не можешь ты:
Всем упоением, всей властью
Бессмертной мысли и мечты.
В душе моей, с начала мира,
Твой образ был напечатлён,
Передо мной носился он
В пустынях вечного эфира.
Давно тревожа мысль мою,
Мне имя сладкое звучало;
Во дни блаженства мне в раю

Believe me: I have learned to covet
620   Your humble joys, your simple state;
When I observe your earth, I love it;
My solitude is all I hate.
I know, I feel: it must be madness!
But hope is in my heart awake,
625   And in the ancient wound, my sadness
Is writhing like a scaly snake.
Without you, who will mark my traces
Through endless years and boundless spaces?
What are the mighty worlds I tread?
630   A shrine whose deity is dead!

Tamara

Away, away, you, sweet seducer!
Away, I do not trust your chant.
Oh, Everlasting One! I can't,
Can't pray! All things are getting looser
635   And slip from my tormented brain.
Your presence will be my undoing,
Your speech will poison me and drain.
Why is it I whom you are wooing?

The Demon

Why do I love you? What will be?
640   Alas, I wish I were a prophet!
I wear a wreath of thorns, but see—
I've come to you and proudly doff it.
I love you more than I can tell,
You are my heaven and my hell.
645   You cannot feel such love! No, never—
Not even you with all your worth!
My passion, longing, hope, endeavor,
They are not for this mortal earth.
Since life began, since God began it,
650   On you alone I've learned to dote;
I've seen your face before me float
In every void, on every planet.
Tamara! I repeat your name,
The name by which I have been haunted;
655   In Paradise it was the same:

Одной тебя недоставало.
О! если б ты могла понять,
Какое горькое томленье
Всю жизнь, века без разделенья
И наслаждаться и страдать,
За зло похвал не ожидать
Ни за добро вознагражденья;
Жить для себя, скучать собой,
И этой вечною борьбой
Без торжества, без примиренья!
Всегда жалеть и не желать,
Всё знать, всё чувствовать, всё видеть,
Стараться всё возненавидеть
И всё на свете презирать!..
Лишь только божие проклятье
Исполнилось, с того же дня
Природы жаркие объятья
Навек остыли для меня;
Синело предо мной пространство;
Я видел брачное убранство
Светил, знакомых мне давно...
Они текли в венцах из злата;
Но что же? прежнего собрата
Не узнавало ни одно.
Изгнанников, себе подобных,
Я звать в отчаянии стал,
Но слов и лиц и взоров злобных,
Увы! я сам не узнавал.
И в страхе я, взмахнув крылами,
Помчался — но куда? зачем?
Не знаю... прежними друзьями
Я был отвергнут; как Эдем,
Мир для меня стал глух и нем.
По вольной прихоти теченья
Так поврежденная ладья
Без парусов и без руля
Плывет, не зная назначенья;
Так ранней утренней порой
Отрывок тучи громовой,
В лазурной вышине чернея,
Один, нигде пристать не смея,
Летит без цели и следа,
Бог весть откуда и куда!

It's you I missed, it's you I wanted.
Oh maiden, if you only knew
My bitter pain, my desperation!
Since the beginning of creation
660 I've never met a thing that's new.
The world is blind to what I do,
Be it perdition or salvation.
My very triumphs leave me bored,
I have defied and fought the Lord
665 And long for reconciliation.
I've tried all things and seen them through;
I could have crushed them, were they greater,
But they are not for such a hater
As stands and pleads this night to you.
670 When exiled from the hallowed places
I started on my mournful way,
I felt that nature's hot embraces
Had closed for me, had closed for aye.
I saw the stars and planets idle,
675 All decked in gold, in garments bridal,
That flowed and flowed before my eyes;
With haloes, one after another
They rolled; alas, their former brother
They did not seem to recognize!
680 Rejected, stifled by my freedom,
I looked in anguish and despair
For other banished souls of Eden,
But even outcasts were not there!
I beat my wings and in a panic
685 Flew off—I cannot tell you why.
My love and pain, my strength titanic
Lost every meaning in the sky;
The world I'd wielded seemed to die.
So in the currents of the ocean
690 A miserable, broken boat
Will aimlessly and sadly float,
Unable to control its motion.
So wanders in the early morn
A fragment of a storm cloud torn,
695 A homeless spot of blackness, as you
Can often see in shining azure.
It drifts, a child of vapors dense,
And no one asks it, where or whence.

И я людьми недолго правил,
Греху недолго их учил,
Всё благородное бесславил
И всё прекрасное хулил;
Недолго... пламень чистой веры
Легко навек я залил в них...
А стоили ль трудов моих
Одни глупцы да лицемеры?
И скрылся я в ущельях гор;
И стал бродить, как метеор,
Во мраке полночи глубокой...
И мчался путник одинокой,
Обманут близким огоньком;
И в бездну падая с конем,
Напрасно звал — и след кровавый
За ним вился по крутизне...
Но злобы мрачные забавы
Недолго нравилися мне!
В борьбе с могучим ураганом,
Как часто, подымая прах,
Одетый молньей и туманом,
Я шумно мчался в облаках,
Чтобы в толпе стихий мятежной
Сердечный ропот заглушить,
Спастись от думы неизбежной
И незабвенное забыть!
Что повесть тягостных лишений,
Трудов и бед толпы людской
Грядущих, прошлых поколений
Перед минутою одной
Моих непризнанных мучений?
Что люди? что их жизнь и труд?
Они прошли, они пройдут...
Надежда есть — ждет правый суд:
Простить он может, хоть осудит!
Моя ж печаль бессменно тут,
И ей конца, как мне, не будет;
И не вздремнуть в могиле ей!
Она то ластится, как змей,
То жжет и плещет, будто пламень,
То давит мысль мою, как камень —
Надежд погибших и страстей
Несокрушимый мавзолей!..

This feeble earth! I could not bear it!
700　These men who always think of gain!
Not long did I belittle merit,
And subtly teach them things profane.
They heard my words and never trembled,
They sold at once their faith and God;
705　I spent my eloquence and rod
On fools, who heartlessly dissembled!
And then in deep ravines I hid,
And, full of malice, all I did
Was fly in desperate abandon
710　And smite my puny foes at random.
On seeing me, a man would urge
His horse beyond the fatal verge;
He'd plead in vain, for I was callous
And only laughed to see him dead . . .
715　I was not happy, for my malice
Was soon by such enjoyments fed.
How often, with a tempest fighting
And churning up the pliant sky,
All wrapped in milky mists and lightning,
720　Myself like thunder, I would fly.
I'd fly to still the murderous hammer
That beat inside me evermore,
To drown my elemental clamor
In nature's elemental roar.
725　What is the tale of men's privations,
What is the story of the grief
Of past and future generations
To just one moment, even brief,
Of my unnoticed tribulations!
730　What are these men, their work and woe?
They came one day, and they will go!
To them the righteous Judge will show
His spirit kind and condescending.
But my despair will only grow,
735　Indeed, it is, like me, unending.
Both day and night it is awake,
Uncoiling like a noiseless snake,
But it may burn, my flesh obsessing,
Or lie, my thoughts like granite pressing,
740　A tomb of passions' wasted ache,
Which even ages cannot break.

393

[Т а м а р а

Зачем мне знать твои печали,
Зачем ты жалуешься мне?
Ты согрешил...

Д е м о н

Против тебя ли?

Т а м а р а

Нас могут слышать!..

Д е м о н

Мы одне.

Т а м а р а

А бог!

Д е м о н

На нас не кинет взгляда:
Он занят небом, не землей!

Т а м а р а

А наказанье, муки ада?

Д е м о н

Так что ж? ты будешь там со мной!]

Т а м а р а

Кто б ни был ты, мой друг случайный,—
Покой навеки погубя,
Невольно я с отрадой тайной,
Страдалец, слушаю тебя.
Но если речь твоя лукава,
Но если ты, обман тая...

[Tamara

Your tale, its end and its beginning—
Why should I know its deathly gloom?
You sinned . . .

The Demon

You did not know me sinning!

Tamara

745   We can be overheard.

The Demon

By whom?

Tamara

By God!

The Demon

He will not leave His garden,
Not earth but Heaven is His sphere.

Tamara

And hell? It will not ever pardon . . .

The Demon

We'll be together there as here!]

Tamara

750   My guest, my visitor clandestine,
You've pushed me to the very brink,
The burning words your thoughts are dressed in
Deep in my very conscience sink.
But if perfidious is your story
755   And if deception is your goal—

395

О! пощади! Какая слава?
На что душа тебе моя?
Ужели небу я дороже
Всех, не замеченных тобой?
Они, увы! прекрасны тоже;
Как здесь, их девственное ложе
Не смято смертною рукой...
Нет! дай мне клятву роковую...
Скажи,— ты видишь: я тоскую;
Ты видишь женские мечты!
Невольно страх в душе ласкаешь...
Но ты всё понял, ты всё знаешь —
И сжалишься, конечно, ты!
Клянися мне... от злых стяжаний
Отречься ныне дай обет.
Ужель ни клятв, ни обещаний
Ненарушимых больше нет?..

Демон

Клянусь я первым днем творенья,
Клянусь его последним днем,
Клянусь позором преступленья
И вечной правды торжеством.
Клянусь паденья горькой мукой,
Победы краткою мечтой;
Клянусь свиданием с тобой
И вновь грозящею разлукой.
Клянуся сонмищем духов,
Судьбою братий мне подвластных,
Мечами ангелов бесстрастных,
Моих недремлющих врагов;
Клянуся небом я и адом,
Земной святыней и тобой,
Клянусь твоим последним взглядом,
Твоею первою слезой,
Незлобных уст твоих дыханьем,
Волною шелковых кудрей,
Клянусь блаженством и страданьем,
Клянусь любовию моей:
Я отрекся от старой мести,
Я отрекся от гордых дум;
Отныне яд коварной лести

Have mercy on me, for what glory,
What gain is it to catch my soul?
Or will you later feel rewarded,
Because I am in Heaven's grace?
760 But others, too, have virtue hoarded,
They, too, avoided all that's sordid
And are as beautiful of face!
No! Listen: a portentous token,
An oath that never will be broken
765 This solemn night from you I want;
Alarm has gripped me in its clutches,
But you, who feel the gentlest touches,
You will not answer with a taunt.
Renounce your evil ways infernal,
770 Renounce and in my presence swear!
Or is it true that oaths eternal
Have not existed anywhere?

The Demon

I swear to you by all creation,
By its unalterable course,
775 By truth with triumph and elation,
By sin with horror and remorse;
By shameful death and bitter mourning,
By hopes of victories unwon,
By seeing you this night, my nun,
780 And by the parting in the morning.
I swear by spirits' mighty legions—
My kin in banishment and woes,
By angels from celestial regions—
My vigilant and ruthless foes.
785 I swear by hell with Heaven vying,
By everything that's sacred here,
By both the glance you'll cast in dying
And your forgotten youngest tear.
By every gentle breath you've taken,
790 And by your wave of silken hair,
By all that leaves us proud or shaken,
And by my love for you I swear—
That I shall never try to shatter
The world of men or God's array,
795 That I shall never tempt or flatter

Ничей уж не встревожит ум;
Хочу я с небом примириться,
Хочу любить, хочу молиться,
Хочу я веровать добру.
Слезой раскаянья сотру
Я на челе, тебя достойном,
Следы небесного огня —
И мир в неведенье спокойном
Пусть доцветает без меня!
О! верь мне: я один поныне
Тебя постиг и оценил:
Избрав тебя моей святыней,
Я власть у ног твоих сложил.
Твоей любви я жду, как дара,
И вечность дам тебе за миг;
В любви, как в злобе, верь, Тамара,
Я неизменен и велик.
Тебя я, вольный сын эфира,
Возьму в надзвездные края;
И будешь ты царицей мира,
Подруга первая моя;
Без сожаленья, без участья
Смотреть на землю станешь ты,
Где нет ни истинного счастья,
Ни долговечной красоты,
Где преступленья лишь да казни,
Где страсти мелкой только жить;
Где не умеют без боязни
Ни ненавидеть, ни любить.
Иль ты не знаешь, что такое
Людей минутная любовь?
Волненье крови молодое,—
Но дни бегут и стынет кровь!
Кто устоит против разлуки,
Соблазна новой красоты,
Против усталости и скуки
И своенравия мечты?
Нет! не тебе, моей подруге,
Узнай, назначено судьбой
Увянуть молча в тесном круге
Ревнивой грубости рабой,
Средь малодушных и холодных,
Друзей притворных и врагов,

A human searching for his way.
I do not want the Demon's laurels,
I want my Lord and love, not quarrels,
I want to trust in peace and grace.
800 Repenting tears will soon erase,
Will wipe from my submissive forehead
All traces of the fire divine;
Men's ignorance in which they've gloried
Will not be a concern of mine.
805 Tamara, can you see me tremble?
I have for you renounced my throne,
You are my one, my holy temple,
In which I kneel and pray alone.
To me your love is like a chalice,
810 Its smallest drop contains our fate;
In love, believe me, as in malice,
I am both adamant and great.
Exempt from hatred and resistance,
I'll take you to the realm above,
815 And you'll be Queen in all existence,
My first and my eternal love.
Unworthy of regret and humble
This tiny Earth will seem to you,
Where things of beauty die and crumble,
820 Where joys are transitory too,
Where awful crime brings forth the gallows,
Where love comes last and fear comes first,
Where evil custom gladly hallows
The meanest, pettiest, and worst.
825 Men only know infatuation;
You must have seen those lovers bold:
Their blood is fire and agitation,
But time goes on, and blood gets cold.
Who can resist—what man? what woman?—
830 A parting from the one adored?
They chase new dreams: for they are human
And feel too soon fatigued or bored.
Fate speaks to you, it's here to tell us
That you belong to me, my maid,
835 That not amid the dull and jealous
You'll drag a paltry life—and fade;
Not 'mid the stupid and pretending,
Whose shining smiles are worthless paste,

Боязней и надежд бесплодных,
Пустых и тягостных трудов!
Печально за стеной высокой
Ты не угаснешь без страстей,
Среди молитв, равно далеко
От божества и от людей.
О нет, прекрасное созданье,
К иному ты присуждена;
Тебя иное ждет страданье,
Иных восторгов глубина;
Оставь же прежние желанья
И жалкий свет его судьбе:
Пучину гордого познанья
Взамен открою я тебе.
Толпу духов моих служебных
Я приведу к твоим стопам;
Прислужниц легких и волшебных
Тебе, красавица, я дам;
И для тебя с звезды восточной
Сорву венец я золотой;
Возьму с цветов росы полночной;
Его усыплю той росой;
Лучом румяного заката
Твой стан, как лентой, обовью,
Дыханьем чистым аромата
Окрестный воздух напою;
Всечасно дивною игрою
Твой слух лелеять буду я;
Чертоги пышные построю
Из бирюзы и янтаря;
Я опущусь на дно морское,
Я полечу за облака,
Я дам тебе, всё, всё земное —
Люби меня!..

XI

И он слегка
Коснулся жаркими устами
Ее трепещущим губам;
Соблазна полными речами
Он отвечал ее мольбам.
Могучий взор смотрел ей в очи!
Он жег ее. Во мраке ночи

'Mid fears and barren hopes unending
840   And labor sadly gone to waste.
I do not want to see you wilted,
From all desires and passions freed,
In prayers inanimate and stilted
That neither God nor people need.
845   Oh maiden born for adoration!
You shall not carry human chains;
You'll live with me, in expectation
Of other raptures, other pains.
Forget your past. Predestination
850   Has left upon your soul its mark,
For both your pain and satiation
This earth is small, this earth is dark.
With spirits beautiful and airy
Your cosmic bedrooms I shall fill,
855   And many an obedient fairy
Shall come and listen to your will.
A magic, luminous tiara
I'll wrest from stars and bring it down.
I'll get the midnight dew, Tamara!
860   And with it wash your dazzling crown.
A ray, from crimson sunset riven,
I'll boldly bring from Heaven's well
And wind you with this glowing ribbon,
Wrapped in a fragrant rose's smell.
865   The perfumed air around your chamber
Will ring with music old and new;
Of Eastern turquoise and of amber
A palace I shall build for you.
Your faithful, your recanting Demon
870   Will fly the heights too high for birds,
Will reach the depths too deep for seamen,
But only love me!

XI

With these words
He stopped, his mouth with passion flaming.
Tamara's lips were his to reach,
875   He bent, her soul and body claiming,
And soothed her with seductive speech.
His eyes, unbearable, unblinking,
Shone fierce; she felt that she was sinking,

Над нею прямо он сверкал,
Неотразимый, как кинжал.
Увы! злой дух торжествовал!
Смертельный яд его лобзанья
Мгновенно в грудь ее проник.
Мучительный, ужасный крик
Ночное возмутил молчанье.
В нем было всё: любовь, страданье,
Упрек с последнею мольбой
И безнадежное прощанье —
Прощанье с жизнью молодой.

XII

В то время сторож полуночный,
Один вокруг стены крутой
Свершая тихо путь урочный,
Бродил с чугунною доской,
И возле кельи девы юной
Он шаг свой мерный укротил
И руку над доской чугунной,
Смутясь душой, остановил.
И сквозь окрестное молчанье,
Ему казалось, слышал он
Двух уст согласное лобзанье,
Минутный крик и слабый стон.
И нечестивое сомненье
Проникло в сердце старика...
Но пронеслось еще мгновенье,
И стихло всё; издалека
Лишь дуновенье ветерка
Роптанье листьев приносило,
Да с темным берегом уныло
Шепталась горная река.
Канон угодника святого
Спешит он в страхе прочитать,
Чтоб наважденье духа злого
От грешной мысли отогнать;
Крестит дрожащими перстами
Мечтой взволнованную грудь
И молча, скорыми шагами
Обычный продолжает путь.

. . . .

Already crushed but still afraid:
880 Those eyes were sharper than a blade.
Alas! He won the wretched maid.
His kiss, the poison of creation,
Deep through his victim's bosom went;
Her shriek, by which the night was rent,
885 Was full of utter desperation,
Of pain and love, and desolation;
A last reproach, a bitter plea,
A shriek of final separation
From things that she would never see.

XII

890 The cloister's wary, aged guardian
Kept after midnight watch and ward.
He walked the pathways of the garden
And beat upon his cast-iron board.
And when the watchman's steps unhurried
895 Had brought him to Tamara's place,
He paused, as if confused or worried,
And for a moment checked his pace.
Beneath the night's impervious raiment
It could have seemed that he alone
900 Had heard a kiss of love's attainment
And then a dying cry and moan.
He looks around; a premonition
Has pierced his heart's unmelting chill;
He views the darkness with suspicion,
905 Of love and beauty thinking ill.
He listens, but the cells are still;
The wind has made the grasses moister,
And far away, behind the cloister,
The river huddles to the hill.
910 Afraid of devilish obsession,
He sends to Heaven his complaint;
He rues his thoughts like a transgression
And says the canon of the saint.
Perturbed, he lifts his trembling fingers
915 To cross his breast and quell the spark,
Then for a moment sighs and lingers
And steps again into the dark.
. . . .

XIII

Как пери спящая мила,
Она в гробу своем лежала,
Белей и чище покрывала
Был томный цвет ее чела.
Навек опущены ресницы...
Но кто б, о небо! не сказал,
Что взор под ними лишь дремал
И, чудный, только ожидал
Иль поцелуя иль денницы?
Но бесполезно луч дневной
Скользил по ним струей златой,
Напрасно их в немой печали
Уста родные целовали...
Нет! смерти вечную печать
Ничто не в силах уж сорвать!

XIV

Ни разу не был в дни веселья
Так разноцветен и богат
Тамары праздничный наряд.
Цветы родимого ущелья
(Так древний требует обряд)
Над нею льют свой аромат
И, сжаты мертвою рукою,
Как бы прощаются с землею!
И ничего в ее лице
Не намекало о конце
В пылу страстей и упоенья;
И были все ее черты
Исполнены той красоты,
Как мрамор, чуждой выраженья,
Лишенной чувства и ума,
Таинственной, как смерть сама.
Улыбка странная застыла,
Мелькнувши по ее устам.
О многом грустном говорила
Она внимательным глазам:
В ней было хладное презренье
Души, готовой отцвести,
Последней мысли выраженье,
Земле беззвучное *прости*.

XIII

She lay as though asleep, for now
She freed herself from her allurer.
920 The veil upon her was not purer
Or whiter than her pallid brow.
Her lashes' thick, untrembling cover
Fell on the eyes whose light had fled.
But, Heavens! Who would not have said
925 That vision in them was not dead
Awaiting daybreak or a lover?
Alas! The sun in glory rose
But did not break the maid's repose.
She lay immovable and tragic,
930 For even love and wizards' magic,
And lamentations' loud appeal
Retreat at death's eternal seal.

XIV

In days of joy and feasting gorgeous
She'd never been so richly dight
935 As when she met her darkest night.
The flowers from the surrounding gorges
(Such was the ancient native rite)
Adorned her with their petals bright.
Her icy fingers' lavish booty,
940 They parted from the world of beauty.
And nothing in her maiden form
Revealed the passions' crushing storm,
Her final, devastating rapture.
Still strangely beautiful, her face
945 Had the serene, unearthly grace,
Of an insensate marble statue
Devoid of feeling, thought, and breath,
Incomprehensible as death.
Upon her lips there stayed imprinted
950 A smile—the last she ever had;
To an observant eye it hinted
Of meditations grave and sad.
It was so eery and disdainful,
Remote from hope, remote from mirth,
955 A trace of thoughts, untold and painful,
A final parting with the earth.

405

Напрасный отблеск жизни прежней,
Она была еще мертвей,
Еще для сердца безнадежней
Навек угаснувших очей.
Так в час торжественный заката,
Когда, растаяв в море злата,
Уж скрылась колесница дня,
Снега Кавказа, на мгновенье
Отлив румяный сохраня,
Сияют в темном отдаленье.
Но этот луч полуживой
В пустыне отблеска не встретит;
И путь ничей он не осветит
С своей вершины ледяной!..

XV

Толпой соседи и родные
Уж собрались в печальный путь.
Терзая локоны седые,
Безмолвно поражая грудь,
В последний раз Гудал садится
На белогривого коня,
И поезд тронулся. Три дня,
Три ночи путь их будет длиться:
Меж старых дедовских костей
Приют покойный вырыт ей.
Один из праотцев Гудала,
Грабитель странников и сёл,
Когда болезнь его сковала
И час раскаянья пришел,
Грехов минувших в искупленье
Построить церковь обещал
На вышине гранитных скал,
Где только вьюги слышно пенье,
Куда лишь коршун залетал.
И скоро меж снегов Казбека
Поднялся одинокий храм,
И кости злого человека
Вновь успокоилися там;
И превратилася в кладбище
Скала, родная облакам:
Как будто ближе к небесам

A message from a lifeless sender,
It was an even stronger mark
Of death and ultimate surrender
960   Than was her eyes' unbroken dark.
Thus, at the hour of sunset solemn,
When the resplendent sunrays' column
Dissolves in its rotation slow,
Caucasian snows on summits distant
965   Retain a dying crimson glow
For only one and hopeless instant.
But never will this feeble ray
Bring warmth to either beast or human,
And never will its light illumine
970   A freezing rider's tortuous way.

XV

A crowd of relatives and neighbors
Have come in tears from everywhere;
Goudál, afflicted with his labors,
In anguish tears his grizzled hair.
975   He mounts. He is prepared for guiding
His clan upon a white-maned horse.
Before them lies a mournful course:
Three days, three nights of cheerless riding!
'Mid bones, of flesh by ages stripped,
980   They made for her a peaceful crypt.
Their ancient kinsman, late lamented,
Had been a famous robber chief.
Like many others, he repented
When pain and illness brought him grief.
985   He promised that in expiation
Of all his bloody crimes and wrongs
He'd build a church 'mid rocky throngs,
Close to the eagles' destination,
Where blizzards sing their joyless songs.
990   Encompassed by the mountains serried,
Where peaks and clouds are wont to meet,
By the surviving tribesmen buried,
The brigand found his last retreat
In the inclement snowdrifts' welter;
995   As though an extra hundred feet
Can warm the body's final shelter

Теплей посмертное жилище?..
Как будто дальше от людей
Последний сон не возмутится...
Напрасно! мертвым не приснится
Ни грусть, ни радость прошлых дней.

XVI

В пространстве синего эфира
Один из ангелов святых
Летел на крыльях золотых,
И душу грешную от мира
Он нес в объятиях своих.
И сладкой речью упованья
Ее сомненья разгонял,
И след проступка и страданья
С нее слезами он смывал.
Издалека уж звуки рая
К ним доносилися — как вдруг,
Свободный путь пересекая,
Взвился из бездны адский дух.
Он был могущ, как вихорь шумный,
Блистал, как молнии струя,
И гордо в дерзости безумной
Он говорит: «Она моя!»

К груди хранительной прижалась,
Молитвой ужас заглуша,
Тамары грешная душа.
Судьба грядущего решалась,
Пред нею снова он стоял,
Но, боже! — кто б его узнал?
Каким смотрел он злобным взглядом,
Как полон был смертельным ядом
Вражды, не знающей конца,—
И веяло могильным хладом
От неподвижного лица.

«Исчезни, мрачный дух сомненья! —
Посланник неба отвечал: —
Довольно ты торжествовал;
Но час суда теперь настал —
И благо божие решенье!

Or counterbalance life's defeat;
As though the dead could come awake!
No! For a buried saint or rover
1000   Both merriment and grief are over,
For they are deaf to joy and ache.

XVI

Through the transparent cosmic spaces,
Away from misery and dole,
Away from death's relentless toll,
1005   An angel flew; in his embraces
He had a sinful human soul.
With words of gentle consolation
He carried her to spheres sublime;
He wept, and his commiseration
1010   Washed off the soul's distress and crime
In Heaven, where blue ether parted,
The hosts were chanting overjoyed,
But lo! before the angel, darted
The Demon from his hellish void.
1015   He darted like a streak of lightning
And stopped the messenger divine,
A child of arrogance and fighting,
He shouted fiercely, "She is mine!"

Appalled by the seducer's vision,
1020   Tamara's soul in horror pressed
To the protective shining breast
And prayed, awaiting the decision.
He stood again before her eyes
But oh! how hard to recognize!
1025   How angry were his frown and glower,
How vicious was his thirst for power,
A thirst for hatred, as of old!
His features at this dreadful hour
Were motionless and deadly cold.

1030   "Away, oh spirit of negation!"
The angel answered in disdain,
"You will not ever rule again.
Henceforward will the Lord ordain,
And you are sentenced to damnation.

Дни испытания прошли;
С одеждой бренною земли
Оковы зла с нее ниспали.
Узнай! давно ее мы ждали!
Ее душа была из тех,
Которых жизнь — одно мгновенье
Невыносимого мученья,
Недосягаемых утех:
Творец из лучшего эфира
Соткал живые струны их,
Они не созданы для мира,
И мир был создан не для них!
Ценой жестокой искупила
Она сомнения свои...
Она страдала и любила —
И рай открылся для любви!»

И Ангел строгими очами
На искусителя взглянул
И, радостно взмахнув крылами,
В сиянье неба потонул.
И проклял Демон побежденный
Мечты безумные свои,
И вновь остался он, надменный,
Один, как прежде, во вселенной
Без упованья и любви!..

———

На склоне каменной горы
Над Койшаурскою долиной
Еще стоят до сей поры
Зубцы развалины старинной.
Рассказов, страшных для детей,
О них еще преданья полны...
Как призрак, памятник безмолвный,
Свидетель тех волшебных дней,
Между деревьями чернеет.
Внизу рассыпался аул,
Земля цветет и зеленеет;
И голосов нестройный гул
Теряется, и караваны
Идут звеня издалека,
И, низвергаясь сквозь туманы,

1035 This maiden was severely tried,
     But all is over, she has died,
     And for her soul you will not rival.
     We waited long for her arrival:
     Her tender soul is one of those,
1040 Whose life is pain without cessation,
     A moment brief of tribulation
     And unattainable repose.
     Of purest ether, in His wisdom
     The Lord once wove their living strings;
1045 The world will never mingle with them,
     Nor will they mix with worldly things!
     The fervent, suffering apostate,
     She drank in agony her cup,
     She yearned for earthly love but lost it,
1050 And Heaven's plains have opened up.''

     The angel made one powerful motion,
     And, disapproval in his gaze,
     Dissolved in the unbounded ocean
     Of the ethereal bluish haze.
1055 The Demon, by the angel worsted,
     Was once again from Heaven hurled;
     He lost the love for which he thirsted,
     And, crushed but arrogant, he cursed it—
     Cursed love, and men, and all the world.

     ———

1060 There stands upon a rocky slope
     Of early days a gloomy token:
     A castle, once its country's hope,
     Today all desolate and broken.
     The ruin tells a silent tale
1065 Of wasted wealth and dead ambition—
     A tragic ghost, an apparition
     That frightens children in the dale.
     Its jagged turrets grimly blacken,
     But in the villages beneath
1070 Sweet-smelling herbs and sturdy bracken
     Have twined into a magic wreath;
     Rich caravans of loaded camels
     Come to this place from distant homes.
     Through mountain mists, through many trammels

411

Блестит и пенится река.
И жизнью вечно молодою,
Прохладой, солнцем и весною
Природа тешится шутя,
Как беззаботная дитя.

Но грустен замок, отслуживший
Когда-то в очередь свою.
Как бедный старец, переживший
Друзей и милую семью.
И только ждут луны восхода
Его незримые жильцы:
Тогда им праздник и свобода!
Жужжат, бегут во все концы.
Седой паук, отшельник новый,
Прядет сетей своих основы;
Зеленых ящериц семья
На кровле весело играет;
И осторожная змея
Из темной щели выползает
На плиту старого крыльца,
То вдруг совьется в три кольца,
То ляжет длинной полосою
И блещет, как булатный меч,
Забытый в поле давних сеч,
Ненужный падшему герою!..
Всё дико; нет нигде следов
Минувших лет: рука веков
Прилежно, долго их сметала,
И не напомнит ничего
О славном имени Гудала,
О милой дочери его!

Но церковь на крутой вершине,
Где взяты кости их землей,
Хранима властию святой,
Видна меж туч еще поныне.
И у ворот ее стоят
На страже черные граниты,
Плащами снежными покрыты,
И на груди их вместо лат
Льды вековечные горят.
Обвалов сонные громады

1075   The reckless river leaps and foams;
        Great nature, as of old, rejoices
        In strength, in beauty's tender voices,
        In flowering spring, and colors wild—
        As does a free and happy child.

1080   But overgrown with weeds and ivy,
        The house is deaf to nature's din;
        So lives a dismal man surviving
        His wife, his children, and his kin.
        Within its walls and panels ancient
1085   New tenants dwell in ceaseless fights,
        Each has its nest and is impatient
        To fly and buzz on moonlit nights.
        The new recluse, a furry spider,
        Spins webs and makes them ever wider;
1090   Green lizards in a playful bevy
        Make merry on the roof and run;
        Below, a snake, keen-eyed and heavy,
        Enjoys in peace the blazing sun.
        It writhes and coils upon the porch,
1095   And, while the sunrays beat and scorch,
        It glitters like a precious weapon,
        First twists, then straightens in the dust;
        So, eaten through by ruthless rust,
        A sword may lie for boys to step on.
1100   The past is gone; its every trace
        Time managed slowly to efface.
        Forgotten is the old disaster,
        And nothing tells the world today
        Of him who was the castle's master
1105   Or of his daughter's grievous way.

        But high above, upon the summit,
        That church remains; one sees it still
        Protected by the holy will,
        Where winter winds and storms benumb it.
1110   As, years ago, it tops the crest,
        Black granite slabs stand at the entry,
        Each like a silent, white-cloaked sentry,
        Each one unarmored, each at rest,
        With sparkling ice upon its breast.
1115   Where all is still, where landslides ended,

С уступов, будто водопады,
Морозом схваченные вдруг,
Висят нахмурившись вокруг.
И там метель дозором ходит,
Сдувая пыль со стен седых,
То песню долгую заводит,
То окликает часовых;
Услыша вести в отдаленье
О чудном храме, в той стране,
С востока облака одне
Спешат толпой на поклоненье;
Но над семьей могильных плит
Давно никто уж не грустит.
Скала угрюмого Казбека
Добычу жадно сторожит,
И вечный ропот человека
Их вечный мир не возмутит.

Snow avalanches sleep suspended
And overhang the mountain tracts
Like frowning frozen cataracts.
The blizzard, when it's there patrolling,
1120 Inspects the guards and sweeps along;
Sometimes it sends a pebble rolling
And starts its howling, mournful song.
A flock of clouds, pursued by thunder
And scattered over pine and birch,
1125 Told by the winds about the wonder,
Will glide like pilgrims to the church.
But people do not come this way
To brush the dust, to sit or pray;
Kazbék, the Tsar of rocks Caucasian
1130 Guards greedily his lofty prey,
And man's ambition and invasion
Will not disturb his royal sway.

Lezginka. (A fast Caucasian dance). Drawing by Lermontov.

V. A. Serov. The Demon. (1891).

Vrubel'. Tamara and the Demon (1890-91).

МОЙ ДЕМОН

Собранье зол его стихия.
Носясь меж дымных облаков,
Он любит бури роковые,
И пену рек, и шум дубров.
Меж листьев желтых, облетевших
Стоит его недвижный трон;
На нем, средь ветров онемевших,
Сидит уныл и мрачен он.
Он недоверчивость вселяет,
Он презрел чистую любовь,
Он все моленья отвергает,
Он равнодушно видит кровь,
И звук высоких ощущений
Он давит голосом страстей,
И муза кротких вдохновений
Страшится неземных очей.

93. MY DEMON

He likes all evils too assemble,
And, when he flies through smoke and cloud,
He looks for elements a-tremble,
For sighing groves and rivers loud.

5   By death and winter followed closely,
'Mid withered leaves he rules alone,
And silent tempests lie morosely
At his imperishable throne.

He laughs at loyalties and treaties,
10   He looks at love with cold disdain,
He does not listen to entreaties,
He is not moved by blood or pain.

His voice of passionate temptation
Makes sounds of noble feelings drown,
15   And lo! the Muse of inspiration
Flees shyly from his awful frown.
1829

МОЙ ДЕМОН

1

Собранье зол его стихия;
Носясь меж темных облаков,
Он любит бури роковые
И пену рек и шум дубров;
Он любит пасмурные ночи,
Туманы, бледную луну,
Улыбки горькие и очи,
Безвестные слезам и сну.

2

К ничтожным хладным толкам света
Привык прислушиваться он,
Ему смешны слова привета
И всякий верящий смешон;
Он чужд любви и сожаленья,
Живет он пищею земной,
Глотает жадно дым сраженья
И пар от крови пролитой.

3

Родится ли страдалец новый,
Он беспокоит дух отца,
Он тут с насмешкою суровой
И с дикой важностью лица;
Когда же кто-нибудь нисходит
В могилу с трепетной душой,
Он час последний с ним проводит,
Но не утешен им больной.

94. MY DEMON

1

He likes all evils to assemble,
And when he flies through smoke and cloud,
He looks for elements a-tremble,
For sighing groves, and rivers loud.
5   He likes the moon when frost is bitter,
The dark and mists that do not clear,
An anguished smile and eyes whose glitter
Is never dimmed by sleep or tear.

2

Beau monde, in spite of all its blindness,
10   Is always his to give advice,
He laughs at every sign of kindness,
He laughs at faith resisting vice.
He does not know commiseration,
He thrives on all this planet shuns,
15   He feasts on blood and devastation
And gulps the choking reek of guns.

3

When one is born for woe and mourning,
The fiend is by the father seen,
He sternly mocks the baby's morning,
20   With savage dignity of mien.
When later death arrives and beckons,
He sees the sufferer again:
He spends with him the farewell seconds,
But not to comfort him in pain!

421

И гордый демон не отстанет,
Пока живу я, от меня
И ум мой озарять он станет
Лучом чудесного огня;
Покажет образ совершенства
И вдруг отнимет навсегда
И, дав предчувствия блаженства,
Не даст мне счастья никогда.

25   This Demon's image superhuman
Will live for aye in me enshrined,
His dazzling brilliance will illumine
By wondrous rays my tortured mind.
Perfection, as I seek and love it,
30   He will display and then recall,
And, having promised things I covet,
Will give me none of them at all.

1830 or 1831

Я не для ангелов и рая
Всесильным богом сотворен;
Но для чего живу страдая,
Про это больше знает он.

Как демон мой, я зла избранник,
Как демон, с гордою душой,
Я меж людей беспечный странник,
Для мира и небес чужой;

Прочти, мою с его судьбою
Воспоминанием сравни
И верь безжалостной душою,
Что мы на свете с ним одни.

95.

'Tis not for bliss or plains Elysian
That I was made of mortal clay,
But why I live through life's derision—
Of that the Lord has more to say.

5   My Demon, born of vice and danger,
With spite and evil filled my breast;
'Mid men, I am a willful stranger,
In heaven, an unbidden guest.

Observe in ruthless meditation
10 The Demon's way and then my own
And trust me that in all creation
We are unique, we are alone.
1831

425

Арбенин
(один)

Бог справедлив! и я теперь едва ли
    Не осужден нести печали
    За все грехи минувших дней.
Бывало, так меня чужие жены ждали,
    Теперь я жду жены своей...
В кругу обманщиц милых я напрасно
    И глупо юность погубил;
Любим был часто пламенно и страстно,
И ни одну из них я не любил.
Романа не начав, я знал уже развязку
    И для других сердец твердил
    Слова любви, как няня сказку.
И тяжко стало мне, и скучно жить!
И кто-то подал мне тогда совет лукавый
Жениться... чтоб иметь святое право
Уж ровно никого на свете не любить;
И я нашел жену, покорное созданье,
Она была прекрасна и нежна,
    Как агнец божий на закланье,
Мной к алтарю она приведена...
И вдруг во мне забытый звук проснулся:
    Я в душу мертвую свою
Взглянул... и увидал, что я ее люблю;
    И, стыдно молвить... ужаснулся!..
    Опять мечты, опять любовь
В пустой груди бушуют на просторе;
Изломанный челнок, я снова брошен в море:
    Вернусь ли к пристани я вновь?
        (Задумывается.)

96. THREE MONOLOGUES BY ARBENIN FROM
THE MASQUERADE
(Act 1, Scene 3)

I

Yes, God is wise to have me bent and buckled,
For in the past I only chuckled,
When husbands looked perturbed or glum.
I jilted many wives and called each man a cuckold . . .
5   Alas, my turn has also come!
I learned to madden a perfidious charmer
   But did not go beyond that start.
Some loved me well, but a protective armor
   Would never let me play my part.
10   I knew the novel's end before I saw the cover
   And, like a child, would tell by heart
   The story of a faithful lover.
The boredom of it made me rave and groan.
But someone helped me; his advice was awful—
15   To marry! Then of course it would be lawful
To live contentedly, unfeeling as a stone.
I went and found a bride and did not even falter.
Oh, she was meek, with nothing gross or sham;
   I quickly brought her to the altar—
20   A pretty sacrificial lamb!
And suddenly my soul, by boredom dried and blighted,
   Gave forth a long-forgotten sound.
I saw I loved her! First I was spellbound,
   And then . . . and then I felt affrighted.
25   To think that in my empty breast
Such love should rage and such a strong emotion!
A battered, broken boat again defies the ocean,
   But will it ever come to rest?

Ты молода летами и душою,
В огромной книге жизни ты прочла
Один заглавный лист, и пред тобою
Открыто море счастия и зла.
    Иди любой дорогой,
Надейся и мечтай — вдали надежды много,
    А в прошлом жизнь твоя бела!
Ни сердца своего, ни моего не зная,
Ты отдалася мне — и любишь, верю я,
Но безотчетно, чувствами играя,
    И резвясь, как дитя.
Но я люблю иначе: я все видел,
Все перечувствовал, все понял, все узнал,
Любил я часто, чаще ненавидел,
    И более всего страдал!
Сначала все хотел, потом все презирал я,
    То сам себя не понимал я,
    То мир меня не понимал.
На жизни я своей узнал печать проклятья,
    И холодно закрыл объятья
    Для чувств и счастия земли...
    Так годы многие прошли.
    О днях, отравленных волненьем
    Порочной юности моей,
    С каким глубоким отвращеньем
    Я мыслю на груди твоей.
Так, прежде я тебе цены не знал, несчастный!
    Но скоро черствая кора
С моей души слетела, мир прекрасный
Моим глазам открылся не напрасно,
И я воскрес для жизни и добра.
Но иногда опять какой-то дух враждебный
Меня уносит в бурю прежних дней,
    Стирает с памяти моей

II

You are so young, fate never crushed or tore you.
In the enormous book of life you've read
The title page alone, and now before you
Lie good and evil: opposite but wed.
5   Your niche is safe and cozy—
Choose any path, the prospects will be rosy,
      And all your past is shining white!
Of our two hearts I am afraid you knew too little
When you accepted me; you love me, that is right,
10   But you . . . you play with feelings rare and brittle,
      Just as a baby might.
I am unlike you, for my love belated
Came to a shipwrecked man who did not see the shore;
I often loved and much more often hated
15   But grieved and suffered even more!
First I would long for all, then mock at all and sundry,
      Pose surfeited when I was hungry
      Or thirst for things despised before.
Hell left upon my life its all-corroding traces,
20   And then I closed my warm embraces
      For all that causes happy tears.
      So did I live for many years.
      That wicked, vicious animation—
      My youthful heart's envenomed guest!
25   With what dismay, what detestation
      I think of it upon your breast . . .
I treated even you with arrogant derision,
      But very soon the hardened crust
Fell off my soul, and my recovered vision
30   Again discerned a world without division,
      And I was born for confidence and trust.
But every now and then a spirit black and tragic
Will take me back to what I left behind,
      And it effaces from my mind

Твой светлый взор и голос твой волшебный.
В борьбе с собой, под грузом тяжких дум,
    Я молчалив, суров, угрюм.
    Боюся осквернить тебя прикосновеньем,
Боюсь, чтобы тебя не испугал ни стон,
    Ни звук, исторгнутый мученьем.
Тогда ты говоришь: меня не любит он!

35   Your smiling glances and your voice of magic.
       While fighting with my past, I wilt and burn
         And seem withdrawn, morose, and stern.
         And then I am afraid to taint you by my touches,
       To frighten you with groans, with something harsh or grim,
40   With sounds extorted by the torment's clutches . . .
       Then you would sadly say, "I am not loved by him."

Кто знает, может быть...
Послушай, Нина!.. я смешон, конечно,
Тем, что люблю тебя так сильно, бесконечно,
Как только может человек любить.
И что за диво? у других на свете
    Надежд и целей миллион,
У одного богатство есть в предмете,
    Другой в науки погружен,
Тот добивается чинов, крестов — иль славы,
    Тот любит общество, забавы,
Тот странствует, тому игра волнует кровь...
Я странствовал, играл, был ветрен и трудился,
    Постиг друзей, коварную любовь,
Чинов я не хотел, а славы не добился.
Богат и без гроша был скукою томим.
Везде я видел зло и, гордый, перед ним
    Нигде не преклонился.
Все, что осталось мне от жизни, это ты:
Созданье слабое, но ангел красоты:
Твоя любовь, улыбка, взор, дыханье...
Я человек: пока они мои,
Без них нет у меня ни счастья, ни души,
    Ни чувства, ни существованья!
Но если я обманут... если я
Обманут... если на груди моей змея
Так много дней была согрета, — если точно
Я правду отгадал... и, лаской усыплен,
    С другим осмеян был заочно!
    Послушай, Нина... я рожден
    С душой кипучею, как лава,
Покуда не растопится, тверда
Она, как камень... но плоха забава

III

You'll laugh at my appeal . . .
You are amused or, shall I say: astounded?
To see my love for you, so tender, so unbounded,
The strongest love a mortal man can feel.
5   Small wonder! Many a civilian
    Woos glory and pursues success;
   A swindler makes his crooked million,
    A scholar makes his brilliant guess.
Some bask in rays of fame and label it attainment,
10   Still others hunt for entertainment;
Some people go abroad, while others like to play . . .
   I, too, began to work, to travel, flirt, and gamble,
    From friends and women learned to stay away,
For fame I dreamed in vain, for rank I did not scramble.
15   When penniless or rich, I felt profoundly bored.
I saw that evil was all people's overlord
    But managed not to tremble.
And now that all that dust is shaken off my feet,
One thing is left: it's you—a creature weak but sweet.
20   Your love, your breath, your eyes, your smile and laughter—
While they are mine, I know that I am whole;
Without them, I shall lose my happiness and soul,
    My life and my salvation after!
But if I was deceived . . . if it is true
25   That you were like a snake upon my breast, if you . . .
If you deceived my hope and mocked at my revival,
If lulled by gentle tricks, I was by you forsworn
    And ousted by a lucky rival!
Oh, Nina, listen . . . I was born
30   With lava in my breast that burned it torrid.
Such lava is like rock, it's hard as stone
Until it melts and boils, and it is horrid

433

С ее потоком встретиться! тогда,
  Тогда не ожидай прощенья —
Закона я на месть свою не призову,
  Но сам, без слез и сожаленья,
  Две наши жизни разорву!

The Masquerade (Pushkin Theater, Leningrad 1917-39). Yu. M. Yuryev as Arbenin. In the long gallery of Arbenins, Yuryev was the most famous.

To meet its rushing torrent; fate alone
Then can protect you, and my passion
35   Will not invite the law that deals with wanton wives;
Without a tear, without compassion—
Myself—I'll sever our two lives!

435

СКАЗКА ДЛЯ ДЕТЕЙ

1

Умчался век эпических поэм,
И повести в стихах пришли в упадок;
Поэты в том виновны не совсем
(Хотя у многих стих не вовсе гладок);
И публика не права между тем.
Кто виноват, кто прав — уж я не знаю,
А сам стихов давно я не читаю —
Не потому, чтоб не любил стихов,
А так: смешно ж терять для звучных строф
Златое время... в нашем веке зрелом,
Известно вам, все заняты мы делом.

2

Стихов я не читаю — но люблю
Марать шутя бумаги лист летучий;
Свой стих за хвост отважно я ловлю;
Я без ума от тройственных созвучий
И влажных рифм — как например на *ю*.
Вот почему пишу я эту сказку.
Ее волшебно-темную завязку
Не стану я подробно объяснять,
Чтоб кой-каких допросов избежать;
Зато конец не будет без морали,
Чтобы ее хоть дети прочитали.

3

Герой известен, и не нов предмет;
Тем лучше: устарело всё, что ново!

97. A FAIRY TALE FOR CHILDREN

1

Unhurried epics are at present rare,
And narratives in verse are out of favor.
It is not right that authors do not care:
Indeed some rhymesters lack poetic flavor,
5 But, nonetheless, the public is not fair.
I will not lavish praise or mutter curses:
I never open other people's verses!
No, not because they are not to my taste—
But you'll agree: what clever man will waste
10 His time on things that make him soft or dizzy?
We've come of age and are so *very* busy.

2

I do not read what others write—that's true,
But just for fun I like to jot and scribble;
My rhymes escape, I hunt for them anew . . .
15 Oh, I adore them quick and smart and triple,
And more than others, liquid rhymes in U.
That's how my story came into existence,
But I shall keep my readers at a distance
By hiding some ambiguous facts, for which
20 Immodest people have the strongest itch.
I'll only add (for children's sake) a moral,
And may it live in written form and oral.

3

My plot is old, my characters are trite;
That's for the best: all novelties are ancient.

Кипя огнем и силой юных лет,
Я прежде пел про демона иного:
То был безумный, страстный, детский бред.
Бог знает где заветная тетрадка?
Касается ль душистая перчатка
Ее листов — и слышно: c'est   joli?..
Иль мышь над ней старается в пыли?..
Но этот черт совсем иного сорта —
Аристократ и не похож на черта.

4

Перенестись теперь прошу сейчас
За мною в спальню: розовые шторы
Опущены, с трудом лишь может глаз
Следить ковра восточные узоры.
Приятный трепет вдруг объемлет вас,
И, девственным дыханьем напоенный,
Огнем в лицо вам пышет воздух сонный;
Вот ручка, вот плечо, и возле них
На кисее подушек кружевных
Рисуется младой, но строгий профиль...
И на него взирает Мефистофель.

5

То был ли сам великий Сатана
Иль мелкий бес из самых нечиновных,
Которых дружба людям так нужна
Для тайных дел, семейных и любовных?
Не знаю! Если б им была дана
Земная форма, по рогам и платью
Я мог бы сволочь различить со знатью;
Но дух — известно, что такое дух!
Жизнь, сила, чувство, зренье, голос, слух —
И мысль — без тела — часто в видах разных;
(Бесов вобще рисуют безобразных).

6

Но я не так всегда воображал
Врага святых и чистых побуждений.

438

25 When I was young and wild and burning bright,
  Another demon made my harp impatient.
  Those childish ravings! That unhealthy light!
  Where is that notebook? Who is she, I wonder,
  That whispers "C'est joli" and takes asunder
30 Its dusty pages with a perfumed glove?
  Oh has a mouse consumed my work of love?
  Today, in devilry I cannot revel:
  This one is courteous and unlike my Devil.

4

  Come with me to a maiden's bedroom! This
35 Will hardly need persuasion or coercion.
  The rosy blinds are down, and you will miss
  Lines on the carpets, each of which is Persian,
  But you will feel the gracious state of bliss.
  The room is still, the drowsy air is laden
40 With virgin breath—the breathing of the maiden.
  Here is her shoulder, and her arms embrace
  A heap of pillows trimmed with costly lace.
  And close at hand, enjoying every feature,
  Stands Mephistopheles, that sadly famous creature.

5

45 Could that be Satan, straight from fiery hell?
  Or just an imp on Hades' humblest level,
  Before whose face the tricksters often fell,
  When, wronged or jealous, they invoked the devil?
  I should have answered all these questions well
50 If fiends wore uniform; then in my loathing
  I'd tell their riff-raff by the horns and clothing.
  For what's a spirit? Nothing but a sprite:
  Life, pressure, feeling, hearing, voice, and sight,
  Plus naked thought, which leaps or slumbers smugly.
55 (Though fiends are normally depicted ugly.)

6

  In olden days I'd often visualize
  The enemy of sacred aspirations.

Мой юный ум, бывало, возмущал
Могучий образ; меж иных видений,
Как царь, немой и гордый, он сиял
Такой волшебно-сладкой красотою,
Что было страшно... и душа тоскою
Сжималася — и этот дикий бред
Преследовал мой разум много лет.
Но я, расставшись с прочими мечтами,
И от него отделался — стихами!

7

Оружие отличное: врагам
Кидаете в лицо вы эпиграммой...
Вам насолить захочется ль друзьям?
Пустите в них поэмой или драмой!
Но полно, к делу. Я сказал уж вам,
Что в спальне той таился хитрый демон.
Невинным сном был тронут не совсем он.
Не мудрено: кипела в нем не кровь,
И понимал иначе он любовь;
И речь его коварных искушений
Была полна: ведь он недаром гений!

8

«Не знаешь ты, кто я — но уж давно
Читаю я в душе твоей; незримо,
Неслышно говорю с тобою,— но
Слова мои, как тень, проходят мимо
Ребяческого сердца,— и оно
Дивится им спокойно и в молчанье,—
Пускай! Зачем тебе мое названье?
Ты с ужасом отвергнула б мою
Безумную любовь,— но я люблю
По-своему... терпеть и ждать могу я,
Не надо мне ни ласк, ни поцелуя.

9

«Когда ты спишь, о ангел мой земной,
И шибко бьется девственною кровью
Младая грудь под грезою ночной,

His image would in splendor rise
And deeply stir my young imagination.
60 A prideful king, he stood before my eyes
But never spoke, his magic beauty shining;
My heart would beat, for things mysterious pining.
So did I dream for years, so did I rave,
Of monstrous visions a defenseless slave.
65 But let me state as early as this proem:
I shook him off: I put him in a poem!

7

Oh, what a weapon for a saucy foe!
An epigram will kill them by the dozen.
And a lampoon or witty skit will go
70 To crush a friend or to destroy a cousin.
But back to business! You already know:
A demon viewed the maiden chaste and gentle.
He did not grow completely sentimental:
It was not blood that in his veins did boil,
75 And, though he loved, he treated love as toil.
His speech was tempting, and he made her hear it.
What do you want? A spirit is a spirit.

8

"You've never seen me, but, my pretty lass!
It is your soul that I am used to reading.
80 I speak to you invisible; alas!
Your heart is deaf to my impassioned pleading
And lets my words and admonitions pass;
I fail to bring you joy and animation.
I'll not disclose my name or appellation:
85 You would be horrified if you could guess
Who loves you so; but I adore you, yes!
According to my style . . . Unlike a human,
I gladly wait and never rush a woman.

9

"When in your sleep, amidst a peaceful rest,
90 You feel your blood within your body surging,
When passions gather in your childish breast,

441

Знай, это я, склонившись к изголовью,
Любуюся — и говорю с тобой;
И в тишине, наставник твой случайный,
Чудесные рассказываю тайны...
А много было взору моему
Доступно и понятно, потому
Что узами земными я не связан,
И вечностью и знанием наказан...

10

«Тому назад еще немного лет
Я пролетал над сонною столицей.
Кидала ночь свой странный полусвет,
Румяный запад с новою денницей
На севере сливались, как привет
Свидания с молением разлуки;
Над городом таинственные звуки,
Как грешных снов нескромные слова,
Неясно раздавались — и Нева,
Меж кораблей сверкая на просторе,
Журча, с волной их уносила в море.

11

«Задумчиво столбы дворцов немых
По берегам теснилися, как тени,
И в пене вод гранитных крылец их
Купалися широкие ступени;
Минувших лет событий роковых
Волна следы смывала роковые,
И улыбались звезды голубые,
Глядя с высот на гордый прах земли,
Как будто мир достоин их любви,
Как будто им земля небес дороже...
И я тогда... я улыбнулся тоже.

12

«И я кругом глубокий кинул взгляд
И увидал с невольною отрадой
Преступный сон под сению палат,
Корыстный труд пред тощею лампадой,

Then it is me, oh unsuspecting virgin!
I talk to you, explaining things with zest.
Believe me, darling, that your secret tutor
95   Can tell you more than any other suitor.
You wonder why? I'll say it all to you:
So many things are open to my view,
Because your earthly bonds I don't acknowledge
And have to bear eternity and knowledge.

10

100   "It happened once and not too long ago:
My way above your city I was wending;
Mysterious night still cast its eery glow,
But in the north the crimson west was blending
With pale and timid daylight. Even so
105   Do words of welcome blend with tears of parting.
I heard strange sounds (for life below was starting),
Which were like ribald words of sinful dreams.
Deep in its bed, the Neva's gurgling streams
Played with the vessels, set them all in motion,
110   And swiftly drove them to the leaden ocean.

11

"The palaces reposed in mute array,
And like a ghost there stood each marble column;
The glinting river's ever-hungry spray
Bathed mighty steps, impregnable and solemn;
115   The traces of the past it washed away,
The traces of events and dealings fateful,
And bluish stars, benevolent and faithful,
Smiled enigmatically from above,
As if this haughty dust deserved their love,
120   As if the sky existed for this planet . . .
And then I also smiled at earthly granite.

12

"I looked around; my glance was deep and shrewd,
It fell on many an unworthy prophet,
On justice sleeping in a happy mood,
125   On hacks who burn the midnight oil for profit,

443

И страшных тайн везде печальный ряд;
Я стал ловить блуждающие звуки,
Веселый смех и крик последней муки:
То ликовал иль мучился порок!
В молитвах я подслушивал упрек,
В бреду любви — бесстыдное желанье;
Везде — обман, безумство иль страданье!

13

«Но близ Невы один старинный дом
Казался полн священной тишиною.
Всё важностью наследственною в нем
И роскошью дышало вековою;
Украшен был он княжеским гербом;
Из мрамора волнистого колонны
Кругом теснились чинно, и балконы
Чугунные воздушною семьей
Меж них гордились дивною резьбой;
И окон ряд, всегда прозрачно-темных,
Манил пугая взор очей нескромных.

14

«Пора была, боярская пора!
Теснилась знать в роскошные покои —
Былая знать минувшего двора,
Забытых дел померкшие герои!
Музыкой тут гремели вечера,
В Неве дробился блеск высоких окон,
Напудренный мелькал и вился локон;
И часто ножка с красным каблучком
Давала знак условный под столом;
И старики в звездах и бриллиантах
Судили резко о тогдашних франтах.

15

«Тот век прошел, и люди те прошли.
Сменили их другие; род старинный
Перевелся; в готической пыли
Портреты гордых бар, краса гостиной,
Забытые, тускнели; поросли

On secret felons, treacherous and lewd.
Among the murmurs that I tried to capture
Some told of grief and some of final rapture,
But, proud or tortured, vice was always there!
130 I heard reproaches in a fervent prayer,
I searched for love but found a gross convulsion,
And all was madness, anguish, and compulsion.

13

"But I observed a house upon the bank
By vulgar sounds and putrid breath untainted,
135 For it was only sunrays that it drank;
A count's escutcheon was upon it painted,
Which by itself bespoke the owner's rank.
The columns crowded, one another chasing,
The balconies' exquisite interlacing
140 Set off the wavy pattern of the stone;
The clear obscure of windowpanes alone
Lent awesome strangeness to the tranquil mansion
And hid what many would not dare to mention.

14

"In days gone by, in happy days of yore
145 The Tsar's retainers thrived in chambers sumptuous;
Such shining retinues we have no more—
Those bearded boyars, wealthy and presumptuous!
I see them dancing on the polished floor:
The candles gutter, orchestras play louder,
150 The locks are gray—nay, not from age, from powder.
A red-heeled foot with nonchalance divine
Beneath the table gives a secret sign,
And many a disgruntled pompous courtier
Calls foppishness a veritable torture.

15

155 "That century is gone, those men are gone,
And ancient names are speedily forgotten,
The famous portraits that in parlors shone
Just gather dust, ridiculous and rotten;
Old gardens are deserted, time goes on.

445

Дворы травой, и блеск сменив бывалый,
Сырая мгла и сумрак длинной залой
Спокойно завладели... Тихий дом
Казался пуст; но жил хозяин в нем,
Старик худой и с виду величавый,
Озлобленный на новый век и нравы.

16

«Он ростом был двенадцати вершков,
С домашними был строг неумолимо;
Всегда молчал; ходил до двух часов,
Обедал, спал... да иногда, томимый
Бессонницей, собранье острых слов
Перебирал или читал Вольтера.
Как быть? Сильна к преданьям в людях вера!..
Имел он дочь четырнадцати лет;
Но с ней видался редко; за обед
Она являлась в фартучке, с мадамой;
Сидела чинно и держалась прямо.

17

«Всегда одна, запугана отцом
И англичанки строгостью небрежной,
Она росла, как ландыш за стеклом
Или скорей как бледный цвет подснежный.
Она была стройна, но с каждым днем
С ее лица сбегали жизни краски,
Задумчивей большие стали глазки;
Покинув книжку скучную, она
Охотнее садилась у окна,
И вдалеке мечты ее блуждали,
Пока ее играть не посылали.

18

«Тогда она сходила в длинный зал,
Но бегать в нем ей как-то страшно было
И как-то странно детский шаг звучал
Между колонн; разрытою могилой
Над юной жизнью воздух там дышал.
И в зеркалах являлися предметы

446

160 This stately house, whose story might have thrilled you,
    Is also dark and has the smell of mildew.
    You might have thought that no one lived inside,
    But someone did, its master had not died.
    A bilious man with features finely chiseled,
165 Thin as a lath, unsmiling, short, and grizzled.

16

    "He ruled his household like a tiny cock
    And would not answer anybody's question.
    He never spoke. He walked till two o'clock,
    Had dinner, slept, or, prey to indigestion,
170 Would to himself this generation mock
    Or read Voltaire's sardonic, acid humor—
    Of things long dead a moribund consumer!
    He had a daughter, who was just fourteen,
    But seldom met her. When the girl was seen,
175 She looked quite prim, and of her youthful fitness
    Her governess was an observant witness.

17

    "She grew alone, her parent always far,
    Her English 'madam' hard and cold as metal.
    A lily of the valley in a jar,
180 A pallid snowdrop, weak in every petal!
    Her childhood left upon her soul a scar.
    As time went on, her life was getting duller,
    Her charming eyes were slowly shedding color;
    She often sat in a secluded nook
185 With some insipid, boring, learned book
    And thought and thought, her brain confused and addled,
    Until reproofed by a despotic adult.

18

    "She would come down, if she were really pressed,
    But in that hall one shrank from making merry.
190 Its musty odor could perhaps suggest
    An open grave, a place in which to bury,
    But not enjoyment, gaiety, or jest.
    The ancient mirrors in the hall were clouded

447

Длиннее и бесцветнее, одеты
Какой-то мертвой дымкою; и вдруг
Неясный шорох слышался вокруг:
То загремит, то снова тише, тише...
(То были•тени предков — или мыши!)

19

«И что ж? — она привыкла толковать
По-своему развалин говор странный,
И стала мысль горячая летать
Над бледною головкой и туманный,
Воздушный рой видений навевать.
Я с ней не разлучался. Детский лепет
Подслушивать, невинной груди трепет
Следить, ее дыханием с немой,
Мучительной и жадною тоской,
Как жизнью, упиваться... это было
Смешно! — но мне так ново и так мило!

20

«Влюбился я. И точно хороша
Была не в шутку маленькая Нина.
Нет, никогда свинец карандаша
Рафаэля, иль кисти Перуджина
Не начертали, пламенем дыша,
Подобный профиль. Все ее движенья
Особого казались выраженья
Исполнены. Но с самых детских дней
Ее глаза не изменяли ей,
Тая равно надежду, радость, горе;
И было темно в них, как в синем море.

21

«Я понял, что душа ее была
Из тех, которым рано всё понятно.
Для мук и счастья, для добра и зла
В них пищи много; — только невозвратно
Они идут, куда их повела
Случайность, без раскаянья, упреков
И жалобы. Им в жизни нет уроков;
Их чувствам повторяться не дано...

448

And made all things look grayish, long, and shrouded,
195   Enfolded in some sort of deathly haze;
Such pictures met the maiden's hungry gaze.
Strange noises could be heard inside the curtain
From restless ghosts—or mice (I am not certain).

19

"What happened? Well, though things around were dead,
200   She learned to listen to the ruins' language.
Her stormy thought flew high above her head
And came with dreams, which did not let her languish—
A noiseless swarm by her seclusion fed.
I stayed with her. To see her passions burgeon,
205   To catch the breath of the enchanting virgin,
To listen and remain disguised and mute!
Indeed, to me it was a new pursuit,
But oh! I felt so meek, so tender-hearted;
I lived enraptured, and we never parted.

20

210   "I fell in love. I tell you: by my soul,
She was divine, my darling little Nina.
I know quite well what beauty I extol,
For even Raphael, even Perugino,
With pencils, brushes, pens and painter's coal
215   Did not depict such grace. Her every motion
Was full of tender and unique emotion,
And from her childhood, from the very start,
Her eyes were always loyal to her heart:
Of all she felt they were a silent keeper;
220   The deepest ocean was not ever deeper.

21

"I understood: her soul was one of those
Which open up in early adolescence
For good and evil, for success and woes.
They go their way, despising people's lessons,
225   Indifferent to contumely and blows.
Led on by Chance, they coolly take its sentence,
Without regrets, reproaches, or repentance;
They don't look back, their feelings don't repeat.

Такие души я любил давно
Отыскивать по свету на свободе:
Я сам ведь был немножко в этом роде!

22

«Ее смущали странные мечты.
Порой она среди пустого зала
Сиянье, роскошь, музыку, цветы,
Толпу гостей и шум воображала;
Кипела кровь от душной тесноты;
На платьице чудесные узоры
Виднелись ей,— и вот гремели шпоры,
К ней кавалер незримый подходил
И в мнимый вальс с собою уносил;
И вот она кружилась в вихре бала
И утомясь на кресла упадала...

23

«И тут она, склонив лукавый взор
И выставив едва приметно ножку,
Двусмысленный и темный разговор
С ним завести старалась понемножку;
Сначала был он весел и остёр,
А иногда и чересчур небрежен;
Но под конец зато как мил и нежен!
Что делать ей? — притворно-строгий взгляд
Его, как гром, отталкивал назад,
А сердце билось в ней так шибко, шибко,
И по устам змеилася улыбка.

24

«Пред зеркалом, бывало, целый час
То волосы пригладит, то красивый
Цветок пришпилит к ним; движенью глаз,
Головке наклоненной вид ленивый
Придав, стоит... и учится; не раз
Хотелось мне совет ей дать лукавый;
Но ум ее и сметливый и здравый
Отгадывал всё мигом сам собой;
Так годы шли безмолвной чередой;
И вот настал тот возраст, о котором
Так полны ваши книги всяким вздором.

In all my wanderings through frost and heat
230 To seek these souls is both my job and pleasure.
I'm such myself—if only to a measure.

22

"When dreams got hold of her, she'd gladly yield,
Enwrapped completely in a sweet illusion;
Her guests arrived, the merry couples reeled,
235 Triumphant music shattered her seclusion,
The perfumed stuffiness was only hers to wield.
And in this tumult, in this glitter royal
A cavalier, invisible but loyal,
A handsome man, whose smile is never false,
240 Would bow and lead her to a brilliant waltz.
Her head was turned, the fiddles sent her spinning . . .
Oh, what a truly beautiful beginning!

23

"Then in her chair she'd for a moment sit,
Her every posture virginally modest;
245 Her foot would show perhaps a tiny bit . . .
But conversation! Oh, it was the oddest,
The most equivocal and full of wit.
Her words were casual, dropped in jest, disarming,
Perhaps too casual, but astute and charming.
250 What next? A stern expression on her face!
He is astounded? Let him know his place!
Her heart beats fast and teaches her the ruses,
Her serpent smile entices and confuses.

24

"Before a mirror she could stay an hour,
255 Forgetful of arithmetic and grammar;
She'd bend her head or pin a pretty flower
And study closely her appeal and glamor.
I stood beside; it was within my power
To help her by advice or friendly nodding,
260 But she was smart and did not need my prodding:
This beauty had a most amazing brain.
Thus years went on and formed a silent chain;
She reached the age on which romances drivel
(You must excuse me if I am uncivil).

451

«То был великий день: семнадцать лет!
Всё, что досель таилось за решеткой,
Теперь надменно явится на свет!
Старик-отец послал за старой теткой,
И съехались родные на совет.
Их затруднял удачный выбор бала.
Что? будет двор иль нет? — Иных пугала
Застенчивость дикарки молодой;
Но очень тонко замечал другой,
Что это вид ей даст оригинальный;
Потом наряд осматривали бальный.

26

«Но вот настал и вечер роковой.
Она с утра была, как в лихорадке;
Поплакала немножко, золотой
Браслет сломала, в суетах перчатки
Разорвала... со страхом и тоской
Она в карету села и дорогой
Была полна мучительной тревогой;
И выходя споткнулась на крыльце.
И с бледностью печальной на лице
Вступила в залу... Странный шепот встретил
Ее явленье: свет ее заметил.

«Кипел, сиял уж в полном блеске бал.
Тут было всё, что называют *светом*...
Не я ему названье это дал,
Хоть смысл глубокий есть в названье этом.
Своих друзей я тут бы не узнал;
Улыбки, лица лгали так искусно,
Что даже мне чуть-чуть не стало грустно.
Прислушаться хотел я, — но едва
Ловил мой слух летучие слова,
Отрывки безыменных чувств и мнений —
Эпиграфы неведомых творений!..»
. . . .

265   "Yes, seventeen! And all that was concealed
And that is now to everyone apparent
Will be uncorked, uncovered, and unsealed.
An aged aunt consults the aged parent:
The military council views the field.
270   They want a courtly ball and are in terror,
Lest all together they should make an error;
Some of the bolder members are dismayed
By the uncommon shyness of the maid,
Still others say that shyness makes perfection.
275   At last the dress was offered for inspection.

26

   "The fateful day arrived. From early dawn,
She was upset and in an awful flurry,
Ripped up a glove, destroyed her finest lawn,
And broke a bracelet, dressing in a hurry,
280   And very soon, unhappy and forlorn,
Was nearly at the end of her resources.
Just then the driver flogged the willing horses.
On stepping out she thought that she would fall,
Approached in tears the overcrowded hall,
285   But walked inside with steps a little firmer—
To be received with an approving murmur.

27

   "The courtly ball was a resplendent view.
The Russian capital's *beau monde* was present.
Beau monde . . . A funny name! Though to a few
290   The world is good, and worldly life is pleasant . . .
But what a change occurred to those I knew!
Here was not one of them who could be trusted,
So even I began to feel disgusted.
I listened closely, and at times I heard
295   A broken sentence, an unfinished word—
Just bits of nameless thoughts and declarations,
The epigraphs to the unborn creations."

POEMS IN FRENCH

Rappelez-moi, je reviendrai.

98.

Quand je te vois sourire,
Mon cœur s'épanouit,
Et je voudrais te dire
Ce que mon cœur me dit!

5   Alors toute ma vie
A mes yeux apparaît;
Je maudis, et je prie,
Et je pleure en secret.

Car sans toi, mon seul guide,
10   Sans ton regard de feu
Mon passé paraîit vide,
Comme le ciel sans Dieu.

Et puis, caprice étrange,
Je me surprends bénir
15   Le beau jour, oh mon ange,
Où tu m'as fait souffrir! . . .
     [?]

457

99.

Non, si j'en crois mon espérance,
J'attends un meilleur avenir.
Je serai malgré la distance
Près de vous par le souvenir.—
5   Errant sur un autre rivage,
De loin je vous suivrai,
Et sur vous si grondait l'orage,
Rappelez-moi, je reviendrai.

[? 1832]

100. L'attente

Je l'attends dans la plaine sombre;
Au loin je vois blanchir une ombre,
Une ombre qui vient doucement . . .
Eh non!—trompeuse espérance—
5   C'est un vieux saule qui balance
Son tronc desséché et luisant.

Je me penche et longtemps j'écoute:
Je crois entendre sur la route
Le son qu'un pas léger produit . . .
10   Non, ce n'est rien! c'est dans la mousse
Le bruit d'une feuille que pousse
Le vent parfumé de la nuit.

Rempli d'une amère tristesse,
Je me couche dans l'herbe épaisse
15   Et m'endors d'un sommeil profond . . .
Tout-à-coup, tremblant, je m'éveille:
Sa voix me parlait à l'oreille,
Sa bouche me baisait au front.
1841

Nevsky Prospekt. Engelgardt's house famous for its public masquerades. Drawing by V. S. Sadovnikov. Lithograph by P. S. Ivanov, 1835.

Ball at Princess M. F. Baratyanskaya's, 1834.

A Fairy Tale for Children. Watercolor by
O. Delavos-Kardovskaya, 1914.

Vrubel'. The Demon's head, 1894.

461

COMMENTARY

Believe me: they'll despise your bitterness and rage;
For them you are a shameless aper,
A mime, a tragic actor, painted for the stage,
Who brandishes a sword of paper.

Commentary

A word born of lightning,
A luminous bubble . . .

This commentary is written for the general reader, not for specialists; thus, I have usually avoided giving references to secondary sources, for the most important of them are in Russian. All the factual information and nearly all the stylistic observations below are taken from other people's works; but the principle of selection and the point of view are mine. The cases in which I attempt an original opinion are few and do not deserve special mention.

Notes in "academic" editions of Lermontov discuss the date of each piece, extant versions and parallels in Russian and Western literatures. These problems will be touched on briefly below. My main aims have been to recreate Lermontov's surroundings, to explain the circumstances under which a poem was written, insofar as those circumstances are important for the understanding of the text, and to draw the reader's attention to the artistry of Lermontov's poetry.

The notes are deliberately repetitive, for my idea was to make each article as self-sufficient as possible. Cross-references and the index, together with the introduction, are expected to turn a mass of disparate remarks into a coherent whole.

I would like to draw the readers' attention to three books, all of which came out after I finished work on my manuscript and so could not use them as much as they deserve. (1) O. V. Miller, *Bibliografiya literatury o M. Yu. Lermontove* (1917-1977) [A Lermontov Bibliography]. Len-

465

ingrad: Nauka, 1980. This is an extremely complete bibliography, with indexes; but it includes only works in Russian and only those published in the Soviet Union. (2) *Lermontov. Kartiny, akvareli, risunki* [Lermontov. Pictures, watercolors, drawings]. Moscow: Izobrazitel'noe iskusstvo, 1980 (162 items, a short introduction, and a few bibliographical references). (3) *Lermontovskaya Entsiklopediya* [A Lermontov Encyclopedia]. Moscow: Sovetskaya entsiklopedia, 1981 (a mine of information, very professional, with numerous entries on style; contains a frequency dictionary, a dictionary of Lermontov rhymes, etc.)

1. Autumn

"Autumn" has the distinction of being the earliest recorded lyric from Lermontov's pen. Undoubtedly, it was not his first, for, according to Lermontov's own recollections, he had been listening to assonances from the age of two. "Realistic" landscapes occur in his longer narrative poems but are rare in the lyrics (cf. the descriptions of nature in Nos. 26, 28, 50, etc.).

The page immediately following this poem in Lermontov's notebook is torn out, so the third stanza may not have been the last one. The lyric does not seem incomplete, but in a typical elegy a melancholy description of nature is usually followed by introspective lines. It was first published in 1889 and enjoys some popularity today; in any case, a recent edition of Lermontov's selected poems for children opens with it.

2. A Monologue

This bitter poem reads like a study for "Meditation" (No. 46), but, although the phraseology is partly the same, the accents are noticeably shifted in the later work. In "A Monologue" "the present generation" is described as a victim of inexorable doom (it is not the fault of a northern plant that it was born in the north), in "Meditation" the poet's contemporaries are made to carry the entire burden of blame. In "A Monologue" the point of view is ethical throughout, whereas the main thrust of "Meditation" is an indictment of people's political and intellectual impotence.

In his youth Lermontov often used blank verse and wrote meditative and narrative meditative poems molded on Byron's "Darkness," "The

Dream," monologues from *Cain*, etc. Later, blank verse reappeared in his *A Song about Tsar Ivan Vasilyevich, His Young Body-Guard, and the Valiant Merchant Kalashnikov* (a variation on a plot from the fifteenth century in *bylina* style, 1837; in an unfinished poem composed in hexameters; in a song from "Tamán' "; and in a short lyric "Speak with Your Voice to Me" (1838:No. 43). In "A Monologue" the last stanza is rhymed, and such a combination of blank verse and rhyme is unique in Lermontov's authorship.

The poem was first published in 1859.

3. A Prayer

The first of several "prayers" (cf. Nos. 35, 37, 51, and 66), it is also Lermontov's earliest poem about the poet and his gift (cf. Nos. 47, 63, 87). It has a structure not unlike that of his 1840 "Thanksgiving" (No. 66), the same type of catharsis, and a similar anticlimax, though the two lyrics are about different things and there are eleven years between them. Line 16 anticipates No. 92:500.

"A Prayer" is definitely the best poem written by Lermontov in 1829. It was first published in 1859.

4. The Caucasus

The Caucasus played an outstanding role in Lermontov's life. In the summer of 1818, when he was only three and a half years old, E. A. Arsényeva (the boy's grandmother) took him to the South, because he was suffering from the consequences of scrofula: he was bowlegged (a defect of which he was never completely cured) and weak. The second journey to the Caucasus took place in 1820 and the third in 1825. In 1825 Lermontov was almost ten years old and remembered everything very well. The natural beauty of the Caucasus made an indelible impression on him. He also had some exposure to Circassian dances and songs and for the rest of his life wrote romantic poems about the Cherkesses. In 1832 he composed the following hymn in rhythmic prose, which in the original sounds like irregular dactyls:

Blue mountains of the Caucasus, hail! You nourished my childhood; you bore me on your wild-looking crests and clothed me in your clouds; you made me friends with the heavens, and since then I have been dreaming always of you and of the heavens. Thrones of nature, from which thunderclouds blow away like smoke! He who but once prayed to the Creator on your peaks will despise life, though at that moment he may have been proud of it. . . .

Often at daybreak I would look at the snows and distant glaciers on the cliffs; they were so shiny in the rays of the rising sun; they were putting on a roseate glitter, while everything was dark down below, and thus heralded morning to the passer-by. And their roseate color was like the color of shame, as if they were maidens who see a man while they are bathing: they are so embarrassed that they forget to cover their bosoms with white cloth.

How I enjoyed your storms, Caucasus! Those loud storms in emptiness, to which caves respond like guardians of nights! . . . On a smooth hill a solitary tree bent by the wind and rains, or a vineyard rustling in a gorge, and an unknown path over a precipice, where, covered with foam, a nameless river is running on, and an unexpected shot, and the fear after the shot: a crafty enemy? or just a hunter? . . . All, all is beautiful there.

The Russian text of the hymn is as follows:

Синие горы Кавказа, приветствую вас! вы взлелеяли детство мое; вы носили меня на своих одичалых хребтах, облаками меня одевали, вы к небу меня приучили, и я с той поры всё мечтаю об вас да о небе. Престолы природы, с которых как дым улетают громовые тучи, кто раз лишь на ваших вершинах творцу помолился, тот жизнь презирает, хотя в то мгновенье гордился он ею!..

———

Часто во время зари я глядел на снега и далекие льдины утесов; они так сияли в лучах восходящего солнца, и в розовый блеск одеваясь, они, между тем как внизу всё темно, возвещали прохожему утро. И розовый цвет их подобился цвету стыда: как будто девицы, когда вдруг увидят мужчину купаясь, в таком уж смущенье, что белой одежды накинуть на грудь не успеют.

Как я любил твои бури, Кавказ! те пустынные громкие бури, которым пещеры как стражи ночей отвечают!.. На гладком холме одинокое дерево, ветром, дождями нагнутое, иль виноградник, шумящий в ущелье, и путь неизвестный над пропастью, где, покрываяся пеной, бежит безымянная речка, и выстрел нежданный, и страх после выстрела: враг ли коварный иль просто охотник... всё, всё в этом крае прекрасно.

Commentary

The similarity between this hymn, "The Caucasus," No. 14, and several other early poems is apparent (cf. the motif of praying on the peak with the subsequent spurning of the human condition). Lermontov used both "The Caucasus" and the hymn, with some slight changes, at the beginning of his long narrative poem *Izmaíl-Bey* (1832). Repetition of the rhyming word in lines 2 and 12 is a feature of the original.

Lines 13-14 are more than a conventional reference to beautiful eyes and an agitated heart. On July 8, 1830, Lermontov made the following entry in his journal:

Who will believe me that I had already known love when I was ten years old! Our large family, Grandmother, aunts, cousins, were staying at a Caucasian resort. A certain lady with a daughter of about nine used to call at my cousins. I saw her there. I do not remember whether she was pretty or not. But her image is still alive in my head: it is dear to me, I cannot say why. Once I remember I ran into the room; she was there, playing dolls with her cousin: my heart fluttered in me, my legs gave way. At that time I had no idea of anything; however, it was a strong passion, even though childish; it was love: I have not loved so since then. Oh! this minute of the first awakening of passions will torment my mind to my dying day! And so early . . . I was mocked and teased, for they noticed excitement in my face: I cried when no one saw me, for no reason at all; I wished to meet her, but, whenever she appeared, I did not want to or was ashamed to enter the room. I did not want to speak about her and would run away when I heard her name (I have forgotten it now), as if afraid that the beating of my heart and my trembling voice might explain to others the secret I did not understand myself. I do not know who she was or where she was from: I would not dare to ask about it even now: they too may ask me why I remember, though they have forgotten; or these people listening to my story may think that I am raving; they will not believe that she existed, and this will hurt me. Fair hair; blue eyes so quick; natural grace—no: I have never seen anything like this since then, or it only seems so to me, because I have never loved as I loved then. The Caucasian mountains are sacred to me. . . . And so early! At ten years of age! Oh, this riddle, this paradise lost will torment my mind to my dying day! Sometimes I wonder at it, and I am ready to laugh at this passion! But more often I feel like crying. Byron says that an early passion means a soul that will like fine arts. I think that there is a great lot of music in such a soul.

This is a touching passage, but its wording is embarrassingly close to that of a corresponding entry in Byron's journal, as given by Thomas Moore (see No. 7 and note).

More on Lermontov's love for the Caucasus will be said in notes on Nos. 52, 90, 91, and others.

Commentary

The song mentioned in line 8 is like many others in Lermontov's works. See especially No. 12 and note on No. 89. "The Caucasus" was first published in 1845, the hymn in 1859.

5. *A Hebrew Melody*

As is the case with many of Lermontov's early lyrics, this "Hebrew Melody" owes much to Byron (see Nos. 7 and 18 and the notes in the Commentary). Among Byron's *Hebrew Melodies* none resembles it rhythmically, but "Sun of the Sleepless" is rather close to Lermontov's poem thematically.

In 1836 Lermontov translated into Russian Byron's Hebrew Melody "My Soul is Dark." The translation is not accurate, but it is one of his best lyrics.

This "Hebrew Melody" was first published in 1844.

6. *An Epitaph*

This poem, strongly reminiscent of Byron's epitaphs, is probably dedicated to the memory of Dmítry Vladímirovich Venevítinov (1805-1827), even though Lermontov wrote his epitaph in 1830. (The first posthumous volume of Venevitinov's poems was published in 1829, and Alexander Odóevsky, the hero of Lermontov's No. 53, also wrote Venevitinov's epitaph in 1830. Both Lermontov and Odoevsky must have been inspired by this edition.) Venevitinov was endowed by nature with every conceivable talent. A master of many classical and modern languages, a painter and musician, a clever literary critic, a journalist, a man of rare personal charm, he was an outstanding lyric poet. Today, his poems, almost all of them four-foot iambics, seem to belong largely to the pre-Pushkin era, but even now an occasional line comes to the reader in all its tenderness and haunting beauty.

Venevitinov had strong Decembrist sympathies and, at least prior to 1825, a great love for Schelling (whose philosophy did not interest Pushkin but played an important role in the development of Lermontov). He was the life and soul of a Moscow philosophical circle, which, like all circles, clubs, and "clandestine societies," was disbanded after December 14. Late in 1826 Venevitinov moved to St. Petersburg. His traveling companion was a Frenchman who had just returned from Siberia: the man had accompanied Ekaterína Trubetskáya to the Nérchinsk mines (Trubetskaya was the first of the Decembrists' wives to share her husband's exile). Immediately upon their arrival in St. Petersburg, both were arrested. No direct allegations were made against Venevitinov, and after several days in custody he was released. At the interrogation he behaved admirably and declared that, though he had not belonged to any of the Decembrists' societies, he could have done so, as he sympathized with the views of the rebels. The arrest seems to have crushed the sensitive and delicate youth. He withdrew into himself entirely. All his last poems are about death, and he died four months later. The immediate cause of his death had nothing to do with police persecutions: he caught cold after a party, while running across the yard to his apartment. But Venevitinov had been coughing ever since the day of the arrest and must have lost all power of resistance. Thus too did Delvig die at thirty of a disease that acquired catastrophic forms after a confrontation with the Chef des Gendarmes Count Benckendorff (the Chief of the Third Section).

The death of Venevitinov at the age of twenty-two made a strong impression on his friends ("How could you allow him to die!" exclaimed Pushkin). For forty years they observed the anniversary of this event (they met for a special dinner, leaving a complete dinner service for "the departed friend") and thus instituted a cult of the young poet. The custom came to a natural end when the circle of worshippers became too narrow.

The second line of Lermontov's epitaph is a borrowing from Venevitinov's poem "The Poet and His Friend":

Nature does not disclose its mysteries to all. We all read it, but who understands it? Only he who from his youth was passionately devoted to art, *who did not spare his life for feelings*, who bought his wreath by sufferings, rose in spirit over the hustle of everyday life and, listening avidly, caught the trembling of his heart as if it were a divine voice.

When Pushkin remarks in *Evgeny Onegin* (I: 7, 1) that his hero knew nothing of the passion "not to spare his life for sounds" and therefore could not learn the difference between iamb and trochee, he is paraphrasing the same line. Pushkin and Venevitinov were friends and distant relatives. If Lermontov's poem is about Venevitinov and not just an ironic autoepitaph, the reference to omens (in the original: "he believed in obscure prophecies and talismans, and love"), may allude to the romance between Venevitinov and Countess Zinaída Volkónskaya. When the young poet left Moscow for St. Petersburg, she gave him her signet, originally found at the excavations of Herculaneum. He never parted with it and wrote several poems about the magic ring. He said that he would put it on either before his wedding or on his deathbed and would like to carry it to his grave. Three hours before his death his friend Alexéy Stepánovich Khomyakóv (a well-known journalist and poet) put the ring on his finger. "Am I going to get married?" asked Venevitinov. "No," answered Khomyakov.

Pushkin also wrote a poem called "The Talisman" about the same signet.

Venevitinov was indeed a "simple-hearted son of freedom." He, as well as Khomyakov, participated in the circle of the *lyubomúdry* ("lovers of wisdom," a translation loan of the word *philosopher*, φιλοσοφος, in the plural), a Slavophile society that studied Schelling and debated the problems of Russia's development (see the note on No. 73). Venevitinov gave strong public support to Pushkin, and the two were planning a journal of their own. In St. Petersburg Venevitinov worked at the Ministry of Foreign Affairs (Office of Records) together with such highly intellectual peers as Vladímir Fyódorovich Odóevsky and S. P. Shevyryóv. The group was known as the Archive Youths, and Pushkin mentions it in *Evgeny Onegin* (VII:49, 1). Venevitinov's early death was a loss whose true significance is impossible to assess, for his genius would undoubtedly have placed him among the greatest Russian men of letters.

Many lines and images in Lermontov's early poetry seem to go back to Venevitinov. His "Epitaph" was first published in 1859.

7. To*
(After Reading Moore's Life of Byron)

Byron was the strongest literary influence of Lermontov's youth (cf. No. 18 and note). In Russia, Byron was treated almost as a demigod. This cult received strong reinforcement after the publication of Thomas Moore's *The Life, Letters and Journals of Lord Byron*. (As is well known, Moore was himself a romantic poet and his *Lalla Rookh* enjoyed as much popularity as any of Byron's Oriental poems. Moore was Byron's close friend and inherited his memoirs; later he destroyed them.) Although the facts of Byron's life had always been common property, in Moore's book the world saw for the first time how Byron the man and Byron the author were manifestations of one colossal individuality.

Like many Romantics, Lermontov existed in an atmosphere of constant interaction between literature and life. Everything that happened to him was immediately transmuted into poems and "psychological prose," i.e. novels and dramas. He compared himself with Byron in even the smallest details. He made Byron's life and works into a mirror that showed him his own reflection and feelings. Two entries from Lermontov's journals show his adoration of the English poet. Both date from 1830, the year the poem "To*" was written. (1) "When I began to scribble poems in 1828 (in the boarding-school), I, as if by instinct, copied them and put them in order; they are still with me. Now I have read in a life of Byron that he did the same; this similarity struck me." (2) "One more similarity between Byron's life and mine. An old woman prophesied to his mother in Scotland that he would be a great man and marry twice. My Grandmother's midwife prophesied the same about me. God grant it! I wish I were as unhappy as Byron." He may have been paraphrasing his own poem when he made Pechórin (*A Hero of Our Time*) say, "So many are those who, when they begin their lives, think that they will finish them like . . . Lord Byron but stay always petty clerks." See also the end of the entry given on p. 469.

Some of those who knew Lermontov misinterpreted his melancholy as a Byronic pose (see notes on Nos. 19, 55, 76). Byronism in Russia soon became a vogue, but this is the fate of every great movement (perhaps only great movements can thus spread and become vulgarized). That dozens of worthless youths and fourth-rate poets struck Byronic attitudes and composed rhymed platitudes cannot detract from either Byron's greatness or Lermontov's sincerity.

Though still imperfect, this early poem contains many features of Lermontov's style. Even the antithesis of the final lines recurs in a later poem (No. 41:1; in the original the similarity is much more patent). It was first published in 1859.

8. A Prophecy

This poem was published in 1862 (without the concluding two lines, which are awkward in the original; the first full edition dates back to 1883). It is often cited as an example of Lermontov's clairvoyance. He seems to have predicted his own death (cf. No. 81) and the future of Russia. But unlike "The Angel" (No. 12) and "A Prayer" (No. 37), this lyric lacks the main ingredient of Lermontov's "mystic" compositions, viz. the all-enveloping ternary meter and a special rocking rhythm. (Lermontov's earlier poems of this nature are all in blank verse.) "A

Commentary

Prophecy'' was probably inspired by the 1830 epidemic of cholera, which began on the Volga and soon reached Moscow, and the "cholera revolts." The expression *black year* was more idiomatic a century and a half ago than it seems today: in Lermontov's time it was used of the Pugachyóv uprising (the greatest peasants' uprising in the history of Russia: 1773-75). The prophecy closely reproduces the progress of the French Revolution, as Lermontov saw it, and the "man with a knife" could have been modeled on Napoleon. A long passage from the narrative poem *Sashka*, in which Sashka's tutor, a French expatriate, tells his pupil of the revolution, reads like a commentary on "A Prophecy," so alike are they in structure and approach.

In the Russian original the title is followed by a latter addition, *Èto mechtá*, "It is a dream." *Mechtá* means a dream in the sense of a longing for something. But when some modern editors assert on the evidence of these words that Lermontov dreamed of, i.e., wished for, a peasant revolution, they give a deliberate and well-calculated twist to the truth, because in Pushkin and Lermontov's language *mechtá* often meant 'vision,' and this is undoubtedly the meaning here. In another 1830 poem Lermontov tells his addressee (presumably, E. A. Sushkóva: see No. 9 and note) that soon he will be cursed by men; then she will remember his prophetic warning and exclaim, "Alas, those were not dreams!" (cf. also No. 11:10 and note).

9. The Beggar

"The Beggar" appeared in print in 1844, when Ekaterína Alexándrovna Sushkóva published twelve poems allegedly dedicated to her by Lermontov.

E. A. Sushkóva-Khvostóva knew Lermontov very well. She was two years older than he (just as Mary Ann Charwort was in 1802 two years older than fourteen-year-old Byron); when they first met in 1830, Lermontov was almost sixteen, and she, eighteen and fully aware of her charms. Lermontov spent four summers near Moscow, in Serednikóvo (cf. the title of No. 10), a beautiful estate that belonged to a family of his relatives and friends the Stolýpins. Sushkova was there too, and her English nickname was Miss Black Eyes. Lermontov was strongly attracted to her. Even in a later lyric (No. 20, 1832) the beautiful maiden is black-eyed and she remained such in the 1837 version (No. 33:5; in the original the girl is called black-eyed and the steed black-maned in the first stanza), that is, long after their dramatic rupture.

Sushkova enjoyed having a lovesick boy in her suite, flirted with him, and tormented him as best she could. Four years after the first summer in Serednikovo Lermontov took revenge on Sushkova: he feigned an affection for her and was graciously received. Sushkova, at that time twenty-two, had every reason to consider herself an old maid (the alarm eventually proved false), whereas Lermontov, an officer and the only heir of his very rich grandmother, was quite eligible as a prospective husband. However, even if Sushkova wanted to marry at all costs, it does not follow that she felt no love for the twenty-year-old Lermontov. When the romance (somewhat in the spirit of "Princess Mary") came to a head, Lermontov sent Sushkova an anonymous letter whose purpose was to make his true intentions clear.

In her middle age she wrote a book of memoirs, and one chapter there was about the first Serednikovo summer. The early stage of their relationships was represented by Sushkova herself and later by the Stolypins in such dissimilar ways and the subsequent events seemed so important to Sushkova that it is hard to judge from the existing sources how deep Lermontov's feeling was in 1830. In 1834, when he was busy turning her head (partly for old memories' sake, partly—that was his explanation—to prevent his good friend Alexéy Lopukhín from marrying Sushkova), he wrote in a letter, dated December 1834, "This woman is a bat whose wings brush against everything that comes her way," and even in one of his 1831 poems he said, "I do not love you," but other lyrics bear witness to his infatuation (in Serednikovo), hopes, and hurt pride.

In Sushkova's memoirs Lermontov is described as a ladykiller whose greatest ambition was to be received in great parlors and whose Muse was she, an unassailable beauty endowed with superior wit and a true understanding of poetry. Unfortunately, Lermontov did have a "shadow" side: The man who emerges from his poems as a thoughtful, educated boy, later a youth writhing under a hostile or simply indifferent look, and finally an extremely sensitive and vulnerable genius had darker aspects to his character, like Byron and like many other people of lesser stature. Thus, it was not difficult to write a caricature of Lermontov. Sushkova exaggerates her role in Lermontov's life (several poems, which she says were dedicated to her, were probably addressed to others), but,

Commentary

contrary to the opinion of some scholars, she does not entirely falsify Lermontov's image; she merely meddles with the chiaroscuro, i.e., she brings many things into relief that should have stayed in the background, and ignores or never notices others. The often cited episode that, according to Sushkova, resulted in the production of "The Beggar" has a genuine ring. She writes that one day a group of young people, including herself and Lermontov, went to the Trinity-Sergius Monastery (*Tróitsko-Sérgievskaya Lávra*, now in Zagórsk).

At the gate we met a blind beggar. In his withered, trembling hand he had a wooden cup, which he held out to us; we all put some small change into it. At the sound of the coins clinking there the poor man crossed himself and began to thank us, saying "God bless you, my good masters. Not long ago some fine folks came here, also young, but they wanted fun and filled my cup with pebbles."

(According to the Stolypins, Sushkova herself gave the old man pebbles! Seems unlikely.) Back at home Lermontov did not take any part in the preparation of the dinner,

he stood on his knees before a chair, and his pencil was quickly covering a scrap of gray paper; it seemed that he did not see us, did not hear our noise, when we were sitting down at table. . . . Having finished his writing, he jumped up, tossed his head, sat down on an empty chair beside me and handed me the poem that had come fresh from his pencil.

Then she gives the text of "The Beggar," almost exactly coinciding with the version known from other sources. Sushkova must have been the first critic of the new poem. Again, if we can trust her, she said, "Thank you, Monsieur Michel for your dedication, and let me congratulate you on how speedily you make the most trivial words into nice impromptus, but will you take some advice from me? Give more thought to your poems and work on them." Today this recommendation makes us wince. ("Very nice, my dear Mozart, but too many notes."—Just as many as necessary, Your Majesty.)

It is clearly a poem written by a very young man, especially the last stanza, but it already has the main features of Lermontov's mature works: the syntax perfectly fitting the content, a beautifully measured rhythm within a traditional meter, a violent antithesis, and a pathetic ending. Some later critics admired it very much, one of them even discussing it in an enthusiastic chapter called "The Rejected Masterpieces" (Lermontov never attempted to see "The Beggar" published).

10. *A Wish*

Lermontov's ancestors on his father's side were Scottish. They traced their origin to the Lermonts or Learmonths of Ercildoune. In the town hall of St. Andrews there are plates enumerating many Learmonths who served as Lords Provosts of the town between 1473 and 1607, though theirs is not an ancient Scottish clan. In the reign of James I, in Scotland's turbulent time, one of the Learmonths (Lermonts) left his home and ended up as an enlisted officer in the pay of the Poles. In 1613, when Bélaya, a small town near Smolénsk in central Russia, was wrested from the Poles, among the prisoners of war were about sixty Scottish and Irish mercenaries, one of them George Lermont. The usual Russian correspondence of George is Yury (Yuriy), a name that stayed in the family. All the foreigners who surrendered at Belaya went over to the Tsar, and George Lermont's aristocratic origin was recognized by the Russians. Later he fought in many wars on the Tsar's side; he perished in 1633. His descendants added -ov to the surname, which was spelled Lermantov. They became completely assimilated but never forgot their glorious past or the participation of their eleventh-century ancestor in the fight of Duncan against Macbeth. They could also take pride in Thomas the Rhymer, the legendary singer, who was called Thomas Lermont (he is the hero of several of Walter Scott's ballads; see below).

The Russian Lermontovs attained neither distinction nor prosperity, but to young Mikhaíl Yúryevich, his father's ancestry was a matter of great importance. Lermontov's grandmother despised her son-in-law, but the boy loved both. He did not try to disentangle his enmeshed loyalties and was deeply grieved when in October 1831 his father died of consumption. The poem he wrote about this event is bitter. Lermontov's mother belonged (on both sides) to the most notable aristocratic families in Russia, and Yúry Petróvich Lermontov was looked down upon by his wife's relatives, so the boy was happy to learn that his father's family was at least equally famous. He found mentions of Duke Lerma in Schiller (*Don Carlos*) and Lesage (*Gil Blas*) and began to sign his poems Lerma. A portrait he painted of the Duke made the Spanish aristocrat look somewhat like himself. He even wrote a letter to the Spanish Academy of Sciences inquiring about Lerma's descendants. He certainly knew Walter Scott's ballads of the Smallholme Baron and of

Thomas the Rhymer: both had been translated into Russian, and he could have read them in the original, for in 1831 his English was quite good. As we know from Lermontov's dating, "A Wish" was written on July 29, 1831, but as early as 1830 in a small poem entitled "Ossian's Tomb," he says that his dormant spirit is flying to this tomb to get a second lease on life from it and to breathe the native wind: "Under the curtain of the mist, under the sky of tempests, amid heaths, stands the tomb of Ossian in the mountains of my Scotland."

A better reading of "A Wish" probably would combine two short lines into one, e.g., "Why was I not born like a bird of the air, like the hawk that is vanishing there? / Why can I not soar over forest and sea and forever be happy and free?" Then, instead of the four-foot amphibrach alternating with the three-foot anapest, we would have the even seven-foot amphibrach with inner rhymes (cf. No. 5).

The poem was first published in 1859.

11. The Cup of Life

Precocity is perhaps the most noticeable feature in young Lermontov. "Young" is a relative concept when applied to a man who lived twenty-six years; in Lermontov's biography it covers the period roughly up to 1835-36. Lermontov never wrote poems resembling those of other youths between fourteen and eighteen. "The Cup of Life" is practically perfect, and nothing is childish in either its allegorical content, beautiful alliterations, or frightening rhythm.

In Lermontov's early works allegories are not uncommon, and, formally, they are simply extended verbal metaphors. Later, allegories become very rare in his lyrics, so that No. 62 (1840 or 1841) is quite an exception. The image of the cup of life was common in the thirties.

The word *dream* (mechtá) in line 11 means 'illusion'; cf. note on No. 8. The poem was first published in 1859.

12. The Angel

Written in 1831, "The Angel" opened editions of Lermontov's *Complete Works* for decades. Like "The Mermaid" (No. 26), it strikes one of the main notes in Lermontov's lyric heritage. The motif of someone coming from afar and trying to remember the music of the previous existence is salient in Lermontov's "folklore" (cf. No. 55 and the passage from *Aoul Bestundjí* quoted in the note on No. 38). His hero carries the curse of looking back at the past, which he not so much recalls as recreates. This past is so distant that it has become almost meaningless, but it is always with him and he clings desperately to it.

A poem like "The Angel" can be read as an allegory, as a symbol, or as evidence of mystic experience. After all, we are dealing with a system of images, not with a religious treatise. The images occurring in "The Angel" are persistent in Lermontov. In a later poem (*Sashka*) he looks at a fiery chain of stars, and it seems to him that there is a pathway between them and the earth that the soul has measured long before; the pathway must have been measured by the soul when the angel was carrying it in his embrace. Even in a work of prose (*A Hero of Our Time*) he says, "When we go away from society with all its conditions and get closer to nature, we turn into children: the soul drops all that we acquired and again becomes as it was at one time and will perhaps be again." Lermontov's early narrative poem *The Angel of Death, The Demon* (No. 92), and Mtsyri's picturesque simile (No. 91:313 ff.) show how real angels were to him.

Lermontov's religious feeling was unlike that of other Russian poets: some felt happy within the framework of Orthodoxy; others recognized the world inhabited by immortal souls as something rational; still others wished to become part of it, but Lermontov seems to have actually perceived that world, to have touched it in his mystic experience. He realized that it would not open to anyone without death and was not afraid to die. But he loved life, and his love of life combined with a longing for an experience after death was the source of his spiritual tragedy (cf. No. 91:128 ff.). True, we know nothing about the religion of Lermontov the man, and it is always dangerous (and wrong) to equate the poet with the private individual. Moreover, Lermontov the man is interesting to us only because he was a great poet; his mystic experience, just as his historical and political views, are valuable to posterity insofar as they are expressed in beautiful lines.

Lermontov is especially vulnerable to rationalistic criticism. He has been praised for his liberal politics, as though he were a journalist, and scolded for his religion, as though he were a doctor of divinity. It is a curious fact that Belinsky, who always supported Lermontov, wrote a cool review of "The Angel." His remark was vague: he said that the reader might have expected more from a poet like Lermontov; he certainly disapproved of the poem's message. (Belinsky's attitude may have

Commentary

been the reason why Lermontov did not include "The Angel" in his 1840 book.)

Lermontov used to recall a song that made him cry at the age of three; it was his mother's song. Like the soul in his lyric, Lermontov tried to remember some distant music, the music that sounded in his heart and broke though every noise of his life.

The poem was published in 1839 in a provincial almanac (in Odessa), and at least thirty composers have written music for it.

13. "I Do Not Love You; I Have Shed"

The words *I do not love you* are rare in Lermontov's works (as they are in general rare in lyric poetry), but in 1831 he wrote a poem to E. A. Sushkóva containing such a hemistich. Otherwise, Lermontov would say something like this only when he looked at a woman whom he could not truly admire, because another woman's image had eclipsed the face he saw (cf. No. 84).

Sushkova, who in 1844 published this poem among several others from her album, claimed that it had been dedicated to her. Later Lermontov wrote another version of the same poem (No. 36), and it is not clear whether the addressee is the same. Lermontov always had his favorite formulas at hand and often rededicated his lines. In No. 13 the strong antithesis and the structure of the concluding two lines are entirely formulaic within Lermontov's poetic system.

14. The Cross on the Rock

M-lle Souchkoff is either E. A. Sushkóva (Khvostóva), the addressee of No. 9, or her cousin E. P. Sushkova ("Dodó"), the future Countess Rostopchiná (see No. 76 and note). The date of the poem is unknown, but it must have been written between 1830 and 1832. The poem sounds like a synopsis of many of Lermontov's later works. As in No. 10, the hero wishes to cast off his human form, and his desire to merge with the universe is akin to his longing for life in death; cf. Nos. 85 and 90:254-55. Lermontov's two main moods, one that incited him to write his iconoclastic, riotous poems and the other so touchingly expressed in Nos. 35 and 51, are both here. He craved infinite heights upon which he would cry and pray and, like *Mtsyri* (91:233-34), become one with a storm, as though a storm could bring him peace (cf. No. 28:9 ff.).

480

Lines 5-6 are even more reminiscent of Pushkin's "Imitations of the Koran" than "Three Palms" (see No. 50 and note).

The poem was made known to editors only in 1870 and first published in 1889.

15. Earth and Heaven

The antithesis of earth and heaven is central in Romanticism (notably so in Byron) and in Lermontov's work, and this early poem contains all the questions and themes to which Lermontov returned for the remaining ten years of his life. His heaven is vague; beautiful sounds reach us from it (cf. No. 12), it sends light to the world of men, but it is far and empty: it bores the Demon and the hero of No. 74. Actually, Lermontov's paradise does not even have to be in heaven: on the bottom of the river, existence is equally attractive and nebulous (cf. No. 26). In Lermontov's poems absolute bliss is attainable only in some special intermediate sphere, in a fairy-tale world, which is both like and unlike our earth and "the other world." His hero is torn by the greatest paradox of being: while we are alive, absolute happiness is beyond our reach, but what comes after death? The youth in "The Mermaid" (No. 26) is dead and still handsome but unable to enjoy love or anything at all. Perhaps for this reason Lermontov's hero yearns to be a raven (No. 10) or even a wave (No. 27), i.e., to be alive, though not as human beings are. Yet, not a single poem by Lermontov has death represented as a desirable end. His hero rather tries to reconcile life and death, soul and body, earth and heaven. Sometimes he envies the heights above and wishes he were a cloud (No. 14) or a star ("Heaven and Stars," 1831), sometimes he is more drawn to earthly existence (as in this poem). The first attitude is naturally expressed in more emotional, the second in more rationalistic verses. He *feels* that his place is far from here (cf. No. 14) but *knows* only what is near, and this earth, of which he is destined to be a part, lays as strong a claim on his soul as the glitter of the remotest star.

The poem was published in 1889.

16. To*

The addressee of this poem is a mystery. Apart from Adam Mickiewicz, who does not seem a very good candidate, two poets have been suggested: Pushkin and Polezháev. Pushkin's attitude toward monarchy and the Tsar was not consistent: he wrote passionate odes to liberty, epigrams on the Tsar and his surroundings, and greetings to the Decembrists in Siberia; but he also loved great dignitaries, if they were his friends, and castigated the "rabble" (whatever the meaning of the word). He glorified Peter I and sympathized with his victims. His flexible mind allowed him to see many points of view. In 1831 he published a poem, "To a Grandee," and his opponents accused him of sycophancy. Earlier, "Stanzas," in which he expressed his faith in Nicholas, shocked even his best friends. At another time he extolled Paskévich for quelling the Poles. Probably in 1835 Lermontov, too, wrote stanzas glorifying the Russian crown (No. 29). In this obscure ode he mentions a poet who, after a long period of silence and inactivity, condemned Russia's detractors. Many words and expressions in "When Tyrants Sin, Why Make a Plea" look like deliberate borrowings from Pushkin.

Another possible addressee is the poet Alexánd(e)r Ivánovich Polezháev (? 1804-1838). A former student of Moscow University, Polezhaev was sucked in by the vortex of reprisals that followed the Decembrists' revolt. The five leading Decembrists were hanged on July 13, 1826. And on July 28, Polezhaev was brought to the Kremlin, where Nicholas himself, who had come to Moscow for his coronation, wanted to see the young man. The Tsar, in the presence of the Minister of Education and the Rector of the University, showed Polezhaev a clean copy of the poem *Sashka* and enquired whether he was its author. When Polezhaev answered "yes," the Tsar ordered him to read it aloud. Hertzen wrote about this episode:

Polezhaev was so excited that he could not read. Nicholas transfixed him with his immovable glance. —I can't,—said Polezhaev. —Read,— shouted the supreme sergeant. This shout gave Polezhaev new strength, and he opened the notebook. At first, it was all he could do to read, but then, feeling more and more animation, he finished the reading in a lively way and loudly. —What will you say?— asked Nicholas when the reading was over. —I'll put an end to this depravity; these are still traces, the last relics. I'll eradicate them.

By depravity the conservatives meant freethinking (in Lermontov's poem the first line, if translated word for word, reads thus, "Oh, do not excuse depravity!"), and the radicals identified depravity with corruption.

Sashka, a 572-line scurrilous poem written in 1825-26, was very popular in Moscow. Although it contained numerous thrusts at religion and priests and several bold political passages, it would hardly have attracted the attention of the Tsar, but for a denunciation of the entire University written by a police colonel; in the denunciation *Sashka* was cited as the freshest and most flagrant example of "depravity." (The same Colonel I. P. Bíbikov later patronized Polezhaev, and Polezhaev fell in love with his daughter; he was of course unaware of the colonel's career). Nicholas had the poet conscripted into an infantry regiment as a noncommissioned officer.

Polezhaev, the illegitimate son of a Pénza landlord and a serf woman, did not enjoy any privileges of the aristocrats. *Sashka*, an autobiographical poem, was composed as a literary parody of Chapter I of Pushkin's *Evgeny Onegin*. Polezhaev graduated in the summer of 1826, one month before the catastrophe. In 1827 he deserted from his regiment (which was stationed in and near Moscow) but soon came back. He was court-martialed, demoted, and continued his service as a private. Nicholas, who was informed of the incident, added the fatal words "without further promotion" to the verdict. In May 1828 Polezhaev was again court-martialed, this time for a breach of discipline, and during the preliminary trial was kept in a damp basement in handcuffs and fetters. In December he was pardoned and sent to another regiment. His new regiment took an active part in the Caucasian war, and Polezhaev spent the years between 1829 and 1833 in northern Caucasus. In 1831, despite the earlier verdict, he was promoted to the rank of an NCO. His two long Caucasian poems *Èrpelí* and *Chir-Urt* were published in 1832.

In 1833 Polezhaev's regiment returned to Russia. Life held no promise for him: he began to drink, and consumption had probably been smoldering in him since 1828. On September 25, 1837, shortly after a severe corporal punishment, he was hospitalized. On December 27, by the Tsar's order, he was promoted from an NCO to a cadet's rank. At that time he already lay in agony. On January 13, 1838 he was moved to an officers' ward and died three days later.

Polezhaev described the Caucasus in very unromantic words. Lermontov, even when he reached the heights of *Valerík* (No. 90) and *A Hero of Our Time*, retained his admiration for the grand scenery of the mountains and for the whole magnificent and awe-inspiring landscape (but of course Lermontov never served as a private!). For Polezhaev the Caucasus was only a dangerous and thoroughly repellent country. His heart went out to the victims of the war, but he extolled Russian generals and had no doubts that the cause of the war was the mountaineers' unwillingness to recognize the legitimate power of the Russian Tsar (of

Commentary

the two poems *Chir-Urt* is especially imbued with this spirit). Polezhaev's
point of view was the most common at the time. With some occasional
reservations it passed into all modern Soviet history books; one can read
there that Peter was justified in wresting the northern territories from
the Swedes because Russia needed the Baltic Sea for the development
of her commerce (both Pushkin and Belinsky thought so too), and that
Russia was obliged to annex the Caucasus, for otherwise England, Per-
sia, or Turkey would have done it. (The latter possibility was alleged
to be a greater evil, either because Persia and Turkey were Muslim coun-
tries, while Georgia was Christian, or—and this is the newest
interpretation—because Russia was at a higher level of cultural develop-
ment than those two, having a revolutionary proletariat that in less than
a century would take over and liberate the downtrodden masses of the
Caucasian population.) Even the Decembrists, who also served as soldiers
in the Caucasian wars, seem to have recognized the legitimacy of Russia's
claims—only they would have liked to see a peaceful, bloodless con-
quest. Pushkin vacillated between the two extremes.

Polezhaev meant a great deal to Lermontov and his generation. He
was a symbol of the political sufferer; he was also the first Russian poet
to place the image of a demon (already introduced by Pushkin: see note
on No. 93) in the center of his spiritual world. Like Lermontov, he was
fatalistic and prone to predicting his grim end (with much better reason
than Lermontov). Whether Lermontov owed something to Polezhaev or
whether they were kindred souls brought up in the same Byronic school
need not concern us here. Polezhaev's fate was known to Lermontov,
and if the poem refers to him it could not have been written before the
close of 1832, the year *Èrpeli* and *Chir-Urt* were published. (If the ad-
dressee is Pushkin, the date must be ca. 1830.)

Both hypotheses may be wrong, for the poem may have had no par-
ticular person in view (cf. No. 67 and note), or it may have been a varia-
tion on a theme by another author. If a choice must be made between
Pushkin and Polezhaev, we will perhaps prefer Polezhaev. But would
anyone who was free and well-off have accused a prisoner in Polezhaev's
position of apostasy, for such a mild offense as a display of official
patriotism? Nor is it really true that Polezhaev glorified the Tsar, even
though he called the mountaineers wild savages and rebels. He had many
good words for Yermólov (see note on No. 80) and especially for his
own benefactor General Alexéy Aleksándrovich Velyamínov
(1788-1838), and at the beginning of *Chir-Urt* he says, "Thus, destroyed

for life, I am eager, by my last blood for my homeland, to wash off my stain! Oh, if long ago it had disappeared with a trace of reproach! . . . I will not betray my Tsar and duty; I follow honor everywhere and will make my way to the star I have lost. . . .'' In *Èrpeli* he also declares that he is "blunting his pen of his own free will without base flattery or embellishments.'' But even broken by fate, Polezhaev remained loyal to his convictions: he refused to add a request for pardon to his poem "A Secret Voice,'' and such a stern man as Hertzen wrote about Polezhaev, "he could not become a police poet and sing Nicholas's virtues.'' If Polezhaev, like many of his fellow-sufferers, had indeed tried to purchase his freedom with a few patriotic lines, everyone would have understood and forgiven him. According to the *Lermontovskaya Èntsiklopediya* (p. 207), he could not have been the addressee of Lermontov's lyric, but this statement is too strong.

The hypothesis that Lermontov's narrative poem *Izmaíl-Bey* was written in direct opposition to Polezhaev does not carry conviction, but later he wrote his own *Sashka* ("Sashka" is a familiar diminutive of Alexander; cf. 53:26). It has nothing to do with Polezhaev, though it contains a reference to the latter's poem.

"When Tyrants Sin, Why Make a Plea" is preserved in Lermontov's notebook known today as Notebook 20; it was first published in 1888.

17. To*

This poem is one of many dedicated to the main heroine of Lermontov's youthful lyrics. The title of some of them is simply "To*," of others "To N. F. I." It is now believed that N. F. I. is Natálya Fyódorovna Ivánova (1813-1875), a daughter of the playwright Fyódor Fyódorovich Ivánov (1777-1816). In all probability, N. F. I. never considered Lermontov as a serious suitor, and Lermontov was hurt by this unsuccessful romance more deeply than by any other rebuff before or after.

Lermontov and Ivanova must have met early in 1830, but in the spring and summer of 1830 Lermontov was in love with Sushkova, so the new romance hardly started before the autumn. Ivanova's father (long dead by that time) had been a friend of A. F. Merzlyakóv, who was one of Lermontov's teachers at the boarding-school and, still earlier, one of his home tutors invited by Arsényeva. If N. F. I. is indeed Ivanova, Merzlyakov could have introduced Lermontov to her. Even the first poems addressed to N. F. I. presage a catastrophe. The woman of his

Commentary

choice (according to Lermontov's sad account) looked at the poet with her clear, pure eyes in utter bewilderment, shook her head, and said that his mind, blinded by a foolish desire, was sick. Their meetings did not last long. In a letter to a friend (June 7, 1831) Lermontov mentioned his pitiful state, constant tears, and grave troubles. It seems that some painful explanation took place at the end of May. That same summer Lermontov wrote a play *A Strange Man*. Its central characters are Vladímir Pávlovich Arbénin (evidently, Lermontov himself) and Natálya Fyódorovna (!) Zagórskina. In the preface he wrote, "All my dramatis personae have prototypes, and I would like them to be recognized; then repentance will perhaps visit the souls of those people." The play depicts Zagorskina preferring Arbenin's friend Belinsky to Arbenin. However, Ivanova did not marry until 1833, so her husband could not have been Belinsky's prototype.

The poems of the N. F. I. cycle are sincere and bitter. Seven months after the rupture, Lermontov wrote a rather inefficient New Year epigram to N. F. I. full of mocking (no longer decipherable) allusions to "spurs, uniform, and moustache." "I Will Not Humbly Beg Your Favor" is a parting letter to N. F. I. It bears no initials at the beginning, but its addressee can be reconstructed. In this case there is no doubt who is meant, but other poems are less transparent, for in 1830-32 Lermontov wrote many lyrics, and it is often a matter of speculation which of the several women whose existence is known to us is the addressee of a particular lyric.

The identity of N. F. I. is one of the most belabored subjects in Lermontov scholarship. Several of Lermontov's biographers, as early as 1910 and 1914-15, hypothesized that N. F. I. was Ivanova. In 1935 an article by Eikhenbaum supported this view. Irákly Andrónikov, at that time Eikhenbaum's student, also published an essay devoted to N. F. I. (1936). Later Andronikov brought out a great number of semi-detective stories and books about "the riddle of N. F. I." The names of his predecessors, including Eikhenbaum who at that time was persecuted as a "formalist"), disappeared from the pages of his post-1936 works, and to millions of people in the Soviet Union Andronikov (a popular writer, amateur actor, and television personality) is known as the only pathfinder. He could as well have deciphered the initials of Mr. W. H. Specialists have always known Andronikov's modest role in this search; besides, his main "witness," allegedly N. F. I.'s granddaughter, is suspect.

Commentary

"I Will Not Humbly Beg Your Favor," the best love lyric written by Lermontov before 1832, was first published in 1859 in a slightly abridged form. The complete text appeared in 1889.

18. *"No: I Am Not Byron, Though I and He"*

As mentioned in the note on No. 7, Byron was the central figure in young Lermontov's spiritual world. Schiller also played a part in his development (cf. note on No. 25), but Byron was worshipped and imitated like no one else. Lermontov knew the English poet in the original and read him in Russian translations, adaptations, and retellings by Zhukóvsky and Kozlóv. In addition, Byron often reached Lermontov as a refracted ray, through Pushkin's Caucasian poems and through the original Byronic poems by Zhukovsky, Ryléev, Kozlov, and Podolínsky. The influence of Byron's *Giaour*, etc. on Lermontov's narrative pieces, including even *Mtsýri* (No. 91), is patent. In lyrics it is difficult to point out borrowings (cf. note on No. 5), but there is great general similarity between the two poets, for the young Lermontov, like Byron, was fond of love lyrics based on meditation and introspection. The man standing behind those poems is a typical Byronic hero.

In Lermontov's early works one can easily find close textual convergencies with Schiller, Hugo, Mickiewicz, and many others, but, surprisingly, Lermontov sounds like none of them. The reason is that only Byron influenced Lermontov by his intonation, by his entire poetic system. It is true that Lermontov borrowed from Byron and his followers a taste for unnatural situations, frenetic types, and exotic settings, elements that are the least important in Byron. But Lermontov would not have become a great poet if he had merely "assimilated" Byron's sorrow and disappointment, if he had put on another man's clothes (as his contemporaries thought he had). The young Lermontov also learned from Byron something less tangible but much more durable—the latter's literary approach to the world.

Byron wrote about the most intimate events of his life with the confidence of someone who is accustomed to stand in the limelight. He never doubted that the world would follow his thoughts and adventures in rapt attention—and the world did. But if in England Byron achieved only notoriety, in the rest of Europe he enjoyed real fame. The cult of Byron was one of the greatest triumphs of nineteenth-century individualism, and this is what was crucially important to Lermontov.

Commentary

In official Russia Byron was a *persona non grata*, looked on as a godless man whose influence should be avoided at all costs. Nevertheless, everybody who could or cared to do so read him. As time went on and hopes for a bright future in Russia gave way to pessimism and gloom, the most important facet of Byron's heritage became his philosophical works. The young Pushkin was inspired by Byron's Oriental poems and by *Childe Harold*. Lermontov, too, was drawn to the Oriental poems (mainly because they acquired enormous popularity as a genre in Russia), but for him Byron became preeminently the author of *Manfred* and *Cain*. Contrary to Pushkin (born in 1799), Lermontov read the whole of Byron at once and could follow any thread of Byron's heritage in any order (for example, in 1830 he translated the beginning of Canto XVI from *Don Juan* and in 1836 paraphrased an extract from *Childe Harold*, though *Childe Harold* antedates *Don Juan* by many years), but the principal impulses that Lermontov received from Byron at each stage of his maturation are clearly discernible.

The first lines of "No: I Am Not Byron, Though I and He" are often treated almost as a manifesto of independence: allegedly, between No. 7 and No. 18, Lermontov realized that he had his own way and answered those who took him for a Russian replica of Byron. To see how wrong this interpretation is, one need only read the poem to the end. Lermontov remained Byron's admirer all his life. The rhetorical "no" in line 1 means just what it says: few can aspire to reach Byron's heights. It is possible that "no" also refers to Lermontov's fate, which is even more tragic than Byron's.

The poem was first published in 1845 and is one of the most popular Lermontov lyrics.

19. "To*"

The addressee of this poem is Varvára Alexándrovna Lopukhiná (1815-1851), the most durable attachment of Lermontov's life (she is the prototype of Vera in his prose works, including "Princess Mary"). Lermontov's relative Akím Pávlovich Shan-Giréy (1818-1883) wrote:

As a student, he was passionately in love, but not with Miss Black-eyes [E. A. Sushkóva; see No. 9 and note (the spelling is Shan-Girey's)] and not even with her cousin [E. P. Sushkóva; see Nos. 14 and 76 and notes] (may the shadow of the famous poetess be merciful to us for this piece of news!) but with V. A. Lopukhiná, young, charming, bright as the day and truly irresistible; hers was an inflammable nature, prone to exaltation, a nature poetic and very attractive. I still remember quite well her gentle look and radiant smile; she was about fifteen to sixteen years of age, while we were children and always teased her; she had a little black birthmark on her forehead, and we tormented her crying, "U Váren'ki ródinka, Váren'ka uródinka" ("Varen'ka has a birthmark, Varen'ka is a fright"), but she, kindness itself, never took offense. Lermontov's feeling for her was almost instinctive, but genuine and strong, and he seems to have preserved it to his dying day, despite some of his later infatuations; it could not (and did not) cast a dark shadow on his existence: on the contrary, at its inception it was reciprocal; in St. Petersburg, in the military school, it was temporarily suppressed by the new surroundings and the cadets' rackety life and after graduation also by new conquests in society and literature; but it at once and strongly came to life when he learned that his beloved had married; at that time the Byronic pose was quite gone.

Lermontov had known Varvara Alexandrovna and her family since 1827 or 1828, but the romance flared up in the autumn of 1831. No. 19 is still somewhat condescending: Varen'ka is not supposed to know what makes or made the poet unhappy, though her love is graciously received. In the summer of 1832 Lermontov left for St. Petersburg, much to the gratification of Varen'ka's parents, for Lermontov was considered feather-brained and unstable. All his poems following the parting are, in a way, like the first one: a superior youth, whose hopes and dreams should be carefully guarded from outsiders, is always ready to teach the less experienced one (Lermontov and Lopukhina identified very strongly with Onegin and Tatyana); he even hastens to say goodbye (No. 23), though sometimes attempts an excuse (No. 21). He predicted that Varen'ka would remember him all her life (and was quite right), but he could not guess that the dull freedom he was so proud of obtaining would become his curse. Shan-Girey mentions Lermontov's "later infatuations," and indeed those were many, but Varen'ka's image became part of him: his early lyrics, his prose, and *The Demon* (No. 92) would never have been what they are without it.

As early as 1832, Lermontov looked back with amazement at his feeling for Varen'ka (No. 24): though quite unlike N. F. I., she proved responsive and lovable. Lermontov could not write directly to Varvara Alexandrovna (that would have compromised her) and therefore addressed his numerous letters to Maríya Alexándrovna, her elder sister (a handicapped, solitary woman, of whom he must have been genuinely fond). However, in 1833 their correspondence flagged, and Lermontov's extant letters are nervous, even apologetic. At the beginning of 1834 Shan-

Commentary

Girey came to St. Petersburg and brought Lermontov Varen'ka's regards, "... tell him that I am at peace, contented, even happy."

I was much chagrined [continues Shan-Girey] that he seemed to take it coolly and did not ask any questions about her. I reproached him; he smiled and said, "You are still a child and do not understand anything." "And you may understand quite a lot, but you are not worth her little finger!" I responded, really angry.

In November 1835 Lermontov graduated from the military school and entered the St. Petersburg *beau monde*. He paid court to E. A. Sushkóva (see note on No. 9), turned her head, then backed out of the unsavory affair in cold blood. When at the beginning of January (1836) Lermontov's relations with Sushkova became known in Moscow, Varvara Alexandrovna agreed to the engagement with Nikoláy Fyódorovich Bakhmétev (1798-1884), a man seventeen years older than herself. In May they were wed.

Around June 20, 1838, Shan-Girey saw Varen'ka and her husband when they were going abroad. "Pale, thin, a ghost of her former self; only her eyes were as shiny and tender as before. . . . She survived him, languishing long, and passed away quietly, about ten years ago as I heard." Lermontov also was sent for, and this was their last meeting.

Lermontov dedicated *The Demon* (No. 92) to Varvara Alexandrovna, and "A Dead Man's Love" (No. 74) must have been written about himself. It is usually believed that *Valerík* (No. 90) is also addressed to her (see No. 90 and note; cf. also note on No. 67). No. 19 was first published in 1876.

20. A Wish

The second part of "A Wish" is informed with the same spirit as the much later "Debate" (No. 80) and gives a good example of how Lermontov was groping toward the impressionism that characterized his best lyrics. In the original the final five lines read, "Let the fountain unceasingly purl in a marble hall and put me to sleep and then awaken me in the dreams of Paradise, while besprinkling me with its cool dust." The antithesis (send to sleep - awaken) and treble feminine rhyme are more important to the poet than the logic of the narrative (who would fall asleep and have beautiful dreams if besprinkled all the time by cold water?). Characteristically enough, freedom for the hero is both wild adventure and absolute repose. Distant echoes of this mixed attitude toward life recur in many of Lermontov's works, even in *Valerík* (No. 90:252-55).

The poem was published in 1841 (posthumously).

21. To*

The heroine of this poem, as well as of No. 19, is very probably V. A. Lopukhiná. In 1832, torn between N. F. I. and Varen'ka, Lermontov wrote many such lyrics, and *en masse* they sound very repetitive. This poem is not better than the others, but it is included here for the sake of its unusual metrical scheme. Compare lines 7-8 with the conclusion of No. 25. ("sorrow defying consolation").

It was first published in 1876.

22. Two Giants

The poem sounds like a fairy tale in verse. The traditional discussion of whether the Russian giant is the Russian people or Tsar Alexander I seems rather pointless, for the poem is frankly allegorical; and independent of a particular author's views, the Russian language was full of such metonymies as "to die for the Tsar" (= to die for Russia: cf. No. 71:13), "the glory of the Russian crown" (= the glory of Russia: cf. No. 29:16, 21-22), and so on. The same expressions, with purely formal substitutions, have continued into the present.

A rather curious hypothesis exists that "a cap of precious metal" (in the original: a cap of solid gold) is not a crown at all but the top of the Moscow bell tower known as Ivan the Great (part of the Kremlin). The hypothesis is quite implausible. The giant of the poem is animated, and the idea that Lermontov means the Tsar (especially in light of No. 29) seems the most reasonable. The first line sets the tone for the whole ballad, and the poem insistently revolves around the notions "head" and "crown."

"Two Giants" was written at the beginning of September 1832 and could have been inspired by the erection of the Alexander Column (Pillar) in front of the Winter Palace (Lermontov had just come to St. Petersburg from Moscow and saw the ceremony). If there is a connection, the identification of the giant with Alexander is all the more natural. Also note the stanza blotted out by the author: "Each of them, with a proud, dark brow, was frightful (strong). But one was seething with malice, the other with contempt." It is hard to imagine a bell tower seething with contempt.

For a broader discussion of Lermontov's attitude toward Napoleon, see Nos. 30 and 60 and notes.

23. To*

It is hard to tell whether this is a dedication to N. F. I. (see No. 17 and note) or to V. A. Lopukhiná (see No. 19 and note). The dramatic tone of the lyric suggests N. F. I., but Lermontov wrote many similar letters. The motifs (the poet who will perish young, the woman who will remember him more in sorrow than in anger, the sounds that are meaningless but sacred), constant antithesis, and an unexpected finale, rather awkward here, are too typical of Lermontov to serve as a good means whereby to identify his addressees. In Lermontov's extant authorship, this is the first poem in which he speaks of sounds in a way closely resembling his celebrated later lyric (No. 59:1-4; see note). Its music is strikingly like that of Byron's "Stanzas to Augusta": ("Though the day of my destiny's over / And the star of my fate hath declined, / Thy soft heart refused to discover / The faults which so many could find.") But the story is all Lermontov's. The poem was published in 1896.

24. "Her Face Is Not the Face of Venus"

The woman in this poem must be V. A. Lopukhiná (see No. 19 and note). A description built on negations (her face is *not* like that of Venus, etc.), almost as in Shakespeare's Sonnet 130 (My mistress' eyes are nothing like the sun), is unusual in Lermontov. But this was the moment when two streams met in his heart: his love for N. F. I. (see No. 17 and note), with all its bitterness and humiliation, and a new feeling for Váren'ka, so he almost unwittingly compares the two. The conclusion of the poem is the first declaration of love for Varen'ka.

Lines 9-12 occur two more times in Lermontov's works: in No. 42:5-8 and in the description of Princess Tamára in *The Demon* (No. 92:155-57).

This poem was published in 1876.

25. A Reed

In his youth Lermontov often wrote ballads of the German type, mainly under the influence of Schiller. He also translated and adapted Schiller into Russian. "A Reed," though an original poem, belongs to this series.

The last two lines of the ballad are close in sentiment to No. 21:7-8.

"A Reed" was discovered and first published in 1875, and it was sometimes performed as a "folk song."

26. *The Mermaid*

Although written at the age of eighteen, it is one of Lermontov's most mature poems. All his life Lermontov was attracted to "intermediate stages" between life and death (cf. note on No. 15). A poet of antithesis and oxymoron, he, nevertheless, felt quite at home in twilight zones. The situation of "The Mermaid" is reproduced in Mtsyri's delirium (No. 91:674 ff.), where a goldfish courts an immovable youth.

Lermontov's mermaid is strangely unlike her folklore namesake, for she is not a seducer but a victim: she is full of love, but her love finds no response. In a much later ballad (No. 86) such a mermaid is cruelly dragged ashore and dies, whispering an inaudible reproach to the prince. Life and death change places even in those of Lermontov's ballads in which he is much closer to folklore than in "The Mermaid", e.g., in "The Terek's Gifts" (No. 52); there the Terek offers dead bodies to "Uncle Caspy" (i.e., the Caspian Sea), and Caspy enjoys these presents. In "The Mermaid" the dead knight almost becomes a symbol. Although this type of symbol is not unique in Lermontov's works (cf. No. 62), he preferred to endow *inanimate* objets with deep meaning (cf. No. 28).

The meter in "The Mermaid" is nearly the same as in No. 12, but the regular use of anacrusis (an unmetrical extra syllable at the beginning of the line) and alternation of short and long lines makes the texture of this poem especially fluid. The same motifs as in "The Mermaid" can be found in Lermontov's later works, but its rhythm is especially typical of his 1831-32 lyrics and ballads. In 1839 Lermontov introduced several insignificant changes into the poem and published it. The Russian text in this book is that of 1840.

27. *"What a Pity that the Maker"*

It may not be immediately obvious that this poem belongs to the same group as "The Mermaid" (No. 26). The two share the sense of detachment, of almost impersonal aloofness. Originally, it was part of the letter to M. A. Lopukhiná (see note on No. 19), written on August 28, 1832, one day after a small flood in St. Petersburg. In 1832, Lermontov returned to the theme "why am I not" several times (cf. No. 10), and

Commentary

the Rousseauian idea of No. 27 (i.e., merging with nature) recurs in many of his later works; the comparison between a human fate and the sea is also common.

The poem was published only in 1863, when some of Lermontov's letters to M. A. Lopukhina became available to editors for the first time.

28. The Sail

The poem was published posthumously, in 1841, and gained immense popularity, enhanced even more by Varlámov's song.

"The Sail" is one of those poetic miracles whose beauty depends on sound symbolism, specific alliterations, order of words, and other components of intonation. What can be salvaged in a foreign language (the general context, parallel constructions, meter and partly rhythm, images, and some sound sequences) does not go far enough. The English-speaking reader may be curious to know the other existing versions of "The Sail" and judge the level of poetic translation from the Russian. Some of these are given on pp. 495-500. My sources were: (1) Anna Heifetz, "Lermontov in English," *The Bulletin of The New York Public Library*. Astor, Lenox and Tilden Foundations, 1942, Vol. 46, pp. 775-90; (2) Richard C. Lewanski, *The Literatures of the World*, Vol. II: The Slavic Literatures. New York Public Library and F. Ungar, 1967. I have also consulted the references in one of the latest English books on Lermontov: Laurence Kelly, *Lermontov. Tragedy in the Caucasus*. London: Constable, 1977. I am aware of eighteen translations of "The Sail". Thirteen are reproduced below. Five could not be included for copyright reasons: "The Sailing Ship" by Frances Cornford and Esther Polianowsky Salaman (in *Poems from the Russian*. London: Faber and Faber Ltd., 1943, 34-35: "White on the blue, the sail has gone, / To vanish with the breeze," etc., alternating eight-, six-, eight-, and four-syllable lines in each stanza; masculine rhyme); "Lonely and far a White Sail Soars" by Bernard G. Guerney (in his *A Treasure of Russian Literature*. New York: The Vanguard Press, 1943, p. 109; masculine rhyme, with one exception); "A Sail" by C. M. Bowra (in *A Book of Russian Verse Translated into English by Various Hands and by C. M. Bowra*. London: Macmillan & Co. Ltd., 1947, 41-42: "A solitary sail that rises / White in the blue mist on the foam", etc.); "The Sail" by Vladimir Nabokov (in his *Pushkin. Lermontov. Tyutchev. Poems*. London: Lindsay Drummond Ltd., 1947, p. 45: "Amid the blue haze of

494

Commentary

the ocean / a sail is passing, white and frail," etc.; odd lines have feminine endings but do not rhyme); "The Sail" by Guy Daniels (in his *A Lermontov Reader*. New York: The Macmillan Company 1965, p. 74: "A lone sail makes a patch of whiteness / Against the blue mist on the sea", etc.; odd lines do not rhyme).

Literal Translation

A solitary sail is whitening
In the blue sea haze.
What does it seek in a distant land?
What did it leave in its native country?

The waves are playing, the wind is whistling,
And the mast is bending and creaking.
Alas! It does not seek happiness,
And it does not flee from happiness.

Under it, there is a stream more luminous than azure;
Above it, there is a golden ray.
But it, rebellious, seeks a storm,
As if in storms there were peace.

(1) The Sail

A solitary sail is gleaming,
  While, through the haze of th' azure, she,
In chase of chance's fortune seeming,
  Far from a cherished home may be.

The waves leap up,—the wind is blowing,
  The mast is bending low and creaks,—
Alas! from happiness not going,
  It is not happiness she seeks.

Beneath her prow blue floods are swelling,
  Above her glides the sunlit fleece,
But still she prays for storms, rebelling—
  As if in storms there can be peace.

(Tr. by Mrs. Heath, "Proceedings of the Anglo-Russian Literary Society," 1897, No. 19, p. 90.)

(2) The Sail

Within the sky's own mist of azure
  A sail is gleaming white and lone;
What seeks he in a distant country?
  What left he, think you, in his own?

The ripples dance, the breezes whistle,
  The mast, low bending, creaks and sighs.
Alas! not happiness pursuing,
  It is not happiness he flies!

Above him, sunlight—blue beneath him
  The sparkling waters curl and crease,
But he, rebellious, woos the tempest,
  As though in tempest found were peace!

(Tr. by Miss H. Frank, "Proceedings of the Anglo-Russian Literary Society," 1904, No. 39, pp. 136-37.)

(3) The Sail

A single sail is bleaching brightly
  Upon the waves caressing bland,
What seeks it in a stranger country?
  Why did it leave its native strand?
When winds pipe high, loud roar the billows
  And with a crashing bends the mast,
It does not shun its luckless fortune,
  Nor haste to port before the blast.
To-day the sea is clear as azure,
  The sun shines gaily, faint the wind—
But it revolting, looks for tempest,
  And dreams in storms its peace to find!

(Tr. by Martha Gilbert Bianchi [Dickinson], in her *Russian lyrics* . . . New York: Duffield and Co., 1916, p. 47.)

(4) The Sail

A lone white sail on the horizon
  Upon the azure sea doth stand.
What seeks he in this foreign region?
  What left he in his native land?

The whistling breeze the mast is bending,
  The playful waves around him rise.
Ah! not for happiness he searches,
  And not from happiness he flies.

The sun is bright as gold above him,
  Light spray below, a snowy fleece;
But he, rebellious, seeks the tempest,
  As though the storms could bring him peace!

(Tr. by Alice Stone Blackwell, "The Russian Review." New York, 1916, Vol. 1, No. 1, p. 33.)

Commentary

(5) The Voyage

Glitters a white, a lonely sail,
　Where stoops the grey mist o'er the sea.
What does this distant search avail?
　At home, unfound, what leaveth he?

Whistles the wind; the waves at play
　Sport round the bending creaking mast;
Ah! not *for* Fortune does he stray,
　Nor yet *from* Fortune flees he fast.

'Neath him, like sapphire, gleams the sea;
　O'er him, like gold, the sunlight glows;
But storms, rebellious, wooeth he,
　As if in storms he'd find repose.

(Tr. by John Pollen, in his *Russian Songs and
Lyrics* . . . London: East and West, Ltd., 1917, p.
24.)

(6) The Sail

A lonely sail is dimly whitening
Within the ocean's azure dome.
What does it seek on the horizon?
What has it left behind at home?

The glad waves play, the glad wind whistles,
The mast is bending like a tree. . . .
Alas, it does not seek for gladness,
And not from gladness does it flee.

The sea is brighter than light azure,
In golden light the sky is drest—
But it is asking for the tempest,
As if in tempest there is rest.

(Tr. by J. J. Robbins, in his *A Sheaf from Ler-
montov*. New York: Lieber & Lewis, 1923, p.
29.)

(7) A Sail

White is the sail and lonely
　On the misty infinite blue;
Flying from what in the homeland?
　Seeking for what in the new?

The waves romp, and the winds whistle,
　And the mast leans and creaks;
Alas! He flies not from fortune,
　And no good fortune he seeks.

Commentary

Beneath him the stream, luminous, azure,
Above him the sun's golden breast;
But he, a rebel, invites the storms,
As though in the storms were rest.

(Tr. by Max Eastman, *The Nation*. New York,
1925, vol. 121, No. 3130, p. 32.)

(8) A Sail

A far sail shimmers, white and lonely,
Through the blue haze above the foam.
What does it seek in foreign harbors?
What has it left behind at home?

The billows romp, and the wind whistles.
The rigging swings, the tall mast creaks.
Alas, it is not joy he flees from,
Nor is it happiness he seeks.

Below, the seas like blue light flowing,
Above, the sun's gold streams increase,
But it is storm the rebel asks for,
As though in storms were peace.

(Tr. by Babette Deutsch. Reproduced by permission of the publisher from Babette Deutsch and Avram Yarmolinsky, *Russian Poetry. An Anthology*. London: Martin Lawrence, 1927, p. 51.)
In later editions (e.g., in *A Treasury of Russian Verse*. Ed. Avram Yarmolinsky, New York: The Macmillan Co., 1949, pp. 88-89), line 10 was changed to: "Above, the sun shines without cease." Line 12: Later "storm."

(9) The Sail

A lonely ship recedes and paler
Appears on seas beflecked with foam.
What seeks the restless, hardy sailor
Renouncing comforts of the home?

While billows rise and winds assemble,
Though swaying masts bend o'er and creak,
Seamen below them never tremble,
But happiness in peril seek.

For such the tide is ever ready,
The sky is clear and bright as gold,
Only a storm-tossed ship unsteady
Can sate their zest for action bold.

Commentary

(Tr. by C. Fillingham Coxwell. Reproduced by permission of the publisher from Coxwell's *Russian Poems* . . . London: C. W. Daniel, 1929, pp. 132-33.)

(10) The Sail

O'er sapphire seas the white mist bleaches
A lonely sail upon the foam,
What seeks she in the distant reaches?
What leaves she in her native home?

The waves make frolic, winds are sighing,
The mast is bending while it creaks;
'Tis not from happiness she's flying—
Ah! 'tis not happiness she seeks!

Beneath, blue streams of light uphold her;
Above, sun's golden beams increase:
But wayward she bids storms enfold her,
As if in storms there may be peace.

(Tr. by Sir Cecil Kisch. Reproduced by permission of publisher and Mr. John Kisch from Sir Cecil Kisch's *The Wagon of Life and Other Lyrics by Russian Poets of the Nineteenth Century*. New York: Oxford University Press, 1947, p. 19.)

(11) A Sail

A lonely Sail afar is gleaming
Across the blue and misty sea:
What happiness, what region dreaming
Far, far from home, what destiny?

The winds cry loud; the mast is creaking
Against the flying waves at play,
No happiness the Sail is seeking—
No bliss at home, nor far away.

The sun shines gold, the sea is turning,
The sounding tide of azure glows.
Yet for a storm his wilder yearning,
As though a storm could bring repose.

(Tr. by Eugene M. Kayden. Reproduced by permission of the publisher from Kayden's *The Demon and Other Poems* . . . Yellow Springs, Ohio: The Antioch Press, 1965, p. 17.)

(12) The Sail

A lone white sail shows for an instant

Where gleams the sea, an azure streak.
What left it in its homeland distant?
In alien parts what does it seek?

The billows play, the mast bends, creaking,
The wind, impatient, moans and sighs . . .
It is not joy that it is seeking,
Nor is't from happiness it flies.

The blue waves dance, they dance and tremble,
The sun's bright rays caress the seas.
And yet for storm it begs, the rebel,
As if in storm lurked calm and peace!

(Tr. by Irina Zheleznóva. In *Mikhail Lermontov, Selected
Works* . . . Moscow: Progress Publishers, 1976, p. 26.)
Permission to reproduce granted by VAAP.

(13) The Sail

A sail lists white against the offing;
A sea mist shrouds it 'round with blue.
What hopes has it in distant mooring?
What fears has it of home, now rued?

Winds are whistling, billows welter;
Its mast bows low with groaning creak.
Away from joy, it craves no shelter,
And not for joy, it dares to seek.

Beneath it—glow of azure current;
Above it—beam of golden sun.
But it, a rebel, asks for torrent,
As if in storm its peace could come.

(Tr. by Hazel Hanley, 1981. Unpublished, by
the translator's permission.)

29. *"Again with Swollen Oratory . . ."*

This is perhaps the most unexpected poem in Lermontov's authorship.
Lermontov's patriotism was of a special kind (see No. 73 and note and
also note on No. 80). He could extol Russian courage in a great battle
(No. 30) or compose a fairy tale, actually a ballad, about 1812 (No.
22), but No. 29 is the only specimen of official smooth-spoken patriotism
from his pen. Its exact date cannot be ascertained, though it was ob-
viously written before "The Poet's Death" (No. 31). Indeed, A. P. Shan-
Giréy remembered that "not long before Pushkin's death, in connec-
tion with political seething in the West, Lermontov had written a piece

reminiscent of the well-known "To the Slanderers of Russia" (by Pushkin), but being, in a way, out of favor with the authorities, never wanted to publish it later, for a very understandable reason." Shan-Girey implies that Lermontov was afraid to be accused of sycophancy, but it is unthinkable that he could have felt too proud of such a poem after 1837. Svyatosláv Raévsky also knew the poem and in trying to save his friend from punishment (see Note on No. 31) quoted the last stanza in his "Explanation" to the police as an example of Lermontov's absolute loyalty, "He heard that some French journal had published slanders about His Majesty and in beautiful verses demonstrated Russian indignation against French immorality. . . . He seems to have written them in 1835."

The poem is evidently incomplete: something is missing in the middle, but there is no gap in the autograph (ellipses were inserted by the bewildered first editor). Shan-Girey was quite right in noticing the similarity between Lermontov's poem and Pushkin's diatribe. But the events that inspired Pushkin to write his lines in 1831 are easy to trace, whereas the immediate cause of Lermontov's outburst (the debates in the French Convent) is rather obscure and petty. The reference to some other poet in the first stanza (Pushkin?) is also obscure (see note on No. 16). Fabricius (Caius Fabricius Luscinus) was a Roman general and statesman (3rd c. B.C.) widely acclaimed for probity in public life.

Shan-Girey wrote his memoirs in 1860 and was not sure whether the poem had ever been published. As a matter of fact, an excerpt from it was published in 1854 and the full text in 1859. In 1860 it was included in Lermontov's *Complete Works* (an edition that Shan-Girey could not have seen).

30. Borodinó

Patriotic poems seldom sound very attractive in another language, and, to make matters worse, "Borodino" is exceptionally difficult to translate. The battle of Borodino was the greatest event in the campaigns of the victorious Napoleon. It is mostly known outside the Russian-speaking world through Tolstoy's description in *War and Peace*. The battle itself took place on August 26 (Old Style; September 7 according to the New style), 1812. Two days earlier (August 24) there was a confrontation at the Shevardinó redoubt. August 25 was spent in preparations on both sides. Stanzas 4 and 5 probably refer to the Shevardino events, stanzas 6 and 7 describe August 25 and the following night, and only beginning

Commentary

with stanza 8 are we shown the battle of Borodino proper. Stanza 3 contains a reference to the long retreat of the Russian army under Barclay de Tolly, the commander later replaced by Kutúzov. The position chosen on August 22 was on the right bank of the Kolochá river, between Dorónino and Shevardino, via the village of Borodino. The redoubt at Shevardino changed hands several times before the Russians retreated. The morning of August 26 began with Napoleon's attack on the fortifications near the Semyónov ravine (the so-called Semyonov flèches), and that is where Lermontov's soldier seems to have been. However, opinions differ as regards the episodes described in the poem, and whether the vantage point is the Semyónov flèches or Raévsky's battery is a matter of dispute.

Like all of Napoleon's major battles, this one was entirely dominated by artillery (which explains Lermontov's choice of an artillery man for the narrator). It cost over 100,000 casualties. Half of the Russian army was destroyed. But the outcome of the battle can hardly be summed up in a simple statement. Napoleon was the first to retreat when dusk fell, but he reported victory in his letters to France. The idea of victory was greatly reinforced when Kutuzov, contrary to popular expectations, decided not to confront the French with the remainder of his forces and preferred to save the soldiers rather than the ancient capital. A week after Borodino, Napoleon entered Moscow. However, the Russian army, though heavily battered, was not crushed, and Napoleon, who had seen so many triumphs, must have been aware of it, for he lost 58,478 men of about 130,000 (the Russians lost 42,238 of 131,548). Neither Kutuzov nor the army recognized defeat: everyone considered that the enemy had been repelled.

Lermontov's description is accurate and agrees quite well with contemporary documents. Many of his relatives took part in the campaign, and one of them was a prominent artillery man, so in his youth the poet must have heard many stories of the great day. Besides, in 1836-37, Lermontov could himself speak of military matters with some degree of expertise. "Borodino" was written in commemoration of the twenty-fifth anniversary of the battle. In 1830 or 1831 Lermontov wrote a shorter poem called "The Field of Borodino" (66 lines). Although full of bombastic expressions, this poem, too, was born of conversations with survivors, and as a result he could transfer several passages from it to the later work. Some sentences in "Borodino" that seem to be romantic clichés are not necessarily such. For instance, the battlefield really was

Commentary

covered with mountains of corpses, soldiers really fell from sheer exhaustion, and so on. To the reader the important aspect is not the absolute historicity of "Borodino," for it is a poem, a "ballad," not an eyewitness report or an article in an encyclopedia; what matters is Lermontov's method of presentation, and "Borodino," in spite of (or perhaps owing to) its somewhat formulaic mode of expression, is as precise and characteristic in its choice of detail as a Russian folk picture of the eighteenth and early nineteenth century.

In Lermontov's narrative two voices are interwoven: that of the veteran and that of the author. They differ stylistically (a difference more apparent in the original) but not formally, for the entire piece (l. 8 ff.) is an old soldier's tale. "Borodino" is the earliest work by Lermontov in which a soldier comes to the foreground (cf. Nos. 71 and 90). Moreover, this common soldier is the hero of the poem. Lermontov's predecessors (for example, Bulgárin, Bestúzhev-Marlínsky, Zagóskin) sometimes described partisans, but such descriptions were marginal and rare, and in all of them the central figure was an officer. Griboédov wanted to write a tragedy entitled *1812* and place a soldier in the center of it, but his draft remained unfinished. So Lermontov's veteran proved to be a novelty in 1837, and his tale, heartfelt and simple, was quite unlike the "anecdotes" that inundated the popular magazines of that time. Lermontov believed that a common man was quite able to form a correct opinion of history, that a soldier could be chosen as a spokesman for all veterans, even his whole generation. Pushkin (who, save for a brief 1828 visit to the Turkish front, did not see war at close quarters) described the battle at Poltáva from Peter's point of view; in spite of his rare historical instinct, his admiration for Rázin and Pugachyóv (the leaders of the greatest peasants' revolts in Russian history), and his knowledge of oral tradition, Pushkin would never have allowed a peasant or a soldier to be the mouthpiece of his ideas. Lermontov made an important step in the direction of Tolstoy, who, incidentally, considered *Borodino* the nucleus of his *War and Peace* (cf. note on No. 90).

"Borodino" was the first poem that Lermontov decided to publish under his name, and he sent it to Pushkin's magazine *Sovreménnik* ("The Contemporary"). Lermontov had not met Pushkin, and Pushkin may or may not have been aware of Lermontov's existence. Lermontov's narrative poem *Khadjí-Abrék* was published in 1835, and Pushkin owned the volume of Senkóvsky's *Bibliotéka dlya chténiya* ("Readers' Library") with this tale. There are no notes in the margin, and Pushkin's laudatory words about *Khadjí-Abrék* reported by Count A. V. Vasílyev are impossible of proof. In the present volume "Borodino" is given before "The Poet's Death" (No. 31), and this is the accepted order in all editions. However, the exact date of the poem is unknown, and it is not impossible (though unlikely) that "Borodino" is later than "The Poet's Death." In any case, Raévsky, in his attempt to shield Lermontov in the winter of 1837 (see note on No. 31), mentioned No. 29 (see note on it) but not "Borodino." Nor did Shan-Giréy remember that "Borodino" had existed before the day of Pushkin's death.

Belinsky in his discussion of "Borodino" made much of the old soldier's words in lines 8-10 (in the original, "Yes, there *were* men in our time, not like the tribe today; it is not you that are giants"). He wrote, "This thought is a reproach to the present generation dozing in apathy, in envy of the great past so full of glory and great deeds." But in "Borodino" this reproach is subdued, not more than hinted at. In a similar manner, the idea of fatalism that became very important in Lermontov's later works (cf. Nos. 54 and 90 and the last tale in *A Hero of Our Time*) is barely indicated in "Borodino" (ll. 13-14). After the army's performance at Borodino, the surrender of Moscow seemed incomprehensible to the veteran, understood only as God's will; this was general opinion in those days.

"Borodino" is the most popular Russian patriotic poem. It received a new lease on life in 1941 (which also happened to be the centennial of Lermontov's death), when the German army approached Moscow.

L. 24/28, 66/70: The repetition of the rhyme is as in the original.

31. The Poet's Death

This poem was a response to the death of Alexánd(e)r Sergéevich Pushkin (January 29, 1837) caused by a duel with Frenchman Georges Dantès (or D'Anthes). Pushkin was married to one of the beauties of his time, Natálya Nikoláevna Goncharóva, and Tsar Nicholas, who was far from indifferent to her charm, insisted on the Pushkins' presence at numerous balls and receptions. The poet's private life became a source of constant malicious gossip. Dantès, a foster-son of Baron van Heeckeren, the then Dutch Ambassador (Envoy), and from January 1837 Pushkin's brother-in-law, openly paid court to Natalya Nikolaevna. One day Pushkin received an insulting anonymous letter and sent a challenge to van Heeckeren (whom he considered the author of the letter) in a doomed attempt to defend his honor. The challenge was taken up by Dantès, and Pushkin received a mortal wound, to the obscene, undisguised glee of the palace clique, which had made his life a nightmare.

Lermontov wrote his poem, without the last sixteen lines, either after Pushkin's death or immediately after the duel, on January 28, for no one knew exactly what was going on at 12 Moika, where the poet was dying. According to Lermontov's friend Svyatosláv Raévsky, who copied and distributed the poem in St. Petersburg, the last lines appeared after a conversation between Lermontov and his relative Nikoláy Arkádyevich Stolýpin:

He (Stolypin) censured Pushkin, said that his behavior in high society had been indecorous, that Dantès had been forced to act the way he did. Lermontov and half of the guests tried to prove, among other things, that even foreigners should spare people distinguished in the country where they live, that Pushkin, in spite of his sharpness, had been spared by two monarchs and that his recalcitrance was not for us to judge.

The outcome of the debate, which took place a week after Pushkin's death, was the passionate finale of the poem.

It must have been more than Stolýpin's opinion that goaded Lermontov into a fury. In the early days of February both St. Petersburg and Moscow buzzed with gossip. Genteel talks in drawing-rooms represented the Russian school for scandal and shaped the attitude of the secret police and court; these talks were the main, practically the only, outlet for aristocratic public opinion. The rabble surrounding the throne, "the hungry, greedy pack" never missed a single detail of Pushkin's life and death. They accused Pushkin and his friends (among them even such well-known courtiers as Zhukóvsky, Vyázemsky, and Pletnyóv) of participating in a secret society, of which Pushkin had allegedly been the greatest inspiration. The grief of many thousand people who said farewell to the dead poet seemed to point in the same direction. Zhukovsky was made to examine Pushkin's extant manuscripts in the presence of a police general, for fear that he would steal some incriminating texts (a denunciation to this effect was sent to the Third Section). Dantès became the hero of several *salons*; for years after 1837 there were grandees who expressed their sympathy with him and defended him against "friends of depravity." During the week between Pushkin's death and the composition of the last sixteen lines Lermontov must have heard speeches like Stolypin's many times. What Stolypin perhaps made especially clear was the future fate of Dantès; he explained that there would be no trial of Pushkin's murderer. And he was right: Dantès was asked only to leave the country, not really for having killed Pushkin but for the duel itself—Nicholas was a severe enemy of duels. Our perception of the thirties and forties in Russia is colored by the deaths of Pushkin and Lermontov and the scenes from *Evgeny Onegin* and *A Hero of Our Time*. But duels were not allowed in the reign of Nicholas I and became prominent again much later, during the epoch described by Chekhov and Kuprín.

It is not known whether the epigraph was present in the poem from the beginning and how it acquired the form in which it exists today. Shan-Giréy and M. N. Lónginov (a literary historian, Lermontov's distant relative) state that it is a passage from A. A. Zhandr's unpublished tragedy *Venceslas*. Andrey Andreevich Zhandr (1789-1873) translated Jean Rotrou's tragedy *Venceslas* but it did not pass the censor, and only Act I and fragments from Act III were published. Alexánd(e)r Odóevsky, Griboédov, and Pushkin found the translation brilliant. However, there is enough evidence to show that Lermontov used Rotrou's original and not Zhandr's paraphrase, for Lermontov's lines do not occur in the published parts of the play, and it is unlikely that he should have had access to the suppressed acts (now lost). The lines in Rotrou corresponding to Lermontov's epigraph are as follows (Act IV, Sc. 5, 1647 version):

Prince et père à la fois, vengez-moi, vengez-vous,
Avec votre pitié mêlez votre courroux;
Et rendez aujourd'hui d'un juge inexorable
Une marque aux neveux à jamais mémorable.

The translation, as always in Lermontov's poetry, deviates from the original. For this reason I considered it necessary to translate the Russian text, rather than reproduce the French lines. (When Lermontov wanted an epigraph in French, he retained the original, cf. No. 49.)

There are two theories concerning the epigraph. According to one, Lermontov added the epigraph later, to protect himself against punishment. Presumably, a direct appeal to the monarch would have meant that the invective contained in the last lines was directed toward certain circles surrounding the throne, whereas the Tsar was exempt from guilt and was even in a position to punish the murderers. This reconstruction of events led to the elimination of the epigraph from most modern editions, but the latest (1980) academic edition of Lermontov again gives the epigraph in the text, not in the notes. According to the other theory, the epigraph belonged to the poem from the very beginning and was at that time the most seditious part of it. The elegy without the last sixteen lines was bold but not catastrophically so, and the epigraph, with its direct appeal for retaliation, must have been the only incriminating element. Count Benckendorff, the chief of the secret police, wrote to Nicholas, "The introduction to this work is arrogant, and the end is shameless freethinking, more than criminal." If the second point of view is correct (and it seems better argued than the first, though each solution has its difficulties), the epigraph was deliberately removed from (not added to!) later copies.

Lermontov was arrested before Raevsky and found himself in very great danger indeed. The Tsar and the police were obsessed with the fear of conspiracies, for Nicholas never got over the Decembrists' revolt, and every protest meant to him an organization to be found and immediately eradicated. Probably no other Russian tsar was so distrustful of his own nobility as Nicholas. The main (and perennial) question that Lermontov had to answer was about his accomplices. If he had refused to answer he could have been made a private and sent to the Caucasus (which would have entailed loss of status as a noble). Polezháev's fate left no doubts about the reality of the menace (see note on No. 16), and Lermontov gave Raevsky away. Later, both Lermontov and Raevsky were sent into exile: Lermontov to the Caucasus, Raevsky to the North, and Lermontov could never forgive himself his disloyalty toward such a good friend, though Raevsky did everything in his power to comfort the poet. A man of rare kindness and integrity, he really bore Lermontov no grudge.

The punishment meted out to Lermontov was mild. The initial reaction of the Tsar was such, "A nice poem indeed . . . I have told the Senior Doctor of The Corps to visit this gentleman and make sure whether he is not crazy; later we will act according to the law." The idea that anyone who opposed the regime or expressed a dissenting opinion was a lunatic took a strong hold of the Tsar. In spite of such an ominous start, Lermontov was not demoted but only transferred to an infantry regiment stationed in the Caucasus. He came to the Caucasus at the end of April or the very beginning of May in poor shape and was allowed to stay in Pyatigórsk until his convalescence. He reported to his new commander in September and thanks to the unremitting efforts of his grandmother was pardoned in October, left the Caucasus in the middle of December, and rejoined his Hussar Regiment of the Guards soon after that.

"The Poet's Death" was first published by Hertzen in 1856 in his

Commentary

London almanac *Polyárnaya Zvezdá* ("The Polar Star"). The text was complete, but the epigraph was missing (a fact always mentioned by those who believe that the epigraph was added later). In Russia the poem was published without the last sixteen lines in 1858, and the full version appeared in 1860. (Nicholas died in 1855, at the end of the Crimean War.) Today Lermontov's poem seems a natural outburst of indignation and grief. The image of Pushkin is vague, almost traditionally elegiac. But this was not the impression those lines made in 1837. Immediately after Pushkin's death, his friends tried to prove that the great poet had been a loyal subject of the Tsar and a good Christian, and since Pushkin's authorship is a whole world, it provides enough evidence for anything. Lermontov was the only one who said openly what everyone knew but did not dare to express. The traditional imagery of the poem does not diminish its force as an important eyewitness report of Pushkin's death and should not conceal from us the author's courage.

Beginning with 1839, Lermontov often met Pushkin's widow (she remarried soon, and her second husband was General Pyótr Petróvich Lanskóy), but only once did he speak to her as a friend. It was in the Karamzins' *salon* (see note on No. 75), when on April 12, 1840 the Karamzins' guests gathered to say good-bye to Lermontov, before he left St. Petersburg for the last time (cf. notes on Nos. 70 and 76). More than forty years later Aleksándra Petróvna Arápova (née Lanskáya) (1845-1919) told of this meeting between Lermontov and her mother:

At no other place did she feel so much at peace as at the Karamzins', where she was always welcome. But in this atmosphere so full of sympathy only one frequent visitor seemed to keep aloof from her, and behind his refinement and good manners she sensed prejudice and hostility. This was Lermontov. Too well-bred to give away a feeling that could have insulted a woman, he always avoided any kind of talk with her and made do with an exchange of empty, conventional remarks. Mother was all the more aggravated by it that much in his poetry, in its melancholy stream, accorded with her moods and awakened in her a responsive echo. There were moments when she wished to speak up, when her admiration for his talent was simply pouring out of her soul, but innate diffidence and some vague fear sealed her lips. Always meeting in the same small circle, they felt the invisible but insurmountable barrier that had grown between them.

There came the last evening before Lermontov's departure. Loyal to his habit, he came to spend it at the Karamzins', to say a sad good-bye to his friends. The company seemed larger than usual, but, succumbing to some inexplicable impulse, the poet, much to Mother's surprise, got hold of the free place near her and immediately started a conversation that struck her by its unusual tone.

Commentary

It seemed that he was trying to look into the recesses of her soul, and, in order to arouse her confidence, he himself began to tell her his thoughts and feelings that had so cruelly poisoned his life; he repented the harshness of his opinions and the relentless finality of his judgment that had often estranged him from perfectly innocent people. Mother understood that this confession was meant as a kind of explanation; she felt that intoxication with young but deserved fame had not killed in him dissatisfaction with life. Perhaps at that moment she caught a kindred echo of the other, mighty, departed spirit, but a lively interest was awakened in her at once; she gave vent to it and in simple, heartfelt words tried to comfort and cheer him up, choosing appropriate examples from her own hard lot. And as the words thus flowed on in an unusual torrent from her mouth, she could see that they were achieving their goal, that the icy crust that had heretofore bound their relations was melting as fast as snow in spring, that Lermontov's plain but expressive face was transforming under the influence of the light from within.

At the conclusion of this talk, which surprised the Karamzins by its length, Lermontov said, "When I think how often we've met here. . . . How many evenings we've spent here, in this parlor, but in different corners! I held aloof from you like a coward giving way to hostile influences. I saw in you only a cold, superior beauty. I was ready to take pride in that I had not joined in the cult reigning here, and only on the eve of my departure I took the trouble to see a woman under this mask, to realize the sincerity whose charm one does not examine but just recognizes, in order to take away an eternal reproof of short-sightedness, a barren regret for the hours stupidly wasted! But when I return I'll know how to earn forgiveness, and, if my dream is not too presumptuous, one day I may become your friend. Nobody can prevent me from expressing to you the dedication that I now feel." "There is nothing I must forgive you," answered Natalya Nikolaevna, "but if you are sorry to leave, now that your opinion of me has changed, believe me, I'll feel happier to stay with this knowledge." . . . I was sixteen . . . Mother told me about their last meeting and added, "It happened that people would do homage to me, but I knew that it was because of my beauty. That time it was a victory of the heart, and that is why it was so precious to me. Even now I am happy to think that he did not carry into his grave a bad opinion of me!"

L. 25. Dantès left France after 1833, for he was an inveterate *legitimiste*. Initially, he tried to settle in Prussia but later came to Russia. There he was received very well and after a nominal examination joined the aristocratic regiment of *cavalier-guardes*. Dantès never learned to speak Russian. Lermontov, like many of his contemporaries, resented the role of foreign aristocrats in the life of Russian society.

L. 35. The poet referred to is Vladímir Lénsky, a character in Pushkin's

Commentary

Evgeny Onegin. Lensky, aged eighteen, Onegin's constant companion and only friend, was in love with Ólga Lárina, whose elder sister Tatyána loved Onegin. Both Onegin and Lensky once went to a ball at the Larins', and Onegin, thoroughly bored, decided to tease Lensky and began to pay court to Olga. Offended and enraged, Lensky challenged Onegin to a duel and was killed. This is one of many echoes from Pushkin in "The Poet's Death."

L. 59. This line is more than a scathing remark. Pushkin was touchy about his genealogy, and, though his name was old enough, his family had lost its importance long before the beginning of the nineteenth century. New names emerged ("upstarts," by the inevitable definition), and the older aristocracy was pushed to the background. Even the rhyme in this stanza occurs in a parallel place in Pushkin's poem "My Ancestry" (which, however, may be due to chance, because this rhyme was common).

32. A Branch from Palestine

The history of the poem is related in the memoirs of Andréy Nikoláevich Muravyóv (1806-1874), a historian of Christianity and at one time a well-known author. Muravyov was a deeply religious man with a strong admixture of bigotry and in his later years a highly placed official. In 1829-30 he went to Jerusalem. In 1832 his two-volume book *A Travel to the Holy Land, 1830* was published in St. Petersburg. Muravyov seems to have met Lermontov in 1834, and considerable disparity in age (eight years) did not prevent them from becoming friends. In August of 1839 Muravyov was the first to hear Lermontov read his *Mtsyri.*

Probably on February 17, 1837, Lermontov came to see Muravyov, in the hope of getting some help from him: "The Poet's Death" had reached the Tsar and Lermontov's situation became really dangerous (see note on No. 31). Muravyov recollected,

Late in the evening Lermontov came to my place and, with animation, read his poem, which I liked very much. I did not find it in any way reprehensible, because I had not heard the last four lines [sic!] that raised such a storm against the poet. The poem circulated in two versions: one with and the other without the addition. . . . He asked me to speak on his behalf to Mordvinov [Alexánd(e)r Nikoláevich Mordvínov (1792-1869), Muravyov's cousin, was the executive director of the Third Section], and on the next day I went to my relative. He was engaged and in low spirits. "You always come with old news," said he,

Commentary

"I've read the poem to Count Benckendorff and neither of us found anything wrong with it." Very glad at having such tidings, I hurried back to Lermontov in order to put him at his ease, but did not find him at home and wrote him, word for word, everything Mordvinov had told me. When I came home, I discovered his note in which he again asked for my assistance because he was in danger. He had waited for me long and on the same sheet wrote his beautiful "Branch from Palestine," which by sudden inspiration poured out from him in my icon room at the sight of the Palestine palms I had brought from the East.

Lermontov was arrested on the next day, and the note written by Muravyov (impounded during the perquisition) might have brought trouble to both of Lermontov's protectors (Muravyov and Mordvinov). Muravyov wrote his recollections in 1871. In 1872, in another work, he also spoke about this poem but traced it to 1836. Lermontov included "A Branch from Palestine" in his 1840 book, and his own date is 1836. If 1836 is correct, Muravyov's version is unreliable. In any case, Muravyov gave Lermontov the branch as a present, and Lermontov meant to dedicate the poem to Muravyov (the dedication was crossed out at the last moment), so the latter's palms could very well be Lermontov's inspiration, even if the verses were not written in the difficult days after Pushkin's death. A certain S. N. Sulima claimed that he had witnessed the moment of the poem's composition, but nothing is known about Sulima apart from these words discovered in his copy of an 1842 edition of Lermontov: "Written by Lermontov in my presence in the apartment of Andrey Muravyov."

A contrapuntal organization of the poem often occurs in Lermontov's lyrics. All is peace and serenity around the branch, but all is secret unrest in the narrator's heart. The whole inquiry is a fruit of Lermontov's methodical mind and agitated soul. The first four stanzas presuppose a world full of harmony; but as the poem advances, this harmony is disrupted, and the fanciful, decorative scenery of an old ballad gives way to a panorama in which tears, wars, and death hold sway. Toward the end all is again tranquil, and the poet looks at the branch almost surprised that such perfection is possible and that such beauty is attainable in this life. He himself is too far from the ideal land of the branch.

Although the poem is full of Pushkinian phrases and resembles Pushkin's "Flower" structurally, the intonation and mood of the two are quite different. Besides, a branch or a leaf torn from the mother trunk is not a chance image in Lermontov's poetics (see No. 83 and note).

511

Commentary

33. The Prisoner

Lermontov wrote this poem, as well as Nos. 34, 35, 37, while he was under arrest after the scandal caused by "The Poet's Death" (No. 31, see note on it). It is an updated version of No. 20, and the alterations caused by the first acquaintance with a real cell in real confinement are all too obvious.

The poem was first published in 1839 and became a popular prison song (with the inevitable distortions and variations). It was put to music by several professional composers as well.

34. The Neighbor

"The Neighbor" was written while Lermontov was under arrest in 1837 (see note on No. 33). We have already been able to note that Lermontov was fond of antithesis and symmetrical constructions. This poem contains one of his most skillful images built along those lines: sounds flow like tears, while tears flow like sounds (cf. No. 92:527-28). As many times later (cf. Nos. 45 and 59 and notes), Lermontov's hero is moved by sounds whose source remains invisible and whose dark purport is hidden from him. But tears of sheer tenderness coming straight from the soul and purifying it are rare in his lyrics (cf. No. 43:10). Rather, his tears will burn a child's cheek (No. 67:15) or even a stone (No. 92:541-46), express sadness (No. 57:30), bitter disappointment (No. 60:67), or impotent fury (No. 91:448). In 1836 Lermontov translated one of Byron's *Hebrew Melodies*, viz., "My Soul is Dark" (cf. note on No. 5); the lines "I tell thee, minstrel, I must weep, or else this heavy heart will burst" must have struck an especially deep chord in him.

The poem was published in 1842 and, like other "prison" poems by Lermontov, is still current as a popular song.

35. "When in a Field of Grain the Wheat and Rye Wave Yellow"

Written while Lermontov was under arrest (see note on No. 33), this poem is close to his most peaceful prayers, and it is the first entirely impressionistic lyric from his pen. It consists of one long complex sentence, and the parallelism of the opening three stanzas, each beginning with *when*, creates a slow but irresistible crescendo resolving in the last four lines, so that the word *then* comes as a breath of relief. The structure of the piece is so tight that little seems to matter in it besides this movement toward the climax (cf. note on No. 37). And indeed, the objects mentioned are of no great importance, for the description depends entirely on the epithets.

It has often been said that Lermontov is sadly wasteful of his verbal resources and that Pushkin would have drawn the same or a better picture with half the words occurring in this poem. No doubt, Pushkin was thrifty where Lermontov was extravagant, but the two poets had quite dissimilar aims and used different techniques. Pushkin was an incomparable master of exact wording. His epithets were rich and many-sided but invariably precise. Lermontov threw about his words like splashes of paint. To judge Lermontov by Pushkin's standards is the same as to reproach Monet or Renoir for not working like Raphael. In his lyrics, Lermontov practically never drew landscapes in Pushkin's spirit (cf. notes on Nos. 1 and 80). Even in his early prose (e.g., in the unfinished novel *Princess Ligovskáya*) factual details were sometimes sacrificed to the general impression. In that novel he said once that the thaw had begun and the sled was gliding through the mist on the fluffy, new-fallen snow. The reason why Lermontov fails to notice that during the thaw snow could not be fluffy does not lie in the lack of professional skill: it stems from the special quality of his vision.

His impressionism notwithstanding, Lermontov must be defended from a common charge with regard to this poem. He has been accused (first by Gleb Uspénsky, later by others) of jumbling together incompatible images: the grain is yellow, the plum is "raspberry-colored," the lily of the valley is bedewed and silvery (an epithet that irritated Tolstoy when applied to lilies of the valley)—and all of them at the same time. But the three opening stanzas do not have to refer to one and the same season. Each tells a story of its own, each singles out a moment of peace, each contributes in its own way to the wavelike movement and the revelation of the finale. The history of literary and art criticism shows how ruinous (to the critic) it is to treat an impressionistic view as a daguerreotype.

This poem is a true religious lyric. Lermontov is not entirely pantheistic in it: although at a moment of supreme peace *man* and *nature* can be welded together (cf. many similar examples in No. 91), *God* and *nature* are separate, because Lermontov's God always remains in heaven. While almost a boy, he wrote a remarkable lyric entitled "Heaven and Stars" about the hero's longing for unattainable heights; No. 14 is a variation on the same theme. Yet, complete dissolution in nature or in God is never achieved in Lermontov's poetry, and the line separating heaven and earth is always present (cf. No. 12 and note). Another "mystic" motif, so important to Lermontov, is barely perceptible in this poem. As expressed so clearly in "The Angel" (No. 12), the soul pining among people half-remembers its home, and the dull sounds it hears on earth cannot replace for it "the music of heavenly grace." In a similar manner the rivulet described immediately before the climax (lines 9-13) murmurs to the hero its mysterious tale (in the original: saga) of the distant place from which it has come, and the tale plunges him into an almost magic sleep.

The poem was published in 1840.

36. *"We Parted, but Your Likeness Stays"*

Lermontov's method of work was special. He constantly returned to his own lines and transferred them from poem to poem. (Cf. notes on Nos. 24 and 30). Since he never meant to publish his early pieces and poetry was simply a way of living for him, these countless repetitions are neither surprising nor embarrassing. There is a great difference between his method and Pushkin's. Pushkin would work on his manuscript, find the best words and, when satisfied, sell his poem to a publisher. Later he would reprint his early poems, even if aware of their immaturity. He seldom changed his old verses, treating them as a fact of history. Nor would he (with the rarest exceptions) reuse his old lines. Lermontov also worked on his drafts (the extant versions bear ample witness to it); but, on the whole, he preferred to write a new variation rather than polish one and the same poem. He had a huge supply of apt phrases, similes, metaphors, rhymes, and entire descriptive passages (cf. note on No. 42) and was forever on the lookout for places in which they could be put to a good use (cf. also note on No. 33).

"We Parted, but Your Likeness Stays" is a modified version of No. 13. The central motif (a portrait on the poet's breast) is a borrowing from Byron. The curious fact is that Nos. 13 and 36 make almost opposite statements in their first stanzas but have the same finale.

This poem was published by Lermontov in his 1840 book.

37. A Prayer

Written when Lermontov was under arrest in 1837 (see note on No. 33) or later in the Caucasus; this poem was published three years later (cf. note on No. 66). Its polyphonic arrangement is not unlike that of "A Branch from Palestine" (No. 32) but more patent: the poet prays for a young girl and at the same time speaks of himself (in lines 3-8). As in No. 35, the effect of this lyric depends not on separate words but on the wavelike movement of the whole. The movement is created by parallel constructions, of which Lermontov was so fond, by multiple antitheses (another favorite device), and by dactylic endings in every hemistich. It is instrumented with the softest vowels, and each of its internal pauses is like a breath of air.

In the original, the dactyls are often inexact (they become amphibrachs because of "wrong" sentence stresses), and the syntax is unusually convoluted.

A rather unsuccessful attempt has been made to connect "A Prayer" with V. A. Lopukhiná (see note on No. 19). The context is too vague for identifying the addressee.

38. "I Am Unwilling to Disclose"

The poem is full of Lermontov's favorite motifs: the mystery of life; a deeply hidden feeling that should be judged by God and not by the mob; unrevealed sufferings; a proud hero who is like a rock among roaring waves. It also contains many of Lermontov's favorite rhymes, and in the original the end of the poem bears a close resemblance to the last stanza of No. 18: it contains the same image and the same feminine rhyme. This is a lyric that Lermontov could have written at almost any moment of his career, except perhaps in 1840-41 (though for some curious reason this is the date for it suggested by Lermontov's contemporaries).

Lermontov was not assuming a pose when he said that he feared the disclosure of his mysterious tale. He knew that nobody would understand or sympathize (and he was of course quite right). At roughly the same time he had Mtsyri exclaim, "And who can tell the world his soul!"

Commentary

(No. 91:83). Much earlier (in 1831 or 1832) he himself said in the dedication to the narrative poem *Aoúl Bestundjí,*

The world did not understand my soul, it does not need one's soul. No one's living eye will penetrate into the obscurity of my soul's mysterious darkness. But in it, closed to the mind, live memories of a distant holy land. . . . Neither light nor the noise of the earth will kill them. . . . I am yours! I am yours everywhere!

Cf. also the last lines of No. 12.

Lermontov did not include this piece in his 1840 book of selected poetry (he probably considered it too personal), and it was first published in 1845 (with a short lacuna).

39. *"Before I've Made My Northern Entry"*

Lermontov, exiled to the Caucasus, left Moscow on April 10, 1837, and returned to it on January 3, 1838 (see note on No. 31), so "past attachments" (in the original, l. 28: "after many years") should not be taken literally. The poem, in a way, anticipates No. 80, in which Kazbék is the central character. For Pushkin and Lermontov, Kazbek was the great symbol of the Caucasus. It is hard to tell whether in his apostrophe to Kazbek Lermontov was influenced by Caucasian folklore. He may have known one of the legends about Kazbek burying a traveler under snow, but no "sources" are needed for this image.

The poem was written at the end of October or the beginning of November 1837 but published only in 1845.

40. *The Dagger*

This poem was first called "A Present." In Georgia Lermontov met Nina Chavchavádze, the widow of Griboédov, and it is believed that she gave him one of her daggers. There was an inscription on it, and originally the poem had an epigraph ("The beautiful maiden read the inscription to me"). Another dagger was given to Alexander Odoevsky (see No. 53 and note).

"The Dagger" is somewhat like the beginning of No. 47 but without its bitterness. It is not one of Lermontov's best works, for it is marred by several drawing-room phrases and trivial images. It also has an unusual finale: direct statements, especially promises to be staunch and loyal, are unusual for Lermontov. Reportedly, Nina Chavchavadze made Lermontov swear "to be loyal to this dagger"; all my data are from V. S. Shaduri's book *Za Khrebtom Kavkaza* ("Beyond the Caucasus's ridge"). Tbilisi: Merani, 1977. In the *Lermontovskaya Èntsiklopediya*, Shaduri mentions Nina Chavchavadze as a *possible* person who gave Lermontov a dagger.

"The Dagger was published in 1841, while Lermontov was still alive.

41. *"My Past is Sad; I Leave it Dreading"*

As late as 1934 two hitherto unknown poems by Lermontov were discovered. One of them began with these lines, "My future is in the mist, /My past is full of anguish and evil . . . /Why did nature not create me/later or earlier?" There followed several verses familiar from "Meditation" (No. 46: 13-16) and from No. 41. In the original the opening stanza of No. 41 runs as follows, "I look at my future with fear, /I look at my past with despair, /And like a criminal before the execution/ Seek in the crowd a kindred soul." Some stanzas and the conclusion do not occur elsewhere. The early poem probably goes back to 1835-36. "My Past is Sad; I Leave it, Dreading" is much more than a mature variant of "My Future Is in the Mist," but the points of similarity are apparent.

The leaf containing this poem and another short elegy formerly belonged to E. A. Karlhoff-Drashusova. She received it from Svyatosláv Raévsky together with a letter in which Raevsky described Lermontov's manner of thinking.

The twenty-line poem belongs to the genre known as *ode pindarique*. It was published in 1845.

42. *She Sings—Each Sound I Hear Her Singing"*

This is the first of a three-poem cycle (Nos. 42-44) containing variations on one and the same theme. They are all about the beauty of a woman's voice and the expression of her eyes, in which the heavens are reflected. Line 2 is also used in *The Demon* (No. 92:508). In Lermontov's poetry, sounds flow like tears and melt like kisses, and the three are almost interchangeable (cf. No. 34 and note). The concluding four lines of this lyric are very close to lines 9-12 from No. 24 (see note

Commentary

on it and cf. note on No. 36) and are also used in *The Demon* (No. 92:155-57).

Nothing is known about the addressee of this cycle. Lermontov's biographer Viskováty proposed S. M. Sollogúb (née Viel'gorskaya, the wife of the writer Vladímir Alexándrovich Sollogúb), a possible inspirer of No. 84, but this is little more than a guess. È. È. Naydich, a modern Lermontov scholar, made an attempt to prove that all three poems, as well as No. 59, were dedicated to Praskóvya Arsényevna Barténeva (1811-72), the Empress's lady-in-waiting and an amateur singer (she was Glinka's pupil). Another name suggested in this connection as the addressee of the small cycle is E. A. Chavchavádze, the sister of Griboedov's widow.

43. *"Speak with Your Voice to Me"*

In his later years Lermontov almost never used blank verse (see note on No. 2). The capricious rhythm of this poem bears some resemblance to the rhythm of his early experiments. In 1831 he wrote several songs, and two of them ("A Yellow Leaf Beats against the Stalk" and "The Church Bell Groans") are excellent. They are not included in this volume, because in translation their beauty does not come through. No. 43 was first published by V. A. Sollogúb (cf. note on No. 42) in 1845 under the characteristic title "An Unpolished Poem" ('Neotdélannoe stikhotvorénie'). Sollogub must have wondered at its meter (it is written in irregular two-foot dactyls), but there is no doubt that the poem is quite finished. It belongs with Nos. 42 and 44.

44. *"Your Eyes, Like Bright Enamel Gleaming"*

As regards its motifs, the poem is related to the previous two and No. 40, but the image of eyes gleaming like enamel does not occur elsewhere.

45. < To A. G. Khomutova >

Ánna Grigóryevna Khomutóva (1784-1856) was a cousin of Iván Ivánovich Kozlóv (1779-1840), a well-known poet. Kozlov began his career as a government official in Moscow, then served in the Regiment of Guards for over three years, and finally transferred to St. Petersburg, again as an official in the civil service. He was bright, cultured, and

518

sociable, but an incurable illness turned his life into misery: in his early forties he was struck blind and paralyzed, and between 1821 and 1840 he led the life of a complete invalid. It was just at this time that he became a professional poet. His original works (narrative poems, elegies, songs, etc.) enjoyed great popularity both among the reading public and among other authors. Pushkin's and Baratýnsky's opinion of Kozlov was of the highest. Together with Zhukóvsky, he was the founder of what may be called the school of Russian poetic translation. Many works by Byron, Thomas Moore, Walter Scott, Wordsworth, Chénier, Ariosto, Schiller, and Mickiewicz (all of whom Kozlov could read in the original) became known to the Russian reader, and though the French and German authors had other advocates, the fame of the English Romantics in Russian would never have been so great without Kozlov. Like other translators of his age, including Lermontov (cf. note on No. 60), Kozlov introduced much of his own spirit into his translations. Byron in Russian was Kozlov's Byron, or Pushkin's Byron, or Lermontov's Byron (cf. note on No. 18).

Today Kozlov is practically forgotten, though his poetry is available in new editions. Almost the only two pieces still included in modern anthologies are his translations of Charles Wolfe's ''The Burial of Sir John Moore at Corunna'' and of Thomas Moore's ''Those Evening Bells.'' The latter enjoys the status of a universally known folk song. ''The Burial . . . '' was also put to music and became a famous dead march, which was performed for years after. Kozlov's original narrative poems, even the once popular *A Black Monk*, are now at best titles mentioned in passing by literary historians.

Little is known of Kozlov's last twenty years, though he had many friends. A. G. Khomutova was his relative on his mother's side. Their friendship is the subject of Kozlov's lyric ''To a Friend of My Spring after Many, Many Years of Absence'' (1838). According to one source, A. G. Khomutova, whose brother General Mikhaíl Grigóryevich Khomutóv was the commander of Lermontov's regiment, showed Kozlov's elegy to Lermontov. Lermontov took it home and on the next day returned it with his own dedication. According to another source, Lermontov wrote this poem after he heard Kozlov's own ''animated story'' about Anna Grigoryevna and their warm friendship. The poem was published in 1844, and the title has been added by the editors.

The lyric is deeply symbolic. Lermontov, whose own vision differed so much from that of others and who saw all objects best when they were at a great distance from him (cf. note on No. 84 and 92:80-82), was somewhat like Kozlov in this respect. Apart from that, it is also a poem about the magic of sound coming from darkness. "The music of heavenly grace" (No. 12:16) and "the speeches whose purport is hidden" (No. 59:2) are present in this lyric like a distant but clearly audible echo.

46. Meditation

"Meditation," published in volume 1 of the *Otéchestvennye Zapíski*, 1839 ("Notes of the Fatherland"), an almanac that carried nearly all Lermontov's works), is one of the most celebrated poems in Russian literature. Like other masterpieces by Lermontov, it was preceded by years of thinking about and testing each expression and image (cf. Nos. 2 and 41: Lermontov knew very well what he was denouncing). Between "A Monologue" and "Meditation" lay not only a decade that turned a talented and honest but precocious youth into a mature poet; in that period was the fateful February of 1837 (see note on No. 31 and the beginning of note on No. 32), when the secret police showed Lermontov all its might. He realized for the first time that the opposite of freedom is not necessarily slavery, tyranny, or something of that sort (frightening but grandiloquent); its opposite turned out to be an ordinary prison, a Siberian mine, or demotion. He was told that if he did not betray his friends ("accomplices"), he would be ground to dust. He cursed himself but obeyed. In the poem Lermontov is far from accusing others: in his own eyes he is part of the despicable generation that will reach old age in shameless inactivity and will leave the stage without "a noise or trace" (words denoting *sound* are always fraught with symbolic meaning in Lermontov's poems). "Meditation" had a great influence on Lermontov's contemporaries and on other poets (the best known example is Turgenev).

The genre of the meditation enjoyed considerable popularity in the poetry of the Decembrists. Especially important were several "Meditations" by K. F. Ryléev (1795-1826), one of the five Decembrists hanged at the order of Nicholas I. In 1839 the title of Lermontov's poem meant much more than it does today. Yet Ryleev's "Meditations" were full of courage and confidence, quite different from Lermontov's gloomy lyric.

47. The Poet

Together with Nos. 49, 63, and 87, this lyric forms a cycle on the theme "the poet and the rabble." All of them say somewhat different things.

"The Poet" is closer to "The Prophet" (No. 87), and the confession of No. 63:92 ff. forms a link with No. 49.

Although the structure of the poem is not very tight, resting only on analogy (the dagger is useless and the poet is useless), in the last stanza Lermontov blends the images of the dagger and of the poet. Iron and metal as symbols of strength also occur in other lyrics (Nos. 40, 55:41).

"The Poet" was published in 1839, soon after it was written.

48. *"A Darling Child I Am Addressing"*

The poem was written in 1839 and published posthumously in 1843. Lermontov sent it in a letter to Alexéy Lopukhín as a dedication to his son Alexand(e)r (1839-1895). Alexey Lopukhin was Varen'ka's brother (cf. note on No. 19) and Lermontov's good friend from 1828 or even 1827. In 1833 Lopukhin fell in love with E. A. Sushkóva, but Lermontov prevented him from marrying her (see note on No. 9). In 1838 Lopukhin married Varvára Alexándrovna Obolénskaya. Since the boy was born on February 13 and Lermontov calls his verse belated, the poem must have been written some time in the spring.

It is easy to guess from Lermontov's wishes what tormented the poet. Lermontov's poems to children are very tender (cf. Nos. 57, 67, and the beginning of No. 91); there is a peculiar sweetness in them without the slightest touch of sentimentality.

49. *"Do Not Trust Yourself"*

Though several verses are strained in this poem (lines 17-22 of the original), it is one of Lermontov's best creations. It bears a resemblance to Tyutchev's "Silentium!" (ca. 1830) and to several lyrics by Blok, but neither Tyutchev nor Blok expressed their ideas with greater mastery, though Lermontov was only twenty-four when he wrote "Do Not Trust Yourself."

"The poet and the rabble" was an important theme in European Romantic literature, and in Russia we find descriptions of poets running the whole gamut from the inspired bard of the Ossianic type to the people's friend, ready to sacrifice his life for them. At one time the figure of a melancholy singer who composed elegies and was disappointed in life by the age of eighteen was very much in vogue. Pushkin's Lensky in *Evgeny Onegin* is a mild parody of this type. But Pushkin was also the

Commentary

first to treat the problem seriously, pointing up its insoluble complexity (cf. note on No. 87 and the description of Charsky given in the introductory sketch). In 1839 the literary type of a God-inspired poet belonged to the past, but the idea of the poet as the rabble's antipode was very much alive, and the epigones of Romanticism were busy furnishing their tables with the baked meats left over from the great masters: those were cold but still quite usable.

The poet in Lermontov's works is indistinguishable from his lyric hero: the narrator of Nos. 46 and 55 is the same man who addresses the Journalist and the Reader (No. 63) and whose two voices (the dreamer versus the skeptic) we hear in No. 49. The bard depicted by Venevítinov and his predecessors in the eighteenth century cannot be called a lyric hero at all, for he was as conventional as Molière's physicians. Even the poet of Pushkin's early "epistles" was not a lyric hero but a type, just like his counterpart in the "epistles" by Zhukóvsky, Bátyushkov, and Yazýkov. Lermontov broke with poetic genres and in his mature years never wrote epistles, elegies, etc. His "Meditation" is the only relic of an older tradition, and he chose this mold deliberately, to contrast his views with Ryléev's (see note on No. 46).

Lermontov's lyric hero is an individual. He is not the product of genre requirements or philosophical conceptions (as is the case with many Slavophiles). Lermontov's poet is part of his generation and, like his lyric hero elsewhere, forms the focus of two crossing currents: he craves the infinite and believes in the great humanitarian ideal, but he knows that his goals are unattainable and says to himself the bitter things that in Russian literature are forever associated with Lermontov. The mature Lermontov not only avoided absolute lyricism, that amorphous fruit of misguided inspiration; he also avoided purely political poems. The greatest intellectual attraction of Lermontov's verses is that his lyrics bear the imprint of his philosophical meditations, and his pieces devoted to the civil theme are deeply lyrical. After Lermontov, genre poems, even if brought to life with the very best intentions, seemed anachronistic. The Lermontov of 1839 still had two years before him; we need only compare the condensed language of "Do Not Trust Yourself," its complex metaphors and constantly varying imagery, with the simplicity of Nos. 71 and 90 to see how rapidly he was becoming a complete master of his inspiration.

Lermontov called on his hero to awaken and serve lofty ideals (No. 47), but he also showed with absolute clarity that the society he knew quite deserved its poets (Nos. 47, 87). "The rabble," whether the concept included the whole world or only the palace clique (cf. No. 31), was as familiar a word to him as to Pushkin. In his youth he repeatedly erected a wall between himself and the mob: cf. the end of No. 18 and one of his 1832 poems that begins as follows,

Yes, I am mad! You are right, quite right. Immortality on earth is ludicrous. How could I wish for fame and glory if you are all happy in the dust? How could I shatter a chain of prejudices by my free mind and take the flame of secret contortions for the heart of poetry? No, I do not resemble a *poet*! I was deceived and I can see it myself; like him, I can be a stranger to the world, but I am also a stranger to Heaven!

In the confession of the Writer (No. 63-92 ff) we find the same idea, and it is repeated in "Do Not Trust Yourself." He continues the poem "Yes, I am Mad": "My words are sad: I know it; but you will not understand their sense. I tear them from my heart in order to tear off my anguish with them."

There is nothing enigmatic in what Lermontov said about inspiration: like every truly great master, he knew that the secret fire consuming the poet is not yet inspiration, because it is formless. His poet (in No. 63) can be feverishly active in the dead of night. In such hours he believes that he has said something great; but what was a volcano at night becomes ashes in the morning. Lermontov was such a sincere author that his verses look like a journal and autobiography, but he knew how to let his poetic lava cool before he showed it to the world. By the age of twenty-four Lermontov as a poet had learned to keep himself completely in check. All his life he altered his own lines and brought many raw drafts to perfection (cf. note on No. 36).

"Do Not Trust Yourself" is unusual in that it gives a sympathetic treatment of the "rabble." Even though the crowd is made up of smiling automata (like dancers at a fashionable ball: No. 55), their masks conceal genuine sufferings. The poet, just because he can dramatize his feelings, is not a whit better than the man in the street. He should be ashamed of his merchandise. This poem has the polyphonic structure of which Lermontov was so fond (cf. Nos. 37 and 56): two voices speak simultaneously, arguing with each other. The poet himself, surprisingly, is ready to join the rabble denigrated in lines 23-24: cf. "Why seek among *us* a physician" (in the original, lines 25-26 are, "What do *we* care whether you suffered or not; why should *we* know about your troubles?"). Later (l. 33), Lermontov says, "each of *them*." The skeptic preaches a sermon to the dreamer and calls the latter's outburst "captive reason's irritation" (an expression that Dostoevsky liked to repeat), but it would be rash to equate either of them with the author. He is far above them, as he is far above his Pechórin. Besides, he loves what he rejects.

The epigraph to the poem is from Auguste Barbier's "Prologue," "After all, what do we care for the vulgar bark of all those yelling charlatans who trade in pathos and invent high-flown words and for all the clowns who dance on the phrase?" But Barbier says, "Que *me* font" (not "que *nous* font") 'What do *I* care' and "*les* charlatans" not *ces* charlatans." Without these two changes, especially without the first, the quotation would hardly have been useful to Lermontov. In spite of the obvious analogy, Barbier - Lermontov, "Do Not Trust Yourself" does not much resemble "Prologue," just as Lermontov's "Poet" (No. 47) is quite unlike Barbier's "Melpomène," though the two have often been compared; the real resemblance is between Lermontov's lyrics, and Pushkin's "Poet" and "The Poet and the Rabble." According to Shan-Giréy, Lermontov (in 1840) did not like Barbier's *Iambes* and praised only eight lines from them (*C'est la mer, c'est la mer, d'abord calme et sereine*, etc.). In general, French Romanticism, including Hugo and even André Chénier, does not seem to have played an important role in Lermontov's development.

"Do Not Trust Yourself" was published in 1839, and it is known that Lermontov looked upon it as his creed. Critics constantly discuss it, but it has never been popular with the general reader.

50. Three Palms

This poem is a good example of Lermontov's poetic method. Whatever his subject in narrative pieces, he was always interested in purely pictorial descriptions. In them he was sometimes carried away by the clichés of album poetry: nouns acquired diminutive suffixes (little hands, little eyes, and the like), the same little eyes looked coyly from under long eyelashes, and so on. His only poem free from these occasional lapses is *Mtsyri* (No. 91). "Three Palms" is also typical in that it contains a hidden challenge to Pushkin, even though the poem's plot could have been suggested by A. I. Filosófov's (see the note on No. 92 about him) stories of a trip to Africa. It is the result, not the source, that matters.

The older Lermontov became, the more he felt drawn to Pushkin's poetry, but as often as not he would take Pushkin's theme and solve it in his own way. "Three Palms" resembles No. 9 of Pushkin's "Imitations of the Koran." In Pushkin's poem, a tired wayfarer is dying from heat and thirst and rebukes God; then he finds an oasis, quenches his thirst, and falls asleep; the magic sleep lasts so long that he wakes up an old man and finds his donkey dead and the oasis dry. Later he is granted youth again, the donkey comes alive, the oasis regains its freshness, and the rejoicing traveler continues on his way. Man and nature become reunited, and death itself turns out to be transient. In Lermontov's ballad, it is harmony that is transient, and death triumphs over it. There is an unmistakable thematic similarity between "Three Palms" and "The Sail" (No. 28), as pointed out by Potebnyá.

The poem, first published in 1839, was discussed from a strictly utilitarian point of view by V. G. Belínsky and later by N. G. Chernyshévsky (Were the palms right in expressing their discontent? Was it a good thing that they perished serving people? etc.)—an interesting episode in the history of Russian radical criticism.

Ll. 27-28. Eyes always flash in Lermontov (e.g., Bela's and Princess Mary's), and everything he admires is made to flash: the Caucasus, Kazbék, two great Caucasian rivers, dew, clouds, foam, snow, leaves, ivy.

L. 32. "Ounce" is definitely a less known English word than its Russian counterpart *bars*. But English Romantics, e.g., Shelley in *Prometheus Unbound*, Southey, and Keats, mention this beast, and I decided not to replace it by "panther" or "leopard." Cf. 91:455 ff.

51. A Prayer

This is one of Lermontov's most musical poems. It was extremely popular in Russia before 1917. As evidenced by O. A. Smirnóva (see No. 68), Lermontov dedicated it to M. A. Shcherbátova (see No. 58 and note). Cf. Lermontov's other "prayer" poems (Nos. 3, 35, 37, and 66).

The poem appeared in 1839, soon after it was written. The Empress liked it very much, and it was probably she who commissioned the "court" composer F. M. Tolstoy ("Theophile") to put it to music as early as February 1841. Since then over eighty composers, including F. Liszt, have chosen this text for their songs.

Commentary

52. The Terek's Gifts

The main "topographical" difference between West European and Russian Romanticism was that French, German, and English authors who extolled the beauty of the East had only a vague notion of it, whereas Pushkin, Lermontov, Bestúzhev-Marlínsky, and others discovered their own promised land, the Caucasus, and knew it intimately (often against their will!). The luxuriant landscape set off the courage of the belligerent mountaineers with their primitive ideas of honor and their ancient songs. The poet's thirst for individualism and grandeur was fully satisfied by the Caucasus. As a result, the Caucasus showed the nineteenth-century Russian reader only its picturesque side (cf. Polezháev's revolt against this tradition: note on No. 16). A somewhat different line is represented by Pushkin's *Travel to Arzrúm* and Lermontov's *A Hero of Our Time*, but this line was not important in their poetry.

"The Terek's Gifts" is characteristic of Lermontov's attitude toward the Caucasus, and it compares easily with Pushkin's lyrics. Pushkin's Terek also "plays in furious mirth, plays like a young beast that has noticed food from an iron cage; it beats against the bank in futile enmity and licks the rocks with its hungry wave." But Pushkin's Terek is crushed by a force greater than its own: "it will get neither food nor comfort: formidably do mute rocks close in upon it." Lermontov's Terek is a symbol of absolute liberty; it robs its own bed of mighty boulders and receives offerings as a deity should. (For Lermontov's love of the Caucasus see also No. 4 and note).

The Terek is a rapid mountain river falling into the Caspian Sea. In folklore the Caspian Sea is often referred to as Caspy. Both *Terek* and *Caspy* are masculine nouns in Russian (hence *Uncle Caspy* and the special nature of the last gift). The narrow canyon through which the Terek forces its way is called Daryál (disyllabic), a popular place-name in Russian Romantic literature. The Cabardínians, as well as the Cherkesses, were specially noted for their courage and in Lermontov's works always stand for the best in the Caucasus. In the original (l. 51) the dead girl's shoulders are called dark-pale. The Cossack mentioned several lines later is a so-called *Grebenskóy* Cossack. The word 'Cossack' referred to several unconnected communities in southeastern Russia. *Grében'* means 'crest', and the name "Grebenskoy" owes its existence to the mountain range on the right bank of the Terek, for Cossack settlements stood opposite the mountain. In *Valerík* (No. 90:106) the man fighting against the *murid* is also a Grebenskoy Cossack.

"The Terek's Gifts" appeared in 1839 and must soon have become popular in the Caucasus; in any case, Ilyá Vasílyevich, a cornet (*khorún-zhiy*) in Leo Tolstoy's tale *The Cossacks* (1852-62) refers to a line in the poem as something that would be equally familiar both to Olénin and himself.

53. *In Memory of A. I. O<doevsk>y*

Alexánd(e)r Ivánovich Odóevsky (1802-1839) was a poet and an active participant of the Decembrists' revolt: on December 14, 1825, he was in Senate Square with a revolver. He spent twelve years in Siberia and was finally, in 1837, transferred to the Caucasus but died there in 1839. He was a brilliant man, though his recorded poetry, almost all written after 1825, is interesting mainly from a political/historical point of view. Today Odoevsky's fame rests on one poem: in 1827 Pushkin sent to Siberia a letter in verse, in which he addressed the Decembrists with words of encouragement and love. The answer was written by Odoevsky, and it circulated widely for decades after. At the beginning of this century Lenin used a line from this poem as the motto for his newspaper *Iskra* ('Spark'). The line runs as follows, "A spark will burst into flame."

In 1837, during his first exile, Lermontov met many of the Decembrists in the Caucasus but struck up a real friendship only with A. I. Odoevsky and, it seems, with A. M. Nazímov. The reason that Lermontov did not get along well with the others is not quite clear. By 1837 Lermontov, who developed fast, had reached a high level of maturity; the Decembrists, however, had had behind them twelve years of trials and mines. Some were physically and morally broken; some regretted their role in the revolt and expected to come home and earn forgiveness. All were bitterly disappointed, tired, and often full of illusions. Nazimov, for instance, felt certain that Nicholas I would soon abolish serfdom. He used to ask Lermontov about contemporary youth, and Lermontov would laugh and answer that the young men he knew only ate, drank, and seduced women. Nazimov was irritated by this flippancy and by Lermontov's irreverent treatment of many matters that seemed important to the Decembrists. However, Lermontov was right when he disbelieved the Tsar, and his "Meditation" shows that he was very serious in his outwardly facetious answers to Nazimov.

But Odoevsky must have struck Lermontov as an ideal hero. Lermtontov borrowed half of the epitaph from his own earlier lyrics and from *Sashka* (cf. note on No. 16; *Sashka* is written in the same eleven-line stanzas as No. 53). Sasha and Sashka are diminutive forms of Alexand(e)r and *Sasha* rhymes with *Russia*.

The poem was first published in 1839 under the title "In Memory of O—y," for Odoevsky's full name could not be mentioned in print, especially in such a sympathetic context.

54. *"He Sat Immersed in Thought on Happy, Feasting Days"*

This poem was first published in 1854 but without the last stanza. The whole text appeared three years later, in 1857. In 1854 the poem was entitled "A Fragment," in 1857 "Cazotte," but neither of the two titles is Lermontov's. It is very probable that the second one was invented by the editors of *Sovreménnik* ("The Contemporary") so that they could publish the final four lines: the lyric acquired an antiquarian ring and, seemingly, lost its political edge. In any case, the situation depicted by Lermontov has little to do with what the French playwright and literary historian Jean-Françoise Laharpe (1739-1803) told the world about Cazotte. Jacque Cazotte (1720-1792), a French mystic and author, was decapitated at the height of the Revolution. His prophecies (*Prophetie de Cazotte*), in which he allegedly announced to everybody present at an aristocratic reception what to expect of the approaching events, were a hoax fabricated by Laharpe.

Fatalism and its consequences were important to Lermontov (as to many Romantics), especially in the last years of his life, as evidenced both by *Valerík* (No. 90) and *A Hero of Our Time*. In this poem the theme of fatalism crosses another one, also prominent in Lermontov's work—"the hero predicting his public disgrace and execution." Cf. No. 72.

55. *"How Very Often at a Fashionable Ball"*

Aristocratic masquerades were the vogue in Pushkin's and Lermontov's time. For Lermontov these fancy dress balls became a symbol of insidious intrigues and moral degradation. The action of his only significant play (a tragedy) has such a setting and is called *The Masquerade* (No. 96), and the word has a wealth of figurative meaning there (see also No. 88 and note).

Commentary

The royal couple also were seen quite often at some of the more fashionable gatherings of this sort, and the Empress's adventures at them were too risky for her status. The exact events that gave rise to Lermontov's elegy are beyond reconstruction, but the poem and its history have become legend in Russian literature.

P. A. Viskováty, Lermontov's first biographer, wrote the following:

On the New Year's Eve, 1839, a brilliant society was invited to the Aristocratic Assembly. Two ladies attracted special attention: one in a blue, the other in a red domino. They were sisters, and though everybody knew who they were the guests respected their incognito and treated them with deference. They must have felt drawn to the young poet and profiting by the freedom that the masquerade offered them said something to him in passing. M[ikhail] Yu[ryevich] gave no sign that he knew who had addressed him, but—his ready wit always at his disposal—retorted at once. He even walked a bit with the luxuriant dominoes, who, quite embarrassed, hastened to take shelter. The act of the young officer seemed to them entirely unexpected and bold out of all proportions. Lermontov's behavior, innocent as it might be, was a breach of etiquette, but the ladies could not report it to anyone. That would have meant making the whole thing public; as it was, the episode was noticed only by a few. But when the *Otéchestvennye Zapíski* published "January 1," many impressions in it struck people as shocking.

Viskovaty implied that the two dominoes were the Tsar's daughters. The censor passed the poem on January 14, 1840, and it appeared that same winter.

I. S. Turgenev, who at that time was a typical romantic youth of twenty-two and the author of numerous imitative lyrics, saw Lermontov at the same ball. His description of Lermontov—written years later, when much of his youthful fervor had cooled off—in Shakhovskáya's *salon* and at a masquerade is famous:

I have seen Lermontov only twice: in the house of the great St. Petersburg lady Countess Shakhovskaya and several days later at a masquerade at the Aristocratic Assembly on the last night of 1839. In Countess Shakhovskaya's parlor, I, a very rare and inexperienced guest at aristocratic receptions, watched from a corner, where I had hidden, the poet whose fame was then at its height. He placed himself on a low stool before a couch, on which, dressed in black, was seated one of the St. Petersburg beauties of the time, the fair-haired Countess Musina-Pushkina, a really charming creature, who was destined to die young. Lermontov was wearing the uniform of his Hussar Regiment of the Guards; he had taken off neither his saber nor his gloves, and stooping, with a sullen expression on his face, cast morose glances at the Countess. She did not speak much to him and preferred to address Count Shuvalov, who was sitting nearby and who also was a Hussar. There was something ominous and tragic in Lermontov's appearance; his swarthy face, his large, immovable and dark eyes emanated some suppressed and sinister force, some meditative disdainfulness and passion. Their heavy look seemed to be oddly out of harmony with the expression of his tender, almost childish and pouting lips. His whole figure, stocky, bow-legged, with a big head on round, broad shoulders, caused an unpleasant sensation; but his inherent power was obvious to all. It is well known that, up to a point, he represented himself in Pechorin. The words "His eyes did not laugh when he was laughing," etc. really appealed to him. I remember that Count Shuvalov and his interlocutor suddenly burst out laughing and laughed long; Lermontov also began to laugh, but at the same time he eyed them both with some offensive surprise. In spite of this, it seemed to me that he loved Count Shuvalov as a comrade and was well disposed toward the Countess. There can be no doubt that following the fashion he put on a kind of Byronic genre, with an admixture of still worse caprices and whims. And how dearly he paid for them! Deep inside, Lermontov must have been profoundly bored; he was stifling in the narrow sphere into which fate had pushed him. At the ball at the Aristocratic Assembly there was a constant vortex around him, someone would accost or touch him every moment; masks followed in rapid succession, but he almost never left his place and listened to their squeaking in silence, turning his dark eyes from one to another. And it seemed to me that I had detected on his face the beautiful expression of poetic inspiration. Perhaps he was thinking of the lines, "The bold and vicious dames with all-too-ready charms unhesitantly lay their hands upon my arms, the perfumed hands devoid of feeling."

However, on December 31, 1839, there seems to have been no ball at the Aristocratic Assembly: according to contemporary reports it took place one day earlier. The royal daughters could hardly have been present at it. The elder (Mariya), married to a foreign duke, was in a rather advanced stage of pregnancy, the younger (Olga) was seventeen and would not have been allowed to go to masquerades and indulge in risky frolics. The Empress, indeed, seldom missed such an opportunity, and it is an established fact that she was interested in Lermontov, in his poetry, and in his friends (a circumstance that precipitated Lermontov's destruction). But it is not known whether Lermontov ever overstepped the line of the permissible or exploited her "incognito." Turgenev did not remember any disruptive episode at the ball (there were about 1,500 guests at it). Besides, it is almost inconceivable that Lermontov should have mocked the Empress or the princesses at a ball and immortalized the event two weeks later in a poem published in one of the most popular almanacs of the time. The author, the editor, and the censor would not have survived such a blunder. In all probability, the direct impetus to the poem was one of the balls, perhaps even the New Year's Eve ball, but nothing out of the ordinary happened at it. Hypotheses concerning the history of the poem are many.

Viskovaty remarked that Count Benckendorff had begun to persecute the poet after the publication of ''January 1, 1840.'' If this is true, ''the verse of steel'' struck the Chef des Gendarmes as more dangerous than ''The Poet's Death'' (No. 31). Benckendorff made no mistake: three years had passed, Lermontov had been given a second chance but spurned it. In Benckendorff's eyes he was beyond redemption.

The landscape described in line 16 ff. is that of Tarkhány, E. A. Arsényeva's estate, where Lermontov spent his early years. The childish romance narrated in such unchildlike words (l. 25 ff.) may be the story of his first love (see note on No. 4) or a reference to his feeling for Annette Stolýpina (though he met her only in 1830 and in Serednikóvo—see note on No. 9—not in Tarkhany).

''January 1, 1840'' is one of Lermontov's poems about sounds (cf. Nos. 12, 23, 45, 51, 59): deafened by the din of the masquerade, almost drowned in the evil whispers and the stupid babble of the guests, he conjures up the tender murmurs of his ''ruined youth'' (cf. No. 84:4). And these murmurs, so weak and perishable, suffuse his soul and triumph over the noise of the ball. The poet is back at home, on the ''fresh and flowering isle,'' where no one will frighten his dream. Time ceases to exist: the fifth stanza (especially lines 25-27) refers as much to the past as to the moment at the ball. ''The poet at a masquerade'' is easily another variation on the theme ''the poet and the rabble'' (cf. No. 49 and note). It is also a reminder of how an artist breaks through the self-asserting and hostile noise of the world to say his quiet word. This motif immortalized in the second movement of Beethoven's Piano Concerto No. 4, is perennial, and for Russian poetry and music the theme of an artist feasting at someone else's table and deriving no joy from it remained central for many years.

Typically Lermontov's is also the desire to transcend the present and shake off the manacles of bodily existence, to merge with nature, to become an organic part of the cosmos. The most dissimilar situations arouse the same reaction in him. He wishes to fly to the land of his legendary ancestors, for, though he has been born in the here and now, his soul is ''elsewhere'' (No. 10); he dreams that he will pray and weep and, cleansed from every impurity, become a cloud driven by the wind (No. 14). At a ball he flies home (No. 55), and in a desert his soul,

Commentary

almost Tyutchev-like, looks at its own body from high up (No. 81). The dying gladiator, in a variation on Byron's theme (1836), sees not "the dissolute Rome" but his native Danube. At the end of his short life he is face to face with the universe, neither dwarfed nor humbled by its greatness: he opens his embrace to it, achieving the state he understands so well and inwardly craves—between life and death, forever incorporated into the harmony of the world (No. 85).

56. "Oh, Boredom and Sadness! And No One Will Rescue or Save"

Solitude is one of the main motifs in Lermontov's poetry. He once (No. 46:8) compared the pastimes of his generation with feasting at a stranger's banquet (cf. also the end of the previous note), and this joyless, strained mirth poisoned every day of his life. Lermontov's personal isolation should not be exaggerated, and his poetry should not be taken for a mirror of his own boredom. Such a well-meaning friend as Shan-Giréy wondered what had made Lermontov a gloomy poet: he had money, position, and women. This seems a naive statement from someone who equates the private individual with the artist. But we, who did not have the advantage of knowing Cornet Lermontov while he was alive and who know only his works, reverse Shan-Girey's mistake; we make conclusions about Lermontov the man from Lermontov the poet; we treat his lyrics as a journal, forgetting that Pechorin, the Demon, and even Lermontov's lyric hero are his literary creations. Lermontov had a number of sincere admirers of both sexes and several worthy friends and he was attached to his relatives, but the poet in him suffered bitterly from the vapidity of his life. Pushkin said in an early "epistle" that he had not entertained the illusion of "love, hope, and quiet glory" too long: all of it had disappeared like a dream, like the morning mist. Lermontov never had any illusions at all. This may have been due partly to his natural melancholy, but the universal appeal of his poetry proves that he said something everyone has felt but has not known how to express. Lermontov lived at a time when the triumph of mediocrity and servility in civil life had become obvious. Everything that seemed to be superior to its neighbor was speedily and efficiently eradicated.

"The Poet's Death" (No. 31) was a cry of uncontrollable despair, "Meditation" (No. 46) a tragic indictment of his contemporaries, "Oh, Boredom and Sadness . . ." a dirge. Lack of sympathy, petty passions

532

unworthy of man, and, in particular, the past that vanishes leaving no trace in the soul (the most frightening thing of all)—such were the subjects of Lermontov's poetry.

Lermontov's lyric is not an ordinary excursion into *Weltschmerz*, nor is it an example of a poet exposing his wounds to the public (cf. No. 49:21 ff). What allows Lermontov the observer of life to walk safely on the edge of the most dangerous precipice in poetry is the constant presence of deep thought. When Nadson, who came soon after, and a whole brood of poets at the turn of the century began to explore the same motifs, the result was catastrophic. Lermontov is banal only when he relapses into the album style—never in his serious works. As an artist, he is saved by his intonation, whose ingredients are constant but almost always appropriate.

Ellipses in the middle are rare in Lermontov's lyrics, so that here they are especially noticeable as markers of sentences that by their nature cannot be finished. As is often the case with Lermontov, the poem contains agitated rhetorical questions (cf. No. 32), movement toward the climax (one is alone—there is no one to love, and love is not worth the effort—the past recedes and nothing is left of it—all passions are transitory—life itself is a joke in bad taste), and a crushing aphoristic finale.

The poem was written and published in 1840, and half of its lines have become proverbial.

57. *A Cossack Lullaby*

As usual (see note on No. 30), Lermontov made no special attempt in "A Cossack Lullaby" to reproduce the exact idiom of his narrator (in "Borodino" he went further in this direction). Some of the expressions in the lullaby are too literary for a Cossack woman, e.g., "Sleep, my angel," but it matters little, for in this lyric the effect is created totally by intonation.

According to legend, Lermontov composed the lullaby in the house belonging to one of the Cossacks; there he found either a baby sleeping alone or a woman rocking a baby. The woman, the boy's aunt (not mother), reportedly was known by name (Dún'ka Dogádikha), a beauty in the village (*stanítsa*) of Chervlyónaya, and the baby was identified as a certain V. E. Verbítsky. The style and content of the lullaby are akin to the songs that Lermontov must have heard on the river Terek,

Commentary

and since the episode that inspired him remains unknown, the details of the local legend, in spite of its outward historicity (names assigned, etc.), should be taken with a grain of salt. There is an eyewitness report by the man who showed Lermontov the place to spend the night. When the two came there, "no one was at home, except the baby sleeping in its cradle." Lermontov liked the house, "sat down at the table and began to jot down something on a piece of paper" and then read the whole poem to his guide.

"A Cossack Lullaby" was published in 1840, but it could have been written two years earlier. Very soon it became a popular folk song. One of Lermontov's fellow officers asserted that Lermontov himself had put the lullaby to music and written it down; however, the score has never been found. There are probably a hundred songs to it. The poem gave rise to several parodies; the most famous among them are those by Ogaryóv and Nekrásov.

58. "To M. A. Shcherbatova"

The poem is dedicated to Maríya Alexeévna Shcherbátova, Lermontov's great inspiration in 1839-40 (cf. also Nos. 51, 65 and notes). M. I. Glinka wrote in his memoirs that Shcherbatova was charming and extremely attractive. Shan-Giréy, Lermontov's relative and friend, remembered twenty years later:

In the winter of 1839 Lermontov was much interested in Countess Shcherbatova (the piece "For Fetters of Duty" is addressed to her). I never saw her, but I know that she was a young widow, and I heard from him that she was more beautiful than words can express. As is apparent from the subsequent events, M. de Barante, the son of the French envoy in St. Petersburg, thought the same of her. The somewhat too obvious preference that she showed the lucky rival made Barante blow up; he approached Lermontov and said, boiling with indignation, 'Vous profitez trop, monsieur, de ce que nous sommes dans un pays où le duel est défendu!' ('You profit too much by the fact that we are in a country where duels are prohibited').—'Qu'à ça ne tienne, monsieur,' answered Lermontov, 'je me met entièrement à votre disposition' ('No matter, I am entirely at your disposal'), and they decided to meet on the very next day; it happened on Wednesday, during the Shrovetide season of 1840.

Lermontov was very lightly wounded and de Barante not wounded at all (Lermontov discharged his revolver in the air), but the duel had cata-

534

Commentary

strophic consequences for Lermontov: he was exiled to the Caucasus again.

Whether the cause of the duel was so simple and whether Shcherbatova was its mainspring has been disputed, but Lermontov's infatuation with her and her feeling for him are beyond doubt. Equally beyond doubt is the jealousy that feeling caused in S. N. Karamziná (see No. 75 and note): cf. her biting remark in a letter to E. N. Meshchérskaya (August 1, 1839), "Countess Shcherbatova again took me in her carriage to Tsarskoye Selo. She is so kind that I will not again call her stupid."

Lermontov's characterization of Shcherbatova needs no commentaries, except perhaps for one detail. When Lermontov was fond of somebody, he always said that this person was in some way like a child: simplehearted, unconventional, close to the soil that nourished him or her. The hero of his epitaph (No. 6), Odóevsky (No. 53), Tamára (in *The Demon*, No. 92), Shcherbatova, Mtsýri (No. 91) are all "childlike." They do not take part in the masquerade of life and approach what Lermontov understood by "natural man."

Shcherbatova was born in the Ukraine, and her maiden name was Shtérich. Her husband died a year after their marriage. Several days after his death she gave birth to a baby who also died very soon. In 1844 she married Colonel I. S. Lutkóvsky.

The Ukraine plays no role in Lermontov's heritage, and this single "Ukrainian" poem from his pen had, among others, a literary impulse. In No. 2 of the *Otéchestvennye Zapíski* E. P. Grebyónka published a lyric called "Declaration of Love," in which he compared the Ukraine to a beautiful maiden and swore allegiance to his native land. Lermontov knew the poem (his own "Bela" was published in the same issue) and apparently borrowed the structure and imagery of his own lyric from Grebyónka. But Lermontov compared a woman to the Ukraine, not the Ukraine to a woman, i.e., reversed Grebyónka's simile (such reversals are typical of Lermontov: see note on No. 62.)

The greatest attraction of this madrigal is its rhythm of a slow waltz, with lines of varying length and feminine rhyme throughout. Lermontov also employed consistent feminine rhyme in other lyrics (cf. No. 62), but the metric scheme of No. 58 is unique in his works. Later, Fet often used such alternations of the two-foot with the three-foot amphibrach. The poem was published in 1842; Shcherbatova herself sent it to the *Otechestvennye Zapiski*.

59. *"So Many Are Speeches"*

Lermontov expressed his deepest conviction when he said that some sounds whose meaning is obscure or insignificant can stir the inmost depths of the human soul. He explored the mystery of the poetic word for years; even this particular lyric is known in three versions (for the earliest see No. 23:9-16).

The concept of sound played an important role in Lermontov's life. At around the age of seventeen (in 1830 or 1831), he wrote a veritable hymn to sounds, and references to echoes, cries, and songs are common in his later works. No. 55 (see note) is about an evil noise that kills the inner music of the heart; the poet's generation will, according to his prophecy, pass "without a noise or trace" (No. 46:38, and see note on this line); Kozlóv is happy to hear the invisible voice (No. 45); the soul brought to this earth from Heaven can never forget the music of its previous existence (No. 12), the prophet is stoned in a noisy town, and so on.

The spirit of music that Schelling, Novalis, and Hoffmann worshipped is ever present in Lermontov's poetry, and this motif is an important connecting tie between Lermontov and European Romanticism. Lermontov was susceptible only to *structural* influences, to the influences of entire systems (cf. note on No. 18), and this is a case in point. But if music had not sounded in his heart, it could not have been so strongly reinforced by the dominant Romantic trend.

The poem was published in 1841, and according to one story, the editor called Lermontov's attention to a wrong grammatical form in line 11 (*iz plámya* instead of *iz plámeni*). Lermontov tried to alter the line but could not think of anything satisfactory and left the line intact. Even if the story is reliable, Lermontov may be spared the charge of faulty usage; in the middle of the nineteenth century, forms like *iz plámya*, which today are current but substandard, did not sound offensive. They occur elsewhere in Lermontov and in other Russian authors (e.g., in Krylóv, whose Russian is superb). The poem's possible addressee is P. A. Barténeva (see note on No. 42).

60. *The Ghost Ship (from Zedlitz)*

The cult of Napoleon constituted an important part of Russian spiritual life in the first half of the nineteenth century. Some echoes of this cult continued until a much later epoch, as evidenced by Marína Tsvetáeva, but after Pushkin, Tyutchev, and Lermontov it lost all social significance, and Tolstoy had nothing but contempt for the French Emperor. It must not seem strange that Lermontov, the author of "Two Giants" (No. 22) and "Borodino" (No. 30), wrote a ballad like "The Ghost Ship": Lermontov was interested in Napoleon's fate from an early age. His first poem on this subject ("Napoleon") goes back to 1829. It is full of Romantic clichés (Lermontov was fifteen years old when he wrote it), and its action is also set on St. Helena. A young bard sings a song in memory of Napoleon: he recounts the Emperor's victories and grieves that the Emperor invaded Russia. At this moment Napoleon's shadow appears and commands the singer to go away, "Let distant scions keep the record of history and my deeds; I will despise their glorification, for I am above praises, glory, and men." Napoleon is depicted in this lyric as a great individual, towering over his contemporaries. Today this figure looks hopelessly hackneyed, but it reflects the attitude of the Romantic age. Beethoven cursed Napoleon as a usurper, and Tolstoy sneered at his pretensions, but to most of those who wrote about him and painted him (in whatever country), Napoleon was a colossus, a demigod, betrayed and captured, but not conquered. The adoration of Napoleon and the cult of Byron were created by the same spirit (cf. note on No. 18). Napoleon's death among his jailers, a picture of a giant overpowered by dwarfs, eclipsed his vanity and his crimes. Byron, Heine, Lermontov, and a host of lesser poets would have agreed that nothing became Napoleon like his tragic end.

In 1830 Lermontov made a prose translation of Byron's poem "Napoleon's Farewell" and wrote two more poems on the same subject: "Napoleon (Meditation)" and "An Epitaph of Napoleon." In the first of them Napoleon is represented as a ghost looking wistfully over the sea at France, his arms crossed on his breast (as in Ch. VII:19 of Pushkin's *Evgeny Onegin*). In the four-line epitaph, Lermontov called Napoleon great and said, "No one reproaches your shadow." In 1831 he produced a short poem entitled "St. Helena." Not unlike the preceding ones, this poem is awkward, important only as a step in Lermontov's development. For the first time we hear the words that Lermontov will repeat years later, "The vicious country did not deserve that the great man should have finished his life in it." Such words could not have been said before the July Revolution (1830). Roughly at the same time, Lermontov wrote "The Field of Borodino" (see note on No. 30) and "Two

Commentary

Giants'' (No. 22), both of them patriotic. In 1840 we find "The Ghost Ship'' and in 1841 "The Last Abode,'' a response to the reinterment of Napoleon (the coffin with Napoleon's remains was brought to Paris late in 1840). "The Ghost Ship'' also may have been inspired by rumors of the reinterment. Lermontov's sentiment in "The Last Abode'' is as follows: Napoleon came and united France; he was glory's favorite child; he ruled over the people who did not deserve such a ruler. Lermontov could have added: he saved your revolution for you (actually, Lermontov said in his early novel *Vadím*, "in ten years he moved us a whole century forward''). Lermontov realized that Napoleon had "murdered the revolution'' (Pushkin's words), but he never forgot Napoleon as he had been at the beginning of his career. Napoleon, in spite of the 1812 campaign, remained for many Russians an example of genius in modern times and a symbol of liberty, a perfect embodiment of the Romantic hero. The halo became, if anything, even brighter after the events of 1830, when "the reign of traders'' had set in under Louis-Philippe.

Though Lermontov added "from Zedlitz'' to "The Ghost Ship,'' his poem is a free variation on the theme equally important to Zedlitz and himself. Lermontov translated European poets (Schiller, Goethe, Heine, Byron, Thomas Moore, Zedlitz, and Mickiewicz), and some of his "adaptations'' are among his best lyrics. Like many nineteenth-century poets, he made no distinction between his original works and translations and indeed his "Pine Tree'' (from Goethe), two pieces from Heine, and "My Soul Is Dark'' (from Byron) are nearly as famous in Russian as his "Sail.'' "The Ghost Ship'' (actually called "The Aerial Ship'' by Lermontov) is a blend of two ballads by Zedlitz, "Das Geisterschiff'' and "Die nächtliche Heerschau.'' The second of them was popular in Zhukóvsky's translation.

The poem was first published in 1840. Its meter and content were used several times for parodies and imitations, and in a grossly distorted form, it had some currency as a folk song.

61. My Neighbor

This is the first of the four poems written while Lermontov was under arrest after the duel with Ernst de Barante (see note on No. 58). The conversational tone of the poem, reminiscent of what is known in Russian musicology as a urban song (*románs* or *gorodskóy románs*), a genre opposed to a "true" peasant folk song, is unusual for Lermontov (but cf. No. 71 and note).

V. A. Sollogúb visited Lermontov when the latter was in custody in the so-called *Ordonnanzhaus* (pronounced *ordonánsgauz* in Russian) and recollected that the heroine of this lyric had really been a guard's daughter and a very beautiful girl. According to Sollogub, her face was pale and expressed the boundless sadness of a downtrodden life. Allegedly, he even saw Lermontov's portrait of the girl. Shan-Giréy left quite a different version in his memoirs:

Here he wrote his piece "My Neighbor." . . . She was really an attractive neighbor, and I saw her out of the window, though there were no bars on the window, and she was not at all a jailer's daughter but probably the daughter of some clerk employed by the *Ordonnanzhaus*, where there are no jailers whatsoever; a sentry with a gun stood at the door all right, and I always left my saber with him.

Shan-Girey's report sounds more trustworthy from every point of view.

The language of Lermontov's narrator is stylistically neutral, and there is no way of determining to what class of society he belongs. This is Lermontov's normal practice; apart from No. 90:227, the only exception in this respect is No. 30, but even there the few "low" words would have been equally natural in the mouth of an NCO or even a captain (cf. notes on Nos. 57 and 71).

The poem originally appeared in 1842.

62. *A Captive Knight*

It is sometimes believed that "A Captive Knight" was written when Lermontov was under arrest, together with Nos. 60, 61, and 63. No direct evidence supports this dating, however, and its somber mood is closer to that of Lermontov's last lyrics. Since many people looking at the world through prison bars have similar thoughts, it is easy to find parallels in literature to this lyric, especially to the first stanza, but probably none of them should be cited as Lermontov's "source."

An entire poem in feminine rhyme is rare for Lermontov (cf. No. 58), and extended allegories are still rarer in his later works (for examples of earlier allegories, see Nos. 11 and 28). He preferred similes and usually compared concrete things with abstract ones, the definite with the indefinite, the close with the distant (cf. note on No. 58). In this he was

Commentary

unique, for, unlike most poets, he sought inspiration from the outward, sometimes invisible world to bring out the essence of clearly discernible objects. In No. 91:167 he says that mountain crests are like dreams, not that dreams are like crests. This reverse perspective is practically the main law of his early poetry: the fire of flickering icon lamps glitters like a thought in the mind oppressed by grief; a person's azure look is quiet as a recollection, as a distant echo of distant mountains; a snake's abode is cold and dark as the mind deceived by dreams, as a life that has no aim, as a cunning murderer's unfinished greeting reflected in his eyes, and so on. Even in his late prose (*A Hero of Our Time*) we find that "it was quiet in the sky and on earth, as in a man's heart at the moment of a morning prayer" and that "the air is clean and fresh, as a child's kiss". In "A Captive Knight" he says that time is his steed, not that his steed is time. Lermontov was surprisingly consistent in keeping all things as far from his eyes as possible (cf. also note on No. 84). The "wrong" placement of subjects and predicates in the third stanza makes the reading and even the understanding of these lines difficult: the voice should fall on the grammatical subjects, because they are the logical predicates of the sentences. For an early example of a reversible simile in Lermontov see No. 34 and note (sounds are like tears, tears are like sounds).

The poem was passed by the censor on June 30, 1841, two weeks before Lermontov's death.

63. The Journalist, the Reader, and the Writer

This poem, reminiscent of a similar "Conversation . . ." by Pushkin, was written in the Ordonnanzhaus after the duel with E. de Barante (see note on No. 61). The first part of it gives an idea of Lermontov's dramatic art. Many of those who knew Lermontov remembered him as a sharp and witty person. In his literary work these qualities emerge only in his play *The Masquerade* (No. 96). His scurrilous poems are seldom amusing to a modern reader. Nor are his album jokes and epigrams funny (cf. the last stanza of No. 75). But he was unrivaled in the art of brilliant repartee; his jibes and caricatures came home at once, and he was much given to pithy aphorisms, as evidenced by his lyrics. Dialogue of the kind he composed in "The Journalist, the Reader, and the Writer" was his true element. Several sentences from this poem are as memorable to a native speaker of Russian as the most familiar quotations from Griboédov's comedy and Krylóv's fables. The second part, the Reader's monologue, is probably the earliest serious description of the creative process in Russian poetry, and it bears a striking resemblance to the corresponding passage from Pushkin (see Introduction, pp. 6-7). Its pathetic tone is somewhat at variance with the elegant, flippant conversation at the beginning and reads like a development of the ideas expressed in No. 49.

The poem contains disguised quotations and direct allusions to the literary scene of the early Forties. The Writer is of course Lermontov himself. The Journalist, the Reader, and the Reader's friend who has talent but does not write anything are also identifiable, though today the allusions are lost, and even literary historians offer conflicting interpretations. The reader is Pyótr Andréevich Vyázemsky (1792-1878), a former friend of Pushkin's, at one time a popular poet and critic and in the late 1830s and 40s a disdainful skeptic and successful courtier, or perhaps A. S. Khomyakóv. The Journalist could have been N. A. Polevóy, also a well-known author, who in Pushkin's days was famous for his liberal sympathies; but by 1840 he had lost them and turned from being Lermontov's supporter into his opponent and detractor. According to another hypothesis, the Journalist is a takeoff on the notorious critic, author, and informer Faddey Bulgárin.

A Hero of Our Time was published in 1840, and the Writer's passionate soliloquy is clearly connected with Lermontov's meditations on the literary merits of his book.

The epigraph has been tentatively identified with one of Goethe's aphorisms.

L. 43. In the Russian intellectual life of Lermontov's time two main groups were central: the Westerners and the Slavophiles (see more about them in note on No. 73). The symbol of Western civilization and Peter's reforms was St. Petersburg (which people called simply Petersburg), while the Slavophiles gravitated toward Moscow. Lermontov was fond of Moscow and felt chilled by St. Petersburg, though his last years were spent there. The line about sharp remarks on Moscow is a transparent reference to the debates of that epoch.

64. < To M. P. Solomirskaya >

Maríya Petróvna Solomírskaya (née Apráksina: 1811-1859) was mar-

Commentary

ried to a brother of Lermontov's fellow officer. When in the winter of 1839-40 Lermontov read his *Demon* in some aristocratic *salons*, Solomirskaya must have been one of his listeners. She is known to have said to Lermontov, while dancing with him at a ball, "You know, Lermontov, I am really drawn to your Demon. . . . His oaths are attractive beyond any measure. . . . I think I could have fallen in love with such a mighty, powerful, and proud creature and sincerely believe that in love, as well as in malice, he would be really loyal and great." (Cf. No. 92:811-12.) When Lermontov was arrested for the duel with de Barante (see note on No. 58), Solomirskaya sent him an unsigned note. Lermontov had probably never seen her hand before and simply guessed the author. The imagery of the poem could have been evoked by their conversation.

The poem was first published in 1842.

65. Wherefore?

According to Eikhenbaum, "Wherefore?" was dedicated to M. A. Shcherbátova (cf. notes on Nos. 51 and 58). Lermontov published it in 1840. It contains all the familiar features of his style: antithesis, steady movement toward the climax, and a chilling paradox in the last line.

66. Thanksgiving

This is the last of Lermontov's "prayers" (cf. Nos. 3, 35, 37, 51). In Lermontov's time there was no strict rule that the Russian forms corresponding to Thee, Thou, Thy when applied to the Godhead should be spelled with a capital letter. In this particular poem Lermontov spelled them with a small letter, so perhaps he addressed a perfidious woman, not God. But the content of the poem, especially of its last lines, can hardly be interpreted as that of a love lyric. Later editors took the poem for a prayer and normalized Lermontov's spelling (in present-day Soviet Russian all these words are again spelled with small letters—see the text facing the English translation). The censor may have misinterpreted the true addressee of the poem, but nineteenth-century Russian censors varied a great deal and would sometimes pretend not to have noticed things that were ambiguous (thus, Goncharóv, the author of *Oblómov*, was a censor and, despite Hertzen's virulent attack on him, a benevolent one;

Tyutchev, indeed a man of very conservative views, was a censor of foreign books. For some reason, a really pious prayer, No. 37, written almost three years earlier, was published later than "Thanksgiving" (both appeared in 1840). The hypothesis that in this way Lermontov tried to atone for "Thanksgiving" or to avert the trouble it might have caused seems, on the face of it, rather thin.

In 1839 V. I. Krásov (1810-1854), at that time Belínsky's great favorite, published in the same almanac as Lermontov his own prayer, banal and devout. Its last line ran as follows, "I thank Thee, Creator, I thank Thee for all." The first line of Lermontov's "Thanksgiving" is almost a word for word repetition of Krasov's conclusion and may have been an answer to that author. Again, "Thanksgiving" sounds somewhat like a passage in *Evgeny Onegin* (VI:45). Both poets wrote their lines at the age of twenty-six, and Lermontov might have been piqued by this circumstance. However, Lermontov's sources are unknown. His works contain dozens of disguised quotations, used approvingly or polemically (those should be distinguished from borrowings, which also are numerous). Independent of the impulse that gave rise to "Thanksgiving," the poem, with its oxymorons, sarcasm, and movement toward the bathos suddenly exploding in the last line, is very characteristic of Lermontov. As regards the message of this lyric, it should be noted that Lermontov was not irreligious (i.e., he was not an atheist and never doubted the existence of God) but often "heretical" and iconoclastic.

67. To a Child

Lermontov's lyrics written between 1837 and 1841 are relatively few, so most of them are well known. *To a Child* is among the less popular poems, despite its outstanding merits. Its stifled syntax and long lines fit the narrator's mood with rare perfection. Enjambment is not uncommon in Lermontov, but he used it economically. This poem probably has five times more run-on lines than any other of Lermontov's lyrics of comparable length. The effect of the device is striking: together with the poet, the reader constantly gasps for air.

Several attempts have been made to find the addressee of the poem, all unsuccessful. (V. A. Lopukhiná [see note on No. 19] indeed had a child, and Lermontov reportedly saw it once, but the child was a girl.)

The poem was published in 1840, the same year it was written.

Commentary

68. To A. O. Smirnova

Alexándra Ósipovna Smirnóva (1809-1882), usually referred to as Smirnova-Rosset (Russian nineteenth-century sources give her name as Rosset, Rossetti, and Rosetti), was the Empress's lady-in-waiting. She met Lermontov quite often, for both were regular visitors at the Karamzíns' salon (see No. 75:15 and note). She presided over her own salon too, and Lermontov was a frequent guest there. Their acquaintance goes back to the summer of 1838. Smirnova was a woman of great beauty and superior intelligence. Pushkin mentioned her in the poem "Her Eyes" (indeed, to say that Olénina's eyes are more beautiful!). Vyázemsky, Rostopchiná, and Zhukóvsky also extolled her. Lermontov wrote about Smirnova (disguised as Mínskaya in "Shtoss"), "Her beauty, rare intelligence, and original view of things were bound to impress a clever and imaginative man. . . ." But the closeness between the two should not be exaggerated. For Smirnóva, Lermontov was first and foremost an ambitious officer. She disapproved of many things he did and had a low opinion of some of his poems ("very bad" was her verdict when she read "The Poet"). Lermontov of course knew it; hence the tone of the poem. When he confessed that in her presence he could never say what he wanted, it was an accurate statement. On May 10, 1841, he mentioned Smirnova in his letter to S. N. Karamziná from the Caucasus, "I wanted to write to some more people in Petersburg, among others to M-me Smirnova, but I was not sure whether she would tolerate such arrogance and thought better of it!" Cf. also what the poet Ya. P. Polónsky, the tutor of Smirnova's children, wrote, "She was the only woman of whose mind, sharp and caustic, even Lermontov was afraid."

Many years after Lermontov's death Smirnova became an intimate companion of Gogol. She is known as the addressee of several letters in Gogol's *Selected Passages from a Correspondence with Friends*. Turgenev knew her too and (at least after 1852) disliked her very much. She is the prototype of Lasúnskaya in *Rudin*. In Chapter 6 of *Rudin* there are these words, "Is it possible that this small, yellow, sharp-nosed woman, not yet old, should once have been a beauty; is she the one in whose honor poets strummed their lyres?" He made disrespectful references to her in his *Fathers and Sons*, *Spring Freshets*, and possibly in *Smoke* ("a dried-up morel").

Commentary

Smirnova was a good friend of the poet P. A. Pletnyóv, Rector of St. Petersburg University, who liked Pushkin but felt unmitigated contempt for Lermontov. Later she was friendly with Count Baryatínsky (he is the general in Tolstoy's short story "A Raid": see note on No. 90); Baryatinsky was Lermontov's former fellow student at the military school, the target of his ribald poem *The Hospital*, the man who hated Lermontov decades after the poet's death. Smirnova's foster-brother A. I. Arnóldi and her uncle N. I. Lórer also disliked Lermontov. So did her husband, N. M. Smirnóv, a highly placed official, but he at least praised Lermontov's poetry. Baryatinsky was sincerely surprised that Viskováty should want to write a biography of Lermontov, when such a man as he himself was still alive and within reach. "Just speak to A. O. Smirnova about it," he said, "I'll introduce you." And indeed, Smirnova advised Viskovaty against studying Lermontov's life. No wonder that when Smirnova wrote her own memoirs (published posthumously in 1894) and an autobiography (published in 1931, almost fifty years after her death), she devoted only several insignificant paragraphs to Lermontov. The episode she relates has a direct bearing on the poem dedicated to her. She writes "Sophie Karamzina told me that Lermontov had felt slighted, because I did not comment on his poem. The album always lay on a small table in my drawing-room. One day he called in the morning, did not find me in, went upstairs, opened the album, and wrote these verses."

The album poem began with the lines enclosed in the translation in square brackets. The reason for this is that Lermontov brought out this poem himself in 1840 without the first quatrain and without the name in the title. The omitted stanza was first published in 1858 (i.e., in Smirnova's lifetime) and later reproduced in 1862. Some critics have argued that the poem will gain if the rejected lines are placed where they belong (some modern editors cite them in the notes). Their opponents refer to the author's intent. The idea that the author's will cannot be violated is quite meaningless in Lermontov's case: almost the entire first volume of his complete works consists of poems never meant for publication at all.

In this book the poem is dated 1840, but there is no certainty that the date is correct. It may have been written at least two years earlier.

69. To a Portrait

The portrait described is that of Countess Alexándra Kiríllovna Vorontsóva-Dashkóva (1818-1856), famous for her beauty both in Russia

545

and Europe. Lermontov saw a 1840 lithograph of her portrait, made in Paris by Pierre-Louis Grevedon (1782-1860). In the Pushkin Museum of Fine Arts (Moscow) there is a portrait of Vorontsova-Dashkova by Zaryánko.

V. A. Sollogúb, a talented author, who, among other things, wrote a book called *Beau monde*, an amusing description of high society and at the same time a rather vicious parody of Lermontov, recollected:

I have seen women much more beautiful and perhaps more brilliant, though Princess Vorontsova-Dashkova was extremely witty; but I have never met in any one of them such a mixture of the most delicate taste, elegance, grace and such sincere merriment, sprightliness and an almost boyish love of mischief. Life welled up in her; it enlivened and made beautiful all that surrounded her.

In the mid 1850s she eloped with a French doctor, who took her to Paris and robbed her. She died soon in absolute misery. Vorontsova-Dashkova's tragic death brought to life Nekrásov's lyric 'Knyagínya'' ('Princess, Countess'), which almost cost him a duel with her husband. In this mocking epitaph, Nekrasov mentioned ''two hurried stanzas by a Russian poet'' dedicated to her; he had in mind Lermontov's verses. Vorontsova-Dashkova was also a mistress of Lermontov's relative and friend Alexéy Stolýpin (nicknamed Mongo); this connection with the fickle and capricious woman ruined Mongo's life. In his younger days Mongo was strikingly handsome and full of life, but, sad as it may seem, it was he whom Turgenev chose for the main prototype of Pável Petróvich Kirsánov in *Fathers and Sons*. Countess R. is Vorontsova-Dashkova.

During his last stay in St. Petersburg, in 1841, Lermontov was a welcome guest in the Princess's salon and even danced at her ball on February 7, which action caused the anger of a Grand Duke (an exiled officer on leave was not supposed to appear at receptions honored by the presence of Royalty).

70. Clouds

''Clouds,'' the last item in Lermontov's book of 1840, was probably improvised by him at the beginning of May in the Karamzíns' salon (see No. 75 and note), before he was sent from St. Petersburg into his second and last exile. Like Lermontov's other improvisations, it was constructed of ready-made blocks. This is not said to belittle Lermontov:

all that is "improvised," from heroic lays to organ fugues, conforms to the same law. The content of this poem had also been prepared by years of meditation. In 1830 Lermontov wrote in his journal,

> At the age of eight I was going alone somewhere in a thunderstorm, and I remember a cloud, which was small as a strip of a black cloak, and it was swiftly flitting across the sky; it stands so alive before my eyes, as if I could still see it.

And, indeed, Lermontov's poems are full of light and dark clouds, mists, and blue smokes. Fibrous and golden, white or dangerous, reflected in the Terek, pursuing the moon, intertwined like snakes, or sleeping on the bosom of an old and solitary cliff, they constitute the most familiar part of his landscapes. And early in life Lermontov chose clouds playing with azure and obeying no force but the winds as a symbol of indifference and rootlessness (a good example in this volume is No. 53:42-44).

The author V. A. Sollogúb recalled the episode of Lermontov's improvisation twice: in a talk with Viskováty (the poet's biographer) and in his own *Memoirs*, but the versions give conflicting evidence. This is the relevant passage from Viskovaty's book:

> Many people came to the Karamzins to say adieu to their young friend, and touched by the attention paid him and the unfeigned love of the selected circle, the poet, standing by the window and looking at the clouds that crawled over Summer Gardens and the Neva, wrote the poem "Heaven's Inhabitants, Friends of Diversity." Sofya Karamzina and several guests surrounded the poet and begged him to read the poem he had just jotted down. He directed to all of us the sad glance of his expressive eyes and read it. When he finished, his eyes were wet with tears.

In *Memoirs* the situation is presented quite differently, and the poem allegedly recited is an extract from *The Demon*—but also about the ever-indifferent clouds! (See No. 92:329-44.)

71. Testament

It would be natural to compare "Testament" with "Borodinó" (No. 30) and *Valerík* (No. 90), for all three are about military life, but the intonation of "Testament" is unique, and only No. 61 is in the same conversational style. "Testament" is probably the warmest and the most touching of Lermontov's lyrics. There is no stylistic indication that its hero is a soldier. An officer, for example, a captain, would have used

the same language and said the same things. The man is, in the idiom
of Lermontov's time, a Caucasian, that is, someone like Maxím Maxí-
mych (*A Hero of our Time*).

The poem was published in 1841, while Lermontov was still alive.

72. *A Plea*

Lermontov returned to the theme of this poem all his life, constantly
visualizing his disgraceful death (usually on the scaffold) and begging
the woman he loved to forgive him and, if possible, not to betray him
(cf. note on No. 54).

Whether the poem was written for V. A. Lopukhiná (see note on No.
19) is uncertain. It appeared in 1841, still in Lermontov's lifetime.

73. *My Native Land*

Lermontov's attitude toward his homeland has been a matter of long and
barren dispute. Lermontov was not a journalist, public speaker, or politi-
cian; he was a poet, and when every line he wrote comes to be quoted
in the court of posterity, the result cannot but appear confusing. Nos.
22, 29, 30, 80, and to a certain extent 90, each in its own way, throw
light on Lermontov's patriotism in the period between 1832 and 1841.
The finales of No. 31 and especially No. 78 tell us more about this mat-
ter. At some moments Lermontov undoubtedly identified Russia and her
history with the glory of the crown.

In the first half of the nineteenth century, defining history was not
an academic question, not, at any rate, in Russia. After the publication
of Karamzín's *History of the Russian State* the Russian intelligencia con-
stantly discussed the problem of whether Russian history "belonged"
to the tsars or to the people. The role of the masses, the attitude of the
educated class toward peasant culture (including popular speech and nar-
rative genres), and many other issues of similar nature were covered
by the term *naródnost'* (relatedness to the people). Practically everyone
swore by the name of the people, but the elastic and resounding word
narodnost' easily justified the most conservative point of view ("the peo-
ple belong to God and the Tsar") and the most radical one ("the people
do not need a monarch; monarchy is hostile to the interests of the peo-
ple"). Again, everyone was for "progress," but there was no agree-
ment as to what progress meant. The main bone of contention was

whether Russia should move along the lines envisaged by Peter I (that is, choose the Western way of development), or retain her national features, reinforce them, and avoid influences from the West. The first party was known as the Westerners; for them St. Petersburg was the symbol of "young Russia" (Pushkin's phrase). The second party went under the name of the Slavophiles, and they looked upon Moscow, Russia's ancient capital, as the spiritual center of the country (cf. note on No. 63:43). Neither trend was homogeneous; both had their "left" and "right" wings, and some prominent figures of that epoch cannot be "classified" at all. All authors were "patriots" and "loved Russia"; the crucial point was not the formula itself but the implications drawn from it.

Lermontov's manifesto is a lyric and should be treated as such, because it bears the unmistakable imprint of his poetic style. For Lermontov, the concept of homeland meant a complete merging with the country's nature and customs. In his choice of "patriotic detail" he was as impressionistic as in many other things. He invariably looked for the most stereotyped symbols. A sail dissolving in a bluish haze signified a solitary and mutinous swimmer to his lyric hero (No. 28); rocks, eagles, racing steeds, and rushing torrents represented home to Mtsyri, a captive boy from mountainous Georgia (No. 91); and ancient castles symbolized Scotland for the young Lermontov himself (No. 10). For this reason, the second part of "My Native Land" is not a mere catalog of Lermontov's favorites. Whatever he might think of sad villages, full garners, dancing peasants, and so on, they were not important items in his life: rather, they were *symbols* of Russia to him, along with the inevitable birch tree. The description is touching, in some places pastoral and sentimental, but, like all impressionistic landscapes, it will not bear close scrutiny. (Cf. Pushkin's description of Russia in *Evgeny Onegin's Travels*: "Inye nuzhny mne kartiny.")

Much more definite (and therefore more difficult to interpret) are the six opening lines. It is clear that seeing war at close quarters had taught Lermontov a great deal, and the glory purchased by blood must have referred to something like the dubious victory on the banks of the River Valerík (No. 90). "The proud serenity" (in the original: the serenity [or: peace] full of proud confidence) was probably a political term. The Decembrists believed that under an ideal regime all citizens would have confidence in their government, and the new order would result in a lasting civil peace and the emergence of pride in the country's leaders and the citizens themselves. The line may mean that Lermontov had little faith in the Decembrists' utopia. According to some critics, serenity (peace) here is an allusion to the confidence the landowners had in their future or to the muteness of Nicholas's Russia, or to the hard-won peace after the French invasion, but those are strained interpretations.

Line 5 sounds like a mild thrust at the Slavophiles. Both the Westerners and the Slavophiles laid claim to Lermontov's poetry; both called it their own. The tendency to present Lermontov as a Slavophile goes back to the end of the nineteenth century, and it permeates Viskováty's biography. The evidence for this doctrine is slight. Lermontov loved Moscow much more than St. Petersburg, but the Slavophiles did not have a monopoly on the love of Moscow. He regarded with disapproval the French way of development after Napoleon, but so did Griboédov and Hertzen, both Westerners. He wrote a variation on a Russian bylina theme (its action is set in the reign of Ivan the Terrible), but history and folklore belong to all, and Lermontov's hero does not resemble the Slavophile ideal. Lermontov was friendly with some leading Slavophiles, but the idea that only people having identical views can be friends was alien to the nineteenth century. Lermontov was a true intellectual; deep, mature reflection is present in all his later poems and in *A Hero of Our Time*, but he did not represent any party, trend, or platform. In "My Native Land" he glorified the poetic Russia, the Russia that only an artist could see. His attachments have Rousseauian overtones, but the music is his own.

In line 7 he calls his love strange. The usual explanation of this strangeness runs approximately as follows. Lermontov could not subscribe to official patriotism (thus, his attitude was at variance, even at cross-purposes, with what was taught by and required of the ruling class); and he was equally indifferent to his country's glorious past (a sentiment incompatible with the very idea of patriotism); finally, it must have been difficult to have amicable feelings for Nicholas's "sordid Russia" (No. 78:1), and Lermontov, like many others (for example, Hertzen and Tyutchev), would almost apologize for his love, a love that was stronger than his "reason." We need hardly decipher Lermontov's epithet in this way and read so much into his words, because everything he wanted to say he says quite clearly, even if some words no longer mean what they meant in 1840. He says that he does not love Russia with a historian's or politician's love ("the glory bought by blood or treason") and that his feeling for her is not fed by any program, whether that of the Decembrists, i.e. Westerners ("proud serenity"), or the

Slavophiles ("the sacred chronicles"). He lets others go their way and is ready to respect their views: glory is glory, whatever its price (it is not called infamy here as in No. 31), the much coveted civil peace is indeed full of proud confidence, and the chronicles are sacred. But *he* loves something quite different, viz. the poetic Russia, where even mournful villages are beautiful (because they are so scenic) and where drunken peasants are attractive (because they are part of the backdrop). He loves the perennial image of his native land. Lermontov's lyric is *a poet's* declaration of love; his love is strange, because it is so utterly selfless.

The poem received approval from both Belínsky and Dobrolyúbov, the two most radical critics of their respective periods (Dobrolyubov was a close associate of Chernyshévsky's), but, curiously enough, neither of them said anything definite about it. According to Belinsky, "My Native Land" was as good as Pushkin's best works. Dobrolyúbov remarked that one could not require from a Russian poet a fuller expression of pure love for the people, a more humane view of their life. But "My Native Land" has little in common with the passages from Pushkin usually cited as parallels, and a trivial mention of drays, garners, and shutters hardly qualifies as "the purest love of the people."

It is not improbable that "My Native Land" was polemically directed against Khomyakóv's poem "Russia." Khomyakóv, a prominent Slavophile wrote, "Flatterers are telling you that you rule half of the world, that your rivers are like seas. Do not believe it, do not listen to it, do not take pride in this strength, this glory, this dust." For Lermontov not everything was dust. He feared that his own love of Russia was more typical of an outsider than of a Russian citizen and wanted to square accounts with his conscience. Friedrich Bodenstedt, who knew Lermontov and was the first translator of his poetry into German, wrote:

Critics were far from unanimous in recognizing his talent; . . . some people thought that Lermontov was too self-willed and insistent in his attempts to swim against the current and behaved in his own country like a beleaguered foreigner. The accusation that he had no real love for Russia made him write his heartfelt poem "My Native Land."

Lermontov was a violent nonconformist and greatly valued his "strangeness" (*A Strange Man* happens to be the title of his early autobiographical drama; cf. note on No. 17), but it was hard to always stand alone.

Commentary

"My Native Land" was published in the spring of 1841, several months before Lermontov's death.

74. A Dead Man's Love

Lermontov's poem was partly inspired by Alphonse Karr's "Le mort amoureux," which appeared in *Les Guepes* in May of 1841. However, an album with Lermontov's autograph goes back to September 1839; in this album, Lermontov's Russian poem also has the title "Le mort amoureux," and this may be too much of a coincidence. Even though Lermontov seems to have known Karr's poem almost two years before it was published, "A Dead Man's Love" is neither a translation from the French, nor a paraphrase of Karr's lyric, because this plot was widely exploited by all European Romantics, especially German. In Russian, Polezháev (see note on No. 16) wrote "A Dead Man Alive" as early as 1828 (published in 1832). Karr may have given a final push to Lermontov, who was particularly interested in the motif of "life-in-death."

The censor passed the poem nine days after Lermontov's death, and it came out in the autumn of 1841.

75. From the Album of S. N. Karamzina

Sófya Nikoláevna Karamziná was the daughter of Nikoláy Mikháylovich Karamzín, the celebrated author and historian. The salon ruled by her stepmother Ekaterína Alexándrovna and herself began its existence in 1826, after Karamzin's death. It attracted the most brilliant writers and scholars of St. Petersburg and was the only fashionable parlor where visitors did not play cards and spoke Russian (otherwise the language of high society was French). Lermontov joined the salon in 1838 as Sofya Nikolaevna's old acquaintance and read *The Demon* (No. 92) and some chapters from *A Hero of Our Time* there.

The present poem is traditionally dated 1841, but as the latest research has shown, it was probably written in 1840. Album poems were seldom or never impromptus, and an extant letter by Sofya Nikolaevna to E. N. Meshchérskaya written in 1839 throws a new light on this genre and on the relations between her and Lermontov.

I gave him—and that long ago—my album to write something there. Yesterday [June 26, 1839] he announced to me that 'when all the people have left, I shall read something and tell him a kind word.' I guessed that he meant my album.

And indeed, when all had left, he gave me the album and asked me to read the poem aloud and tear it up if I did not like it: for he would then write another one. He could not have guessed better. The poem, very poor indeed, written on the last page of the album, contained nothing but commonplaces of the worst sort. He said that he was afraid to write amidst so many celebrities, most of whom he had never met. He felt among them like an awkward débutant entering a parlor where he is unable to follow the ideas and conversations but smiles at jokes, pretending that he understands them, and at last, embarrassed and confused, sits down sadly in a small corner, and that is all. 'Well?' 'To tell the truth, I don't like it. Too banal, and the verses are insignificant.' 'Tear them up.' I did not wait for him to repeat it, ripped the leaf out of the album, tore it to small pieces and threw them to the floor. He picked them up and burned them over a candle, but he blushed and laughed in a strained way, I must confess. Mother says that I am crazy, that what I did is silly and insolent. She finally drove me to tears and made me repent, though I insist (and it is quite true) that I could not have given a stronger proof of my friendship and respect for the poet and the man. He also said that he was grateful to me, that I had done him a service since I considered him above childish vanity and that he wanted the album back, because now his honor was at stake. Finally, he left, rather embarrassed, and I was very ill at ease. I look forward to meeting him in order to dispel the unpleasant impression.

The poem that has survived Sofya Nikolaevna's friendly criticism and that editors call "From the Album of S. N. Karamzina" is serious and deep in spite of the facetious and not very funny ending. Lermontov began *in medias res*, as if continuing a conversation memorable to both. It is tempting to suppose that the conversation was about Romanticism and Pushkin, for some of Pushkin's strophes from *Evgeny Onegin* (VI:43-44) say the same things in almost the same words as in Lermontov's miniature. "Ugly beauty" is a striking oxymoron and the key phrase in the poem.

A. O. Smirnóva is the addressee of No. 68. Lermontov alluded to the bold anecdotes that she liked to tell. Smirnova was extremely witty, and Myátlev regarded her as the real inspirer of his humorous poem about M-me de Courdukoff, a Russian innocent abroad. Sásha is Alexánd(e)r Nikoláevich Karamzín, the historian's son, who was twenty-six or twenty-seven at that time, also a brilliant conversationalist and a poet. Íshka Myátlev is Iván Petróvich Myátlev (1796-1844), an author and well-known wit. Both Pushkin and Lermontov loved him (Lermontov and Myatlev even exchanged dedications), and others, Turgenev among them, were fond of his works too.

Commentary

The poem, without the last four lines, was published at the very end of 1841 (after Lermontov's death but apparently by Sofya Nikolaevna's permission). The concluding stanza became known to the public only in 1916.

76. To Countess Rostopchina

Evdokíya Petróvna Rostopchiná (née Sushkóva: 1811-1858), a cousin of E. A. Sushkóva (see note on No. 9), was a popular poetess in the 1830s and 1840s. Several years before her death she became friendly with Dumas père, who spent some time in Russia. In 1858 she wrote him a long letter in which she recalled her acquaintance with Lermontov. Dumas published it in *Le Caucase. Journal de voyages et romans* 19, 1859, 147-50 (Paris). The letter is very interesting and clever. Lermontov and Rostopchina first met in Moscow and Lermontov dedicated to her several poems, "The Cross on the Rock" (No. 14) and "Dodó" (a New Year madrigal) among them. The madrigal follows the laws of the genre, but one can still feel that Lermontov had the highest opinion of Rostopchina's ready wit and independent judgment. And indeed, even when she was very young, she did not allow anyone to tell her what to do. Rostopchina shocked society by her resolution to write and publish poetry. She admired the Decembrists for their heroism and martyrdom and was herself respected and loved by many of her brilliant contemporaries. In the 1850s, Rostopchina cursed her past and began to extol the Tsar, and she was as adamant in her recantation as in her heresy.

When Rostopchina and Lermontov met for the first time, she felt entirely unimpressed by him.

He had a very plain appearance, and this lack of physical beauty, which later gave way to the force of expression and nearly vanished when his genius transformed his plain features, was striking even at his young age. It determined the way of thinking, tastes, and attitudes of the young man with a passionate mind and boundless ambition. Since he did not believe that he could enjoy success, he decided to seduce or frighten and draped himself in Byronic clothes, which was all the vogue then. Don Juan became his hero—moreover, his model; he acted mysterious, gloomy, sharp. This childish game left an indelible imprint on his quick and impressionable imagination; since he passed himself off as a Lara or a Manfred, he became like them.

Lermontov and Rostopchina did not see each other for ten years and met again when Lermontov came to St. Petersburg for the last time in

554

the winter of 1841. Both were common visitors of S. N. Karamzina's salon (see No. 75 and note), and Lermontov also saw Rostopchina at her own receptions. This time they became friends at once. As her brother S. P. Sushkóv said,

Both were almost of the same age, . . . both were very clever and witty, both were poets from early youth, both belonged to the same layer of society, had mutual friends, and both, young as they were, had already suffered from disappointments and hardships, each in a different way.

Lermontov's furlough was drawing to a close.

He was very unwilling to leave, he had all kinds of forebodings. At last, at the end of April or the beginning of May we met for a farewell supper to wish him a happy journey. I was one of the last to shake his hand. . . . During the whole supper and before his departure Lermontov spoke of nothing else but his impending death. I tried to make him stop it and began to laugh at his seemingly groundless forebodings, but they affected me too and gripped my heart. Two months later they came true, and a revolver shot for a second time robbed Russia of a precious life that was her national pride.

Shortly before he left Rostopchina dedicated to Lermontov a lyric entitled "Farewell." In return, Lermontov gave her an album with his poem "I've Always Known: One Star Received Us." Several days after Lermontov's departure from St. Petersburg a book of Rostopchina's poems came out. She sent him a copy with the dedication, "To Mikhail Yuryevich Lermontov in token of amazement at his talent and of sincere friendship for him himself." But the book reached Pyatigórsk too late. After Lermontov's death Rostopchina wrote an elegy "To Our Future Poets," in which she lamented the early and unnatural death of Russia's literary geniuses, and another called "An Empty Album." The latter, composed in blank verse, is very close to some passages from her memoirs.

"To Countess Rostopchina" was first published in 1841.

77. The Pact

This is a late version of a poem written in 1832 (at that time it was called "To a Seducer" 'K prelestnitse'). Lermontov reworked the last eight lines; the other changes are minor. Prostitutes, "fallen women," etc., are not uncommon characters in Lermontov's narrative poetry, and they are always described with sympathy and compassion. However, the image of the heroine is vague (is she indeed a fallen woman?). Lermontov often described situations that are realistic and clear only at first sight (cf. Nos. 38 and 41). The poem was published in 1842.

78. *"Farewell, My Russia, Sad and Sordid"*

In a literal translation the poem reads as follows, "Farewell, unwashed Russia,/ Land of slaves, land of masters,/ And you, blue uniforms,/ And you, people, devoted to them./ Perhaps beyond the wall of the Caucasus,/ I will hide from your pashas,/ From their all-seeing eye,/ From their all-hearing ears." The poem may have been written in 1841 in connection with the last exile, when Lermontov was ordered to leave St. Petersburg in forty-eight hours; but the exact date is unknown.

Blue uniforms were worn by gendarmes. *Pashas* and *ears*, both words in the genitive plural, make a perfect rhyme in Russian, but, regardless of the rhyme, *pasha* is an excellent word in this context. (*Viziers* is an obvious choice here. The same rhyme (viziers-ears) is in Guy Daniels' translation.) For political reasons the poem was suppressed for many years. It was first published in 1887 (with the word *tsars* instead of *pashas*); the Russian variant given in this book came out only in 1890. The 1890 text had a note at the end, "Recorded from the poet's mouth by a contemporary."

79. The Cliff

In 1841 Lermontov paraphrased two poems from Heine: "Ein Fichtenbaum steht einsam" and "Sie liebten sich beide, doch keiner." Both are about solitude and an unrequited feeling, and both are among Lermontov's highest achievements. "The Cliff," which is an original lyric, is part of this small cycle, and it carries one of Lermontov's favorite motifs. In his poetry cliffs often stand alone, separated from other cliffs (as in No. 91:156 ff.), and proud sufferers are likened to them (cf. No. 38:11 ff. and also No. 76:17-18).

Lermontov was fond of clear-cut juxtapositions; cf.: "the blind beggar was cruelly deceived, and I was deceived in the same way" (No. 9); "the dagger has become a useless toy, and the poet has lost his importance" (No. 47), etc.; but he also used allegories that he did not turn into fables. Thus, "The Cliff" lacks a moral beginning with some such

Commentary

words as "And so do we . . ." or "Are we not as well . . . ?" which inevitably accompanied older Russian elegies.

The poem is written in the five-foot trochee, a meter that Pushkin never used at all and Lermontov only twice: here and in No. 85. "The Cliff," published in 1843, proved a great favorite with Russian composers (about sixty songs).

80. The Debate

Apart from stating that the Caucasus was *the* country of Russian Romanticism (cf. notes on No. 39 and 52) and the main source of Lermontov's literary inspiration (see No. 4 and note), one should bear in mind that Russia waged endless local wars there, trying to subjugate the mountaineers and annex their territory (see note on No. 16). The attitude toward the Caucasus remained one of the main political issues of Nicholas's epoch. "The Debate" was written in 1841 and, together with *Valerík* (No. 90), it gives us some insight into Lermontov's position. But the texts of both poems should be used with great caution in deriving any political inferences, because as constantly stressed in these notes (see especially note on No. 73), the poems are literary works, not versified manifestos. This is especially true of "The Debate," in which the descriptive aspect is paramount.

In the poem *Izmaíl-Bey* (1832 or later) Lermontov wrote the following, "Submit, Cherkess! Both West and East may soon share your fate. The hour will come, and you yourself will say with pride: 'I know I am a slave but a slave of the tsar of the universe.' " Even in the prologue to *Mtsyri* (No. 91) he spoke of Georgia flourishing under the protection of friendly Russian bayonets (the tone of the preceding lines is perhaps ironic, but the conclusion seems to be quite serious). *Valerik* is devoid of the belligerent mood that inspired the lines from *Izmail-Bey*, and in "My Native Land" he refused to feel elated at the sight of the glory bought by blood (No. 73:3). In "The Debate" the fall of the Caucasus and its conquest by Russia are taken for granted and, what is more, Lermontov gave a very sympathetic description of the Russian army and its leader (lines 81-84).

This leader was General Alexéy Petróvich Yermólov. Two more references to Yermolov occur in this volume: No. 90:68 and No. 91:27, but he is mentioned by name only in *Valerik*. Yermolov, an active participant of the war against Napoleon (he distinguished himself in the battle of Borodinó), was known in 1812 as a brave officer and a skillful intriguer against Kutúzov. Between 1816 and 1827 he served in the Caucasus and enjoyed tremendous popularity in the army. He was democratic in his habits, and Nicholas suspected him (with good reason) of Decembrist sympathies. In 1827 his corps was taken away from him, and after that he lived in Oryól (central Russia), in Moscow, and in a village near Moscow, sometimes visiting St. Petersburg. He remained the center of attraction for many outstanding people; at one time, Ryléev and Kyukhelbéker wrote odes to him, and Griboédov was his friend. Pushkin (in 1829) considered it an honor to meet him, but Pushkin had mixed feelings about Yermolov as a man. Some of Yermolov's older admirers, e.g., Griboedov and Kyukhelbeker, were later disappointed in him: Yermolov was a sly and slippery politician. He could have changed the history of Russia but chose not to do so; his contemporaries believed that if he had supported the Decembrists' uprising both the monarchy and serfdom would have fallen, and Russia would have become a republic in 1825. Yermolov's name was a symbol of Russian victories in the Caucasus, which means that he drowned that country in blood. He was more hated and feared by the natives than any other Russian military commander. Lermontov was going to write a historical novel about the Caucasian wars under Yermolov (like Pushkin before him!), and there is no knowing what he would have said there; but whenever Yermolov's name comes up in Lermontov's extant works, the tone is invariably one of respect.

The censor may not have recognized the allusion to the banished general, but the likelihood of such naïveté is not great. Besides, there was no ban on Yermolov's name, as evidenced by "Maxím Maxímych" (a tale in *A Hero of Our Time*) and No. 90:68. Lermontov left his poem to the editor of a Moscow almanac with the request to publish it "just as it is, without any comments, with his signature." This is sometimes interpreted as meaning that Lermontov wanted to avoid too overt a reference to the general who was in Nicholas's disfavor. But what editor would have wanted to add such references, if they were really dangerous? The reasons for the request must have lain elsewhere. Lermontov had published most of his poems in Kireévsky's *Otéchestvennye Zapíski* (cf. note on No. 55), but "The Debate" was submitted to the *Moskovityánin* (*The Moscovite*), a new organ of Moscow Slavophiles (see note on No. 73). Whatever Lermontov's sympathies, he realized that "The Debate" would look strange in the *Otechestvennye Zapiski*. Incidentally, Belínsky, whose view of poetry was utilitarian (see note on No. 12), disapproved of the poem as a whole (but enjoyed its descriptive passages). Lermontov did not mean to sever his relations with Belinsky and Kireevsky, even though Kireevsky had brought out Sollogúb's *Beau Monde* (see note on No. 69), but was probably afraid that the appearance of "The Debate" in the *Moskovityanin* would be taken as a decisive step in the direction of the Slavophiles and a challenge to the *Otechestvennye Zapiski*. So he preferred to see his poem published without an editorial flourish of trumpets. It can also be added that shortly before Lermontov wrote "The Debate," S. P. Shevyryóv subjected Lermontov's works to an unfavorable review in the *Moskovityanin* (the main emphasis was on the lack of originality in Lermontov's poetry). A. S. Khomyakóv, Lermontov's friend and a leading Slavophile, believed that giving such a fine poem to the *Moskovityanin* was Lermontov's tactful answer to Shevyryov's treatment, and there is no reason to disagree.

Lermontov's description of the Russian army is so placardlike that a search for the old general's identity may seem futile. But no doubt the leader meant is Yermolov: The earliest proof comes from Alexandre Dumas (père) who in the course of his travel in the Caucasus (1858) translated the poem into French; and in his publication *Le Caucase. Nouvelles impressions de voyage*, II. Bruxelles 1859, p. 267, he spelled out Yermolov's name. He even sent his translation to Yermolov with a courteous letter. Lermontov met Yermolov during his last furlough in the winter of 1841 and wrote his poem after this meeting (which need not have been the first of its kind). It is also known that Yermolov was infuriated when he heard of Lermontov's death.

Kazbék and Èlbrús are the highest peaks in the Caucasus, and Kazbek looms large in Russian Romantic poetry (cf. 39:3, 90:217, 91:passim). "The Debate" contains recognizable echoes of Caucasian folklore, but to stage such a dialogue as constitutes the story of this poem Lermontov did not need any native legend (for a similar conclusion cf. note on No. 39).

More relevant than Lermontov's occasional borrowings from the mountaineers' tales is his Romantic position as late as 1841. In "The Debate" the conquest of the Caucasus is not the only theme: equally prominent is the eternal Romantic theme "man versus nature". For Lermontov's earlier (1839) treatment of it we can turn to "Three Palms" (No. 50), where the solution is traditional: man is hostile to nature and ruins it.

Commentary

Probably without being aware of it, Lermontov reproduced in "The Debate" much of the composition of "Three Palms." Both have a somewhat similar conversation at the beginning (the palms complain of their useless beauty and long for the appearance of man; the mountains discuss man's intrusion), followed by a lengthy description of a great mass of people (in the original the verbal overlap is easily noticeable, partly because Lermontov constantly repeated his favorite expressions). The finales, too, are similar: in one poem, the palms are cut and the oasis runs dry; in the other, Kazbek realizes that he is doomed and stays forever silent. (In the note on No. 50, it was pointed out that "Three Palms" and "The Sail" are also structured somewhat alike.) Man triumphing over Kazbek is a grander subject than the Russians annexing the Caucasus, and in the poem Kazbek is not a symbol of Cherkess or Chechen liberty: it stands for all nature, just as the approach of the Russian troops signifies not only the advances of the Russian crown but also the advent of civilization. The optimistic, jubilant picture in the second part of the poem suddenly ends on an almost tragic note, for it is sad to see the fall of a beautiful giant under the axe of a crafty dwarf. The two themes in "The Debate" run parallel; whereas one is self-asserting, the other is melancholy, even pathetic. The conquest is inevitable (and there is obvious, though hardly joyful, recognition of this fact in the poem), but it will bring in its wake the death of proud and primitive nature. Lermontov the Russian officer and Lermontov the poet seem to hold conflicting views in this tale.

The poem has many other historical overtones. "The Debate" was written when the Slavophiles and the Westerners were discussing the destiny of Russia: should she go along with the rest of Europe or retain at all costs her unique national traits? Unlike several of his contemporaries (notably Victor Hugo), Lermontov believed that the East would remain dormant forever, and his rather sarcastic, even if pictorially attractive, treatment of the Oriental powers, as well as the indication that Russia is neither in the East nor in the West, but in the North, must have been a much more meaningful, even explosive, statement in those days than now. But as mentioned above, Lermontov was a poet, not a politician or a journalist, and it would be rash to use his verses to enlist him in one of the two intellectual camps.

Lermontov's descriptive method in this poem is all his own. His eye shifts from one detail to another with a methodical precision unusual in lyric poetry. Just as in No. 32 the hero asks the branch every possible question and in No. 60 Napoleon calls each of his old supporters to be reminded of all the places where he lost them, so here Kazbek sees the forces moving in perfect order, one regiment after another: banners, cannons, horses, and even the general. The countries of the East are enumerated like paragraphs in a history book. Each of them has its own color, so the whole begins to resemble an administrative map. Naturally, in the first part adjectives predominate and in the second, verbs of motion. This style is more common in Lermontov's legends, ballads, and scenes from folk life, but when the hero and the narrator merge, as in Nos. 73 or 90, his language changes entirely, and instead of the terse, rough-hewn sentences of ''The Debate,'' we find long and difficult syntactic periods, asides, double entendres, and all the devices that make up his ''mellow'' style. Lermontov must have especially enjoyed writing ''The Debate,'' for in it he employed to the full his gift of seeing and describing distant objects (cf. note on No. 62). Kazbek looks at the world from high up, not unlike the Demon flying over the Caucasus (No. 92:33ff.). The result is diagrammatic and maplike.

81. The Dream

Several circumstances made this poem famous immediately. The main reason is that it reads like a grim prophecy: in the same year (1841) Lermontov himself lay dead with a smoking wound in his side. In the original, the country where the man is having his last dream is given by name, Daghestan, and line 1 is built on a very powerful alliteration, the sounds *d* and *n* serving as its kernel.

To what extent its source is an early conversation with Sushkóva, a Cossack song, reminiscences of *Evgeny Onegin* (V1:32), or a story by one of the officers (such a story is extant) is unknown; all these and many other possibilities have been discussed in Lermontov scholarship. The most inspired poems, as Anna Akhmatova once put it, grow from nondescript rubbish. Whatever the source of ''The Dream,'' its theme, like every theme in the mature Lermontov, goes many years back. At the age of sixteen or seventeen he wrote several poems about death. In one of them the narrator is asleep and then wakes up, but his awakening is also sleep (cf. the nightmare in Gogol's *Portrait*).

''The Dream'' was published in 1843.

Commentary

82. Tamara

Queen Tamára, or Thamar (all *h*s in Georgian names are mute), is one of the central personages in Georgian medieval history. She ruled Georgia from 1184 to 1213 and conquered the neighboring Armenians, Turks, and Persians, and many small mountain tribes. Tamara stands for the Georgian Renaissance, and ancient Georgian poetry extols her. Even the name of the Ossetian epic hero Soslán has been identified with that of her husband. Shot(h)á Rustavéli was her courtier and represented her as T(h)inat(h)ín in *The Knight in the Tiger Skin* (or *The Man in the Panther's Skin*). In his prologue, Rustaveli apostrophizes the Queen by her real name. In epic tradition, Thamar is a woman of great intelligence and incomparable beauty. In several Georgian historical books, she is described as a protector of learning and religion, unlike the heroine of the legend that inspired Lermontov's poem. Many ruins in Georgia bear the name of Thamar's castle, and one of them can be seen in Lermontov's drawing. Lermontov was the first to identify the inhabitant of this particular castle with Tamara; his predecessors mentioned a certain Darya, a fictitious character (the name is a back formation from Daryál). As a heroine of oral literature, Darya was a queen or a sorceress famous for her cruel amorous feats. Similar adventures were ascribed to Queen Tamara's sister. In some tales, the sister's name was also Tamara (a typical folklore plot: two sisters, sometimes twins, one of whom is pious and virtuous, the other self-serving and living for pleasure; the real Tamara's sister was called Rusudán and was a kind and virtuous woman). Lermontov may have heard a tale in which the rapacious owner of the castle was Tamara; but many castles in Georgia allegedly were built for Tamara, so the replacement of Darya by Tamara could have taken place under his pen. It is also possible that Lermontov knew a story about quite a different Tamara, a seventeenth-century queen of western Georgia; this Imeritan queen was a skillful intriguer and the wife of many kings.

Although the femme fatale is a familiar character in nineteenth-century balladry, this motif was first introduced into Russian literature by Pushkin's *Egyptian Nights* (which ends in a poem about Cleopatra) and "Cleopatra." Pushkin focused his attention on the psychology of Cleopatra, while the erotic element merely formed a background for a "historical elegy." *Egyptian Nights* remained unfinished, but Lermontov's indebtedness to Pushkin's poems is beyond doubt. Thus, in

"Cleopatra" there are three claimants for the Queen's love: a warrior, a sage, and an unknown youth (and it is believed that the youth would have triumphed over the mercenary woman and opened to her the nature of real love). In "Tamara" we also hear about three men, but here they are a warrior, a sage, and a shepherd. Lermontov's femme fatale does not change toward the end. Nor does she sell her love: she is genuinely enamored of each of her successive victims; hence the tale's tragic tenor. The entire machinery of the poem, with its assonances, parallel constructions, and violent contrasts, emphasizes the essentially lyric nature of the tale. Pushkin's language is always compressed and terse, whereas Lermontov's descriptions are impressionistic and vague. He has Tamara meet her lovers fully dressed (in the original: "on a soft eider-down bed, decked out in brockade and pearls"), because the words create a romantic atmosphere, and the picture becomes beautiful; neither he nor anybody else, it seems, noticed the incongruity of this detail. It is also typical of Lermontov that he found a Caucasian setting for his legend.

"Tamara" was published in 1843.

83. The Leaf

Numerous attempts have been made to find the "sources" of this poem, that is, to discover a folk song or a lyric in German or French from which Lermontov could have borrowed his images. But most of the imagery in it belonged to all Romantics, and at least some of it occurs in Lermontov elsewhere. Thus, Mtsyri (No. 91:105) compares himself with a leaf torn from a tree. A precocious fruit, which hangs alone among the leaves and will be burned by the sun and wither when the others will bloom, is perhaps the most familiar image in Lermontov's poetry (very often in his early lyrics; cf. No. 41:16 ff. and No. 46:13 ff.). Plantains (plane trees), too, are mentioned in many of Lermontov's Caucasian works (they and pyramidal poplars were his favorite trees), and an oak tree must have meant a great deal to him as a symbol; cf. No. 85. This lyric has many features of a ballad: a love story as the mainspring of the plot, passionate wooing, the impossibility of a union with a proud beauty, and a tragic finale accentuated by an abrupt antithetic ending.

The poem is a transparent allegory, and, though it would be pointless to try to identify the beauty who turned down the poet in his second exile (in Russian, *leaf* is a masculine noun, and *plantain* feminine), Lermontov was too obvious a prototype for the homeless oak leaf tossed

by every wind: he had just arrived in the South from St. Petersburg and
was sure that he would die soon.

The poem was first published in 1843.

84. *"No, 'Tis Not You for Whom I Am Aflame"*

Viskovátov relates the following episode that concerns Sófya Mikháylov-
na Sollogúb, the author's wife.

The poet used to look at her with his expressive eyes, which had a magnetic
influence, so that one involuntarily turned in the direction from which they looked.
My husband—remarked Sofya Mikhaylovna—hated Lermontov watching me like
this, and once I said to Lermontov, when he began to stare at me in his usual
fashion, "You know, Lermontov, that my husband does not like your manner
of watching me so closely; why, then, do you keep annoying him?" Lermontov
did not answer anything, got up, and went away. On the next day he brought
me the poem "No, 'Tis Not You for Whom I Am Aflame."

However, on the evidence of Odóevsky's album, the poem must have
been written after Lermontov's departure from St. Petersburg, and it is
now believed that his addressee was Ekaterína Grigóryevna Bykhovéts,
Lermontov's distant relative and constant companion of his last months
in Pyatigórsk. Judging by the extant letter in which she recounts her
meetings with Lermontov before the duel, Bykhovets, though pretty, was
a woman of very ordinary intelligence and culture. She says that she and
Lermontov have been so friendly that she has become known to all as
Lermontov's *charmante cousine*. She also makes the following remark,
"He was passionately in love with V. A. Bakhmetyeva [V. A. Lopukhiná's
married name: see note on No. 19]; she was his cousin; I think he loved
me only because he found some resemblance between us, and it was about
her that he always talked." The hypothesis that the poem is about
Lopukhina seems very strained to me, the more so that the woman whom
he describes as his beloved is obviously dead. This difficulty is usually
explained away by reference either to the figurative use of the words *long-
dead* and *vanished* in the last two lines or to Lopukhina's unhappiness
in marriage. But it is enough to reread the journal entry cited in the note
on No. 4 or some of Lermontov's youthful poems addressed to Rostop-
chiná and his cousin Annette Stolýpina, to see that many romances might
have inspired Lermontov's recollections. He himself said in the narrative
poem *Sashka*, "So what? At fourteen I suffered from every woman's mug

Commentary

and naively tried to convince the whole world that they were absolutely alike.''

In addition, two early poems, both imperfect but thematically close to "No, 'Tis Not You for Whom I Am Aflame," show how regularly Lermontov returned to the theme of this lyric. The first of the two poems ("To *") is an elegy written by Lermontov in 1829 at the age of fifteen or sixteen. These are its opening lines, "Do not attract me with your beauty! My spirit is now extinguished and old. Ah! It has been many years since another look became imprinted on my mind!" ("Ne privlekáy menyá krasóy"). The second dates from 1830 or 1831.

I saw her once in the merry tumult of the ball; I think she wanted me to pay attention to her; the tenderness of her eyes, the swiftness of her movements, the natural brightness of her cheeks, and the fullness of her bosom—all, all would have filled my mind with fascination, if I had not been carrying the burden of quite a different, senseless desire; if before me there had not flitted a shadow with a vacuous taunt, if I only could have forgotten the other features, the colorless face, and icy looks!" ("Ya vídel raz eyó v vesyólom víkhre bála").

The poem is a perfect example of Lermontov's vision (see note on No. 62). He saw distant things better than those in immediate proximity and had little to say about the objects before him. At best, those only sharpened his perception of something hidden from other people's view. From Lermontov's pen a poem like "No, 'Tis Not You for Whom I Am Aflame" could not insult: its addressee was simply too close to be his inspiration. His love for Lopukhina was unchanging because he lived away from her; it is true that he never forgot her, but other women shared Varvára Aleksándrovna's lot of being admired as shadows of his past.

The poem was first published in 1843.

85. "All Alone Along the Road I Am Walking"

Few masterpieces of Russian poetry enjoy the reputation of this lyric. All the elements important to Lermontov came together in it: his solitude, great and all-embracing as the cosmos; unification with God, which he always experienced when nature enveloped him, whether it was a field of grain or a tranquil starry sky; life-in-death, as manifest in his many angels, mermaids, drowned but desirable maidens, and delirious youths; sounds coming from nowhere and outwardly meaning little but conveying so much that even mutinous souls, like Mtsyri's or his own, could at last find peace; the tragic conflict between the beauty of the world and despair in his heart. The poem, written in the rare five-foot trochee (cf. No. 79), is full of unobtrusive assonances, alliterations, and vocalic groups, and therefore every line seems longer than it actually is—as long as the poet's way to eternity through the night. Any translation of this poem (and there is a good translation of it into German by Rilke, for instance) must remain a weak shadow of the original.

Shining stars arouse meditation in many, but Lermontov, by instinct, always chose the time of day in harmony with the age and mood of his hero (which does not of course mean direct correspondence). Thus, most of *The Demon* (No. 92) is enacted to the crimson light of sunset; on the contrary, *Mtsyri* (No. 91) is shot through by morning light, which later gives way to the fierce light of noon but never to that of sunset (as, for example, in No. 34). Pechórin's despair plays itself out against the background of the setting sun.

While writing his poem, Lermontov could have been inspired by Heine's "Der Tod, das ist die kühle Nacht." Lermontov liked Heine (see note on No. 79), but "influences" are hard to prove, unless we speak of the interaction of entire aesthetic systems, as was the case with Byron's influence on Lermontov (see No. 18 and note).

The poem was published in 1843.

86. The Sea Princess

This is Lermontov's last ballad. The poem is written in masculine rhyme throughout, and a strong syllable at the end of each line emphasizes its dactylic nature. It is the only poem by Lermontov in which an intruder triumphs in a kingdom not his own. But even he wins a dubious victory. The situation of this ballad is almost an echo of what happens in "Taman'" (a tale from *A Hero of Our Time*).

The poem was first published in 1843.

87. The Prophet

This lyric, first published in 1843, seems to be a direct response to Pushkin's "Prophet." Pushkin's poet pines away in a desert from "spiritual thirst," and an angel, "a six-winged seraph," endows him with the gift to see things previously hidden from view and hear every sound in the universe. After that, the angel sends the poet into the wide world to burn the hearts of men with the newly acquired speech. Lermontov picks up where Pushkin left off and relates what happened to the prophet in the world. But Lermontov's "Prophet" lacks the Biblical solemnity of Pushkin's work.

"The Prophet" sums up Lermontov's thoughts on the relations between the poet and the rabble (cf. No. 49 and note). The hero of Pushkin's "The Poet and the Rabble" despises the mob and peremptorily commands it to go away; his inspirations are not for those who expect poetry to be of practical value. In Lermontov's lyric, the prophet would be happy if the mob understood him, but his bid for hearing falls on deaf ears. Pushkin let the poet triumph, at least in a moral sense; Lermontov sent his "false prophet" to a desert as an outcast. Pushkin could despise the rabble and keep his dignity, but he could also hope that one day all nations would worship his memory (he never tried to be consistent). Lermontov saw his generation hounding the poet out of life. Like the hero of No. 85, his prophet walks along his road alone; the universe is beautiful, the worlds, conforming to the Rousseauian ideal, listen to his speech, as they listened once to the angel's song (No. 12:3-4); but there is a heavy load on the prophet's heart: the grief of a great man who knows that it is a shame to be admired by the intellectual riffraff (cf. No. 53:49-52), the stupid and the smug, but who almost against his better judgment suffers from solitude and longs for their worthless recognition.

88. *"A Half-Mask on Your Face, Mysterious and Teasing"*

The poem is late, but its exact date is unknown. It gives a rare example of Lermontov feeling happy at a masquerade (cf. No. 55). As is usual for Lermontov, a hidden object stirs him more deeply than an object in full sight, and his real happiness lies not in the possession of someone or something he loves but in lifelong recollections of the beauty once seen: cf. Nos. 12, 33, 91, etc. Lermontov's characters shy from material contacts with what is dear to them. His Pechórin is afraid that he will be coerced into marriage; Mtsyri does not dare to approach the Georgian girl (but once she is gone, he thinks and dreams of her; and her song, like the Angel's tune in the lyric [No. 12], is buried in his breast forever); the Demon is happy only while wooing Tamara (when he kisses her, she dies [No. 92:872 ff]). Lermontov was fond of the word "mysterious," because he heard echoes and discerned shadows better than most others. His method of "reconstructing" a beauty from two features is also very

Commentary

typical: he prefers a hint and a detail to the whole (cf. the description of Arab women in No. 50).

The poem was first published in 1843.

89. The Deserter (A mountaineer's legend)

Lermontov wrote many narrative poems about the Caucasus. *Mtsyri* (No. 91) and *The Demon* (No. 92) belong to this series, but their message is so universal that it overshadows their ethnic (Georgian) background. Other poems, especially those based on Circassian and Daghestan folklore, are reworkings of ancient legends. Lermontov wrote most of them very early, and they have minimal artistic value. But *The Deserter* is traceable to 1838 and, though not a great poem, it is very good. It was apparently influenced by Pushkin's *Tazít*, also a poem of unfulfilled revenge.

The Circassian girl's song, with a few changes, was transferred to this poem from *Izmaíl-Bey* (there it is called "Selim's Song," but Selim is a young girl wearing man's clothes). The song is apt and tells Haroun more than a threat or a curse could. Lermontov's female personages (Tamára [No. 82], the Cossack mother [No. 57], the smuggler in "Taman'," the Georgian girl, and the goldfish in *Mtsyri* [No. 91]) often sing, whereas the men are susceptible to the songs (Mtsyri, the Demon, Tamara's lovers; Pechórin remembers every word of the smuggler's song, and Bèla's song is of decisive importance to him).

It is probable that Lermontov heard some legend of a deserter, for similar songs were recorded in his lifetime, and the mountaineers did not forgive traitors.

90. Valerík

On June 10, 1840, Lermontov arrived in the Caucasus, where his commander was General Galaféev. Galafeev's forces consisted of ten and a half infantry battalions, two Cossack regiments, and twenty-nine cannons. The expedition to Chechnya Minor began on July 6. The place-name *Chechnyá* (rhymes with *spa*) is derived from the ethnic name Chéchen (cf. No. 57:11, where an angry Chechen is "crawling, knife in hand"). The battle at the river Valerík took place on July 11, and a contemporary report, which has come down to us, shows that Lermontov's description is remarkably accurate. Lermontov himself

568

demonstrated great courage on that day and was cited for bravery, but the Tsar crossed his name from the list, and Lermontov did not receive any decoration. Shortly after the battle, Lermontov wrote to his friend Alexéy Lopukhín,

Something happened every day, and one engagement was rather hot, and it lasted six hours. We had only four thousand infantry, and they had about six thousand; and we fought the whole time with bayonets. We lost thirty officers and about three hundred privates; they left six hundred bodies lying. . . . Imagine: the ravine where the battle took place smelled of blood an hour after the end of the engagement.

It can be easily seen that *Valerik*, unlike "Borodinó" (No. 30), is not a description of a military confrontation. The story of the "massacre" occupies ten lines of the text. "Borodino" is full of patriotic animation and really is devoted to a battle, not to long meditation before and after it. Comparison of the two poems has become a commonplace of Lermontov scholarship, and it is certainly true that Lermontov, whatever he thought of the Caucasus in its relation to Russia, could not feel inspired by the slaughter he had witnessed: there was a vast difference between saving Russia from Napoleon and butchering the Chechens and Cherkesses in order to annex their mountains and valleys. It is also true that in 1836 Lermontov had not yet seen war, and for his generation the horrors of Borodino were eclipsed by its historic mission. In 1840-41 Lermontov realized for the first time that in battle, personal courage, the sense of duty, and many other excellent things had as their natural complement oceans of blood. One could remain an exemplary officer and a brave man, but corpses would pile up and stink just the same.

He also noticed that encounters with death had dried up his soul. The world of drawing-rooms and masquerades began to look ridiculous, but at the same time loss of friends failed to impress. In Russian literature Lermontov was the first to notice the absolute apathy of a shaken soul. It was not the resignation of Macbeth sated with murder: it was the indifference of Camus's *L'Etranger*, whom Lermontov anticipated by a whole century. In everyday life, Lermontov was often rude but never callous, and his feelings after the battle of Valerik are a terrible indictment of war as an institution. Cf. the following passage from the memoirs of the historian Yúry Fyódorovich Samárin (1819-1876), who often met Lermontov in 1838-41,

We talked long. He showed me his drawings. Recollections of the Caucasus enlivened him. I remember his poetic story of the battle against the mountaineers,

Commentary

in which Trubetskoy was wounded. . . . His voice trembled, he was about to start crying. Then he felt ashamed of it and hoping to wipe out the first impression began to discuss why he was so moved, explaining all by his nerves worn out by the heat. It was Lermontov all over.

Lermontov's deep and tragic thoughts on war and peace were a source of inspiration to Tolstoy, who never concealed his indebtedness to Lermontov (cf. "A Raid" and note on No. 30). *Valerik* is often praised for its realism and naturalism, but, actually, Lermontov is thrifty here, saying only as much as is absolutely necessary. The illusion of naturalism is created by the masterful choice of detail.

Valerik is the summit of Lermontov's lyric poetry. The frame of it, in which he addresses the woman he loves, contains many of his best lines. The letter, quite deliberately of course, mirrors the design of Tatyana's letter to Onegin (and of every well-structured "oration of conviction"). An introduction sets the tone and contains an apology for something that perhaps should better have been left unsaid (a typical device); it is followed by numerous details arranged on an ascending scale; and the climax (with two peaks, to show death "in general" and "closeup") takes us back to the beginning and is reinforced after a catharsis by the author's contemplation of nature. Tatyana's epistle has quite different subject matter (no death, no war, no horrors), but its framework is the same, and in literature structural resemblance may sometimes mean more than similarity in the plot. Thus, Lermontov's *Masquerade* (cf. No. 96) is very much like *Othello* in terms of the intrigue, but it is hard to think of two tragedies that have so little in common. Even Tolstoy's "A Raid," which shares almost every important detail with *Valerik* and contains references to and direct quotations from Lermontov, seems remote from *Valerik*, so different are the poetic systems of the two authors. But Pushkin's verses come to mind the moment we open *Valerik*:

> I write to you . . . Your humble debtor . . .
> It could not, could not be more plain,
> And you are free to read this letter
> And punish me with your disdain.
> But you, I think, are kinder, better,
> And, pitying my wretched state,
> You will not leave me to my fate!

The supposed addressee of Lermontov's poem is V. A. Lopukhiná (see note on No. 19), but it is unbelievable that Lermontov should have finished his letter to her on such a sarcastic, almost contemptuous, note. *Valerik* is the author's condensed biography: he starts like a disappointed lover, passes through the inferno of the battle, and emerges many years older (thus, Romeo and Hamlet appear as impetuous youths and end up wise and weary men). But even the transformed Lermontov would hardly have spoken to Lopukhina in such a patronizing, condescending way; nor would the beginning of the poem fit the circumstances of his romance with Varvára Alexándrovna. Someone like Countess Èmíliya Kárlovna Músina-Púshkina, who must have meant more to Lermontov than we are aware of and whose heart, according to Lermontov's facetious 1839 epigram, was like the Bastille, would be a better candidate. (Also note that Russian, like French and German, distinguishes between intimate and formal address; and the form of address in *Valerik* is in the plural, which is quite inexplicable if Lermontov meant Varen'ka.)

The original autograph of *Valerik* is lost, but Lermontov's "rough draft" has survived. Another copy of the manuscript, bearing the title *Valerik*, was brought to Yu. F. Samarin from the Caucasus by Lermontov's fellow officer Count I. Golítsyn. It has the inscription "The author's present" and contains eleven lines absent from the published (1842) version. Whether Lermontov wrote his poem immediately after the battle in 1840, or some time later, is unknown. As a rule, *Valerik* is given among Lermontov's lyrics. But it is closer to his narrative poems; in any case, it is much longer than even the longest ballads, e.g., Nos. 30 and 80.

L. 68. Yermólov: see note on No. 80.

L. 73. A peaceful Tartar means a Muslim who recognized the Russian rule (a very common phrase in the "Caucasian" literature of the nineteenth century). In those days the ethnic name Tartar was often applied to the Azerbaijanis, but in *Valerik* it probably referred to a Kumýk (the Kumyks are a Turkic tribe).

L. 80. Lermontov studied the languages of the Caucasian natives and was reliable as an ethnographer, so "guttural speech" is probably not just a verbal embellishment. The most "guttural" pronunciation is believed to be that of the Veinakhs.

L. 101. The word "murid" had a number of meanings, the main one being "a Muslim and a sworn enemy of the infidels (Christians)."

L. 121. Ghikhi (in Russian, stress falls on the second syllable; pronounce: Ghe-hé) or Ghekhi is a village in Chechnyá, not far from the Valerik.

L. 129. Ichkéria, the legendary homeland of the Chechens, bordered on Chechnya Major, south of the Térek and the Súnja, and was inhabited by the Ichkerians. In 1839 Shamil, the leader of the war against the Russians, had his residence there.

L. 227. Kunák means "friend" (the original Turkic meaning is "guest"). Russian stories and poems about the Caucasus are full of native words. I excluded from my translation those that have become universally known in Russian (e.g., *aul*, pronounced *ah-ool*, "village," and *saklya*, "hut"), for, at least today, they are stylistically neutral and the English text would have gained nothing if they had been preserved. *Kunak*, however, is not so common as *aul*, etc., and I have retained it for the sake of the local color. The name Galoob (its exact transliteration from Russian is Galub) is borrowed from Pushkin's *Tazit* (cf. note on No. 89), where it is a misspelling for Gasúb. Lermontov's choice is odd, because the name Galub does not exist (it is a distortion of Gasub or Gashub) and has nothing to recommend it except Pushkin's authority. Originally, Lermontov hesitated between Yusup (Yupus in the manuscript is apparently a slip of the pen) and Akhmet.

L. 229. Valerik is a river in Chechnya, a tributary of the Sunja. Its Chechen name is Valarkhi, and the Veinakhs call it Valarg. The older form was Valaran khi "the river of men's death" (men as opposed to women! a female counterpart also exists); the ending -an designates the genitive case, and it is often lost in colloquial speech. The form that Lermontov must have heard is Valarig. The grim name of the river, which can go back to ancient battles with the Alans (Ossetians), was fully justified in 1840. (My ethnographic and linguistic commentary is borrowed from the article by B. S. Vinogradov and V. B. Vinogradov, " 'Rechka smerti' i mechta o mire" [The river of the dead and a dream of peace] in: B. S. Vinogradov [ed.], *Lermontovsky sbornik. 1814-1964.* Grozny: Checheno-ingushskoe knizhnoe izdatel'stvo, 1964, pp. 161-81, esp. p. 167, note 2, and pp. 169-72, 176-78.)

91. Mtsýri

Mtsýri was probably written in 1839; in 1840 it appeared in the first and only book of selected poetry that Lermontov brought out in his lifetime. A youth in a monastery is a central figure in Lermontov's works.

Commentary

In 1830, at the age of sixteen, he wrote a poem entitled "On a Picture by Rembrandt." (Lermontov was fond of Rembrandt: cf. *Sashka* I:99/11.) The picture represented a Franciscan monk, and the poem began as follows, "I see a half-open face vigorously drawn; is it not a famous fugitive in a monk's sacred clothes? Perhaps his mind is killed by a secret crime. All is dark around: his haughty look burns with anguish and doubt." Roughly at the same time Lermontov made a characteristic entry in his journal, "Notes of a young monk who is seventeen years old. Lived in a monastery since childhood; read nothing except the Scriptures. His passionate soul is longing for something. Ideals . . ." The plan outlined in this entry materialized in two ways.

First, he wrote a poem *The Confession*. It is comparatively short, barely one third of the length of *Mtsyri*. Apart from the prologue, which tells the story of a young Spaniard awaiting his sentence in a monastery jail, and the conclusion, *The Confession*, is a tale addressed by the prisoner to a monk. The Spaniard's crime is obscure ("nobody knew or could have known anything about it"), but later we learn that it has something to do with the young man's tragic love, and in the epilogue, when a nun hears the bell tolling for the executed youth, she gives a piercing shriek and her heart breaks of grief. The Spaniard is a monk. Though he refuses to disclose ("sell") his great secret to the confessor, he does say something about his childhood. He was brought up in a monastery, but, unlike Mtsyri, he is dying in his homeland: the action is set on the banks of the Guadalquivir, the favorite river of Russian Romantic poetry. The Spanish fashion coincided with Lermontov's own predilections: in his youth he believed that his ancestor had been Count Lerma (see note on No. 10), and there are several proofs of his love of Spain, a drama in verse, *The Spaniards*, among them. *The Confession* partly imitates Byron's *Giaour* and *Parisina* and is written in masculine rhyme, following the example of *The Prisoner of Chillon*. Despite its vagueness and relative insignificance, it contains many good lines, some of which are to be found in *Mtsyri* intact.

In 1833 Lermontov began to write a novel. It is called *Vadim* and is devoted to the great peasants' uprising under Pugachyóv. Vadím is a hunchback, and this is Vadim's story.

I was taken to the monastery out of compassion; they fed me, because I was not a dog and could not be drowned; within the walls of the cloister I spent my best years; within the stifling walls, deafened by the chiming of the bells and the singing of the men dressed in black and therefore believing that they were closer to Heaven, oppressed, because I was a freak, . . . because I am ugly. . . . To pray! . . . In my heart there was nothing but curses! Often, as evening drew near, when the roseate rays of the setting sun played on the pinnacles and brass bells, I left the sacred gate and from the hill, where a dilapidated chapel stood, admired my jail (it looked beautiful from afar!); clouds drew my imagination to their airy wings. . . . No one in the monastery sought my friendship or my companionship; I was alone, always alone . . . my soul dried up; it needed freedom, the steppe, an open sky. . . . How awful it is to stay in a white cage of brick and to judge winter and spring by a narrow path leading from the cells to the church; not to see the clear sun otherwise than through a long latticed window and not to dare to speak of things not mentioned in such and such a book. . . . One can easily despair.

Soon after this, Vadim "fled from the monastery and became a beggar."

In 1835-36 Lermontov approached the same subject again, this time in the poem *Boyar Orsha*. (Boyars were the upper nobility and later the richest landowners in Russia from the foundation of Kievan Rus in the tenth century until approximately the sixteenth century. The estate was abolished by Peter I.) Like *The Confession*, *Boyar Orsha* is a love story. The epigraphs (sometimes slightly changed) are from *Parisina* and *Giaour*, and the lines introducing Chapter 1, "Then burst her heart in one long shriek,/And to the earth she fell like stone/ As statue from its base o'erthrown," immediately remind one of the finale of *The Confession*, but the resemblance between the poems is not great.

The story can be summarized as follows. Boyar Mikhaíl, known as Boyar Orsha, is a favorite vassal of Ivan the Terrible (sixteenth century). In spite of the Tsar's protection, he is unhappy at court and is allowed to return home, where on the bank of the river Dniepr, close to the Lithuanian border, his house stands desolate and uncared for. At home he also feels miserable, even though he has a beautiful daughter, and one night he calls his trusted slave Sokól (the name means 'falcon') and asks for a story that will dispel his sad thoughts and lull him to sleep. Sokol tells him a short tale of an old and feeble tsar whose main treasure was his daughter. He kept her under lock and key, but one day, when he decided to make sure of her chastity, he stole into her chamber and found his daughter sleeping with his stableboy. He had them put into a barrel and thrown into the sea.

Orsha takes the hint and goes to his daughter's bedroom. Behind the closed door he hears two voices. The man (his name is Arsény) is telling the young girl that ever since a monk delivered (actually, sold) him to her father he has been planning to flee to Lithuania. But he is so much in love with her that he could not leave Russia. Tomorrow they will both flee. In the Lithuanian forests, a gang awaits him. At this point Orsha pushes the door open, his daughter falls to the floor in a swoon (this is the place where Lermontov uses the lines about a shriek from *The Confession*), and Arseny is bound hand and foot and taken away. Orsha leaves the room, turns the key three times in the lock, and throws it into the river.

Chapter 2 also has an epigraph from Byron, "The rest thou dost already know,/And all my sins, and half my woe,/But talk no more of penitence." Arseny will be tried by the monastery court. Father Superior, old and blind, but alert as in his youth, is sitting near Orsha and announces to Arseny that men will never forgive him his last sin but that he may turn to God and confess. Arseny's speech, interrupted by Orsha himself, by one of the monks, and by Father Superior, is the best part of the poem. It contains some verses form *The Confession*, and several passages in it are familiar from *Mtsyri*. Arseny does not know where he was born. As a child he was given to the care of the monks, and once he ran away from the monastery. That was his first moment of freedom. Although the main instrument of Arseny's undoing is his love for Orsha's daughter, he is formally accused of underhanded dealings with the forest people. He is convicted and taken to the monastery prison. But at night his friends manage to saw through the bars on his window, and he escapes. Chapter 3, again introduced by two lines from *Giaour* (" 'Tis he! 'tis he! I know him now/ I know him by his pallid brow"), has nothing to do with the *Mtsyri* plot. In this chapter Orsha, at the head of his men, repels an attack by the Poles. Arseny is on the enemy's side. The two meet when Orsha is mortally wounded. In answer to Arseny's questions he says that his daughter has been waiting for her beloved ever since that terrible day. Arseny hurries to Orsha's house, opens the door of the bedroom and finds the girl's decomposed corpse.

Boyar Orsha was published in 1842, and *The Confession* found its way into print as late as 1887. Lermontov, of course, would never have brought out *The Confession*, and would hardly have published *Boyar Orsha*. Today both poems are interesting only as steps toward completing *Mtsyri*, undoubtedly the best work from Lermontov's pen. Its masculine rhyme, with sometimes four and even five repetitions of the same sound sequence, makes the poem flow rapidly onward. As for the content, it is the epitome of Lermontov's poetic world. A young boy, a captive, half-remembers his homeland, which is like Paradise, and whatever happens to him in this life cannot deafen the music within his soul, the music he brought from afar. He is a monk and consequently a prisoner (cf. below). He is solitary, dreams of freedom, and, when he obtains it, it is the Romantic freedom with thunder, lightning, and wild beasts. Freedom in *Mtsyri* is an escape from dingy cells and a complete merging with nature. Nowhere else in Lermontov's works can we find such a passionate longing for action. Lermontov's lyric hero usually is unhappy because he is alone and bored; what he sees around him is despicable, and what he is allowed to do is not worth doing. Mtsyri, on the contrary, has a great aim, but it willfully evades him, and to prove himself, he is ready for anything. Thus, he provokes the ounce. To be sure, Lermontov could have borrowed the motif from Victor Hugo (*Han d'Islande*) or from Caucasian folklore; but the ultimate origin of the episode is of no importance, the more so because in folklore a beast must be overcome for the hero to be able to advance, whereas Mtsyri fights to give vent to his passions, and the ounce, described with obvious sympathy, is sacrificed for no practical reason. Mtsyri's great despair, his shyness in the presence of a girl, his exuberance—everything meets in his soul at this terrible moment, reaches its culmination, and is finally redeemed. After the fight nothing is left for Mtsyri to do, and with inexorable logic he is made to come full circle and die in his prison.

The poem has a most skillful accompaniment: a howling storm attends Mtsyri's escape, and three songs mark his progress (the Georgian girl sings a simple tune that haunts him; the goldfish, like the mermaid of his early lyric [No. 26], tries to entice him with her mirthless serenade, and over his body a friend will sing words of love). *Mtsyri* passes through every mood of Lermontov's poetry: he is rebellious, tender, flippant, sad, and finally at peace with himself. The end of the poem is not a betrayal of the hero's lofty ideals: Mtsyri has done what he could, and now nature will pay him homage. Nature first met the youth like a brother, then burned him dry and put an insurmountable barrier in his way, but in the final passages man and nature are united again, and the Caucasus will send Mtsyri a greeting from its summits: he has striven hard, embraced a storm, and has deserved this last sign of recognition. Mtsyri will die, as Lermontov wanted to die (No. 85): with trees whispering above his grave and death itself resembling a peaceful dream.

Commentary

Although it is not immediately obvious, the alternatives facing Mtsyri are also those of Lermontov's lyric hero. He can choose between submission and riot, prefers riot, and is rewarded in the usual way: "A crown of gold is not your crown" (No. 16:6); "They put a laurel wreath with thorns upon his head" (No. 31:46); "What are to you the thorns of their abhorrence/ Or wreaths of praises, equally inane?" (No. 53:51-52); likewise *Mtsyri*: "A withered leaf upon my head/ Was like a wreath of thorns; (ll. 607-8). In marked contradistinction to Lermontov's early Bryonic heroes, Mtsyri rejects feminine charms. Later the goldfish offers him perennial peace again. The goldfish bears a strange resemblance to the Georgian girl, for both are associated with water and both sing haunting songs. (The original also has some verbal overlap between the two descriptions, but this is because of Lermontov's method of using standard epithets [cf. note on No. 80, where "Three Palms" and "The Debate" are compared]). The goldfish is a replica of the mermaid from No. 26. The mermaid and the goldfish want their beloved wayfarers to stay where they are and feel content. They implore them to dissolve their will in the measured rhythm of the waves. The temptation they offer is strong, for "It's sweet to laugh at every warning,/ Enjoyment from deception reap/ And fall into a dreamless sleep/ With dreams of an approaching morning" (No. 90:252-55). It is the temptation of fatalism so important to the older Lermontov (cf. note on No. 90); the prospect of giving oneself up to fate must have seemed especially enticing to a man exhausted by endless and vain strife. An attentive reader will also notice that Mtsyri, unable to find his way, weeps like Pechórin when the latter fails to overtake Vera (cf. note on No. 34), that Lermontov's favorite rhymes, word groups (e.g., "fresh isles," No. 55:35 and *Mtsyri*, line 637), metaphors, and epithets all turn up in *Mtsyri*. But it is even more noticeable how unique *Mtsyri* is. *Mtsyri* depends for its appeal on direct statements to a much lesser degree than any of Lermontov's lyric poems. Although it has a lot of "extraneous" matter: recollections, landscapes, etc., its symbolic message is subtly grafted on the narrative, and it has a perfect structure: it never rambles, its digressions are carefully thought out, and nothing said in its twenty-six chapters is irrelevant.

Perhaps the main reason that *Mtsyri* is all of a piece lies in the author's treatment of nature. In *The Demon* (No. 92) the pictures of the Caucasus are memorable but scenic; in *Mtsyri* they are as integral to the story as any of the narrative episodes. The hero's heart beats more strongly at the sight of a pigeon looking for shelter in the storm (5), but he himself is brave and greets this storm (8). Freedom for him is first and foremost native landscape (6-7); he is indistinguishable from the wild creatures of the forest (9, 16-17); in the solemn chorus of voices praising God there is no voice of man, but Mtsyri hears them all (11); the sun and the moon closely follow him, as they always follow a boy in a fairy tale; the formidable wood he tries to pass is also from a fairy tale, and the entire drama unfolds itself against the backdrop of distant but grand mountains. So the final reconciliation between the hero and nature is not only an expected conclusion, an appropriate Rousseauian note from the poet who always sought peace in storms, but also a skillful bringing together of the two planes of the poem (those of man and nature), a masterful, even necessary, formal device.

The symbolic value of *Mtsyri* is quite apparent. It is a poem about the impossibility of regaining freedom. The curse is not so much outside the hero as within him, even though Mtsyri, unlike John Bunyan's Pilgrim, has to overcome many physical obstacles. Lermontov's poem is not a medieval allegory, not even an allegory in the spirit of ''A Captive Knight'' (No. 62), but the obstacles described should not be taken quite at their face value. The monastery, so often called a jail in the poem, is not a fortress. A stormy night creates a proper atmosphere for the escape, but Mtsyri could have fled at any other time. The monks are not cruel people. They saved him from death when he was a child and try to find him after the storm, moved entirely by concern; they are semi-kind, to use Vadim's phrase. Although Mtsyri has sworn to himself to run away one day, he does not do anything practical to ensure his success. Born in the Caucasus, he does not even think of the route he will eventually take. But *Mtsyri* is poetry, not a biography, and its verses easily make up for the seeming absurdity of the plot. Also, Lermontov cared for the idea, for the symbolic, more than for the verisimilitude of the tale. He himself knew that the fatal flaw was in the hero, not in the circumstances. Mtsyri says that he resembles a flower grown in a prison yard; used to poor soil and darkness, he withers once he is exposed to the sun (l. 588 ff.). He does not find his way home, because he does not know the way. It would have been ludicrous to have Mtsyri prepare food and maps in advance: on his map, home would have remained a blank. Thus, the plot is not so absurd after all. As always in literature, that is meaningful and justifiable which serves an artistic aim.

Now that almost a century and a half have passed since the time when

Commentary

Mtsyri was written, its symbolic message is more potent than it may have been in 1839, but no doubt even then the poem was broader than its plot. Today we are apt to ignore the plot and treat it as a conventional framework for a Romantic tale. Many details escape us. One of them is the fact that Mtsyri's confessor is a Benedictine, or black, monk (this is what he is called in the original) and that the theme of a monastery was very important to Lermontov. Mtsyri himself calls his monastery a jail, but Lermontov, who wrote a number of genuine prison poems (Nos. 33-34, 61-62), remained true to his initial plan and made his Spaniard, Arseny, and Mtsyri monks, not captives. Mtsyri wilts in his monastery, and a holy convent does not save Tamara (in *The Demon*) from the greatest temptation of her life. Lermontov's monks and nuns are invariably rebels. We have seen that Lermontov could feel at peace with his God: his prayers and his lyrics "When In a Field of Grain the Wheat and Rye Wave Yellow" (No. 35) and "All Alone Along the Road I Am Walking" (No. 85) are as sincere as anything he wrote. He was not irreligious, but recognition of God in Heaven does not mean that he liked all the institutions of official Christianity. The idea of No. 15 remained with him all his life: Mtsyri is ready to give up Paradise in exchange for a moment of earthly bliss (ll. 716-22), and there are even stronger statements in the extant draft copy (see below and cf. the hero of No. 74, who is unhappy among "the disembodied" because he cannot find his beloved there). At a time when Russian sentimental poetry, greatly encouraged by pro-government criticism, extolled cloisters as quiet havens, as shelters in a stormy life where passions were subdued, as desirable abodes for all, Lermontov wrote a violent anticlerical poem. He could see the Everlasting when a winding brook murmured its "mysterious saga," when distant stars shone upon his way, but not in a dingy monastery cell. If the epigraph to *Mtsyri* is really from *Spiridion* (see below), the reconstruction of Lermontov's approach to his plot becomes even more plausible. *Mtsyri* is a defense of freedom in its most abstract (romantic) form, and monasteries are a symbol of repression and the strongest obstacle between man and his right to exercise his will.

Mtsyri is free of the drawing-room infelicities that mar many of Lermontov's works, including even some passages in *The Demon*. Muravyóv, to whom Lermontov meant to dedicate "A Branch from Palestine" (see No. 32 and note), recollected,

One summer evening I called upon him and found him at his desk, with a glowing face and fiery eyes, which were especially expressive in him. 'What's the

matter with you?' I asked. 'Sit down and listen,' he said and at the same mo-
ment, in an outburst of ecstasy, read to me, from beginning to end, the whole
of his marvelous poem *Mtsyri* ("novice" in Georgian), which had just come
from his inspired pen. . . . Never had any tale made such a strong impression
upon me.

This episode must have taken place on August 5, 1839, and in a historical
perspective it looks somewhat ironic, for Muravyov became a Christian
writer, and no one left so many heartfelt passages on monasteries as he.
On May 9, 1840, Lermontov recited the scene of Mtsyri's fight with
an ounce at Gogol's birthday party. *Mtsyri* had a lasting influence on
Turgenev's narrative poems, and Turgenev was the first translator of
Mtsyri into French. "Its rhythm," said Turgenev in the preface, "has
once been compared with the work of a prisoner, who unremittingly
knocks with double raps at the wall of his dungeon." Many echoes from
Mtsyri are heard in Nekrasov's poem *On the Volga* ("Na Volge") and
in other Russian authors, as late as Gumilyóv.

The epigraph. The original epigraph is written in Church Slavonic
and has no reference, apart from I Kings (i.e., I Samuel). The passage
is easy to find. It is I Samuel 14:43, "And Saul said to Jonathan: Tell
me what thou hast done. And Jonathan told him, and said: 'I did but
taste a little honey with the end of the rod which was in my hand, and
behold I must die.' " Lermontov's quotation does not correspond ex-
actly either to the English or to the Russian text, and it is hardly due
to chance that he fails to mention chapter and verse. Though the sentence
is from the Old Testament, he must have come across it elsewhere and
noticed how well it fitted his poem. Again, it must have happened at
the last moment, for initially the epigraph was in French, "On n'a qu'une
seule patrie" ('One has only one homeland'), probably a paraphrase
of F. de La Mennais's maxim, "Il n'y a d'amis, d'epouses, de pères
et de frères que dans la patrie. L'exile partout est seul" ('We have
friends, spouses, fathers, and brothers only in our homeland. An exile
is always alone'). E. A. Vágin (*Novy Zhurnal*, 1978, pp. 82-91, in Rus-
sian) seems to have found the correct source of Lermontov's epigraph.
At the end of 1838 and the beginning of 1839 George Sand was bring-
ing out her new novel *Spiridion* (in *Revue des deux mondes*). In 1839
it appeared in book form. The action of the novel is set in an Italian
monastery, and its central character is a young novice passing through
many bitter trials. He seeks advice from an old monk; the monk is first
hostile to the novice but then takes pity on him and says the following

Commentary

words (in Latin), "Gustavi paululum mellis et ecce nunc morior." Lermontov's epigraph is a word for word translation of this sentence into Church Slavonic.

The hero of *Spiridion* is otherwise quite unlike Mtsyri, and Lermontov had started thinking of a young monk "in captivity" long before George Sand wrote her novel; it is also sometimes believed that Mtsyri had a partial prototype. But Lermontov probably knew *Spiridion* and may have noticed that the Latin adage in it would make a strikingly appropriate epigraph to his poem. While translating the epigraph into English, I deliberately chose not to use the corresponding passage from the King James Bible.

L. 2 ff. Two Caucasian rivers. The original gives the names of the rivers: they are the Kurá (rhymes with *hurrah*) and the Arágva (the same in l. 635). Lermontov described the ancient Svéti-Tshkovéli ("Life-giving Pillar") Cathedral at Mtskhet with its burial vault of the last Georgian tsars, Irákly II and George XIII. Mtskhet was the first capital of Georgia (= Iberia, Colhis) until the sixth century A.D. The cathedral was erected in the eleventh century, destroyed by Tamerlane, and rebuilt in the fifteenth century. In the eighteenth century Georgia was hard-pressed by the Turks and the Persians, and in 1783 accepted vassalage to Russia in exchange for assistance. George XIII abdicated in 1801. Lermontov writes of these events with barely perceptible irony and seeming approval.

L. 27. The Russian general mentioned here is Yermólov, as transpires from Lermontov's drafts (see note on No. 80).

L. 83. A very common statement in Lermontov (cf. No. 38 and note).

L. 85 ff. Another recurring motif: one's life, a string of years, even eternity, are less valuable than one moment of extreme bliss (cf. No. 23:17-20).

L. 105. The same image in No. 83.

L. 154. It is characteristic of *Mtsyri* that inanimate objects in it are almost human (trees stand in a circle like dancing brothers; two rocks long for a meeting); even the ounce (l. 488) moans like a man, and it is only people that are inhuman.

L. 156. Cf. note on No. 79.

L. 166. This line, also occurring in *Izmaíl-Bey*, is a good example of Lermontov's rhythmic experiments. Not only are the mountains phantasmagorical: the line itself is as broken as they.

L. 259. Snakes are often mentioned in Lermontov's Caucasian poems, and the image is approximately the same everywhere. In both *Mtsyri*

Commentary

and *The Demon* (No. 92:734-37, 1092-99), they appear at the moment when all hopes are shattered, as a symbol of final defeat.

L. 286 ff. This is a reference to the Georgian legend of the giant Amiráni who was hurled down from Heaven and sank into an abyss.

L. 422. After this line there was another long passage later crossed out by Lermontov:

> New visions then began to rise
> And float before my tortured eyes.
> I saw a steppe; its edges lay
> Consumed by darkness, far away,
> 5 And clouds, a shaggy, stormy throng,
> Were driven fast and flew along.
> I did not even start to trace
> The way of that fantastic race;
> A wildly snorting, frightened steed
> 10 Would never run at greater speed . . .
> But lo! The plain resounds and moves,
> It seems that many thousand hooves
> Dig all at once into the ground . . .
> Surprised, I shyly looked around
> 15 And saw a horseman strongly built
> Who seemed to ride at me full tilt;
> And then another . . . more and more . . .
> All dressed in wondrous clothes of war.
> Soon sturdy helmets came in sight,
> 20 Wrapped in bashlýks¹ of shining white.
> Each armed, each in a red beshmét²—
> Such were the horsemen whom I met.
> They whistled madly, riding on.
> I watched their eyes—they burned, they shone.
> 25 Each galloped past, within my reach,
> And well do I remember each.
> The monkish garb I'd always worn
> Aroused in them surprise and scorn.
> They laughed at me and drove ahead;
> 30 My heart became a piece of lead,
> I could not breathe for shame and pain.
> Behind the men who crossed the plain
> My father rode; with sudden force

1. A warm cloth hood with long ear flaps.
2. A narrow-sleeved garment worn by men in the Caucasus.

He checked the movement of his horse.
35 He raised his white bashlyk, and then
I saw those features once again.
A night between two autumn days
Is not as dark as was his gaze.
He smiled—that smile at his approach
40 Contained a bitter, stern reproach.
He waved to me; his arm was strong,
He called his son to come along,
But drained of will and words, I stood,
As if my feet were chained or glued.
45 Like someone dead, I did not cry;
Nor did I send him my reply.

L. 458. Cf. what is said about the ounce in note on No. 50.

L. 542. In the draft this line was followed by a passage excluded by Lermontov from his final version.

This place, this wood I seemed to know . . .
I felt deep horror and dismay!
The measured stillness of the day
Broke up. There came a sound—and yes!
5 Its meaning was not hard to guess.
I heard the toll expand and swell:
It was the cloister's biggest bell.
That toll of death! . . . It made me smart,
For it was coming from my heart,
10 As if a blade anew, anew
Were cutting up my breast in two.
Oh Lord, I thought, why did you give
All things to me with which to live:
An avid mind, a mighty frame,
15 Desires and youth, a thirst for fame?
Why did you tie me with a chain
But fill my heart, my breast, my brain
With love of freedom? Tell me, why
Of all whom you created, I
20 Should live in prison—live and die?
I was not good enough to save,
You saw me blind but never gave
A candle to dispel the dark;
And look: a wolf has learned to bark.
25 So I complained, so clamored there
In pain and absolute despair;

It was my grief that yelled and screamed.
Old man, you think I'll be redeemed?
I felt that fate had played me false;
30 Before, I had not known such falls:
Each hour had brought its tiny ray,
With which to live, to hope, and pray . . .
And then the days I'd spent with you
Arose before my eyes anew:
35 The humble church you used for prayer,
The images—all hostile stare:
Each was a picture of some saint
Hung on the walls with cracking paint;
One could not find a single nook
40 To hide from that unyielding look.
You barred each shining, merry beam,
And when I watched the sunrays gleam,
To leave you was my only dream.
Life, passions broke into my cell,
45 They called upon me to rebel,
And tears, my captive childhood's salt,
Did not allow me to exalt
The Lord; I could not glorify
Him, Who decreed that only I
50 Should live in prison—live and die . . .
The sound of that prophetic toll
For many years had wrung my soul.
I listened and I knew at last
That, whether I was slow or fast,
55 I should not find my home and past.
My courage failed; a deadly chill
Came over me and sapped my will;
It was the cold that people feel
When hearts in them are cut with steel.
60 How I despised my pain and fear!
I could not shout or shed a tear.
I lost; the things I'd tried to seek
Had not been destined for the weak.
At last, at last I understood
65 And crushed my stupid hopes for good;
Thus does, I heard, a snake pursued
Itself destroy its frightened brood . . .
Well, tell me truly: have I not
Deserved the weakling's shameful lot?

584

L. 586. Cf. No. 49:4. Mtsyri speaks the usual language of Lermontov's lyric hero, and there is no attempt in the poem at the linguistic local color. But Mtsyri's confession is not so full of abstract words (both nouns and adjectives) as Lermontov's other works, and the expression "the mind's disease," which is a variant of "captive reason's irritation" (No. 49:4), is not typical of this poem.

92. The Demon

The Demon is the most famous Romantic poem written in Russian. Its plot, a number of verses from it, and even the names of its protagonists have become an integral part of Russian spiritual life. It is also the last great Romantic work in the Russian language, though some echoes of it are easily discernible in post-Lermontov literature, and the image of the Demon recurs even in twentieth-century poetry, the latest universally known example being Blok's *Retaliation*.

Lermontov was by no means the first to make a fallen angel (Lucifer, Mephistopheles, Satan) his hero. He had a long line of predecessors: Dante, Milton, Goethe, Klopstock (*Messias*), Chateaubriand, Southey (*Vision of Judgment*), Byron (*Cain* and other "demonic" poems), Thomas Moore (*Lalla Rookh*), Alfred de Vigni (*Eloa*) and, in Russia, Zhukóvsky, Pushkin, and Polezháev (see note on No. 16), to mention only the most illustrious names. But no one returned to this subject with such regularity as Lermontov. The Demon as a special type—the embodiment of wickedness and vice, a symbol of gloom and sorrow, a great seducer, or a sinner longing for God and the ideal—pursued him from early adolescence. It does not matter that Satan was a central personage in European Romanticism and that Lermontov's taste coincided with the fashion of his time. Sources and parallels excite only literary historians, not authors; each outstanding poet creates a universe of his own, which is as sovereign in its rights as each individual human being, who, as well, has ancestry and establishes contacts with the world at large.

It is customary to distinguish eight redactions of *The Demon*. The earliest (1829; Lermontov was fifteen at the time) contains several poetical fragments and two prose outlines, the second of which sums up many of the motifs of the later versions. The opening and meter are as we know them from the canonized text. The next redaction dates back to the beginning of 1830. It is much longer than the first (442 lines); the heroine, so far nameless, is a nun, probably Spanish. Seduced by the Demon, she dies, and her soul goes to hell. In the summer of 1831 Lermontov wrote a fragment about the Demon, and this fragment is usually referred to as the third redaction, though there is no unanimity among Lermontov scholars as to which redaction is the third and which the fourth. The meter of the fragment (iambic pentameter) bored Lermontov almost at once, for after line 56 he jotted down the following words, "I wanted to write this poem in verse, but no—prose will suit it better." Also in 1831 Lermontov wrote two narrative poems, *Azrael* and *The Angel of Death*, both distant variations on the same theme, and toward the end of that very productive year, he finished the fourth redaction of *The Demon*, actually a reworking of the second. There are 516 lines in it, including a twenty-line dedication ("Accept my gift, oh my Madonna!"). The addressee of the dedication could have been either N. F. I. or V. A. Lopukhiná (Varen'ka), for in the autumn of 1831 the painful romance with N. F. I. came to a sudden end and a new love brought new inspirations to Lermontov (see Nos. 17, 19, 21, 23, 24, and Commentary). It is not improbable that the poem was written for N. F. I. but later "rededicated" to Lopukhina. In the fourth redaction, Lermontov wrote the nun's song, several landscapes, and an important dialogue (more about this dialogue will be said below).

In 1832 Lermontov thought of writing a poem whose outline has survived.

The Demon Plot. At the time of the Jews' Babylonian captivity (from the Bible). A Jewess; a blind father; he first sees her when she is asleep. Later she sings to her father about old days and about the closeness of an angel; etc. as before. The Jews return home, but her grave remains abroad.

"He" is of course the Demon; "etc. as before" must have referred to the previous redaction. This idea did not materialize, but Lermontov's lyrics and longer narrative poems of 1832 are full of reminiscences from *The Demon*. His early novel *Vadim* (1832-34) develops the demonic theme, applied, for the first time, entirely to mortals. A new redaction (fifth) was probably begun at the end of 1832, finished early in 1833, and slightly revised in the same year. This last "youthful" version contains 517 lines: about 200 were transferred from the previous redaction, but the rest of them were written anew. Among the new verses we find the Demon's monologue "Why do I love you?" (639 ff. of the present edition) and his oath (773 ff.), though the oath lacks the all-conquering passion of the canonized text. The poem was rapidly taking shape under the pen of the eighteen-year-old author.

Commentary

The action of Lermontov's mature narrative poems is usually set in the Caucasus. The same is true of the last redactions of *The Demon*, and that is why only the sixth redaction, dated September 1838, is immediately recognizable as the "real" *Demon*. Although Lermontov returned to his poem after an almost four-year interval, the Demon's type had been with him all that time, as evidenced by his play *Two Brothers* and especially by his drama in verse *The Masquerade* (see No. 96 and note). The impetus for a complete revision of the poem came from Lermontov's brief encounter with the Caucasus during his first exile (1837). At once everything changed, as if by magic: the heroine became a Georgian princess with a father and a bridegroom; the abstract and conventional southern landscape came alive; there appeared scenes describing the life of medieval Georgia; the poem acquired its two-part structure (though not exactly the same division into chapters as later); several hundred lines were written just for this version; and the actions of the characters received new and incomparably more convincing motivations.

A version of *The Demon* dated February 25, 1842, was discovered only in 1939 in Yerevan (the capital of Armenia). Since it was found so late, it lacks the distinction of having a number, but it differs considerably from the other versions and contains about a hundred totally original lines. It is not clear whether the Yerevan version precedes or follows the sixth redaction, with which it has almost everything in common. The 1838 redaction was presented to V. A. Lopukhina with a special dedication. The seventh redaction is less than two months younger than its predecessor (December 4, 1838). Its existence has been called in question, because neither the original nor an authorized copy of it has survived. However, according to a contemporary report, there once existed a notebook folded in two. Only its right-hand side was written up, while the left-hand side remained clean. This was presumably the seventh redaction, and it has an unusual history. By the end of 1838 *The Demon* had become so popular that even the court wanted a recital. The recital took place in February 1839, with V. A. Peróvsky (a natural son of Count A. K. Razumóvsky, a man interested in literature) as a performer, and Lermontov introduced many corrections for the occasion. According to the same report, the corrections were jotted down on the left-hand side, so that the seventh redaction became a draft of the eighth. Later, A. I. Filosófov, who brought out the first complete edition of *The Demon* (see below) wrote on the title-page of the autograph he used (which has survived) that the text had been copied from Lermontov's manuscript with all the changes, alterations, and corrections. This inscription was made two months after Lermontov's death (September 13, 1841; Lermontov was killed on July 15), and Filosofov must have used the folded notebook. He also dated the "clean" version: December 4, 1838. Since the reconstructed seventh redaction was completed in December and the recital at the court took place on February 8 and 9, 1839, the seventh redaction was converted into the eighth during the intervening months (December-January).

There is a tradition of long standing, which goes back to the contemporary report mentioned above, to push the date of the last redaction as much forward as possible (to 1840-41), but in all probability Lermontov did not return to his poem after December 1838-January 1839. Lermontov's *Selected Works* often close with *The Demon*, which is indeed his most memorable, even if not most perfect, poem, but there is little that can justify this practice on purely chronological grounds, for *Mtsyri* was written in 1840.

Filosofov reproduced Lermontov's corrections in his notes and thus saved the seventh redaction. The seventh redaction is somewhat longer than the sixth, and the chapters are numbered. Part 1 was transferred almost without changes, but Part 2 was reworked in many places. Thus, the last redaction of *The Demon* is the so-called court version. However, many scholars tend to discount it, because they believe that the latest changes are merely a tribute to censorship. For instance, in the sixth redaction, after Tamara's funeral the Angel flies to her grave and implores God to forgive the young sinner. The Demon flies to the grave too and does not try to fight for Tamara's soul. Lermontov does not say whether she will be saved (in the earlier redactions he vacillated between perdition and salvation); in the court version, the Demon's defeat is beyond doubt, and in the last scene he is depicted as a loathsome devil. This finale could have been caused by the necessity to make the poem more palatable to the august audience, but Lermontov replaced many other "neutral" passages as well. Whether he improved or spoiled them is debatable, and the answer is largely a matter of taste.

Lermontov did not make a serious effort to publish *The Demon*, though in March 1839 it was passed by the censor; despite this permission, spiritual censorship (the censorship that dealt with matters of religion) did not allow its publication, and for a long time *The Demon* was disseminated all over Russia in manuscripts. Soon after Lermontov's death Kraévsky, the editor of *Otéchestvennye Zapíski*, announced the appearance of *The Demon* in his almanac but again ran afoul of the censor. The galley proofs have miraculously come down to us and make it clear that Kraevsky used a defective copy of the eighth redaction, which he patched up here and there with passages from the sixth (1838) redaction. In 1842 Kraevsky published several extracts from the poem, but the first full text of *The Demon* appeared in print fourteen years later, in Karlsruhe (Germany). The edition was prepared by A. I. Filosofov (compare above) and brought out in 28(!) copies. In 1856 *The Demon* was published in Berlin by Schneider, whose text is a combination of the sixth and eighth editions. In 1857, both editions were repeated.

The Karlsruhe edition played an outstanding role in the history of Lermontov scholarship. It was accepted as the most reliable version of the poem and canonized; only the dialogue between Tamara and the Demon (1. 742 ff.), which is not to be found in the 1856 edition, goes back to the 1857 edition. Most modern editions reproduce this dialogue preceding the Demon's oath, and its legitimacy has caused heated debates. The Demon, as he appears before Tamara, is a confirmed and straightforward opponent of God. He does not conceal his intentions, and Tamara has little reason to say, "But if perfidious is your story, and if deception is your goal. . . ." She may doubt his readiness to start a new life but not his iconoclastic words, so the dialogue does not fit the context and Lermontov was right in excluding it. The only reason for including it in the present translation is that most modern editions print the dialogue in full.

I will pass over the recent attacks on the Karlsruhe edition, because they are hardly justifiable, and go on to the artistic problems of the poem, for *The Demon* has attracted the attention of scholars interested in its every aspect, and textual criticism, though of prime significance in this case, is only the thin edge of the wedge.

Let us first of all cast a brief look at the story itself, as we know it from the Karlsruhe version. The Demon, called the "spirit of banishment" in the opening line of the original, was at one time "a pure cherub," and the whole universe treated him as a dear friend. "The happy firstborn of creation," full of love and faith, he was eager for knowledge and used to watch the wandering caravans of luminaries. Later he calls himself the king of knowledge and freedom and promises to let the world wither *in ignorance* without him (803-4). Nothing at all is said about the causes of his downfall. In one of his soliloquies addressed to

Commentary

Tamara he mentions God's curse, but the sense of the quarrel remains obscure. We learn only that the moment the curse was pronounced, nature lost all interest in its beloved child. Stars and planets, which used to greet him with their sweetest smiles, stopped recognizing the outcast. In utter despair the Demon flew through boundless space and became the arch-seducer of men. Like all devils portrayed in Russian literature from Lermontov to Bulgákov, this Demon felt disgusted with men's petty passions, cruelty, and lack of integrity. Men succumbed to him at once. They turned out to be easy prey, and for a short while the Demon entertained himself by deceiving wayfarers. He appeared before benighted horsemen in the shape of a will-o'-the-wisp, and the unsuspecting travelers who followed him fell into the precipice. Killing innocent men was even more boring than buying them by the thousand, and the Demon wrapped in mist and lightning would often emulate storms in the vain attempt to forget the past. But his sorrow never gave way, and only hatred and indifference stayed in his soul. When we first see him, he is, according to his own words, the murderer of hope, the scourge of his slaves on earth, Heaven's foe, and the evil force in nature (though at the same time the king of knowledge and freedom), feared and detested by all. The beauty of nature has no appeal for him, and the luxury of God's creations fills him with contempt, envy, or abhorrence.

Everything changes when he meets Tamara, the only daughter of Goudál, a mighty Georgian prince. Tamara, evidently bereft of her mother a long time before, grew up not entirely sheltered from the labors of everyday life (such as carrying water from the river below to her huge, gloomy castle). At last the day comes for her to leave her native home for the home of her husband. She is the most beautiful maiden under the sun, and her bridegroom can hardly wait to see her. While his caravan is making its slow and perilous way along the river Arágva to Goudal's house, Tamara is playing and dancing with her friends. Lovely and innocent, full of unfeigned simplicity, she gives herself up to the merriment with a mixture of abandon and sorrow, for she fears her future; soon she will become a slave of her husband's kin, and secret doubts cast a shadow on her clear features. It is at this moment that the Demon sees her from high up in the air and is touched. Something suddenly melts in him, "a forgotten and beneficial sound filled the barren desert of his silent soul," and he revives. Sweet dreams start haunting him again, and he remembers the language of his glorious past. Both Tamara and her bridegroom have to pay for the Demon's awakening, because the Demon is jealous of the young man and gets rid of him without any compunction. The Demon inspires the youth with such a strong passion for Tamara that he neglects the ancient rite and does not stop to pray before a local saint's relics. Unprotected by this saint, he falls dead in a quick skirmish with the Ossetians, who waylay rich caravans in those parts. The Demon adds one more rider to the long list of those whom he has killed in days of yore. The horse brings the corpse of the ill-starred bridegroom to Goudál's court.

While Tamara is weeping on her bed, the Demon approaches her with the first of his irresistibly seductive speeches. These speeches, which follow one another in quick succession, are among the greatest achievements of Russian Romantic poetry. Tamara, even in her deepest despair, does not turn a deaf ear to the Demon's supplications. Once (I, 16) she actually sees him, though of course in a dream; the Demon is full of unearthly beauty, and his look is a blend of love and sorrow. She guesses that her visitor is not an angel, because there is no halo on his curls (!); nor is he a gloomy spirit of hell, "a vicious sufferer." No! He is like a clear evening; neither day nor night, neither darkness nor light. This is perhaps the most astounding characterization of the Demon in the whole poem, whatever its literary sources.

Broken-hearted and disconsolate, Tamara refuses to choose a new husband from a host of suitors and forces Goudal to send her to a monastery. A widow-bride, like Pushkin's Xenia Godunóva, she seeks the holy refuge not only because she is unhappy after her bridegroom's death; she hopes that as a nun she will stop hearing and stop inviting the seductive voice of the evil spirit. Her plan fails, and the Demon keeps tempting her in her cell and even in the chapel as strongly as before. Finally, he comes to Tamara's monastery cell. He is no longer a callous, heartless devil: he enters the cell ready for peace, with a soul open for love and brimming with the desire to start a new life. But instead of Tamara he sees the Angel, trying to protect his charge. The old malice flares up in the Demon. He defies the Angel, claims Tamara for himself, and drives away his opponent, who recognizes his defeat at once. In a welter of passionate expectation and fear, Tamara asks the Demon to leave her, if his intentions are not honorable, and the Demon answers with his great oath, which is the climax and the most famous part of the poem. He promises Tamara the whole universe in exchange for a paltry human lot and at the end of his speech touches Tamara's lips with his own. This kiss kills Tamara, and the suspicious night watchman hears her last, piercing scream.

Tamara's relatives bury her in a grave on an almost inaccessible summit, and one of God's angels (*the* Angel) carries her soul to Paradise. Once more we meet the Demon. Now his eyes are malice itself, and his immovable face breathes the cold of death. He has come to claim Tamara's soul, but the Angel brushes him aside: Tamara has suffered so much that her death expiated her guilt; now she belongs to God. Worsted, as once before, the Demon curses his dreams and stays alone to nurse his hurt pride.

With time, Goudal's castle crumbles, and spiders, snakes, and lizards play their games within its walls. Only the church over the family crypt survives. The poem closes with a description of the graveyard that has received the coffin with Tamara's remains.

The principal problem of *The Demon* is the character of its protagonist. It is immediately clear that the poem does not go back to any particular episode in the Scriptures, though Tamara, as well as all her relatives, is Christian. Lermontov, in whose vocabulary the words for Lord and God were very common, never used the name of Jesus Christ, even when he spoke of redemption and salvation. The Demon is not the Christian devil; he is strongly reminiscent of Milton's and Byron's Lucifer. Most Russian prerevolutionary scholars applauded Lermontov for allowing the Angel to defeat the Demon. They were glad that the poet and his heroine had come to terms with God. Since the revolution, Lermontov has always been praised for his rebellious tendencies (a fighter against monarchy, a fighter against religion, etc.), and the finale of *The Demon* has seemed unexpected and unmotivated to many. It has become customary to explain away the Angel's victory as a deplorable tribute to censorship: presumably, Lermontov could not afford a different dénouement in his court version. In more recent times, there have been attempts at modifying the extreme position of the second school. B. T. Udódov, the author of numerous works on Lermontov, including a formidably huge book (Voronezh 1973; 700 pages), insists that Lermontov's finale is natural and owes nothing to the pressure of censorship. He argues that the Demon wanted a living, loving Tamara; her soul, especially the soul that sought protection on the Angel's breast, would have been of no use to him, and he chose not to struggle for it.

Commentary

Several difficulties are involved in this discussion. As evidenced by such lyrics as Nos. 3, 35, 37, 51, 66 in the present volume, Lermontov's attitude toward God was complex. His poetry reflects two moods: in some lyrics he openly challenges God, in others he is completely at peace with the world and the Creator. Even Mtsyri, who in a passage not included in the printed text (again, it is believed for fear of the censor!) defies God's wisdom and curses his fate in the most un-Job-like fashion, immediately asks the old monk, "You think I shall be forgiven?" (p. 584, line 28; note on No. 91). So there is nothing really unexpected in the poem's conciliatory finale. On the other hand, censorship was a tangible force in the history of Russian nineteenth-century literature, and many books were maimed by it and by "self-censorship," as the practice of the preventive expurgating of one's works came to be named in later days. Lermontov himself rewrote the whole of *The Masquerade* [No. 96] in a futile attempt to see it on the stage, so again there is nothing improbable in the suggestion that by sending Tamara's soul to Heaven Lermontov wanted to gratify the censor.

The main weakness of this seemingly hopeless controversy is that both schools of thought ("Tamara was saved, because Lermontov was a good Christian" versus "Tamara was saved, because Lermontov gave in to external pressure") treat these plot elements as "real" rather than as literary facts. Both schools and Udódov interpret Lermontov's text as they would a police record. But the Demon and Tamara are products of a certain literary approach to life, not of life itself. The questions about why Pushkin married Natalie Goncharóva and why Lermontov did not marry Varen'ka Lopukhina are not of the same order as why Tatyana, though still in love with Onegin, preferred to stay with her old husband and why the Demon failed to get possession of Tamara's soul. Literature is not a transcript of life, it does not even "reflect" life: all art distorts its object, and that is why it is *art*. Literature goes to life for inspiration, borrows its material from life, and then processes it. Once a fact of life becomes a fact of art, it must submit only to the laws of art. "Art for art's sake," this bugbear of "progressive" criticism, does not mean an art interested only in itself. This unhappy formula stresses only the independence of literary laws. Literature, language, painting, music, come from "life" in order to turn into self-contained and self-governed systems: "The summer's flow'r is to the summer sweet, though to itself it only live and die." A scholar who undertakes to write a book about

Commentary

Hamlet's childhood remains outside literature, because Hamlet never was a child, and his age changes, depending on the requirement of the dramatic situation.

Thus is it also with Tamara and the Demon. The poem belongs to two systems: one is Lermontov's own poetics, the other the literature of Lermontov's day. The Demon and Tamara live in these two artificial worlds and are subject to their laws. In Lermontov's larger works, apart from his so-called ironic poems, the finale is invariably tragic (just as is the case with Dostoevsky). Pechorin loses the woman he loves, torments those who love him, and dies young. Mtsyri perishes in a hopeless attempt to find home. Kaláshnikov is dishonored and later executed. All Lermontov's plays are tragedies. It is also significant that Lermontov's hero, in spite of his bravado, is usually afraid of women and spends his passion in mockery or in tempestuous but inefficient wooing. It always happens that at the decisive moment he is prevented from being united with the object of his love. Mtsyri has a good excuse for not approaching the Georgian girl, but the others end up like Mtsyri. Grigory Alexandrovich Pechorin (*A Hero of Our Time*) is shockingly cruel to Princess Mary, and his strange triumph comes when he is able to say, "I do not love you" to her, whereas Vera (a sad failure from an artistic point of view) is allowed, almost forced, to slip away. Georges Pechorin, the protagonist of *Princess Ligovskaya*, plays the central role in the distasteful farce according to the Lermontov-Sushkova model: he poses as a lovesick suitor, only to tease his quarry. Lermontov seems to have been such a man himself. He loved V. A. Lopukhina but did not marry her; there were rumors of his marrying Shcherbatova, but again he never proposed, though the feeling was reciprocal. At one time he was in love with Sushkova (how much in love is evidenced by his revenge) but was snubbed by her and never let bygones be bygones: when he grew up he almost ruined her. The fleeting romance with N. F. I. was a hard trial to the young Lermontov, but if we can trust the pattern, nothing would have come of this infatuation either, even under the best of circumstances. He paid his court to E. A. Klingenberg, N. P. Verzílina, and Nataliya Martýnova; he followed È. K. Musina-Pushkina like a shadow. To make up for the collapse of so many strong attachments, he wrote "hussar" poems whose smutty language is often an end in itself; Pushkin's obscenities are full of charm, but the culminations of Lermontov's ribald poems are embarrassing. Lermontov's hero is like his creator: brilliant, effusive, tender, or harsh, as the case may be, but always barred

Commentary

from consummating his union with the woman. In lyrics he is deceived by the woman; in most dramas, in *A Hero of Our Time*, and in *The Demon* he himself is the deceiver, but the result is the same. Lermontov lacked Pushkin's universality and never broke the circle he had circumscribed in his youth. Whether Lermontov tried to live up to his own literary creations or whether he wrote to get rid of his obsessions, as he intimated in his *A Fairy Tale for Children* (No. 97:65-66) is something we will never learn. In any event, the Demon did not win Tamara and later did not get Tamara's soul, because that would have meant the attainment of happiness by the hero, and such a solution was impossible to Lermontov the poet. He could not conceive of a happy end, just as Dickens could not finish his early novels on a discordant note.

The other system that should be taken into account is that of Lermontov's contemporary literature. Lermontov inherited from Pushkin and partly from European Romantic tradition a scheme according to which a talented but bored young man, someone who is too bright to serve the establishment, meets a woman of exceptional purity. The man usually experiences a longing for an undefined ideal. Sometimes he has a vague revolutionary past (like Pushkin's Aléko in *The Gypsies*); though he is not worldly, the woman he meets prefers him to her other suitors or chooses him herself. The hero is, however, not worthy of her love: he spurns it, runs away from it, or, overpowered by jealousy, even kills the woman (like Aléko and Arbenin in *The Masquerade*). As characters in poems and novels such women were barely outlined and hardly carried more conviction than Lermontov's Vera. Among the talkative and inept "superfluous men" of Russian literature the Demon occupies a prominent place. As bored as they, as tired of being bad, as clever as the best of them, more sinned against than sinning, the Demon meets Tamara, who has no independent role to play. She is born to provide help to the hero, a help that will not save him. She asks questions to which the Demon gives his eloquent answers. It is not relevant whether a certain number of selfless and heroic women actually lived at that time. In literature they signify a pure function and are not meant to be married. Even Tatyana—who is definitely less shadowy than Lermontov's Vera, Turgenev's Natalya (*Rudin*), and Goncharov's Olga (*Oblomov*)—does not follow Onegin at the end of the story. Pushkin is known to have said, "Imagine what my Tatyana has done: she married an old general!" This statement is always cited to prove that Pushkin was faithful to "the truth of life" and wielded no absolute power over his characters. This is a wrong conclusion. Pushkin could allow his heroine to marry an old general but never to be united with a man like Onegin, for the story had to end in the hero's disaster, and here Pushkin was no more free than Lermontov: Onegin's type inevitably carried the seed of self-destruction. When Lermontov attempted to marry the Demon's mortal counterpart (Arbenin) to the woman he loved, he had to invent a new motivation for the catastrophe and came up with an insignificant intrigue.

One more circumstance makes the movement of the plot natural and easy to understand if we agree to view the poem as a literary artifact rather than a transcript of life. The crux of the matter is that the Demon is not quite real. Here we must again return to Pushkin. In her letter to Onegin Tatyana says that Onegin had haunted her dreams and become dear to her long before they met, so that when he actually appeared, Tatyana *recognized* him. "Who are you," asks Tatyana, "my guardian angel or a perfidious seducer?" It is hard to believe that the quotation is not from *The Demon*. Tatyana's infatuation with the image she herself conjured up can perhaps be explained as a usual Romantic cliché: a provincial girl given to reverie and introspection, brought up on French novels, she pays the usual price for her childish ideas. Even her fear of an almost supernatural demonic seducer, which comes to the surface in her dream, is perhaps part of this price. But for Lermontov, dreamland is more tangible than the outside world (Pushkin never crossed this line). Surrounded by vicious ladies at a fashionable ball, his hero "shuts off" the scene before his eyes and sees himself a child back at home, so that the pictures of the past come out much more real than the ball (No. 55). In another poem (No. 88) the action is again set at a ball, but this time the hero is quite happy. He meets a woman whose face is hidden under a mask, but he creates her image from the few clues at his disposal and falls in love with the product of his imagination. The dying gladiator and Mtsyri have beautiful visions of their past. The hero and heroine of "The Dream" (No. 81) testify to the ultimate triumph of dream over reality. The Demon belongs to the same twilight area between reality and fiction. There is no doubt that he exists (because Lermontov tells us so), but at the same time he is largely evoked by Tamara; he is part of her erotic dreams. Although he is free to seek his pleasure by day as well as by night, he never shows himself to her before sunset. She invites him, and he comes; he is *her* Demon, the materialized longing of her soul.

All this is not meant to carry Freudian connotations. Lermontov's neuroses, let alone Tamara's, are no concern of ours, for Lermontov is a private individual, and Tamara is fictitious. Of real importance is that Tamara is not alone among Lermontov's characters who hear voices. The man pursuing a mask at a ball (No. 88) is one of them too. The most striking evidence, however, is the tale called "Shtoss" (recently translated into English by David Lowe. See Carl R. Proffer, ed., *Russian Romantic Prose*. Ann Arbor: Translation Press, 1979, pp. 198-209). The hero hears a voice telling him an address in St. Petersburg. He finds the place, rents the apartment (which happens to be empty), and falls victim to an evil spirit living in a portrait on the wall. The hero is described with the greatest sympathy, and his fight against his obsession is as hopeless as Tamara's attempt to hide in a monastery. A number of literary creations are akin to Lermontov's *Demon*. Such are, for instance, Shakespeare's ghosts seen only by some, such are many fantasies of E. T. A. Hoffman and Gogol. The Demon is like twilight: neither darkness nor sunshine, neither night nor day; as long as he wanders through space, his color is neutral. He becomes irresistibly handsome when he meets Tamara and repellent after her death. His appearance depends on the development of the romance. When Tamara dies, he becomes redundant (the ghost returns to the picture on the wall). His triumph over the Angel in the finale would have meant the collapse of the whole literary structure of the poem. As mentioned above, the Demon followed Lermontov all his life, and he knew the force of this phantom. He even tried to cut one diamond with another and wrote a self-parody (*A Fairy Tale for Children*, No. 97), but hardly exorcised the devil. Lermontov's Demon came only to those who waited for him, and Lermontov never stopped waiting.

The Demon is a typical Romantic study in the relations between good and evil. Lermontov believed that no one is only good or only bad and that an almost imperceptible line separates light from darkness in a human soul. His ideas on this subject were close to Schelling's (as were many other ideas in Lermontov's philosophy and aesthetics). According to Schelling, a cornerstone of true philosophy is freedom, defined by him as the ability to create good and evil, for man is a receptacle containing the entire might of darkness and light, the extreme depth of an abyss, and the highest limit of the heavens. Readers of *A Hero of Our Time* will remember many pronouncements to the same effect and know that Pechorin's ethics are elusive. He imbibed all the diseases of his age (so he is "bad"), but he is the most brilliant, the most sensitive, and the most attractive figure in the novel (so he is "good"). Another striking example of Lermontov's "dialectics" is his drama *Two Brothers*. Superficially, it is a weak play with a rather worthless plot, but in spite of all this *Two Brothers* is part and parcel of Lermontov's heritage. The opponents—the "good" brother Yury and the "bad" brother Alexander—are not replicas of Schiller's brothers. Alexander is the villain of the drama, but it is he who is Lermontov's mouthpiece, and it is his monologues that we later hear from Pechorin.

The *Demon* is as complex as *A Hero of Our Time* and *Two Brothers*. The Demon is the only character in the poem who is entirely free; for this obvious reason he is both "nature's evil" and the "king of knowledge." At one time he defied God and is doomed to stay an exile forever. Contrary to Milton and Byron, Lermontov did not represent his protagonist as a great rebel, and if we feel a measure of sympathy for him, it is because he is the poem's tragic hero and a victim of God's wrath. It is his position in the story, not his character or deeds, that elevates him. He is partly responsible for the corruption of the human race (although people succumbed to temptation at once and deserve no pity); and with such a catastrophe as backdrop, the death of a few benighted riders that he has on his conscience does not look like a serious crime. The Demon, with his neutral color, appears before us as a bored misanthrope, not as the king of evil. Andrey Sinyavsky, who, as it seems, has come closer than anybody else to the true understanding of Lermontov's poem, remarks (in his article on socialist realism) that the Demon is typically Russian: too inconstant in his pursuit of evil to be a full-fledged devil and too inconstant in his repentance to become reconciled with God. Likewise, the Angel is not the embodiment of goodness, conventional as he is. He cannot defend Tamara, and he is too feeble to function as the Demon's opponent. He is a messenger of God, and his victory is not a triumph of good over evil, just as his defeat in the first encounter does not mean that good was worsted. The Angel is "good," because he carries Tamara's soul to Paradise, but he is "bad," because but for him the Demon could perhaps have been saved. No wonder that Tamara is torn between the two forces fighting for her: she is ready to love the Demon but his first kiss kills her. Even after her death, the expression on her face is somewhat ambiguous. In meditating on Tamara's fate Lermontov approached the area that was later so thoroughly explored by Dostoevsky: superhuman suffering and expiation.

The Demon, Tamara, and the Angel constantly find themselves

representing their enemies' sides: the Demon forgets his all-consuming hatred and is ready to beg for God's forgiveness, Tamara does actually forgive her bridegroom's (and her own prospective) murderer and returns his love, and the Angel leaves Tamara at the mercy of his great antagonist. Thus do they play their tragic game, and no one emerges victorious from it. Only nature, which is for Lermontov synonymous with the Caucasus, stands above it all, as it does in the poetic obituary of Odóevsky, in *Valerik*, and in *Mtsyri*.

Lermontov's views on good and evil were very early identified with those of his characters, and his critics concluded that Lermontov stood on the side of evil. Nothing could have been further from the truth. If inspiration in a poet tells its own story, then Lermontov's case is unambiguous. The Demon is a bored observer of life at the beginning of the poem and a loathsome spirit at the end. He is irresistible only while he is in love and ready to become reconciled with God; compare his beautiful monologues in Tamara's bedroom and cell with the curt and peremptory speeches addressed to the Angel. We know from "Do Not Trust Yourself" (No. 49) that Lermontov was actually afraid of spilling the music of his soul, of selling its "storm and thunder" to the mob. Even if he was akin to his own Demon, he was fully aware of his demonic powers and constantly fought against the temptation to use them. He knew that his genius could conquer the world but renounced his claims for fear of disturbing one trusting soul or making one child sadder (No. 63, 157 ff.). Here again he anticipated Dostoevsky, who owed as much to Lermontov as did Dostoevsky's antipode Leo Tolstoy.

L. 1. The first line of the poem is as old as the earliest version of *The Demon*. The literal translation of it runs as follows, "The melancholy Demon, the spirit of banishment." It is one of the most familiar quotations in Russian.

L. 34 ff. Kazbék is the highest summit of the Caucasus; it is repeatedly mentioned in Lermontov's poetry. Daryál is a canyon in the Caucasus, the bed of the river Terek in the area of its rise (cf. Nos. 4, 39, 52, and notes; cf. also No. 90:216-18 and No. 91:735).

L. 38. "The lioness with a mane" has puzzled many commentators, but this phrase occurs in all the reputable copies of *The Demon*.

Ll. 31-53. The impressionistic landscape of great heights and depths, with a furious river leaping over stones and clouds above, but without any people seen anywhere, is typically Lermontov's. The vocabulary of the original is unusually solemn. Note that Lermontov's personages, so very much alike at first sight, differ in their attitude toward nature. Mtsyri and Pechorin are far from indifferent to the beauty of the surrounding world, while the Demon is only bored by it. Lermontov could not have chosen a more telling detail. See note on ll. 329-44.

Ll. 80-82. The simile is characteristic. Almost everyone else would have said that a beautiful girl's eyes shine like stars, but Lermontov consistently compared distant objects to those in his immediate field of vision, rather than the other way about.

L. 92. Actually, *Goudál* should rhyme with *shall*, not with *wall*. The Russian spelling of the name (in transliteration) is *Gudal*. The root of this proper name is *Gud(a)*; according to legend, Guda was a mountain spirit who fell in love with a mortal girl, so the name of Tamara's father is richer in immediate tragic associations than it seems to a Russian (or any other non-Georgian) reader. It has been suggested that Goudál's prototype was Prince Gul'bát Chavchavádze and that Lermontov described his castle in lines 89 ff.

L. 99. The Arágva is a tributary of the Kurá. At the confluence of the two rivers there was a monastery, which Mtsyri saw at the end of his wanderings (see No. 91:2 and 635 and note on l. 2). The Arágva rises in the canyon called Guda; the name of the spirit mentioned in the previous note comes from Gúd-gorá, the mountain towering over the river. (It is the same type of back formation as Darya from Daryál—see note on No. 82). See also line 185.

Ll. 100 and 102. Of the two words explained by Lermontov in the footnotes the first is now in common use in Russian.

L. 114 ff. This description is reminiscent of a passage in *Evgeny Onegin* (I: 20) and gave birth to many echoes and imitations.

L. 135. Peri: a Persian fairy, a beauty. This word—used by Lermontov—was a great favorite in Russian and English Romantic poetry.

Ll. 154-57. Cf. No. 24: 9-12 and No. 42: 5-8.

Ll. 166-67. A beneficial sound rising from the bottom of the soul is one of Lermontov's most constant images.

Ll. 170-74. Cf. l. 11-12.

L. 181. Lermontov's hero never forgets anything.

L. 196. Sinodál is Tsinondáli (in eastern Georgia).

L. 205. Karabákh is a mountainous area in Azerbaijan. Sorrels of the Karabakh breed have been famous since ancient times.

L. 235 and 238. In the Russian text each of these two lines has a footnote. Lermontov calls the stirrup resounding (234) and explains why he says so; the second note is on the word meaning 'Cossack cap' (like a bearskin).

L. 242. This description has caused many surprised protests from those who know that the Georgians are anything but timid.

L. 271. Cf. No. 89:1.

L. 286. Ossétia is a region in Central Greater Caucasus. The Ossetians are an ancient people famous in legend. They speak an Iranian language, and only some of them are Moslem (others are Eastern Orthodox).

Ll. 290-91. . . . *fell* . . . *fallen* . . . is an attempt to render Lermontov's probably unconscious but very effective pun (. . . *zapalyónny* . . . *pal*).

Ll. 329-44. Clouds aimlessly floating in the sky is a recurring image in Lermontov's poetry. The Demon, who in the opening stanzas feels only contempt for and hatred of nature, is now singing a song about the beauty of the aerial ocean. This love-sick devil is no longer blind to the appeal of God's world.

Ll. 432-49. In lines 31 ff. we see the earth from above. The description begins with Kazbék shining like "the diamond's facet," Daryál, and the Terek. As the Demon starts descending, he begins to discern small rills with variegated stones on the bottom, rose bushes, and even caves. Lermontov has often been admired for his cinematographic view, and twentieth-century cameramen repeat with amazement that the Caucasus seen from an airplane looks exactly like what the Demon saw in his flight over Georgia. Equally masterful is the description in II: 3. Here the eyes of a nun investigate the world lying outside the monastery wall, and we are shown only what Tamara herself could have seen. Kazbék is the first thing the Demon observes from above; for Tamara it is the last.

L. 453. Muezzins are Mohammedan officials who call to prayer (Lermontov's word).

Ll. 458-61. The image of a Georgian maiden going to the river to draw water is an echo of lines 97-99. The circumstances have changed, and a picture of something so simple and ordinary reinforces—in a most subtle and unobtrusive way—the idea of forfeited happiness. A Georgian maiden is also mentioned in the description of nature, lines 80-82. A beautiful woman is part of beautiful nature to Lermontov; cf. the appearance of a girl in Mtsyri (No. 91:342 ff.), the hero's vision at a fashionable ball (No. 55:13-30), and the description of Shcherbátova (No. 58).

Ll. 459-69. Note seven rhyming words (459, 460, 461, 462, 465, 468, 469); this is Lermontov's (and Byron's) favorite technique, and there are many similar instances in both *Mtsyri* and *The Demon*, though seven is the greatest number.

Ll. 480-86. The reference is to Amiráni (See 91:286 ff. and note). It is a curious fact that in this passage the chained spirit of Georgian legends is associated with Tamara, rather than the Demon.

Ll. 527-28. Cf. No. 34:23-24 and note.

L. 630. A familiar image in Lermontov; cf. 98:12.

L. 987 ff. The description of Tamara's tomb on an inaccessible summit can go back to the cycle of Georgian legends about the interment of Queen Tamara (about whom see note on No. 82).

L. 1018. The same exclamation as in line 577 (and as in Tatyana's dream).

93. My Demon

In 1824 Pushkin published his poem "My Demon" (followed by several others on the same subject). This is what he said:

In the days when all the impressions of life—the maidens' glances, the noise of groves, the singing of a nightingale—were new to me, when lofty feelings, liberty, glory, love, and the inspiration of art so strongly excited my blood and threw a sudden shadow of melancholy on the hours of hope and joy, then an evil spirit began to visit me. Our meetings were sad: his smile, wondrous look, and caustic speeches poured cold poison in my soul. He tempted Providence, he called the beautiful a dream, he despised inspiration. He trusted neither love nor liberty; he mocked life, and there was nothing in all nature that he wanted to bless.

Strangely enough, the literary critic who reviewed this poem (in 1825) thought that he had recognized the Demon's prototype, namely Alexand(e)r Raévsky. Raevsky's contemporaries found something hellish in him, discovered a blend of vanity, perfidy, and malice in his soul, contempt for people, extreme egoism, and a stern mind devoid of nobility. Reticent and reserved, arousing in people something that oppressed them, he, according to his own father, was capable of a passionate outburst, friendship, sacrifice, magnanimity, and sometimes one word from him would expiate a hundred sins. Raevsky said once, "I am sad as always, my existence is more senseless than ever, and I see no comforting hope from any direction." These words were pronounced several years after 1825, and his friendship with Pushkin goes back to earlier days. Pushkin was attracted to Raevsky by "a peculiar charm, which consisted in sharp and acrimonious negation."

Pushkin meant to publish an answer to the reviewer but never did it. In a short note dated 1825, which was brought out as late as 1874, he wrote,

I think the critic went astray. Many people share his opinion, some even pointed to the concrete person presumably described by Pushkin in his strange poem. They are hardly right; at least I see in "My Demon" a different and more moral aim. In the prime of life the heart not yet dampened by experience is open to everything that's beautiful. It is trusting and tender. By and by the eternal contradictions of being produce doubts in it—a feeling that is painful but not durable. It disappears but destroys forever the best hopes and the soul's poetic prejudices. It is not for nothing that the great Goethe called the eternal enemy of the human race *a spirit of negation*. And did Pushkin, too, not mean to embody in his demon this spirit of *negation and doubt* and delineate in a compact picture his characteristic features and his influence on the morals of our age?

The end of Pushkin's reply reads like a passage from Lermontov's preface to *A Hero of Our Time*; both men gave the most general description of their generation and sent gullible critics tracking prototypes.

The similarity between the two poems entitled "My Demon" is obvious and several phrases were borrowed by Lermontov from Pushkin without changes. "My Demon" is Lermontov's first extant attempt to deal with the image that was destined to pursue him all his life. It was published in 1859.

94. My Demon

This poem, first published in 1889, shares the title and the opening lines with the preceding one. Otherwise, it is quite an independent lyric. Characteristically, the Demon is here not only a symbol of melancholy, cruelty, and gloom but also a source of wondrous light, the future king of knowledge. By the age of sixteen or seventeen, Lermontov must have realized that he would not be able to shake off his demon; hence the tenor of the conclusion.

L. 20. Cf. No. 91:193.

95. 'Tis Not For Bliss Or Plains Elysian

This short lyric, published in the same issue of the *Otéchestvennye Zapíski* (Vol. 125, 1859) as the early version of "My Demon" (No. 93), is typical

Commentary

of Lermontov's style, and all the motifs are familiar: God and angels versus the Demon, solitude, worthlessness of life, and so on. Note the rhyme in the second stanza (danger: stranger; in the original, izbránnik: stránnik), which also occurs in "I Am Not Byron" (No. 18:2-3).

96. Three Monologues by Arbénin from The Masquerade

The Masquerade, written in 1834-35, is a drama in four acts. Its hero, Evgény Arbénin, is married to a young woman called Nina. Early disappointments and demonic passions (about which we learn from Arbenin's speeches) have left an indelible mark on his soul. At a fashionable masquerade Nina falls victim to a traditional intrigue: she loses her bracelet, and Arbenin is led to believe that his wife has been unfaithful to him. He poisons her and immediately discovers the truth.

Monologue 1 describes Arbenin waiting for his wife late at night, when the masquerade is nearly over. Monologues 2 and 3 are given after his suspicions have been aroused.

97. A Fairy Tale for Children

The poem was written in 1839-40 and published posthumously in 1842. At that time it won the approval and admiration of several discerning critics; today it is known mainly to specialists, but it is undoubtedly one of Lermontov's masterpieces. It is unfinished and consists almost entirely of Mephistopheles's monologue (Stanza 8 ff.). The heroine's name must have been dear to Lermontov; in any case, there is a very early lyric from his pen called "To Nina" (a 1829 translation of Schiller's "An Emma"), and Arbénin's wife (in *The Masquerade*: No. 96) is also Nina. Lermontov used the same eleven-line stanza in his long poem *Sashka* and in the obituary of Odóevsky (No. 53), in the latter with a slightly modified system of rhyming. The devil of this "fairy tale" was meant as a parody of the great Demon briefly described in Stanzas 3 and 6, but, as the tale goes on, this mischievous spirit almost imperceptibly acquires the familiar features of Lermontov's hero, and in the last stanza the speaker seems to be the poet himself.

Ll. 12-16. There is a similar place in Pushkin's narrative poem *A House in Kolómna*, and Lermontov's predilection for rhyming words in "fluid u" finds ample proof in his works.

Commentary

L. 28. On December 16, 1843 a certain N. Ulyánov wrote the following letter to Kraévsky, the editor of *Otéchestvennye Zapísky*:

Dear Sir: In 1833 I received from one of my friends verses entitled *The Demon*. At that time no one was of course particularly concerned about the works of some cadet, and the notebook with the verses was lost. When finally *Lermontov's Poetical Works* were published and I read, among others, his poem *The Demon* written in 1839, I remembered a number of places familiar to me from some source. I was especially struck by the poet's words in *A Fairy Tale for Children* [gives ll. 25-31]. The last verse turned out to be prophetic. At long last, a month or so ago, after many efforts I regained that notebook, and I hasten to send it to you, so that you can treat your subscribers to this titbit for the New Year. This notebook is not my property.

The notebook in question contained the fifth redaction of *The Demon*.

L. 29. It is nice (French). In Lermontov's time French was the main, often the only, language of the Russian upper class.

Ll. 50-51. The passage is probably a self-parody too, for Tamara tried to identify her strange visitor just by his "uniform" (No. 92:385-91).

Ll. 67-70. This is a close paraphrase of *Evgeny Onegin* VI: 33 (Pushkin's digression after Lensky's death in a duel).

Ll. 78-99. A parody of the Demon's monologue in Tamara's bedroom (No. 92:593 ff.).

L. 100 ff. Here Mephistopheles sees St. Petersburg exactly as the Demon sees Georgia: from high above (No. 92:31 ff.), and his description of human depravity is close to the Demon's description of people and their petty passions. Like Pushkin in *The Bronze Horseman*, Lermontov gives a lyrical sketch of a white night in St. Petersburg, but Lermontov did not like St. Petersburg, and his intonation is very different from Pushkin's.

L. 141. In the original the windows are called transparently dark. I think it is a borrowing form Byron's *Parisina*, which Lermontov knew very well (see note on No. 91). *Parisina* opens with an anthologized description of twilight, with its "clear obscure, so softly dark, and darkly pure," and I risked using Byron's oxymoron in my translation.

L. 177 ff. Nina, like many of Lermontov's characters, has an unhappy childhood whose scars never heal. She resembles Tamara in that she has only one parent, a father (despotic and seemingly inefficient), and lives in a world created by her own imagination. Cf. Stanza 21 and No. 92: 1039 ff. She also resembles Mtsyri, for, like him, she is a flower that has grown in prison (line 179, cf. No. 91:587-601).

Ll. 215-16. Cf. No. 92:154-57 and note.

Ll. 257-60. Both Nina and Tamara are pursued by the demons that suit them perfectly.

L. 276 ff. The passage reads like a condensed description of Natásha Rostóva's first ball in Tolstoy's *War and Peace*.

98. *"Quand je te vois sourire"*

French was the language of everyday life in Russian high society. Both Pushkin and Lermontov wrote most of their letters in French, and spoke French at receptions, and on other social occasions. They also composed some poetry in French. Lermontov's extant poetry in French is, however, scarce.

Translation: When I see you smile, my heart bursts into bloom, and I would like to tell you what my heart says to me. Then my whole life passes before my eyes, and I curse and pray, and cry in secret. Because without you, my only guide, without your fiery look my past seems empty, like Heaven without God. And—a strange whim!—I notice that I bless the beautiful day—oh, my angel!—when you made me suffer.

The poem was published in 1859.

99. *"Non, si j'en crois mon espérance"*

Translation: No, if I can believe my hope, a brighter future is before me. In spite of the distance, I shall be with you in my recollections. Wandering on another shore, I will follow you from afar; and if a storm breaks out over you, call me: I will return.

The poem was published in 1882.

100. *L'attente*

Translation: Expectation. I am waiting for her in a dark valley. At a distance I see a wraith, a wraith that slowly approaches. But no! Hope is treacherous! It is an old willow swinging its dry and shining trunk. I bend and listen long: It seems to me that I hear the sound of light steps on the pathway. No! It is a leaf rustling in the moss, a leaf moved by the fragrant night wind. Full of bitter thoughts, I lay myself down in thick

grass and fall into a deep sleep. Suddenly I start and wake up: her voice
has whispered something in my ear, her mouth has kissed my forehead.

The poem was published in 1887.

INDEXES

General Index

General Index

Bodenstedt, Friedrich, 551
Bol'shoy svet. See *Beau Monde*
Boris Godunov. See Pushkin, A. S.
Borodinó, the battle of, 501-2 (No. 30), 504, 558, 569
Bowra, Cecil M., 494 (No. 28)
Boyars, 574
The Bronze Horseman. See Pushkin, A. S.
Bryúsov, V. Ya., 16
Bulgákov, M. A., 590
Bulgaria, 21 (Note 4)
Bulgárin, F. V., 503, 541 (No. 63)
Bunyan, John, 578
"The Burial of Sir John Moore at Corunna." *See* Wolfe, Charles
Bykhovéts, E. G., 564 (No. 84)
Byron, George G., 15, 19, 21, 26, 29, 30, 469, 470 (No. 5), 472, 473 (No. 7), 474 (No. 8), 475, 481 (No. 15), 487-88. 489. 512 (No. 34), 514 (No. 36), 519, 530, 532, 537, 538 (No. 60), 566 (No. 85), 573, 575, 577, 585 (No. 92), 592, 598, 602, 605
"An Album Piece," 5
Cain, 467 (No. 2), 488 (No. 18), 585 (No. 92)
Childe Harold, 19, 488 (No. 18)
"Darkness," 466 (No. 2)
Don Juan, 5, 20, 488 (No. 18)
"Dream," 467 (No. 2)
epitaphs, 470 (No. 6)
The Giaour, 487 (No. 18), 573, 574, 575
"Hebrew Melodies." *See* "My Soul Is Dark" and "Sun of the Sleepless"
Lara, 554 (No. 76)
Manfred, 488 (No. 18), 554 (No. 76)
"My Soul Is Dark," 5, 470 (No. 5), 512 (No. 34), 538 (No. 60)
"Napoleon's Farewell", 537
Parisina, 573, 574, 605
"The Prisoner of Chillon," 573
"Stanzas to Augusta, 492 (No. 23)
"Sun of the Sleepless," 470 (No. 5)
Byronism in Russia, 473 (No. 7), 484, 489, 554 (No. 76)

Cabardinians, 526
Cain. See Byron, George G.

Camus, Albert, 569
L'Etranger, 569
Caspian Sea, 493 (No. 26), 526
Le Caucase. Journal de voyages et romans, 554 (No. 76)
Le Caucase. Nouvelles Impressions de voyage, 559
Caucasus, 4, 5, 9, 10, 16, 483-84, 507, 515 (No. 37), 516 (No. 39), 526, 527 (Nos. 52 and 53), 544, 557-61 (No. 80), 562-63 (No. 82), 568-69 (Nos. 89 and 90), 571, 572 (No. 90), 576, 577, 578, 581, 587, 599, 601
Cazotte, Jacque, 528 (No. 54)
Censorship, 542-43 (No. 66), 558, 588, 589, 592, 593
Charwort, Mary Ann, 474 (No. 9)
Chateaubriand, Alphonse de, 585 (No. 92)
Chaucer, Geoffrey, 26
Chavchavádze, E. A., 518 (No. 42)
Chavchavádze, Gul'bát, 600
Chavchavádze, Nina, 516 (No. 40), 517 (No. 40), 518 (No. 42), 600
Chechens, 560
Chechnyá, 568 (No. 90), 572 (No. 90)
Chekhov, A. P., 30, 506
Chénier, André, 519, 524 (No. 49)
Cherkesses, 467 (No. 4), 526, 557 (No. 80), 560, 568 (No. 89), 569
Chernets. See A Black Monk
Chernyshévsky, N. G., 525 (No. 50), 551
Chervlyónaya, 533 (No. 57)
Childe Harold. See Byron, George G.
"Cleopatra." *See* Pushkin, A. S.
Colhis, 581
"Conversation of a Bookdealer with a Poet." *See* Pushkin, A. S.
Cornford, Frances, 494 (No. 28)
Corot, Jean-Baptiste C., 17
Cossacks, 526, 533 (No. 57), 568
The Cossacks. See Tolstoy, L. N.
Coxwell, C. Fillingham, 499 (9)
Crimean War, 508
Custine, Astolphe L. L. de, 3
La Russie en 1839, 3

Daghestan, 561 (No. 89), 568 (No. 89)
Daniels, Guy, 495, 556 (No. 78)

General Index

General Index

General Index

General Index

General Index

General Index

Súnja, 572 (No. 90)
"Superfluous men," 595
Sushkóv, S. P., 555 (No. 76)
Sushkóva, E. P., *See* Rostopchina, E. P.
Sushkóva-Khvostóva, E. A., 48 (Fig. 2), 49
(Fig. 3), 474, 480, 485 (No. 17), 488
(No. 19), 490 (No. 19), 521 (No. 48),
554 (No. 76), 561 (No. 81), 594
Sveti-Tskhoveli Monastery, 581
Symbolists, 16, 21

"The Talisman." *See* Pushkin, A. S.
Tamára (Queen), 562, 602 (No. 92)
Tamerlane, 581
Tarkhány, 3, 4, 531
Tarlínskaja, Marína, 24-25
Tartars, 571
"Tayny golos." *See* "A Secret Voice" (the
same as "Dukhi zla")
Tazit. See Pushkin, A. S.
Térek, 526, 533 (No. 57), 547 (No. 71),
572 (No. 90), 599, 601
"Terek." *See* "The Terek"
"The Terek." *See* Pushkin, A. S.
The Third Section, 471, 505, 510 (No. 32)
Thomas the Rhymer. *See* Lermont, Thomas
"Those Evening Bells." *See* Moore,
Thomas
Tiflís (*now* Tbilísi), 135 (Fig. 15)
"To Chaadaev." *See* Pushkin, A. S.
"To a Friend of My Spring After Many,
Many Years of Absence." *See* Kozlov,
I. I.
"To a Grandee" *See* Pushkin, A. S.
"To Our Future Poets." *See* Rostopchina,
E. P.
"To the Slanderers of Russia." *See*
Pushkin, A. S.
"Der Tod, das ist die kühle Nacht." *See*
Heine, Heinrich.
Tolstoy, F. M., 525 (No. 51)
Tolstoy, L. N. (Leo), 3, 30, 501 (No. 30),
503, 513, 527 (No. 52), 537, 545 (No.
68), 570, 599, 606 (No. 97)
The Cossacks, 527 (No. 52)
"A Raid," 545 (No. 68), 570

War and Peace, 501 (No. 30), 503, 606
(No. 97)
Tomlinson, Charles, 25, 26
A Travel to Arzrum. See Pushkin, A. S.
A Travel to the Holy Land in 1830. See
Muravyov, A. N.
Trinity-Sergius Monastery, 476
Tristan. See Gottfried von Strassburg
Tróitsko-Sérgievskaya Lávra. *See* Trinity-
Sergius Monastery
Trubetskáya, E. I., 470 (No. 6)
Trubetskóy, S. V., 570
Tsárskoye Seló, 535
Tsvetáeva, M. I., 537
"Tsvetok." *See* "The Flower"
Tsygane. See The Gypsies
Turgenev, I. S., 3, 520 (No. 46), 529, 544,
546 (No. 69), 553, 580, 595
Fathers and Sons, 544, 546 (No. 69)
Rúdin, 544, 595
Smoke, 544
Spring Freshets, 544
Turkey, 484, 503
Turks, 562, 581
Tyútchev, F. I., 3, 12, 14, 25, 28, 30, 521
(No. 49), 532, 537, 543 (No. 66), 550
"Silentium!", 521 (No. 49)

Udódov, B. T., 592
Ukraine, 535
Ulyánov, N., 605
Uspénsky, G. I., 513

Vágin, E. A., 580
Valerík, the battle of, 549, 568-69 (No. 90)
Valerík (river), 568 (No. 90), 572 (No. 90)
Váren'ka. *See* Lopukhina, V. A.
Varlámov, A. E., 494
Vasílyev, A. V., 504 (No. 30)
Veinakhs, 571, 572 (No. 90)
"Vel'mozhe." *See* "To a Grandee"
Velyamínov, A. A., 484
Venceslas. See Rotrou, Jean and Zhandr, A.
A.
Venevítinov, D. V., 43 (Fig. 1), 470-72,
522

620

The Lermontov Index

Lermontov Index

[1]An attempt has been made to gather up all the important motifs of Lermontov's poetry under this rubric. Motifs have been understood very loosely and include both typical situations and recurring images. The only other motif index cutting across Lermontov's entire heritage can be found in the *Lermontovskaya èntsiklopediya,* but the compilers of that motif index have preferred to discuss Lermontov's pivotal themes rather than the motifs in the broad sense of the word. The entries (each of which is devoted to a separate motif) are freedom and will, action and exploit, solitude, wandering, banishment, the native land, memory and oblivion, deceit, revenge, peace, heaven and earth, sleep, play, road, time and eternity, traces, love, death, and fate.

Lermontov Index

Napoleon in Lermontov's works, 491 (No. 22), 537-38

Natural man. *See* Motif index

Pantheism. *See* Religious feelings

Parents. *See* Life and Character

Parodies of Lermontov, 534 (No. 57), 538 (No. 60)

Patriotism, 500-1, 537-38 (No. 60), 548-52 (No. 73), 569

Phrases from Lermontov's poems that have become familiar quotations, 533 (No. 56), 540-41 (No. 63), 599

Political poems, 522

Psychological prose, 472-73 (No. 7)

Pushkin's death. *See* Life and character

Pushkin and Lermontov juxtaposed, 14, 15, 18, 511, 513, 514 (No. 36), 524-25 (No. 50), 532 (No. 56), 549, 551, 557 (No. 79), 562-63 (No. 82), 596, 605

Religious feeling, 479, 513-14 (No. 35), 543 (No. 66), 565 (No. 85), 579, 593
  iconoclasm, 480 (No. 14), 543 (No. 66), 593
  mysticism, 473 (No. 8), 479, 514 (No. 35)
  prayers as lyrics, 467 (No. 3), 512-14 (No. 35), 525 (No. 51), 542 (No. 66), 579

Romances with women. *See* Life and character

Romanticism. *See* Romanticism in the *General Index*

Rousseauism, 494 (No. 27), 550, 567 (No. 87), 578

Schelling's influence on Lermontov, 470 (No. 6), 597

Scurrilous poems, 540 (No. 63), 594

Slavophiles. See Westerners and Slavophiles, Lermontov's relations with

Soldier as hero, 503

Sources of Lermontov's poetry, 9, 470 (No. 5), 471, 487 (No. 18), 492 (No. 23), 510 (No. 31), 511, 514 (No. 36), 516 (No. 39), 524 (No. 50), 536 (No. 59), 539 (No. 62), 543 (No. 66), 551, 552 (No. 74), 561 (No. 81), 563 (No. 83), 566 (No. 85). *See also* Byron, George G. in the *General Index*

Style. *See* Method, style, technique

Technique. *See* Method, style, technique

Translator of poetry, Lermontov as, 470 (No. 5), 488 (No. 18), 506, 519, 538 (No. 60), 556

Vision, 11, 12, 13, 18, 513, 519, 561 (No. 80), 565 (No. 84), 567 (No. 88), 600. *See also* Method, Style, Technique: cinematographic technique

Westerners and Slavophiles, Lermontov's relations with, 550

Works and the First Lines in English and Russian

(The page numbers in bold type refer to the texts of the poems; the pages containing the main discussion of each item are given in italic.)

Index of Works and First Lines

Index of Works and First Lines

Index of Works and First Lines

Index of Works and First Lines

Anatoly Liberman, born and educated in Leningrad, worked as a research fellow in Indo-European linguistics at the Academy of Sciences of the U.S.S.R. from 1965 to 1975. He is now a professor at the University of Minnesota, where he has taught in the German and Scandinavian departments since 1975. Liberman is the author of books and articles on linguistics, literature, and English as a second language, and he is a translator of English and Russian poetry. The University of Minnesota Press published his *Germanic Accentology: Volume I. The Scandinavian Languages* in 1982.

St. Louis Community College
at Meramec
Library